Citizen Bachelors

Citizen Bachelors

MANHOOD AND THE CREATION OF THE UNITED STATES

John Gilbert McCurdy

CORNELL UNIVERSITY PRESS
ITHACA AND LONDON

First published 2009 by Cornell University Press

Printed in the United States of America

Library of Congress Cataloging-in-Publication Data

McCurdy, John Gilbert, 1972–
    Citizen bachelors : manhood and the creation of the United
States / John Gilbert McCurdy.
        p. cm.
    Includes bibliographical references and index.
    ISBN 978-0-8014-4788-4 (cloth : alk. paper)
    1. Bachelors—United States—History—17th century.
2. Bachelors—United States—History—18th century.   3. United
States—Social life and customs—To 1775.   4. United States—Social
life and customs—1775–1783.   I. Title.

    HQ800.3.M38   2009
    306.81'520973—dc22

2008045803

Cornell University Press strives to use environmentally responsible sup-
pliers and materials to the fullest extent possible in the publishing of its
books. Such materials include vegetable-based, low-VOC inks and acid-
free papers that are recycled, totally chlorine-free, or partly composed
of nonwood fibers. For further information, visit our website at
www.cornellpress.cornell.edu.

Cloth printing   10   9   8   7   6   5   4   3   2   1

Contents

Illustrations

Acknowledgments

In December 1997 I went to see a production of Tchaikovsky's *Nutcracker Suite* with two male friends. Sitting there in the balcony of a Kansas City theater, surrounded by married couples and small children, I felt a certain amount of smugness. Weren't we fortunate to live in a time where one could choose to remain unmarried? I thought back to the story of Tchaikovsky's own troubled marriage and how familial expectations had tormented this man. How different it must have been to have lived so many years ago when marriage was not a choice but an obligation. Once the production began, however, I became fascinated with Drosselmeyer, the mysterious godfather who presents the nutcracker to little Clara and who magically controls the action from behind the scenes. In the ballet, he appears without children of his own or even a wife. This man was obviously unattached and this implied no malevolence. I began to rethink my smugness about the present and my perceptions of the past. Maybe the unmarried had played a larger role in history than I had once believed.

The following year I initiated a research project on the unmarried in American history. I turned to the era that I knew best—early America—and began to explore the role of the single man in the colonial and Revolutionary eras. Were there any single men three and four hundred years ago? If so, what did people think about them and what was it like to have been one? How had being a bachelor changed over time? The following pages contain my answers.

The debts—both financial and personal—that I have accrued over the past decade working on this book are numerous. My first and greatest debt is to my parents, Gilbert and Beverly Lankford McCurdy. Not only did they pay a great deal of money for my education, they helped me eke out an existence as I completed my graduate studies and traversed the country searching for research materials. More important, they provided moral support and inspiration. I dedicate this book to them. I am also grateful to my sister Anne Kirk and her family.

I am also indebted to the mentoring of several historians. As my graduate advisor, David Thomas Konig provided invaluable insights that helped me sharpen my eye as a historian and my skills as a writer. In addition to Professor Konig, several members of the Washington University faculty tolerated my constant talk of bachelors and helped point me in the right direction, including Iver Bernstein, Conevery Valenčius, Andrea Friedman, Daniel Shea, Andrew Rehfeld, and Erin Mackie. Several historians outside of St. Louis have also been invaluable to this project, especially those graduate students and faculty members that I met at the McNeil Center for Early American Studies. I could not have completed this project without the careful comments of Daniel Richter, George Boudreau, Dallett Hemphill, Thomas Foster, Sean Goudie, Lorri Glover, Lisa Wilson, Anne Lombard, Richard Ryerson, Tammy Miller, and Susan Klepp. I am also indebted to several people for their inspired citations, help with translating French, and general encouragement including Philip Greven, Joshua Greenberg, Suzanne Marshall, Daniel Vickers, Carole McCann, Carole Davidson, and Daniel Polley. Finally, I must thank my colleagues at Eastern Michigan University who have helped me stay focused on my research despite expectations of teaching and service, especially Steven Ramold, Kathleen Chamberlain, James Egge, and Stephen Jefferson.

I have also been the beneficiary of funding from several organizations and institutions who made it possible for me to pursue sources up and down the Atlantic seaboard, to take time to think and write and rewrite, and to present various draft forms at professional conferences and informal conversations. While working on this project, I received generous funding from Washington University in St. Louis, the McNeil Center for Early American Studies at the University of Pennsylvania, Eastern Michigan University, Moravian College, the American Antiquarian Society, the Library Company of Philadelphia, the David Library of the American Revolution, the Virginia Historical Society, and the North Caroliniana Society. I am also grateful to Eastern Michigan University for helping to defray the costs of publishing this book.

Portions of this book have previously appeared in print. Much of my discussion of the Pennsylvania bachelor tax appeared as "Taxation and Representation: Pennsylvania Bachelors and the American Revolution" in the *Pennsylvania Magazine of History and Biography* 129, no. 3 (July 2005): 283–315, while my discussion of the Pickering brothers in chapter 4 is a condensed version of what appeared as " 'Your Affectionate Brother': Complementary Manhoods in the Letters of John and Timothy Pickering" in *Early American Studies* 4, no. 2 (Fall 2006): 512–45. I thank both journals for allowing me to reprint portions of these articles.

To come full circle, I return to my bachelor friends. Having read enough acknowledgments in scholarly books, I know that this is the place where I am supposed to thank my spouse, partner, and/or children for their support. In light of the subject of this book as well as my own bachelorhood, I thought it more appropriate to thank some of the single men and women who have inspired, consoled, and frustrated me over the years: Daniel Polley, Julie Visocsky, Kendra Knight, Matthew Richardson, Douglas Ross, Larry Barker, Michael Fisher, Gary Kotraba, George Boudreau, Michael Drake, John Paul, Liz Taylor, Sinderella, JoAnn Kennedy Slater, Kathey Klozik, Marlen Harrison, and Brenda Wilson.

Citizen Bachelors

Introduction

BACHELORS IN EARLY AMERICA

November 1772 was a particularly gloomy month for young James Madison. Fifteen years later he would write the U.S. Constitution, thirty-seven years later he would be inaugurated as the fourth president of the United States, yet all of this was too far off for the twenty-one year old to see. Madison wallowed in his own loneliness, trapped at Montpelier, his father's plantation in rural Orange County, Virginia. Like the country, then locked in a decadelong struggle with Great Britain, Madison seemed unable to declare his independence. The year before he had graduated from the College of New Jersey (which later became Princeton) and had subsequently begun a course of study in the law. Yet the return to his paternal residence had reduced him to a subordinate state. In economic terms there was little difference between him and his twelve-year-old sister Nelly. In a society that ranked one's value in terms of acres of land and number of slaves, James Madison had neither. He was the master of nothing and no one.

As winter approached Madison expressed his pessimism to William Bradford, a friend from college. In a letter dated November 9 Madison blamed his pitiful situation on his sickly nature, claiming "my sensations for many months past have intimated to me not to expect a long or healthy life." The two men had kept up a lively correspondence since departing Princeton. Bradford kept Madison up to date on their friends, especially those who married. Such news only depressed Madison further as his lack of an estate kept him from even contemplating wedlock. He worried that he would remain forever unmarried and become a subject of vicious gossip. In his letter Madison warned Bradford, who was then living in Philadelphia, not to "suffer those impertinent fops that abound in every City to divert you from your business and philosophical amusements." Although Madison did not to include himself in this group, his disgust with men of "vanity and impertinence" repeated a popular link between unmarried men and moral depravity.[1]

For all of Madison's pessimism, his situation was far from bleak. Although his economic situation kept him from achieving mastery and attaining a family, he was no dependent. His race, class, and gender provided him with opportunities that few other members of the Montpelier estate had. Moreover, his status as a bachelor conferred on him masculine autonomy that gave him agency. Even though he lived under his father's roof, Madison was not his father's pawn. Colonel Madison was no stern paterfamilias and placed no pressure on James to assume control of the estate. Instead, he allowed his eldest son to choose his own vocation, which James did by taking more advice from his friend Bradford than from his father. Madison also enjoyed considerable personal liberty, including sexual liberty. Although his strict morals demanded chastity, Madison was regularly titillated by Bradford's stories of men who did not wait for marriage to engage in intercourse. In one letter Bradford told of a classmate who "put the Cart before the horse" and became "a father before he was an husband." In another he joked that he had access to a pamphlet titled "On the Management of Children." "When you are married I will send you one—or sooner, if you please," he noted wryly.[2] Most important, Madison's status as an unmarried member of his father's household did not prevent him from taking an active role in politics. Two years after his glum letter to Bradford, Madison was elected to the Orange County Committee of Safety. He then ascended to the Virginia House of Delegates and the Council of State, quickly becoming one of the most influential men in Virginia. In the end Madison was well into his forties before he married and took control of his father's estate. In the meantime he discovered that bachelorhood conferred upon him all the privileges of manhood including personal, sexual, and political liberty.

James Madison lived in an era of dynamic change. In the second half of the eighteenth century the thirteen colonies separated from Great Britain and created a new nation. Concurrent with the creation of the United States was the rise of the bachelor as a distinct identity defined by masculine autonomy. The bachelor stood on equal political footing with any married man, and although his reputation could be linked to sexual immorality, he had access to the full rights of American citizenship. To be sure, there had always been unmarried people in America but they had not always had the freedoms that men of James Madison's generation took for granted. When the first English colonists settled along the Atlantic seaboard in the early seventeenth century, the lives of single men were severely circumscribed by law and custom. Those who lived under their fathers' dominion had no freedom of movement, could not joke about or engage in sex, and were entirely devoid of political rights. None of these restrictions were new or unique to America; they had defined the single state in England for centuries. That they changed and why they changed is an important chapter in the history of the United States. Not only does it help us to understand how the man we remember as "the father of the

Constitution" could be a bachelor, it sheds new light on our understandings of gender in early America and the creation of American citizenship.

The Bachelor and American History

The word *bachelor* dates back more than seven hundred years and since then the basic definition has remained the same. First and foremost, a bachelor is an unmarried man. Unlike imprecise terms such as *single* and *unmarried*, bachelor refers only to men who have never been married. Other terms are applied to unmarried women (spinster, widow) and to men who were once married (widower, divorcé). Implicit in the definition is an element of agency: a bachelor is able to marry but has not done so. A bachelor is thus an adult man, physically and legally capable of marriage, and so underage boys are necessarily excluded. To be sure, there is a gray area between bachelor and husband when it comes to informal unions. Benjamin Franklin never officially married Deborah Read because no one could confirm the whereabouts of Read's first husband. The couple spent forty-five years together and had two children, so few consider Franklin a bachelor even though he never married in the eyes of the law. In the twenty-first century homosexual men in committed relationships exist in a similarly gray area. In most states such men are not legally husbands, yet it would be unfair and incorrect to deny their unions. In spite of these gray areas, we can define the bachelor as an adult man who, regardless of sexual orientation, has never legally wed and is not in a de facto marriage.

Defining who is a bachelor is only half the challenge. When we discuss bachelors in the present day, we are often building on assumptions and employing connotations that go far beyond a man's lack of a wife. For example, every year *People* magazine publishes a list of the fifty hottest bachelors. In recent years the list has included movie stars, entrepreneurs, musicians, and even the man second in line to the British throne. The magazine prints several alluring photos of these men on beaches or in fast cars, looking vibrant and powerful. In its own way *People* captures the connotations of bachelorhood in America today. To be a single man is to be masculine and autonomous, self-sufficient and successful, attractive and sexual. Bachelorhood is thus the very essence of masculinity: pure manhood uncorrupted by familial duties and unrestrained by female influence. Of course, *People* only depicts bachelorhood in its most attractive light. Elsewhere a far darker image of the single man takes precedence. In Congress representatives debate the problem of men who abandon their children with more conservative members demanding legal incentives to encourage marriage. When violent crime in America fell in the late 1990s, statisticians correlated domestic tranquility to a decreasing number of young and single men. Likewise, social scientists wonder about the presence of so many young and unattached men in hostile Muslim nations and the shortage of eligible women in China. Self-help manuals continue to sell briskly, with the most popular topics being love and finding a mate. The potent masculinity so alluring in *People* can also mean broken families, crime, terrorism, and personal despair.[3] In other words, the bachelor is more than just an unmarried man: he is a powerful symbol of manly independence. In a country divided by culture wars this makes him a Rorschach test: depending on one's point of view, the bachelor is either the embodiment of personal freedom or another symptom of a society bereft of family values.

Where do these ideas come from? How far back into the American past can we go to find the origins of the modern identity of the bachelor? And what are the origins of the debate surrounding the bachelor? Have Americans always been of two minds when it comes to unmarried men? For the most part historians of the United States have located the origins of the bachelor at the turn of the twentieth century. Several historians, most prominently Howard Chudacoff, have argued that over the course of the nineteenth century industrialization and immigration brought large numbers of young men to the cities. This was the first time in American history that so many people in their late teens and twenties had been away from the control of their parents and the restrictive expectations of their communities. Accordingly, these men took advantage of the situation. They did not marry quickly, as their parents had, but spent their days and spare change in saloons, gymnasiums, and amusement parks. In time this brought the rebuke of moralists who condemned such irresponsibility and self-indulgence. The bachelor—and the debate over his existence—first appeared a century ago.[4]

Although historians acknowledge that the turn of the twentieth century was "the age of the bachelor," they tend to have a far more dismal assessment of the single life in earlier eras. In the preindustrial age the family was the central institution of American society and anyone who deviated from it was deemed a threat. In other words, there was no debate over bachelorhood in the seventeenth and eighteenth centuries; single men were universally unwelcome. "Bachelors were rare and were viewed with disapproval," writes Arthur Calhoun in one of the first histories of the American family. "They were almost in the class of suspected criminals." To prove his point Calhoun cites a 1636 Massachusetts law that forbid single people from living alone and the existence of a tax on bachelors in Maryland during the Seven Years' War (French and Indian War).[5] Although much of Calhoun's work has been revised by subsequent studies of the family, his assessment of the miserable status of colonial bachelors largely has gone unchallenged. A subsequent historian theorized that Virginia's great planters replaced indentured servants with African slaves after their bachelor former servants launched Bacon's Rebellion, while another speculated that being single subjected men to accusations of witchcraft in seventeenth-century New England. Within the past decade historians have argued that bachelorhood was viewed by colonial Americans as a sign of moral depravity and that the founders of the republic saw bachelors as disorderly men against whom responsible manhood was defined.[6] Before the age of the bachelor, there was no place for the more positive view of the unmarried man or the liberties that define bachelorhood today.

The inherent flaw in the prevailing interpretation is that nearly all who have written on the early American bachelor have done so in the context of the family.

Beginning with marriage and family as normative inevitably leads historians to define the bachelor as abnormal and to dismiss him as immature, unmanly, or corrupt. This view changes if we begin with the bachelor as the subject and place him in the larger context of early American history. A recent study of novelist Charles Brockden Brown demonstrates that men in the 1790s found places in men's magazines where they were not ashamed to identify as bachelors. Similarly, a study of spinsters and widows in eighteenth-century Philadelphia reveals that a number of women enjoyed the independence that came with being single.[7] Both of these studies began with the unmarried rather than the family and consequently both discovered places and times in early America where unmarried people were not deemed pariahs but maintained a considerable degree of freedom. However, the two studies are rather narrow in their focus and thus neither one attempts to challenge the orthodox view of Calhoun and others. Yet their conclusions suggests that if we make the bachelor the focus of study and examine him in the broad context of early American history, the prevailing view that all single life was abysmal before the twentieth century might have to be revised.

Our contemporary perception of what it means to be a bachelor emerged over the course of the colonial era. A review of the laws, literature, and lives of the seventeenth and eighteenth centuries reveals that there was actually little interest in single men in the early years of settlement. Although a number of men were unmarried, few Americans discussed their positive or negative attributes. This changed in the second half of the seventeenth century due to a variety of factors. Change started when lawmakers became concerned that married men were unduly burdened by the cost of raising children and thus began to place higher taxes and other civic obligations on single men. At the same time political and popular authors investigated the bachelor as they considered matters of the heart. Convinced that people who married did so because of love, writers asked why certain people did not marry and soon began theorizing about the pathology of the bachelor. Change also came at the individual level. Economic and social changes allowed new freedoms for the young man who had left his father's house but who had not yet married and become a father himself. These changes worked in concert with one another to forge the unique bachelor identity that we know today.

Then as now there was considerable disagreement over what to make of the bachelor. Some viewed him with open hostility. Although it is hyperbole to label early American bachelors criminals, lawmakers in nearly every colony did require single men to pay higher taxes than married men, to enroll in the military so that married men did not have to, and to serve prison sentences from which married men were routinely excused. Bachelors also became the object of ridicule and scorn in weekly newspapers and in the pamphlets that traversed the Atlantic Ocean. Some single men even internalized these assaults and wondered, like James Madison did in the fall of 1772, if they could be successful if they never married. Yet this was only half of the story; the bachelor was also the beneficiary of unintended consequences. Laws that placed greater duties on single men had the effect of politicizing bachelors. Many of the men affected by the laws had never voted and had never had any formal role in politics, but after they were required to pay taxes and perform other civic duties, they became increasingly interested in their political rights. Similarly, the unflattering literature had the effect of bringing about a sense of group consciousness. Before dissections of the bachelor became common, unmarried men tended to exist in a nebulous world somewhere between childhood and adulthood. Now they had an identity with which they and thousands of other American men could identify. Being labeled a bachelor was an insult for some but others took pride in an identity that bestowed upon them unquestioned masculinity and an enviable amount of freedom. Bachelors demanded more personal liberties including the right to engage in sexual intercourse without legal retribution. By the time of American Revolution the bachelor was able to successfully formulate a case for why he should have the same rights as married men such as suffrage, freedom of assembly, and unhindered sexuality.

In effect, we have an incomplete history of the bachelor. To be sure, the single man did reach an unheralded apogee at the turn of the twentieth century, yet the seeds for this age of the bachelor were planted at least a century before. We thus do not merely need to acknowledge that life for the unmarried was not as bleak as historians have long portrayed it as. Rather, we need to explore the unmarried man in his early American context and understand how he went from being a relatively unimportant figure to the center of a great American debate.

What Makes a Man?

By establishing that the present-day identity of the bachelor emerged in the colonial era rather than at the turn of the twentieth century, we can better understand gender in early America and its relationship with citizenship and sexuality. Within the last decade researchers in the field of men's studies have explored the basic components of masculinity and have sought to establish what makes a man. Early American historians have contributed to this exploration and now several excellent works exist that explain the dimensions of seventeenth- and eighteenth-century manhood. We have learned that colonial society expected its men to progress from boyhood to manhood by achieving a series of benchmarks in adolescence and young adulthood. A man had to gain control of his passions and subject his baser instincts to societal expectations. He had to demonstrate his competence in a vocation and win the approval of his father in order to receive his inheritance. When this happened he could then acquire the ultimate indicators of manhood: marriage, an independent household, and fatherhood. We have also learned that early Americans also understood manhood in relation to those who *could not* control their passions—such as women and boys—or those who *would not*—such as men who failed to acquire a vocation, establish a household, or marry and father children. It is thus not surprising that historians of early American manhood have universally painted the bachelor as the antithesis of colonial manhood. "In the eyes of the majority of adults, bachelors were never really men," writes Anne Lombard.[8] Mark Kann asserts that the founders viewed the bachelor as a "man-child who did not merit the rights of men, fraternal respect, or civil standing."[9]

In essence, these historians have defined the parameters of normative manhood, an important first step in establishing a history of early American manhood. However, this has led them to mistake those men who did not fit the mold as aberrant and problematic. Such a narrowly dichotomous view of manhood has been rejected elsewhere in men's studies and we need to do the same in early American history. In her groundbreaking studies R. W. Connell has asserted that there is not one masculinity but many different masculinities and that these have to be understood in relation to one another.[10] This is true for the bachelor, who was not the antithesis of early American manhood but a variation on it.

There were always exceptions to the rule that one had to be married to be a man. In medieval England priests and dons were lifelong celibates who were able to claim the full privileges of manhood.[11] What was true for the university professor in 1400 was true for the bachelor writ large in 1600 and 1800. Marriage by itself never entitled one to manhood nor did being unmarried disqualify one. Mastery—meaning the ownership of property, the possession of a profitable vocation, and/or the establishment of an independent household—was always more important than marriage. Poor men could marry, but if they became destitute the courts had no qualms about breaking up their families. Conversely, the man who acquired a landed estate was entitled to the full political, economic, and social rights of manhood, even if he was unmarried. As a result, early America was filled with husbands who never were really men and bachelors who became well-respected governors and ministers.

We may also consider how changing ideas about manhood affected the bachelor. Over the course of the colonial era the requirements for entrance into manhood changed dramatically, allowing more and more individuals to claim the privileges of men. In the early years of American settlement bachelors who were not masters had little access to masculine power. Typically these single men were young and propertyless and thus they existed as economic dependents living under another man's roof and taking their orders from him. They were men, but because of their lack of mastery, they had no political standing, were not free to move from place to place, and were severely limited in terms of sexuality. There was essentially no difference between the single man who was not a master and other economic dependents such as children, servants, and women. Gender was less consequential than mastery and thus early seventeenth-century laws made little distinction between young and propertyless single men and young and propertyless single women.

This was not the case for long. Indeed, the most important part of the history of the bachelor in early America is how young and propertyless single men transitioned from dependents similar to single women to independents similar to married men even though they did not become masters. The laws that placed greater civic obligations on bachelors applied largely to young and propertyless single men, the very men who had had no political standing. Moreover, the obligations were uniquely masculine duties such as military service that were not applied to women. As a result, the bachelor laws not only politicized single men, they masculinized them. Literary attacks on bachelors had a similar effect. Authors rarely made distinctions based on age or rank, but treated all single men the same. The wealthy old miser was an object of numerous lampoons but he was nothing more than an extreme version of the young and propertyless bachelor. All single men shared the uniquely masculine traits of independence, personal autonomy, and unrestrained sexual desire. As colonial society began treating young and propertyless bachelors as men, and as these men grew into their new identity, manhood became a more inclusive category. Marriage and mastery continued to make the man, but so too did political obligations and a new masculine ethos that included a healthy sexual appetite. As young and propertyless bachelors became men, they separated themselves from single women. The eighteenth-century laws that required unique obligations for bachelors ignored spinsters, while the literature that spoke of the potential dangers of a bachelor's agency dismissed single women as completely passive. Mastery became less important than gender. Thus, while bachelors internalized a sense of empowerment, single women continued to be subordinate to their fathers, restricted in their movement, and lacking sexual freedom.

This division of gendered power ultimately had a profound effect on the development of American citizenship. The creation of the American republic introduced the idea of commensurate rights whereby a person earned privileges such as suffrage through the performance of obligations such as military service and the payment of taxes. Young and propertyless bachelors benefited from this idea of commensurate citizenship. For over a century they had been obliged to perform military service and pay special taxes, and so by the time of the American Revolution they were able to make a compelling case for suffrage and equal treatment under the law. In so doing, these bachelors were the first disfranchised group to gain equal rights. Other groups excluded from political participation in the colonial era had much less success gaining entrance to citizenship during the Revolution. Women—both married and single—found themselves excluded from voting in all states but one. Commensurate citizenship disadvantaged women since only a handful joined the army during the war, and only unmarried property owners paid taxes. As a result, there was a growing cleavage between political experience of men and women in the last quarter of the eighteenth century.[12] Young and propertyless bachelors improved their status by claiming that all men regardless of marital status or social standing were equal. This, in turn, had the effect of distancing them from their single sisters and may have slowed women's access to political rights.

Of course, manhood is not all about political rights or economic status. It also involves less tangible qualities such as honor and reputation. It does not necessarily follow that because propertyless bachelors gained the right to vote that they earned respect as men. For instance, we might consider the reputation of the fop in early America. Some historians have argued that the denigration of effeminate men was an attack on bachelors because single men were perceived to be homosexuals. Although this conclusion yields considerable insight into the evolution of sexual identity, it underestimates the complexities of the bachelor's masculinity and sexuality. It is certainly true that some colonists saw the bachelor as effeminate and morally depraved in a way that implied homosexuality, but the bachelor could also be the manliest of men and heterosexual to a fault. The bachelor's gender identification certainly could be problematic, although sometimes it was because he was too manly and at other times it was because he was not manly enough.[13]

As a result, we have to be careful about asserting that the bachelor was a proxy for the homosexual in early America. Beginning with Michel Foucault, historians of sexuality have largely accepted the social constructionist view that while some men in the ancient, medieval, and early modern world had sex with other men, they were not homosexuals. The term homosexual was not coined until 1868 and the idea of an exclusively homosexual identity did not appear until the early twentieth century.[14] However, there has been considerable revision of this point, with some historians claiming there was something very close to a homosexual identity before the American Revolution.[15] What are we to make of this? Were bachelors in the colonial era primarily seen as unable or unwilling to marry women because they preferred to have sex with men? These questions are inadequate in part because they involve mistaken ideas about eighteenth-century notions of sexuality. Sexuality was undergoing tremendous change in the century before the Revolution. Americans had begun to decouple sex and procreation but Freud had yet to formulate an understanding of desire as being determinative of sexual identity.[16] The early American bachelor's sexuality straddled this divide and often created as much confusion as it did clarity. It had long been considered problematic by moralists and lawmakers who demanded total abstinence for all unmarried people. However, as the bachelor emerged as a unique identity, Americans reconsidered single sex and asked if one variation was more depraved than another. They did worry that bachelors were sodomites, but they also worried about bachelor fornicators. Indeed, far more ink was spilled by moralists agonizing over a new breed of bastards bankrupting taxpayers than was invested in innuendos about effeminate men. In time Americans would conclude that heterosexual bachelor behavior was preferable to homosexuality, but in 1800 this was far from assured.

Early American bachelor sexuality thus cannot be confined to a simple homosexual/heterosexual dichotomy because it often contravened and confused this anachronistic division. Instead, we have to consider bachelor sexuality as a whole and understand how the perception of different sexual acts evolved over time. At the same time, the unsettled sexuality of the early American bachelor may offer some insight into the evolution of the modern-day homosexual. Historians seeking a gay American history have often looked to sodomy trials, curiously affectionate correspondence, and attacks on effeminate men to find the roots of the modern gay identity.[17] Yet being a homosexual is not simply about sex acts and gender inversion. It is also about the disavowal of traditional marriage, the building of a subculture made up almost entirely of other men, and the assertion of a greater degree of sexual license. In this, the emergence of the bachelor is integral to the history of gay men.

Overview of the Book

This book is divided into five chapters. Chapter 1 establishes how the single state was viewed and experienced in sixteenth-century England and seventeenth-century America. The diversity of the single state retarded any notion of a coherent bachelor identity because issues of mastery were considered more important. The next three chapters explain how and why this changed. Chapter 2 examines the laws that singled out unmarried men and how these laws served to legally segregate bachelors from other dependents. Chapter 3 focuses on the cultural conversation that accompanied the new politics of bachelorhood. As political theorists issued calls for new laws to encourage marriage, essayists and pamphleteers challenged this idea and popularized new characterizations of bachelors who valued their freedom and resisted state control. Chapter 4 examines the experience of American bachelors as recorded in diaries, tax rolls, and belles lettres. Bachelorhood was not merely a political construct or a cultural idea: it was a lived experience, as witnessed by the fact that young men's lives became increasingly vibrant over the eighteenth century. Chapter 5 brings the themes of politics, culture, and lived experience together in the context of the American Revolution and its immediate aftermath to demonstrate how the emergence of bachelorhood informed the creation of American citizenship.

In this book I examine the bachelor through a wide-angle lens in an attempt to demonstrate broad cultural changes. Instead of focusing on a single author or city, the parameters have been expanded to the transatlantic Anglophonic world over the course of the seventeenth and eighteenth centuries. This approach necessarily sacrifices some degree of detail but it opens the topic to a level of national import and allows us to mark regional variations. It also allows us to see change over time more clearly.

The sources examined for this book come from all thirteen colonies as well as Great Britain, although most of the focus is on Massachusetts, Pennsylvania, Maryland, and Virginia. These locales witnessed the most dynamic discussions of the bachelor and produced the richest historical record. Moreover, although a wide variety of sources have been consulted, the focus here is largely on three types of records: statutory laws and evidence of their execution, ephemeral literature such as political pamphlets and periodicals, and the personal reflections of the unmarried such as diaries. For the most part, the analysis of these sources is handled separately. The decision to do so stems from organizational convenience. The material here could have been organized around region or time period without significantly altering the findings. However, separating the materials does make it clear just how diverse the discourses surrounding bachelorhood could be. Lawmakers, authors, and bachelors often agreed but just as often they held completely different ideas about what it meant to be a bachelor in early America.

The grand chronological scope of this book necessarily required sacrifices. Bachelors in this book are presumed to be free and white. Thousands of African Americans were kept single by the cruelties of slavery and white indentured servants were legally prohibited from marriage by their contracts. However, these men have been excluded because when colonial lawmakers and authors wrote about bachelors, they nearly always presumed freedom and whiteness. Similarly, although religious communities such as the Moravians offer a unique perspective on the single life in the colonies, they too have been excluded. Because of their German background and isolation from American society writ large, these communities had little effect on the changing connotations about what it meant to be a bachelor. Some attention has been paid to single women, especially as their experience compared to that of single men, although this book does not purport to be a comprehensive account of the spinster experience.

1

"Unmarried Men Are Best Friends, Best Masters, Best Servants"

SINGLES IN EARLY COLONIAL AMERICA

Being a single man in colonial Massachusetts certainly had its downsides. At least it did for Stephen Hoppin, Junior, who in 1672 was summoned before the selectmen of Dorchester to account for his life. Standing alone before them, Hoppin listened carefully as the five councilors inquired into the details of his existence. They had received word that he was not regularly employed, a situation they assumed was due to his living situation. Whether he resided on his own or with his brother is not clear; either way the young man lacked a proper master to keep his shoulder pressed firmly to the wheel. What did he have to say for himself, the selectmen wanted to know, and how did he plan to remedy the situation?

Stephen Hoppin no doubt knew that his masterless days were nearing an end when he received his summons to appear before the selectmen. Four years earlier the General Court of Massachusetts had determined that too many young people in the colony were living without proper supervision. Such youths were wasting their days in idleness, breaking the Sabbath, and even engaging in sexual deviance. While the Puritans acknowledged the potential in all people to fall subject to sin, they believed the young to be particularly susceptible to temptation. Because of this, the General Court ordered the various towns "to dispose of all single persons and in-mates within their Towns to service."[1] Throughout Massachusetts local selectmen went about ensuring that every young person received the proper supervision of one who could monitor his or her actions. The town of Dorchester dutifully complied with the General Court's request and warned sixteen young men to house themselves with a local family or else the town council would do it for them.

Forewarned, Stephen Hoppin came to his examination prepared. When the selectmen asked him how he planned to follow the dictates of the General Court, he replied that a local man named Joseph Long owned a boat and had agreed to hire him to tend it. Such a situation would provide an income and, nominally at least, a master for Hoppin. At this point the selectmen no doubt conferred among themselves. This young man's answer was troublingly unorthodox. Although employment might keep him busy, it did not sound like Joseph Long was interested in taking Hoppin into his home and family. They thus rejected Stephen Hoppin's proposal and directed him to seek a more suitable master.[2]

Of the five selectmen who decided Stephen Hoppin's fate, one could claim to know better than the others what God demanded of Dorchester, its leaders, and its young men: William Stoughton. Stoughton had only joined the town government the year before but he was one of the most pious men in Massachusetts. Born in Dorchester to a founder of the colony and a hero of the Pequot War of 1636–37, Stoughton was raised to be a child of the covenant, receiving proper instruction from his father, his minister, and his Harvard masters. He traveled to England during that country's civil war to aid the Puritan cause and soon began preaching Calvinist doctrines from the pulpit. When the revolution came to an end in 1660, Stoughton returned to Massachusetts and began preaching a no less stern theology in Dorchester. He supplied the town's pulpit for nearly a decade, and although the church leadership repeatedly offered to make the position permanent, Stoughton declined, opting instead to leave the ministry and enter public service. As a selectman, Stoughton honed his skills as a holy inquisitor. Twenty years later, his experience of grilling people like Stephen Hoppin would prove useful as he faced down the men and women of Salem. It was Stoughton who took control of the Court of Oyer and Terminer and it was Stoughton who dismissed skeptics that did not believe a person should be executed on the basis of spectral evidence.

The juxtaposition of Hoppin and Stoughton is striking: one at the top of the society, a forty-one-year-old master and landowner who enforced the law and spoke the word of God; the other at the bottom, an idle youth without a household who broke the law and subverted the will of God. Yet both men were single. Although Hoppin's marital status was identified by the law, Stoughton's was no less certain. He went to his grave without ever taking a wife, a fact made emphatically clear a century later when the Dorchester faithful erected a tombstone for him that read *Vir Conjugij Nescius* (a man to wedlock unknown).[3] Both single men, their experiences could not have been more different. Indeed, neither man appreciated the irony of a lifelong bachelor examining another bachelor for being single.

The interaction of Hoppin and Stoughton is emblematic of how the earliest American colonists viewed marital status. For most of the seventeenth century, singles were divided into two groups: those who were masters and those who were not. The former did not concern anyone. A man who held property and who assumed patriarchal duties, even if he was not actually a husband and father, took his place among the other masters of a community. Nowhere in seventeenth-century America did the lack of a wife prove to be a bar to either political or religious leadership. In fact, those few authors that pondered the existence of single masters speculated that there might be a positive connection between the lack of a family and the faithful execution of one's vocation. By contrast, the bachelor who lacked property had no claims to mastery and was thus a dependent. A propertyless single man was typically in a liminal position between childhood and mastery, waiting until he could marry and establish a household. Until he did so he held the same social position in society as a woman, child, or servant.

Our story begins in England on the eve of American colonization. There were a considerable number of men without wives in early modern England yet they had no collective identity. The lack of marital status did not unify all single men in any meaningful way. Mastery underscored all aspects of manhood in this era and divided unmarried men into two groups: older men who maintained independent households and young men who were propertyless. When sixteenth-century English writers referred to *bachelors* they invariably meant the latter group. This division remained largely de facto until the economic crisis of the sixteenth century led Parliament to codify it in a series of labor laws. In effect, English society deemed young and propertyless single men to be more like women and children than like masters. The law restricted sixteenth-century bachelors in their political rights, economic and geographic independence, and sexuality. Conversely, it largely ignored older, propertied single men.

The first settlers in England's American colonies brought these basic understandings of marital status with them. As in England, single men consistently maintained a large presence in the colonies. Yet the distance from England and the specific conditions of life in the wilderness set the stage for the emergence of a uniquely American understanding. New England colonists replicated the English labor laws, although their lackluster enforcement and short duration ultimately negated their importance. In the Chesapeake a surplus of single men forced the alteration of English ways of thinking about unmarried men. Bachelors were not singled out for unique legal treatment. Instead, the consistent shortage of marriageable women created a class of single men who were neither true masters nor true dependents. This in turn led the men to redefine what it meant to be a bachelor. In effect, the magistrates in Massachusetts and single men in Virginia challenged English notions of the single life and forced Americans to begin discussing what role marital status should play in a person's life. Out of the discussion that ensued, the present-day identity of the bachelor began to take shape.

In this chapter I begin with a brief survey of bachelors in England before colonization, looking in particular at ideas of service and mastery. Ideas of sexuality in the context of unmarried men are also explored. I then turn to the experience of single men in New England and the Chesapeake in the first three quarters of the seventeenth century. Due to the dearth of popular literature and diaries, the evidence for this chapter is mostly drawn from the laws and their execution. Although this was not the only arena where ideas about bachelorhood emerged, it was one of the first and often the most dramatic.

The Unmarried in Early Modern England

Early modern England was full of single people. In most preindustrial societies it was common for nearly everyone to marry and for them to do so at a young age, but England contravened this trend. A reconstruction of data from several English parishes indicates that the average age at first marriage for people born in the second half of the sixteenth century was twenty-eight for men and twenty-six for women. Likewise, demographers have estimated that as many as one in five people born in the second half of the sixteenth century reached the age of forty having never married.[4] As a result, men without wives and women without husbands constituted a constant presence in sixteenth- and seventeenth-century England. Despite their numbers the unmarried were a fragmented group, dispersed throughout society without a collective identity. Most were young and propertyless people living in service in a master's household, yet a sizeable number were masters in their own right. Although there was a great deal of anxiety about the first group, early modern Britons believed the latter to be normal and, at times, even admirable.

The position of the unmarried in early modern England is readily apparent in the 1599 census of the County Middlesex village of Ealing. A microcosm of sixteenth-century English society, Ealing was an agricultural community with a sprinkling of merchants and artisans. Most of the 426 residents of Ealing were married adults or minor children living in two-generation households. The number of parents and children was typical for the early modern era but so too were the 140 unmarried adults—almost one-third of the total population—who constituted the rest of the town.

Singles in Ealing varied widely in age and social position. Among the more prominent unmarried men was Peter Haywood, a seventy-eight-year-old merchant and widowed father who lived with his single son, Thomas, a thirty-eight-year-old schoolmaster. Like Peter Haywood, many Ealing singles had once been married. There were more than a dozen widows or widowers trying to raise small children by themselves including the town's vicar, Richard Smart, who lived with his four teen-aged children. There was also a sizable contingent of people who had never been married. Seven singles lived with married siblings or other relatives. An equal number headed their own households. Thirty-year-old tailor John Millet maintained a house by himself, as did three other single men and three widows. Some of the never married opted for companionship and made households with other singles. Richard Geyle, a twenty-six-year-old "bailiff of husbandry," kept house for an absentee landlord with two husbandmen and a shepherd.

The largest number of unmarried adults were "servants": workers living with masters who were not their parents. This group of well over a hundred included Elizabeth Gardyner, the "waiting gentlewoman" for the wife of the justice of the peace, and Peter Burgess, a bricklayer's apprentice. Most single servants worked in husbandry or performed domestic chores. All told, about one quarter of Ealing's population consisted of unmarried live-in workers, the vast majority of whom were in their teens and twenties. Almost 80 percent of Ealing's male residents between the ages of fifteen and twenty-four were servants as were about half of Ealing women of the same age.[5]

The place of singles in Ealing was typical of early modern England. The unmarried held a variety of occupations, social positions, and roles in the kingdom. By far the vast majority of unmarried people were young, but a significant minority were older, some previously married and others never married. Most owned no property, although some were householders who constructed alternative families with unmarried relatives or same-sex peers. Single women were about as numerous as single men, but because of gender differences in the life cycle, there tended to be more widows than widowers and more young single men than young single women.[6]

There are many reasons why singles were so numerous in early modern England. The most important was no doubt the centrality of the independent household. It would be difficult to overestimate the importance of the household in early modern England. It was the bedrock of the polity and the first order of government, fulfilling many functions that would later be assumed by the state. The head was required by law to make sure that all members of his—and occasionally her—household were sufficiently fed, clothed, housed, put to useful labor, and kept out of trouble. To enforce his rule, the householder exercised considerable power over his dependents, occasionally meting out corporal punishment. Known as a family governor, the head acted as the intermediary between the state and the household members. He was responsible for the family's lands, any property taxes, and all poll taxes that might fall on his dependents. If his land had an annual income of forty shillings or more, a householding man had the right to vote in county elections.[7] The establishment of a household was largely contingent on the inheritance or acquisition of property. In order to support one's wife, children, and servants, a householder had to have sufficient land to grow crops and raise livestock or he had to have tools to practice a trade. The person who did not have such economic means was thus discouraged from taking on dependents. This more than anything delayed and denied wedlock to early modern Britons.[8]

Young men who did not have the resources to become householders were expected to live and work in the houses of masters. It was an old English custom that young people should leave their parents' homes in their early teens and go to work for another family. In the parlance of the day they were known as servants and their employment accomplished several important goals. It allowed for the reallocation of labor by taking young people from households where there was little or no work to be done and placing them in situations where labor was needed.[9] Through service a young man could acquire experience in husbandry and a young woman could learn the art of housewifery. Regardless of gender, servants typically earned wages that they could use to set up an independent household later in life. Service among the young was so widespread in early modern England that the majority of young people entered into some kind of labor contract and 90 percent of servants were under twenty-five.[10] As was the case in Ealing, service could take on numerous forms including apprenticeship although the primary work for young men tended to be work in the fields, tending crops and raising livestock. Service had the added advantage of guaranteeing that each young person had a master to ensure that he or she did not become idle or immoral.

Economic factors alone do not explain why Britons married late and many remained single for life. Rather, there were deep cultural values that protected and even promoted the unmarried state. Catholic dogma had long insisted that ministers remain unmarried and these teachings were not entirely exorcised with the Protestant Reformation. Instead, the process whereby the control of the English Church passed from the bishop of Rome to the king of England initiated an early and important discussion of the relationship between marital status and morality. A series of vociferous critics, such as Erasmus, Martin Luther, and the English Puritans, attacked priestly celibacy as the epitome of hypocrisy. "Fearefull haue beene the effects of this Diabolicall doctrine," wrote William Gouge in 1622, who claimed that "fornication, adulterie, incest, Sodomie, buggerie, and what not" had been the results of the Church's prohibition on clerical marriage.[11] These and other Protestant theologians demanded that wedlock be promoted especially among the ministry, citing St. Paul's admonition that it is better to marry than to burn with passion (1 Corinthians 7:9). Calvinist author William Perkins proclaimed that marriage "is a state in it selfe, farre more excellent, then the condition of single life."[12] Gouge compared celibacy and marriage, declaring that there was no contest as to which was the more acceptable: "If these two be duly poised, and rightly weyed, we shall finde single life too light to be compared with honest marriage."[13]

Yet as was the case with the Reformation generally, many Britons were reluctant to embrace radical change and so they remained largely ambivalent on the issue of priestly celibacy. The monarchy straddled the issue. Although neither Henry VIII nor Elizabeth I allowed Parliament to grant legal status to clerical unions, the royal courts made little effort to prosecute ministers who married and the Thirty-Nine Articles of Religion stated that "Bishoppes Priestes and Deacons are not commaunded to vowe the state of single life without mariage."[14] The indecision among the monarchy and episcopacy generally reflected the mood of the general populace. Many people and priests continued to believe that religious dedication demanded celibacy, or, as Francis Bacon wrote: "A single life doth well with Church men: for charity will hardly water the ground, where it must first fill a poole."[15] The vicar of Ealing notwithstanding, most Anglican clergymen before 1600 remained single.[16]

Even among radical Puritans, the single life was not entirely rejected. In the *Institutes of the Christian Religion,* John Calvin acknowledged Christ's revelation in Matthew 19 that some people were called to be eunuchs in service to God: "The Lord affirms that continence is a special gift of God, one of a kind that is bestowed not indiscriminately, not upon the body of the church as a whole, but upon a few of its members."[17] Calvin's English disciples followed his lead and acknowledged that there would be Christian celibates in any society. William Perkins wrote that because of Adam's original sin, it had become necessary for a number to remain unmarried, "since the fall, to some men who haue the gift of continencie, it is in many respects farre better then marriage." Perkins detailed why this was, explaining that celibacy "maketh him much more fit and disposed to meditate of heauenly things, without distraction of mind" and "freeth a man from many and great cares of household affaires."[18] In 1663 Quaker William Smith wrote that "singleness is a good state," explaining that "in that state Temptations may be resisted as easily as in any state whatsoever out of the Life, and they that walk in the Light, and with the Light, are kept single every way."[19] These sentiments remained the caveat to the otherwise promarriage message of the Puritans and their theological descendants.

Besides economics and theology, there were many other reasons why early modern Britons did not marry or married late in life. Some vocations attracted more single men than others. The military offered opportunity and adventure to young soldiers without much money and to elite officers denied inheritances by laws of primogeniture. The lack of a wife and family made distant travel and long periods away from home easier to stomach and for these reasons Britain's New World empire filled with unmarried men in uniform. Low pay made other occupations unattractive to men with families to support and thus the ranks of schoolmasters were filled largely with recent college graduates.[20] In such positions the unmarried made a personal sacrifice that benefited the community as a whole. Francis Bacon wrote that "certainly the best workes, and of greatest merit for the publike, have proceeded from the unmarried or childlesse men," since such men bestowed upon the commonweal the "affection and meanes" that married men reserved for their wives and children. Ultimately, some people chose to remain single because it was more attractive than marriage. "But the most ordinary cause of a single life is liberty," opined Bacon. He added that greed was also a common cause, noting that "there are some foolish rich covetous men, that take a pride in having no children, because they are thought so much the richer."[21] Religious writer John Mayer connected the single state to immorality, complaining that "many young gallants in these times, very incontinent, yet wil not marry, but rather burne in lust, or wallow in the mire of vncleannesse with harlots."[22]

The diversity of reasons that people remained single also speaks to a greater cultural value in early modern England: personal autonomy in the decision to wed. For well over a thousand years the Roman Catholic Church had insisted that the marriage ceremony continue without interference from ministers, parents, or state officials. If two people had reached physical maturity and they were not related, already married to other people, or members of a religious order, then all that was required for them to be married in the eyes of the Church was an exchange of vows in the present tense and consummation. The ease of marriage frustrated secular lawmakers but the Church remained adamant that marriage was a decision to be made only by those entering into it.[23] In England the Reformation did little to impede ecclesiastical control of marriage and it was not until 1753 that the state began legislating requirements for legal unions.[24] Likewise, parents were often frustrated by the Church's rules on marriage and tried repeatedly to gain a say in spousal choice. But parental control had its limits. Families rarely arranged marriages and the parental prerogative proved a veto that a child could override so long as he or she was willing to forego an inheritance.[25]

To be sure, most people in early modern England married and did so before they reached their late twenties. Likewise, the choice of when and whom to marry was rarely an entirely free choice as it was typically manipulated by parents, neighbors, and community leaders. Yet in a culture where the individual had, in principle at least, ultimate authority over the decision of whom to marry, there existed the possibility that a person might choose *not* to marry at all. Even in their charge that some people remained single for immoral reasons, Bacon and Mayer conceded that it was ultimately up to the individual to make the choice. Neither man called for the unmarried to be penalized or argued that marriage was the best option for all. Instead, the decision to marry was a personal one that depended upon a complex set of factors including resources, vocation, and personal taste. Efforts to contravene this right were viewed harshly by Britons who resisted efforts to pressure people into marriage. Even as views of the single life changed, the principle of personal choice remained dear to Britons and later to Americans.

"Where As Thise Bacheleris Synge 'Allas'"

Although early modern England debated priestly celibacy and contemplated the connection between marital status and morality, there was one aspect of the single life upon which nearly everyone agreed: the young and propertyless were not entitled to the privileges of manhood. When authors of the era referred to bachelors, they typically meant men who were young, irrational, and not yet prepared for the responsibilities of mastery. Such men had not yet learned to control their natural impulses toward idleness and immorality and thus they needed older, more established men to guide them. Some bachelors never matured and never attained manhood although it was not assumed that simply being unmarried made one a degenerate. Britons in the sixteenth and seventeenth centuries recognized that young single men were in a liminal position, yet unlike later writers they deemed this life stage utterly unmanly.

The word *bachelor* is believed to have entered the English lexicon in the fourteenth century. Previously, the nouns *virgin* and *maiden* as well as the adjective *single* had referred to unmarried people regardless of gender. Before the fourteenth century the word *bachelor* described a young or novice knight who followed the colors of another, thus linguists have suggested that the word comes from the French *bas chevalier,* meaning *low knight.* Over the course of the thirteenth and fourteenth centuries the term came to signify a man who had received the lowest degree at a university or a junior member of a guild. Lexicographers have also speculated that bachelor may also derive from the Latin *baccalarius,* an eighth-century term for a rustic man who worked another man's land. Given the large percentage of single men who worked as servants in husbandry, the connection between the land and the single state is obvious.[26] Regardless of exact origin, bachelor from the start implied youth, inferiority, and service.

The first major English author to use the term bachelor was Geoffrey Chaucer whose *Canterbury Tales* features a number of comical young men. In "The Merchant's Tale," Chaucer describes bachelors with a light invective that retains its resonance six hundred years later:

> Where as thise bacheleris synge "allas,"
> Whan that they fynden any adversitee
> In love, which nys but childyssh vanytee.
> And trewely it sit wel to be so,
> That bacheleris have often peyne and wo;
> On brotel ground they buylde, and brotelnesse
> They fynde whan they wene sikernesse.
> They lyve but as a bryd or as a beest,
> In libertee and under noon arreest,
> Ther as a wedded man in his estaat
> Lyveth a lyf blisful and ordinaat
> Under this yok of mariage ybounde.[27]

Here bachelors are childish men made ridiculous by their pursuit of love. They pitifully seek freedom, not as independent men but as irrational beasts. Such bacheleris are sophomoric figures, closer to children than to married men with property.

Youth, dependence, and the bathos of romance also surfaced in the plays of William Shakespeare. The prototypical Shakespearean bachelor is Romeo Montague, the lovesick young man who casts off the concerns of a family feud to follow his heart. The bawdy nurse in the play even chides Romeo for what he is, advising: "Marry, bachelor."[28] Yet Romeo was like many of Shakespeare's young single men in being focused on the immediate gratification of alcohol and sex and wholly lacking the mature judgment of an older man. In the first part of *Henry VI* a shepherd refers to a bastard daughter as "the first fruit of my bach'lorship," a pointed reference to a single man's sexual incontinence.[29] Shakespeare often made light of the impudent nature of bachelors, having a young man confidently decry the restrictions of marriage only to rue his words later on. While marching off to war in the first act of *Much Ado about Nothing,* young Benedick laughs at cuckolds and curses marriage, swearing, "I will live a bachelor." But when he meets Beatrice in act 2, Benedick clarifies his earlier vow: "When I said I would / die a bachelor / I did not think I should live till I / were married."[30]

In effect, liminality defined bachelorhood in early modern England. As social commentators of the time understood it, the bachelor was at a midway point in the seven ages of man. Having progressed past the stages of infancy and boyhood, he stood as a student or a soldier; having abandoned the teachings of his mother for masculine instruction, he was not yet ready for the responsibilities of a jurist.[31] In other words, a bachelor lacked mastery. Legally able to marry and physically able to father children, he did not have the basic maturity required of a man. Until a bachelor abandoned his juvenile need for freedom, his reckless impatience, and his wont to continually fall in love, he could not be a householder, a husband, a father, or a master.

As men-in-training, bachelors engaged in activities that Britons chalked up to the foibles of youth. Most young men spent a least a decade living as dependents in the households of other men, working as servants or apprentices in anticipation of the day when they could become masters themselves. In such situations they were constrained in their movements, yet by virtue of their gender they had a greater degree of physical mobility than female servants. Specifically, unmarried men engaged in the bachelors' social round, a gathering of young men at the local alehouse far away from the watchful eyes of parents and masters. Temporarily freed from the responsibilities of service, they demonstrated self-mastery by being able to consume large amounts of alcohol and gained acceptance in the eyes of their peers by bragging about sexual conquests. Most masters and authorities tacitly allowed the bachelors' social round, although drunkenness and sexual bravado tended to confirm the participants' immaturity.[32]

Bachelors were also treated as creatures in need of extra supervision lest their immaturity harm the social order. Idleness and repeated drunkenness were not acceptable, nor was sexual incontinence. Early modern Britons saw humans as naturally sinful creatures that lacked industry, sobriety, and chastity. It was thus up to the community to inculcate such values in young men. English society as a whole called on young men to learn self-control, and religious conservatives such as the Puritans issued constant admonitions. "Another Sin whereunto Young Men [are] addicted, is Wantonness and Uncleanness," wrote Thomas Gouge in *The Young Man's Guide*. "O young Man, dost thou love thyself, or any thing that thou hast?" Gouge asked. "Abstain then from Fornication and Uncleanness, whereby thou sinnest against thine own Body and bringest a Consumption and Rottenness upon it." John Mayer was equally adamant in his denunciation of sexual liberties by young men and offered a prescription whereby they could keep themselves chaste. First, a man was "to beat downe the body, and bring it into subjection, as the Apostle [Paul] did." For this, Mayer recommended constant prayer and the forgoing of "meates and drinkes as inflate and lift vp the body and prouoke to fleshlinesse." Second, a bachelor was to be mindful of his companionship and "abstaine from the company of a woman in priuate." To such writers, young men's sins were contagious and a total reformation was required. As Gouge noted: "When Men are idle, they have no Business but to Sin; but when Men are busy in their Calling, then they have no Leisure to Sin."[33]

The sexual appetites of single men were perhaps the most disturbing aspect of bachelorhood for early modern England, since men who had neither learned self-control nor married were susceptible to all types of sexual vice. In his discussion of "Wantonness," Thomas Gouge divided the "Kinds and Degrees of this Sin" into both "Contemplative Uncleanness" and "Practical Uncleanness," meaning both what went on in young men's minds and what they actually did. Among the latter, Gouge differentiated between fornication, adultery, incest, polygamy, and rape or ravishment, all which had to be resisted by young men. Gouge also discussed homosexual acts in passing, citing St. Paul's rebuke of the sodomite—which he translated as "effeminate"—and noting how "the Lord rained Fire and Brimstone upon Sodom and Gomorrah."[34] For commentators of the era, single men were incontinent creatures whose lusts were universal and without limits. Gouge was uninterested in drawing distinctions based on men's predilections and did not acknowledge anything resembling sexual orientation. Although historians have begun to argue that people of the early modern era may have understood sexual attraction between men to be natural and even tolerated some homosexual relationships, for moralists such as Gouge the emphasis was not on accepting young men as they were but on persuading them to renounce all forms of nonmarital sex.[35] Only when a single man became completely chaste was he ready to abandon celibacy.

Occasionally, perceptions of bachelorhood extended to men who were no longer young. The archetypal bachelor who never matured was Shakespeare's Sir John Falstaff. A fat, drunken, and lascivious old bachelor, Falstaff first appears in part 1 of *Henry IV* as a fellow reveler of young Prince Hal. For the majority of the play the two men indulge in drinking, fornicating, and thievery, with Falstaff serving as an antimentor for the prince, instructing him in all things sinful. At the end of the play, however, Hal renounces both his life of vice and Falstaff. Having outgrown the bachelors' social round, the future King Henry V leaves behind the pathetic old Falstaff to take up the mantle of responsible manhood as he prepares to inherit his father's throne. In *King Henry V* Henry marries for dynastic purposes, ensuring peace between England and France, but Falstaff never reforms. He never becomes a responsible master, husband, or father. In the characterization of Falstaff, the aged single man is really no different than a young one. They act the same, suggesting that the associations of immaturity and bachelorhood transcended age.[36]

Yet Falstaff was somewhat of an anomaly. Shakespeare included many unmarried men in his plays who were not young or overgrown bachelors including priests, knights, and elderly fathers. Indeed, such men were not bachelors in the parlance of the era, that is, their social status or vocation bestowed on them the maturity and manhood denied young single men. No one confused the indecisive and immature Hamlet with his recently married Uncle Claudius or the doting widower Polonius. A man who was the master of a household though he lacked a wife was not associated with the irresponsibility of youth. What made Falstaff like Prince Hal was his lack of masculine responsibility: he had no land, no vocation, *and* no family. If he had had the first two, the third would have been a moot point.

As a result, although young and propertyless single men did not possess manhood because they lacked the self-control necessary for mastery, there were plenty of older single men who were not bachelors. Recent work on manhood in late medieval Europe has revealed the existence of not one but three types of manhood that

Figure 1. "Sir John Falstaff." Before the eighteenth century, bachelorhood was a mark of youth and dependence, and thus unmarried masters were not considered bachelors. However, bachelorhood did encompass those men who continued in idleness and immorality well into middle age, such as Shakespeare's Sir John Falstaff.

Source: Original Letters &c. of Falstaff: Selected from Genuine Manuscripts Which Have Been in the Possession of Dame Quickly and Her Descendants Near Four Hundred Years (Philadelphia: Desilver, 1813), frontispiece. Reprinted with the permission of the American Antiquarian Society.

coexisted without conflict, each of which was symbolized by and connected to different vocations. There was the knight whose chivalrous masculinity stood in opposition to femininity by his dominance over other men, the university scholar whose use of rationality contrasted with the beastlike nature of unlearned men, and the craft worker who stood against boyhood and achieved mastery over other men through economic means. Among these different groups, marriage mattered more to some than others in defining manhood. The presence of a wife and dependents helped to assure a tradesman's position as petit patriarch while the celibate dons at the academy managed to erect their own standards of manhood in a community wholly removed from the world of women and children. In each case it was mastery that made the man, not marriage. Mature responsibility in the form of diligent industry, sober judgment, and sexual continence were what separated men from bachelors.[37]

Regulating the Unmarried

In his essay "Marriage and the Single Life," Francis Bacon reflected on the many different roles single men played in early modern England and observed that "unmarried men are best friends, best masters, best servants." Yet he qualified this endorsement, adding that the unmarried were "not alwayes the best subjects; for they are light to runne away; and almost all fugitives are of that condition."[38] Bacon was not the only early modern Briton to draw this conclusion. In the middle of the sixteenth century England experienced economic change and dislocation, causing lawmakers to fear the breakdown of the traditional order. Locating the problem as being one of too many bachelors, Parliament forced the young and propertyless into a state of dependency. In so doing, they codified the differences between unmarried men for the first time in English history. Single masters were entirely exempted from the laws while those who were not masters were reduced to a legal status indistinguishable from that of a woman or a child. A fear of too many bachelors also produced the first laws against singles' sexuality.

England in the sixteenth century underwent a complex agricultural revolution in which communal farms were replaced by individual lots. The process of enclosure fenced in common fields and deprived small landholders of grazing rights while the practice of engrossing turned entire villages into sheep ranches. To compound the problem, England simultaneously experienced unprecedented population growth: between 1541 and 1651 the kingdom's population doubled. Although agricultural and manufacturing output swelled, the economy could not keep pace with the increasing number of people. Unemployment grew rampant and those who did find work had to contend with food prices that were increasing at twice the rate of wages. Consequently, poverty and vagrancy multiplied on a scale previously unknown in England. In the 1520s the population of the destitute reached 20 percent, and it approached 30 percent by the turn of the seventeenth century. As conditions worsened, much of the population took to the road in search of employment or sought handouts from local authorities. With the emergence of this highly mobile class of masterless men, authorities began to fear that the traditional order was breaking down. They concluded that the problem was too many singles. The solution was to force their attachment to households and ensure they had masters to set them to work.[39]

Historically, English authorities had relied on custom and economic necessity to prompt young people into service. The reality was that very few people, especially the young, could afford to live on their own. However, the state did intervene if the relationship between master and servant became strained. When the Black Death created a shortage of workers in the fourteenth century, Parliament stepped in to ensure that workers did not demand higher wages than masters could afford.[40] Two hundred years later the situation seemed equally dire and Parliament again took action. Lawmakers identified the large number of vagrants swarming the English countryside as the main problem and enacted a series of poor laws to stem the rising tide of the destitute and transient. The poor laws directed that those unable to work due to age or physical condition be cared for at minimum expense to the state, while those who could work but refused to do so be dealt with severely. Parliament ordered the poor to seek public assistance only in the towns where they had been born or had labored for at least a year. Beggars were to be whipped or jailed, and the laws included provisions "for settinge to worke all such p[er]sons maried or unmaried havinge no meanes to maintaine them[selves]."[41]

As this passage indicates, the poor laws were written either without reference to marital status or were explicitly inclusive of both single and married people. Once a person had become a destitute transient, it mattered little what his or her marital status was.[42] Yet Parliament quickly realized that it might be able to prevent the growth of the poor if it took proactive steps to keep people from descending into poverty. Lawmakers saw young single people as the best candidates for prevention. Such a choice made sense on many levels. For one, the unmarried were more mobile than those who had wed. In the town of Haverling, two-thirds of men who appeared on the 1562 list of servants never again appeared in the town records as either servants or householders.[43] Similarly, a study of the vagrant population of England from 1560 to 1640 reveals that between 40 and 80 percent of all vagabonds were single men and that about half were under twenty-one years of age.[44] Mobility worried the authorities because it raised the specter of vagrancy. It was also the case that singles could be saved in a way that married people could not. Tradition insisted that a married couple be allowed to maintain an independent household, and so when such couples became vagrant, the local authorities had the unpleasant task of breaking up families and binding children into service. It was much easier to place a young person into a stable household before he or she married or conceived a child out of wedlock.

The poor laws were one half of a two-pronged attack on vagrants. Building on medieval legal precedent, Parliament enacted a series of statutes that tightly regulated workers and ensured that all who could work did so. In addition to setting wages, the laws meted out jail time for any person who departed a job before fulfilling his or her contract, imposed compulsory labor on those without visible means of support, and required certain agricultural workers to serve by the year or part of the year but never by the day. Unlike the poor laws, the labor laws made explicit reference to marital status. "An Acte concernyng reteynyng of Jo'neymen," passed by Parliament in 1549, required that "no p[er]son or p[er]sons unmaried shall be hiered or reteigned" as journeymen clothiers, weavers, tailors, and shoemakers "for any les tyme then for the space of oon hole qarter of on hole yere." The same act demanded "all servaunts of husbondrie unmaried and whiche have not bene maried" serve by the year.[45] The Statute of Artificers, passed in 1562, expanded these obligations by requiring apprentices to serve until twenty-four years of age, obligating servants to give their masters a quarter year's notice before departing, and ordering that people brought up in a trade remain in that trade. It also augmented the constraints on singles, demanding yearly service from

> every p[er]son being unmarried, and every other p[er]son being under thage of thirty yeres after the Feast of Easter next [who] shall marrye, and having been brought up in any of the said Artes Craftes or Sciences, or that hathe used or exercised any of them by the space of three yeres or more, and not having Landes or Lyves of the clere yerely value of fourtye shillinges, nor being worthe of his own Goodes the clere value of tenne poundes.[46]

Known collectively as the statutes of laborers and artificers, the 1549 and 1562 laws required that every single person in England contract by the term, attach himself to a settled household, and submit to the authority of a master.

Building on the cultural perceptions of the single state, the statutes of laborers and artificers applied almost exclusively to the young and propertyless. The 1549 act justified its existence by beginning, "whereas many yonge folks and servaunts of sundrye occupacons, beinge ones oute of their appenticehodes or their yerely retayned s[er]vice." The man who never acquired property and never married might find himself endlessly constricted by the laws, since there was no maximum age for men stated in the statutes. Similarly, the 1549 act applied only to people "whiche have not bene maried," thus omitting widowers. The statutes also did not apply to those who owned real property worth forty shillings or moveable property worth ten pounds. Since 1430 a forty-shilling freehold had been the minimum amount of land required to vote in parliamentary elections, thus the requirement of service did not apply to people who were full participants in the English polity.[47]

Occupation was largely unimportant in the statutes of laborers and artificers. Lawmakers wrote both acts to include as many types of workers as possible, from servants in husbandry to apprentices and journeymen. Gender was also largely irrelevant. In case anyone thought otherwise, the 1562 law contained a provision specifying that "any suche Woman as is of thage of twelfe yeres and under thage of fourtye yeres and unmarried" was to be put to service. Although authors such as Chaucer and Shakespeare capitalized on the distinctly male traits of bachelors, lawmakers were uninterested in such distinctions. The single man who was not a master had no claims to manhood and thus was to be treated the same as a single woman. This law thus reaffirmed the distance between sixteenth-century English bachelors and men.

Court records indicate that laws regulating the service of singles remained on the books for nearly two hundred years and were vigorously enforced well into the

Figure 2. "Hoeing." Seventeenth-century Americans made little legal distinction between single men and single women. If a single person was young and propertyless, he or she was required to submit to the authority of a master, refrain from sexual activity, and perform valuable labor.

Source: Harvest Home: Representing the Progress of Wheat in a Series of Elegant Engravings (Philadelphia: Johnson and Warner, 1809), eighth image. Reprinted with the permission of the American Antiquarian Society.

second half of the eighteenth century.[48] A historian studying County Essex has observed that the "refusal by single men . . . to take service on demand, was frequently reported to the petty sessions by the parish constables."[49] Specifically, several unmarried men were reported for being "masterless men and other that work at their own hand contrary to the law" or for working "about by the day," thus violating the requirements for quarterly and yearly contracts.[50] Court records indicate that a number of single women were prosecuted under the laws, suggesting that the authorities, like lawmakers, saw little difference among people who were young and propertyless. Although most jurisdictions prosecuted more men than women, a majority of the presentations under the statutes of laborers and artificers in at least one county were single women.[51]

In addition to requiring the service of young and propertyless singles, Parliament also used the economic crisis of the sixteenth century to begin regulating the sexuality of the unmarried. Since the thirteenth century most matters relating to marriage and sexuality had fallen under the purview of the Roman Catholic Church, which set the penalties for sex outside of marriage and meted out punishments through an elaborate system of ecclesiastical courts. The only instances in which the state contravened the Church's authority on matters of sexuality were cases of rape and the abduction of women.[52] The Reformation challenged the status quo as radical Protestants contended that the church courts' typical penalties of fines, shaming rituals, and threat of excommunication were ineffective at stemming the assault on God's commandments. Such true believers, most notably the Puritans, demanded that the state assume total control over matters of sexuality. Tudor monarchs largely resisted these demands with the exception of buggery, which Parliament made a capital crime in 1534.[53]

In a society obsessed with the ill effects of too many masterless men, one did not have to be a radical Protestant to see the wisdom in keeping imprudent couples from producing more vagrants and idlers. Bastard children fell upon the charity of the local parish, which had to raise taxes in order to provide for them. In an attempt to reduce the number of "Bastards begotten and borne out of lawfull Matrimonye," the state began to exert greater control over issues relating to fornication and bastardy in the last quarter of the sixteenth century. In 1576 Parliament approved a new poor law, stating that local justices of the peace "shall and maye by their discretion take Order aswell for the punishement of the Mother and reputed Father of suche Bastarde Childe." Although lawmakers left the sin of fornication to the church courts, the 1576 poor law asserted an explicit moral rebuke of those who committed "an Offence againste Gods Lawe and Mans Lawe" by their "evell Example and Encouradgement of lewde Lyef." In practice, most civil magistrates who heard bastardy cases only extracted fines from male offenders, although some took the opportunity to lecture offenders on why a father should marry the mother of his child.[54]

Although the bastardy provision of the 1576 poor law was far less important than the statutes of laborers and artificers, it was another means by which the state problematized single men. By transforming bastardy into a crime against the state, lawmakers further reduced bachelors, this time to criminals. In a parallel to the division between single men in the labor statutes, the fathers of bastards were singled out for harsh treatment but noncriminal single men were left alone. Given that the bastardy law was part of the poor law, it is probable that the same men prosecuted for their sexuality were also forced into service under the statutes of laborers and artificers. The bastardy law also opened the door for further civil legislation against the unmarried. If the state was able to fine men who conceived children outside of marriage, then there was little to stop it from also punishing all types of nonmarital sex. Although English lawmakers largely left these matters in the hands of the church courts, the thrust of the 1576 poor law set the stage for American colonists to assert more control over the sex lives of bachelors.

The Unmarried in Early America

A hundred years after the first colonists landed in Jamestown, Robert Beverley looked back on the first century of life in Virginia. Writing his history at a time when marriage and family in Virginia were commonplace, Beverley was struck by the unique demographics of the colony's early years:

> Those that went over to that Country first, were chiefly single Men, who had not the Incumbrances of Wives and Children in England; and if they had, they did not expose them to the fatigue and hazard of so long a Voyage, until they saw how it should fare with themselves. From hence it came to pass, that when they were setled there in a comfortable way of Subsisting a Family, they grew sensible of the Misfortune of wanting Wives, and such as had left Wives in England, sent for them; but the single Men were put to their Shifts [set to work].[55]

Beverley's retrospective assessment was correct: the settlement of the English colonies in America began with single men. Among the 104 men and boys who landed at Jamestown on May 13, 1607, nearly all were unmarried, including early leaders John Smith and George Percy. From that point on, unmarried adults would constitute a considerable minority of the colonial American population. Yet as Beverley's passage indicates, not all single men shared the same fate. Wealthy and powerful men acquired wives in short order while those at the bottom of the social ladder became servants. Such conditions mimicked the experience in England. Beverley's history also suggests subtle differences between single life in the New World and the Old World, specifically an exclusive focus on men and a lack of laws demarcating differences between the unmarried. For the first two generations of life in America, the treatment, perception, and experience of single men was largely the same as it had been in sixteenth-century England, yet subtle differences were also planted from the very start.

When discussing marital status in early America, the most important question is the most difficult to answer: How many single people were there? Historians have long insisted that the unmarried constituted a negligible minority despite a constant stream of case studies that suggest otherwise. Thus when Richard Middleton asserts "one myth about the colonial family which has proved grounded in reality is that nearly everyone married," he proceeds to spend more time qualifying his assertion than demonstrating it. In truth, it is impossible to quantify marital status in colonial America due to the paucity of sources as well as the dramatic regional and cultural variations. No mechanism existed in colonial America to regularly count the number of colonists or to inquire into the basic aspects of their lives. Occasionally, a new governor would demand a census to know how many men were able to bear arms, although such inquiries rarely concerned themselves with which men were husbands and which were not. In fact, only three colonywide censuses survive in which the census takers asked about marital status: New Hampshire's counts from 1767 and 1773 and Connecticut's from 1774. All three reveal a surprisingly large number of unmarried adults. Twenty-six percent of people ages twenty to seventy were unmarried in Connecticut as were thirty-seven percent of sixteen- to sixty-year-old men in New Hampshire. To be sure, neither colony distinguished between the never married and the previously married, and both included people just past the age of puberty. Nevertheless, these figures do suggest that Middleton is exaggerating when he claims "in most colonies single people comprised a mere 3 percent of the population."[56]

Lacking comprehensive counts, we are left to generalize about the number of singles based on anecdotal evidence and case studies. Although it is unclear how representative these may be of early America writ large, some patterns are discernable. First, there were more singles in societies that depended on unfree labor than in those that did not, the most obvious example being early Virginia and Maryland. James Horn estimates that between 70 and 85 percent of arrivals to the Chesapeake in the seventeenth century were indentured servants. As a rule, these servants were young and male. Passenger lists from the 1630s reveal that almost half were between the ages of twenty and twenty-four and that men outnumbered women by a ratio of six to one. Because of these patterns single men remained a sizable minority of the Chesapeake a generation after indentured servitude had been replaced by African slavery. In their examination of testate records, Lois Green Carr and Russell Menard discovered that over a quarter of the men in southern Maryland who died with estates between 1658 and 1705 had never married. Although the Chesapeake is the classic example of a society dominated by too many men, indentured servitude supplied workers to all of the colonies, creating a constant presence of young single men throughout seventeenth-century America. Once the colonists began replacing white servants with black slaves, the gender disparity—and thus the presence of unmarried men—continued. Among slaves in the mainland American colonies, there were on average 130 men for every 100 women for most of the eighteenth century.[57]

Second, there tended to be more single men among the first generation of settlers. Robert Beverley's observations about the early Chesapeake are borne out in the Virginia Muster of 1624–25. This rare seventeenth-century census offers a detailed list of the 1,218 people who called Virginia home. Reflective of immigration patterns, the muster reveals that more than 75 percent of the population was male and nearly 60 percent were between the ages of fifteen and twenty-nine. Of the 1,218 inhabitants, 507 (42%) were servants, and of the servants 437 (86%) were white men. Given these dimensions, it is not surprising that almost 70 percent of adult Virginians were single. Yet not all single men were servants. Of 309 households, 86 (28%)

consisted of one person—almost always a single man—and another 8 households were headed by two men. Similar patterns are discernable among other immigrants. Passenger lists reveal that three out of every five persons who sailed to New England during the first two decades of settlement were male. When Germans began arriving in the eighteenth century, they came in similar proportions. Indeed, right up until the American Revolution men consistently outnumbered women among immigrants regardless of status or place of origin. Although not all male immigrants were single, the demographic disparity suggests that there was a constant influx of men without wives and families, especially in port cities and in those locales that absorbed large numbers of immigrants such as the Pennsylvania backcountry.[58]

Third, cultural variations meant that there were more single people in some locales than others. Through a detailed analysis of two monthly meetings, Robert Wells has established that 12 percent of Quaker men and 15 percent of Quaker women made it to age fifty having never married. Subsequent studies by Barry Levy and Susan Klepp have confirmed these findings. The presence of so many unmarried people among a sect known for its esteem of marriage and family is perplexing unless one accepts the argument made by Karin Wulf that Quakerism included an implicit acceptance of the unmarried. Yet it was apparently not only the Quakers that were content to have so many singles in their midst. A study of urban Jews in late-eighteenth-century America indicates that a third who lived to age fifty never married. A lack of female coreligionists may account for this disparity. Alternately, an increased number of bachelors may have stemmed from the constraints of specific vocations. Throughout the colonies certain professions continued to attract more single men than others. In addition to the military and schoolmastery, the sea attracted unmarried men and thus villages of unattached fisherman, such as Marblehead, Massachusetts, kept a presence of singles on the periphery of New England. Ultimately, a number of people did not marry for reasons that are difficult to explain. A 1698 enumeration of Bedford, New York, indicates that a third of the adult population was unmarried despite gender parity. Likewise, 9 percent of eighteenth-century Yale graduates died having never married. Such men clearly could not claim poverty or a lack of eligible women.[59]

As was the case in England, the vast majority of colonial Americans married. Yet the evidence—however incomplete it may be—suggests that we should not necessarily conclude that marriage was universal or that the single life was any less common in early America than it was in sixteenth-century England. A similar conclusion can be reached by looking at the average age at which the American colonists married for the first time. Eighteenth-century New England was a good place to be in the marriage market as most women who married did so around age twenty-two or twenty-three and most men around twenty-five or twenty-six, both two years younger than their English counterparts. However, most people living in other places and times in early America had a much different experience. On average, men in eighteenth-century Germantown and Bethlehem, Pennsylvania, did not marry until age thirty. The same was true for male immigrants to the seventeenth-century

Chesapeake.[60] Although servitude and a lack of eligible partners no doubt played a part in the delay, early America was full of unfree workers and places with unequal sex ratios. Accordingly, we should not assume that most American colonists married any more quickly than their English ancestors had.

Cultural understandings of the unmarried also crossed the Atlantic. Yet the laws, literature, and lives of the unmarried proved far more volatile than the demographic situation. Despite a consistent contingent of single people, ideas about them changed radically over the course of the seventeenth and eighteenth centuries, allowing a new connotation of bachelorhood to emerge. This change was slow, subtle, and not without contradictions. Yet the discourse on the single life began in the earliest years of settlement and American ideas about bachelors soon diverged from English ones.

Family Government in New England

Colonial New England has long enjoyed the reputation as a family-centered society. A number of families came over on the *Mayflower* and the Great Migration of the 1630s was full of fathers, mothers, and children. In part, this was a result of the high premium Calvinists placed on the family and the religious meaning assigned to the household. As in England, the household was the primary locus of political power and economic regulation, but among the Puritans it also took on religious significance. Engaged in building the New Israel, the New England faithful sought to disseminate their beliefs to their children and bring them up in the ways of the Lord. Accordingly, Puritan families not only worked together, they prayed together, read the Bible together, and sought to divine whether they were predestined or not together. Religious imagery filled understandings of familial relations and the family became the model for the society writ large. Selectmen served as "fathers of the towns," and the family was known as "a little commonwealth." As a result, household heads in New England assumed great responsibilities. In the first years of settlement the colonial governments gave masters near absolute authority over their dependents. Although this power was subsequently revised to allow the church and the state more authority over the lives of individuals, New Englanders embraced the stern paterfamilias as society's central figure.[61]

The Puritan view of the family informed ideas of the single state in early New England. As the Puritans established communities, they relied on the paternal leadership of masters regardless of marital status. Edward Alleyn was an early town father of Dedham, Massachusetts, despite never marrying. He had a hand in the town's incorporation, held a number of local offices, and was a deputy to the colony's representative assembly, the General Court. Alleyn's prominence was due in part to his wealth. Early records name him as a "gentleman" and he acquired a town lot as well as a 350-acre farm. Yet it was not only Alleyn's money that commanded the respect of his community. He was a devout Puritan and one of only eight people deemed sufficiently predestined to join the local church when it formed in 1638.[62]

Conversely, those single men who were young and propertyless came under intense scrutiny. As he sailed to America aboard the *Arabella*, Massachusetts governor John Winthrop observed fistfights between young men as well as a young woman who nearly drank herself to death. Of the latter he noted: "We observed it a Common fault in our yonge people, that they gave themselues to drinke hott waters verye immoderately."[63] Winthrop and other Puritan leaders recognized that young men were in a transitional state, still learning self-mastery and preparing to receive the Holy Spirit. To aid the process, they believed that the young needed more supervision and parental guidance. As Anne Lombard has explained, men in early New England were discouraged from learning manhood from their peers and wasting their time drinking and whoring as part of a bachelors' social round. Instead, they were expected to hew closely to the commands of their fathers and to achieve manhood by putting away childish things. As a result, bachelor freedoms proved far more circumscribed in New England than in the old country.[64]

Toward this end, Winthrop and other early New Englanders crafted a legal code that strengthened the position of the family and reduced young and propertyless singles to dependency. The General Court of Massachusetts passed one law that required parents to teach their children the "ability to read & understand the principles of religion & the capitall lawes of this country" and another that prescribed death for "a stubborne or rebellious sonne" who would not "obey ye voyce of his fathr or ye voyce of his mother."[65] The General Court also made sure that other household dependents would be orderly by prescribing the duties of servants and fixing workers' wages. It was in this same vein that Massachusetts first identified the unmarried. On December 13, 1636, the General Court ordered "that all townes shall take care to order & dispose of all single p[er]sons & inmates wth their towne to servise, or otherwise."[66] Connecticut and Plymouth adopted similar laws within a year, as did New Haven and Rhode Island some time later.[67]

The family government laws have received considerable attention over the years from historians. Edmund Morgan, John Demos, and others have suggested that laws requiring single people be put to service were evidence of the Puritans' hostility toward unmarried people. However, this argument misinterprets early New England understandings of the single state. The laws did not seek to punish people for being unmarried nor did they try to encourage youngsters to marry more quickly. Instead, they mimicked the English statutes of laborers and artificers by ensuring that any young and propertyless person found to be masterless would be assigned to a household.[68] The English labor laws were consistent with the Puritans' notions of family order and they were appropriate given New England's economy. Whereas colonies in the Chesapeake profited from monoculture plantations worked by indentured servants and later African slaves, New England retained the English pattern of dividing the land into small farms for subsistence agriculture. It was more efficient for families to work these holdings, and if fathers and sons proved unable to supply the necessary labor, native-born servants in husbandry were hired. As had been the case in England, hired workers in New England were typically unmarried people in their teens or early twenties who contracted to work by the year and lived with their masters. Such workers were critical to the success of the economy; even if the Puritans had wanted to eliminate all unmarried people, they could not have done so. The laws existed so that every young man had a master to ensure his compliance with the laws of the colony and the laws of God.[69]

The New England family government laws closely followed the English statutes of laborers and artificers. As in England, the distance between master and servant was far more important than differences of sex, age, or occupation. Accordingly, Connecticut's law applied only to people who were "neither maried nor hath any servaunte, & be noe publicke officer." There were also subtle differences in the laws that separated England and America as well as the individual colonies. Most colonies left out any reference to age, but as the primary purpose was to restrain the young, some made this explicit. Rhode Island's law specified that "any young man though above twenty-one years of age" was to be placed with a family and Connecticut's law singled out the "young" specifically. The New England laws also were mute on issues of occupation and length of service and thus did not demand a person work by the year nor did they distinguish between journeymen and servants in husbandry. The most important distinction was the coded discussion of gender. Like the English laws, the Massachusetts and Plymouth statutes applied to every single person and the New Haven law explicitly named the "single person of either Sex." Yet not all colonies were so inclusive. The laws of Connecticut and Rhode Island applied only to the offending "young man."

Subtle differences in language gave way to profound differences in enforcement, especially with respect to gender. Whereas English authorities regularly prosecuted single women for being out of household government, New England's efforts fell almost entirely on bachelors. Magistrates worried about men who lived alone. John Littlehale of Haverhill, Massachusetts, appeared before the Essex County Court in 1672 because he "lay in a house by himself contrary to the law of the country, whereby he is subject to much sin and iniquity, which ordinarily are the companions and consequences of a solitary life." Although the record does not specify what type of iniquity Littlehale was engaging in, the court ordered the twenty-one year old to place himself with a family within six weeks or have the Haverhill selectmen do it for him. Failing to heed the court's direction, Littlehale would be placed in the local house of correction.[70] Concerns about immorality also brought young men who lived together to the attention of the courts. In 1653 Teague Jones and Richard Berry appeared before the Plymouth Colony General Court for keeping house together and were ordered to live apart. A contentious pair, the two had first appeared together before the court four years earlier when Berry accused Jones of "sodomy, & other vnclean practisses allso with Sara, the wife of Hugh Norman." Sodomy—the act of sexual intercourse between two men—was a serious charge in seventeenth-century America and could bring the death penalty in most colonies. Although Berry later admitted the sodomy charges were untrue and was whipped for making a false accusation, the two men lived together anyway and apparently brought out the worst in each other.[71] Although the courts stepped in to keep single men from living apart or together, they rarely took similar action against single women. Masterlessness in New England was a masculine crime.

The uneven application of the family government laws may stem in part from the lackluster enforcement of the statutes overall. Despite the occasional involvement of the courts, the burden of enforcing the family government laws fell mostly on the towns. This was appropriate since New England selectmen were well versed in disposing of idle servants and warning out strangers. Yet records indicate that most towns ignored the family government laws unless and until prodded to action by the colonial governments. The records of Dedham, Massachusetts, are entirely absent of any action against singles for the first generation of settlement, suggesting a general ambivalence about the living situation of young singles in their midst. Indeed, the first mention of masterless youths appeared in 1662 when the town considered "whether Such younge men as liue in the Towne and not vnder parents or masters dispose but in there imployment are at there owne dispose." The selectmen were not considering reducing these young men to dependence but rather whether or not they should "be accounted Inhabitants & to doe sume worke in the high wayes as other inhabitance doe."[72] In other words, Dedham pondered whether living on their own made young men responsible for communal labor or if such obligations were the responsibility of employers. In a move that completely inverted the intention of the 1636 law, the selectmen ruled that the young men were on their own.

Dedham was hardly unique. Throughout New England towns took great liberty to interpret the laws as best suited the situation. New Haven town records from April 1686 chronicle an incident in which "John Osbell a single man upon his request had liberty graunted him to live by himselfe for the present untill the Towne see cause to alter." Osbell was a man of some means who had accrued property in New Haven, and who apparently lived peaceably by himself without any complaints of idleness or disorder.[73] More common were cases in which single men gained permission to live together. In 1652 Windsor, Connecticut, allowed Isaac Shelton and Samuel Rockwell to "keep house together" so long as "they carry themselves soberly and do not entertain idle persons, to the evil expense of time by night or day."[74] In both cases single men had to request the right to be their own masters and they had to give assurances that they would not fall into idleness and immorality. Although this was in keeping with the spirit of the law, it presumed a masculine autonomy available to well-behaved young and propertyless single men, a presumption not anticipated by the statute itself.

Time and again the towns' defiance of the family government laws attracted the attention of the colonial governments. In 1668 Massachusetts complained that "it doth appear that the Select men are negligent in executing the Laws therein mentioned" and announced that it would begin fining those towns not in compliance with the law. Where the selectmen failed to act, the General Court would "dispose of single persons, stubborn Children or Servants to the house of Correction, according to the intent of the Law." Lest any town cite a precedent of inaction, the

Court voided "any Law, Custom or Usage to the contrary." Each town was required to submit "a List of the names of those young persons within the Bounds of
your Town" who were not "under Family Government."[75] Throughout the colony
selectmen responded accordingly. In Dorchester in 1669 sixteen men were called
before the selectmen and warned "to take inspection of their orderly walking [in-
vestigate their behavior] and submitting to family government."[76] That same year
Dedham went so far as to demand appearances from adult sons who lived with
their parents and issue superfluous orders such as "Ezra Morse is alowed to be
vnder his mothers gouernmt."[77] Having disposed of their single men, the towns
took no further action on the issue and called no unmarried men before the council
for the next three years. Apparently, the General Court had intended for the towns
to enforce the law more than once and so it turned the matter over to the county
courts. In 1671 the Essex County Court ordered "that the selectmen observe the
court orders carefully," and the Middlesex County Court issued a similar rebuke
the following year.[78] Once again the towns acted dutifully. Dorchester presented
two men for living out of family government in 1672 and another in 1673. Dedham
in 1672 called all single men living out of family government to appear before its
selectman and did so annually for the next six years.[79] Other colonies may have
struggled with their towns as the assemblies in Connecticut and Plymouth also
reiterated their commitment to the family government laws at midcentury.[80]

In essence, there was a basic disagreement in New England between the colonies
and the towns, and also between the theological understanding of youth and how
the colonists actually treated young men. At the heart of this debate were basic
issues of manhood and the role of single men in society. Although the colonial government insisted on the need for all masterless men to be placed under the control
of a master, the towns as well as bachelors insisted on the right of the individual to
be responsible for himself. Clearly there were limits. Those men who earned the
privilege of living outside of family government had to renounce indolence, drunkenness, and sexual mischief. In effect, single men on their own had to live as if they
had masters. Yet this was an opportunity available to men alone. Women did not
make the same transition from dependent to master but were expected to remain
under the rule of a man for their entire lives. Whether single or married, a woman
was not to live alone, and thus the towns received no petitions from unmarried
women seeking permission to assume the duties of mastery. In a pattern that would
repeat itself again and again over the next century, bachelors were able to use their
gender to assert their independence and autonomy while single women remained
dependents.

In the end, the towns and the single men triumphed. After the 1670s the issue of
masterless men in Massachusetts was quietly forgotten. The General Court never
again raised the issue and 1677 was the last year that Dedham set aside a portion
of the town meeting "to setel the younge persons in such familyes in the Towne as
is most sutable for thier good."[81] By 1691 whatever interest there had once been in
the law had disappeared from the colony. That year Massachusetts received a new

charter and was compelled to reissue all laws, making sure that they were in compliance with the statutes of England. Although the family government law would have met this criterion, the legislature made no provision for single people. In 1703 the General Court did add language to the poor law ordering that "no single person of either sex, under the age of twenty-one years, shall be suffered to live at their own hand, but under some orderly family government."[82] However, by limiting the application of the family government law to poor children, the legislature severely limited the scope of the original statute. In the other New England colonies the family government laws died such a quiet death that it is difficult to pinpoint the exact moment when the statutes expired. One historian has argued that the 1636 law of Connecticut continued in force until the general revision of the statutes of 1821, making the law "the oldest statute provision on our records not previously repealed, expressly or by implication." In the town he examines, however, this historian finds that the law was last applied in 1699.[83]

To be sure, communal values and economic realities meant that most single men continued to place themselves under the rule of masters. In his autobiography, Benjamin Franklin remembered a time in the 1720s when "my Brother being yet unmarried, did not keep House, but boarded himself and his Apprentices in another Family."[84] Yet by the fourth quarter of the seventeenth century the state no longer took an interest in forcing the dependence of freemen. It was about this time that bachelor freedoms began to emerge in New England. Authorities looked the other way as Harvard students engaged in the excessive drinking and mischief making. At the same time, a group of young men in Boston established the Friday Evening Association of Batchelors in 1677. Although it would take another century for bachelorhood to emerge as an expression of masculine autonomy, the seeds were well planted by the 1670s.[85]

Sex and the Single Man

As John Winthrop and the other founders of New England formulated a plan for regulating young men, they worried about what would happen if bachelors became masterless. The young man who lived outside of the stern command of a paterfamilias would inevitably become idle and descend into a life of immorality, of drinking, gambling, and breaking the Sabbath. Yet the worst crime was sexual incontinence. In his diary Winthrop time and again noted the "lustes of youthe," such as in 1631 when "a yonge fellowe was whipped, for soliciting an Indian Sqa to incontinencye," or eleven years later when "a servant in Salem, about 18 or 20 years of age, was found in buggery with a cow, upon the Lord's day."[86] Proper parental guidance could have negated such crimes, but once they had been committed, they were such an affront to the laws of God that only a civil magistrate could mete out proper punishment.

Back in England the Puritans had complained about leaving sexual offenses in the hands of the church courts. The "bawdy courts," as they called them, meted out penalties that were insufficient to discourage immoral behavior and that ignored biblical proscriptions. Free to craft their own legislation in New England, the Puritans quickly went to work. They made marriage a wholly civil institution and gave control over sex crimes to the secular courts.[87] The most heinous of acts, such as adultery, rape, sodomy, and bestiality, were all declared capital offenses. To make sure that everyone knew these laws came from God, Massachusetts cited passages in Leviticus and Deuteronomy alongside the laws when it first published them. Laws were also passed banning sex with girls under ten years of age, polygamy, incest, and the murder of a bastard child to conceal pregnancy, although the penalties for such crimes were less than death.[88] None of these laws made any reference to marital status. In part, this appears to have been a consequence of using the Bible as a guide since the Old Testament made no distinctions between bachelors and husbands when it came to sodomy and rape. It also appears that while early New Englanders worried about the lusts of youth, they did not necessarily connect moral depravity to the single state. When Plymouth governor William Bradford bemoaned the "sundry notorious sins" such as sodomy and bestiality that broke out in 1642, he wrote of "not only incontinency between persons unmarried, for which many both men and women have been punished sharply enough, but some married persons also."[89] Nor were singles prosecuted more often than married people for the most heinous crimes. To be sure, when New Haven put to death William Plaine because he committed sodomy and "corrupted a great part of the youth of Gilford by masturbation," John Winthrop remarked that sodomy "tended to the frustratinge of the Ordinance of marriage & the hindringe of the generation of mankind." Yet Winthrop admitted that Plaine was "a married man." Indeed, Winthrop was far more concerned about Plaine's atheism, heresy, and that he was "a monster in humaine shape" than his marital status.[90] If anything, New Englanders proved more determined to constrict the sexuality of married men. Because colonial law defined adultery as when "any man shall have carnall copulacon with another mans wife," a married man who had sex with a single woman could be tried under a lesser charge. Yet Bradford denounced this exemption and demanded that husbands who engaged in extramarital affairs with single women be prosecuted for the capital crime of adultery.[91] In short, it was a lack of mastery and not the lack of a wife that predicted a man's sexual immorality. Early New Englanders did not assume that bachelors were nascent homosexuals or more likely to commit violent sexual acts.

The one area of sex crime legislation in which New England lawmakers made special provision for the unmarried was fornication. By definition, fornication was committed when a single woman engaged in intercourse. The marital status of the man was usually not specified but typically the man was also unmarried. More often than not, those presented for fornication were young people who had given in to temptation and whose actions had resulted in the birth of a child. Many of these couples were already betrothed or at least had been contemplating a union when they engaged in coitus and thus many took the woman's pregnancy as a sign that they should marry. Records of fornication prosecutions in the Essex County Court between 1641 and 1685 show that 61 percent of couples had already wed before they faced a magistrate. In Plymouth during the same time the number of married couples presented for fornication outnumbered unmarried ones by almost three to one. Those couples that formalized their unions were rewarded for their initiative. Married couples were often given the option of paying a fine. Fornicators who resisted marriage were typically whipped instead.[92]

For lawmakers, the courts, and the community as a whole, it was critical that couples who had conceived a child enter into wedlock. A single mother inevitably became impoverished, thus placing new mouths on the poor relief rolls. Marriage, on the other hand, ensured a father's financial support and established a household for the orderly governance of offspring. Early New England lawmakers looked to England for precedent, specifically the 1576 poor law that charged magistrates with determining the father of a bastard. They also found inspiration in Deuteronomy 22:28–29, which ordered that a man who lay with a virgin must pay a fine to the woman's father and take her as his wife. Toward this end, New England lawmakers included provisions in their fornication laws that encouraged marriage. In a statute replicated in all the New England colonies but one, Massachusetts ordered that a couple convicted of premarital sex be punished "either by enioyning to marriage, or fine, or corporall punishmt, or all or any of these, as the iudges shall appoint, most agreeablie to the word."[93]

A unique addition to the New England law code, the enjoin-to-marry provision became a tool for magistrates to push reluctant couples toward wedlock. When Matthew Stanley appeared before the Essex County Court with Ruth Andrewes on the charge of fornication in December 1649, the magistrates ordered the two be fined fifty shillings or whipped, but added that the punishment "be remitted if they marry together." The couple wed and later moved to Topsfield where they raised several children.[94] As this case illustrates, the enjoin-to-marry clause was almost always offered to a couple in lieu of a fine rather than as an ultimatum. This is not to say that the courts did not exert pressure on the couples that approached extortion. In November 1669 the Essex County Court fined William Sanders four pounds for fornication with Mary Vocah, provided that the judgment be halved if Sanders married Vocah. As the couple was confined to prison until they paid the fine, the offer effectively persuaded the two to wed.[95]

Despite the effectiveness of the enjoin-to-marry clause, it remained an underutilized provision of New England law. Of more than three hundred cases of fornication presented to the Massachusetts General Court, the Essex (Massachusetts) County Court, the Suffolk (Massachusetts) County Court, and the Plymouth Colony General Court in the seventeenth century, only six involved orders to wed. The vast majority of persons were either fined or whipped while the rest were either acquitted or faced uniquely humiliating penalties including having to wear a scarlet letter.[96] Although many of the fornication cases involved couples who had already married, the reluctance of courts to use the law indicates a larger discourse on the role of the state in regulating the actions of unmarried men. As was the case with the family government laws, a number of single men defied the law and the courts largely tolerated their disobedience. Once again New Englanders proved accepting of the type of bachelor freedom that the region's founders had sought to extinguish.

Although magistrates were never very comfortable employing the enjoin-to-marry provision, by the fourth quarter of the seventeenth century single men had become increasingly defiant of any attempt to push them toward marriage. When Joseph Cowell appeared before the Suffolk County Court in April 1673, he confessed to the charge of "too much familiarity" with Mary Hunter. In response, the court ordered Cowell to be whipped with thirty stripes and to pay four shillings a week in child support "until hee either marry with her or this Court take further Order." Cowell ignored the court's offer to wed Hunter and appeared again nine months later on charges of fornication with a different woman.[97] When John Ring and Martha Lampson appeared before the Essex County Court seven years later, the court ordered the couple whipped or fined, but "if said John should, within six hours or before noon on this Sept. 29, 1680, marry said Martha, their fines were to be reduced. If he refused, he was to be bound for the maintenance of the child." Facing marriage or child support, Ring chose the latter.[98] In addition to their willful defiance of the law, male fornicators increasingly turned a deaf ear to the pressure of friends, family, and neighbors. Although most early New Englanders wed before they faced sentencing, only nineteen of fifty-two men tried for fornication in Suffolk County, Massachusetts, in the 1670s had married their partners at the time of presentment.[99]

As was the case when the colonists began flouting the family government law, the Massachusetts assembly attempted to reign in the growing problem of sexually incontinent single men. In 1665 the General Court approved a law whereby a freeman convicted of fornication could be disfranchised.[100] But the courts proved even more reluctant to enforce this law than the enjoin-to-marry clause. Out of three hundred fornication cases, in only one was a man threatened with disfranchisement, and in that case the law was used to compel the man's appearance after he had repeatedly ignored the court's summonses.[101] More important, disfranchisement was hardly an effective deterrent when most of the offenders were young men who owned no land and thus could not vote anyway. It also avoided the most important issue: child support. Accordingly, in 1668 the General Court tried again. This time, it adopted a bastardy law that demanded that any man "legally convicted to be the father of a bastard child, he shall be at the care & charge to majnteyne & bring vp the same." Tired of single men challenging the claims of pregnant women, the assembly deputized midwives to examine single mothers during delivery about the child's paternity and to relate their findings to the court. If this method proved inadequate, then "the man charged by the woman to be the father . . . shall be the reputed father, & accordingly be ljable to the charge of maintenance."[102]

An effective bastardy law ultimately served as the compromise between the colony's desire that fornicating singles marry and the colonists' preference that the freedom of the single man be preserved. After 1682 Massachusetts magistrates no longer pressured couples to wed. In 1703 Connecticut became the last New England colony to remove the enjoin-to-marry clause from its fornication law.[103] However, single men could not fornicate with impunity. They still faced social pressure from the community to marry their partners and the courts demanded that they provide financial support for any children they fathered. There was no sexual revolution in the last quarter of the seventeenth century like there would be a century later; although the laws changed, sexual incontinence remained illegal and immoral.

New England's shift toward bastardy laws effectively separated free white men from other nonmasters. In practice, the region's fornication laws had always been more gender neutral than its family government laws as women and men often received the same punishment. Indeed, the enjoin-to-marry clause may have worked to the advantage of pregnant single women whose partners might otherwise have abandoned them. Conversely, the bastardy laws advantaged bachelors at the expense of single women. First, the offending man only had to pay child support while the woman had responsibility of raising the child. The courts typically required that men pay for the woman's lying-in period, put up a substantial bond, and pay two to three shillings per week in cash, corn, or other provisions until the child reached the age of seven and could be put out to service. However, several men tried to abbreviate the length of time they were required to pay child support including Josiah Clarke who obtained permission to put out his bastard at the age of two.[104] Second, with the implementation of the bastardy law, the fornication law largely became a tool for punishing single women and men of color. Cornelia Hughes Dayton has found that in the New Haven courts, no white man accused of fornication confessed his crime and pled guilty after 1701, and that after 1745 the towns ceased to prosecute men for bastardy altogether. Similar trends appeared in Massachusetts almost as soon as child support was introduced. In this, the option to dispose of one's sexual indiscretion through monetary means alone became a privilege afforded to wealthy and free white men alone. While single women struggled to raise their children by themselves, servants and those single men who could not afford weekly payments continued to be whipped for fornication. When Nimrod, an African American, was found guilty of fornication in 1685, the Plymouth General Court ordered that he be whipped and put to service to raise eighteen pence a week in child support.[105] In a trend that would become common in the eighteenth century, the New England courts ceased to treat single men the same way they did women, children, and servants.

In a parallel to the demise of the family government laws, the New England bastardy laws placed the onus of personal responsibility on young men. They had to make decisions about their sexuality and regulate their own desires. In part, this sense of individual choice had always been lurking just below the surface. The choice of whom, when, or whether to marry had always been left up to the individual and, even with their fixation on the family, the Puritans had not negated this right. Indeed, the failure of the enjoin-to-marry clause may have reflected a larger cultural discomfort with anything that hinted at disturbing this sacred privilege. An individual, especially one who had already fathered a child, could be pressured, cajoled, or shamed into marriage, but the state had no right to force a person into marriage. Even as critics took aim at bachelorhood in the eighteenth century, Americans would never impinge on this basic personal right. Appropriately, at the beginning of the eighteenth century, New England divines praised personal responsibility when it came to single men and sexuality. In a 1704 sermon Boston pastor and Harvard president Samuel Willard looked not to the law to restrain the impulses of young men but the admonitions of faith. "As to those who never entred into a State of Marriage," Willard wrote, "it is their Duty to maintain Modesty, in Thoughts, Words and Actions; and with great Sobriety to wait the Time when God shall call them to Change their Condition."[106]

Batchelors Hope in the Chesapeake

In exploring the transmission of ideas about the unmarried from England to America, New England serves as a tidy example. Because of the region's economy and Puritan ideology, the colonists adopted English cultural perceptions and statutes, gradually modifying them to fit their own experience and beliefs. By contrast, the movement to the Chesapeake was messy and abrupt. The first English settlers in Virginia looked not to replicate England in America but to exploit the region's resources. When they failed to find gold, the colonists profited from having indentured servants grow tobacco on large plantations. The dual expectation of adventure and reliance on unfree labor meant that the population remained overwhelmingly male for the first century of settlement and that family life materialized slowly. In this environment the English rules for the single state made little sense and were generally ignored. In their place a new idea emerged: the free and autonomous American bachelor.

In his 1584 manifesto of colonization, Richard Hakluyt popularized the idea of America as a dumping ground for England's single men. Observing that England was "swarming at this day with valiant youths, rusting and hurtful by lack of employment," Hakluyt recommended putting such men to work in a colony mining gold and producing naval stores.[107] Although it would be more than twenty years before a permanent English colony was established in the New World, Hakluyt's ideas would be central to the first century of settlement in the Chesapeake colonies of Virginia and Maryland. From the beginning the Virginia Company imported thousands of young, single men from the lowest ranks of English society to serve as hewers of wood and drawers of water. Initially their presence proved destabilizing, but once the settlers at Jamestown discovered the profits of growing tobacco, such men became the backbone of the economy. They arrived primarily as indentured servants and often found life in America harsher than it had been in England. Cruel treatment and insufficient food, clothing, and shelter were common, as was an early death.[108]

Lawmakers in Virginia and Maryland gave masters broad powers over their indentured servants. Within the first generation of settlement the two assemblies enumerated the penalties for servants who ran away, committed fornication, or resisted the command of their masters. Although the masters' power had limits, the government allowed planters to lengthen the terms of ill-behaved servants and even sell them like property. Such prerogatives were loosely based on England's poor laws and statutes of laborers and artificers, although neither gave masters so much power over their workers. Masters also had the right to keep their servants single. One could give a servant permission to marry, but the man who lacked an independent income would have been unable to support a wife—that is, if he could find a wife at a time and place where there were six male servants for every female one. The law also gave masters the power to prevent informal unions. If two servants engaged in a clandestine marriage or conceived a child out of wedlock, the master could punish them with extended service.[109]

Most indentured servants were too preoccupied with staying alive to worry about marriage. On average, one of every two servants died before they completed their four- to seven-year indentures. Those who outlived their contracts often spent a number of years as hired servants, working for wages in anticipation of purchasing land. The treatment of hired servants was much the same as indentured servants. In 1619 the Virginia assembly, the House of Burgesses, approved a statute barring indolence, stating that "if any man be founde to live as an Idler or renagate, though a freedman, it shalbe lawful for that Incorporation or Plantation to which he belongeth to appoint him a M[aste]r to serve for wages" at least until that man "shewe apparant signes of amendment."[110] Other imitations followed as the colony adopted maximum wage limits, allowed masters to prosecute hired servants who left before their contracts expired, and required vagrants to provide security for good behavior. Hired servants tended to contract for a year at a time and thus they could more easily leave an abusive master. They also received wages for their services, pay they could use to later purchase land and become masters themselves. A study of former indentured servants in Maryland freed before 1660 indicates that a majority obtained land and that many held public office.[111] Of course, these men still had to contend with a chronic shortage of eligible women. Through the end of the seventeenth century, men outnumbered women in the Chesapeake by a ratio of two to one. Consequently, 20 percent of men died unmarried in seventeenth-century Norfolk County, Virginia, as did 30 percent in neighboring Lancaster County. In contrast, spinsters and widows were almost nonexistent.[112]

Because the seventeenth-century Chesapeake was largely a society of single men, the very essence of what it meant to be a bachelor changed. In England and New England, single and unmarried were legal shorthand for the young and propertyless, people who needed the supervision of a father or master lest they descend into idleness and immorality. In this context, singleness was as temporary as youth, and if the men and women in question could be kept out of trouble long enough, they would become responsible masters and mistresses. Such assumptions fell flat in the

Chesapeake where bachelorhood stretched well past thirty for most men and was permanent for many.

The clearest indication of a change was in the lack of attention to marital status in the laws of Virginia and Maryland. At its first meeting in August 1619, Virginia's newly formed House of Burgesses approved the Chesapeake's first law to differentiate between single and married men. A prohibition "against excesse in apparell," the law demanded people dress according to their station and assessed fines on a man "if he be unmarried according to his owne apparell, if he be married, according to his owne and his wives, or either of their apparell." The extent of enforcement of this sumptuary statute is uncertain, although the legislatures of Virginia and Maryland never revisited the law or updated it. Indeed, with the exception of this one law, neither Chesapeake colony explicitly mentioned marital status in its statutes for the first two generations of settlement.[113]

Legal attention to bachelors did not appear in the Chesapeake until 1658 and even then it was highly qualified. As in England and New England, it was illegal for unmarried people in Virginia and Maryland to engage in intercourse. Although records indicate an official lack of concern when free people copulated, lawmakers and magistrates took a far different position when freemen fornicated with servant women. In the first two generations of settlement, a sizeable number of women who immigrated to the Chesapeake were indentured and placed in the fields alongside male servants. In such a setting it was probably inevitable that problems would arise. By the 1640s legislators began to respond to planters' complaints about freemen engaging their female servants in secret marriages or impregnating them. Of the various remedies, one clearly evoked the enjoin-to-marry provisions of New England: the Maryland fornication law of 1658. In addressing the issue of freemen who impregnated female servants, the Maryland Assembly looked both to compensate the master for the lost service of the mother and to prevent an illegitimate child from becoming a burden to taxpayers. Toward this end, the assembly sought to encourage marriage where appropriate. According to the law, a freeman who conceived a child with a servant woman under the promise of marriage had to make good on his pledge. The statute stated that "if any such mother as aforesaid be able to prove by such testimony or confession as aforesaid that the party Charged (being a single person and a freeman) did before the begitting of such Child promise her Marriage, That then hee shall performe his promise to her, or recompense her abuse, as the Court before whom such matter is brought shall see Convenient, the quallity and condition of the persons considered."[114] In other words, if a single freeman coaxed a servant woman into intercourse by pledging marriage, it would not be sufficient for him to pay child support. He had to keep his promise.

Although Maryland's fornication law remained on the books well into the eighteenth century, the official encouragement of marriage proved the exception rather than the rule.[115] In Maryland freemen who committed fornication but who had not promised marriage were ordered to pay child support, while male servants faced extended service. In Virginia the promise of marriage was not even taken into account.

In 1643 the General Assembly ordered a freeman guilty of fornication to "give satisfaction" worth double the value of the woman's service to her master and to remit five hundred pounds of tobacco to the parish.[116] When this failed to deter eager bachelors, Virginia simply increased the penalties. In 1658 the legislature ordered freemen who married servant women to pay the woman's master fifteen hundred pounds of tobacco or serve him "one complete yeare."[117] Four years later the colony ordered men convicted of sexual relations outside of marriage to pay five hundred pounds of tobacco to the parish and "put in security to keep the child and save the parish harmelesse."[118] In other words, Virginia simply avoided the debate of whether the state should encourage marriage or what the actual limits on a single man's sexuality should be. As long as a freeman compensated the master for a servant's lost work and indemnified the community against child support, his actions went unmolested by the law.

The overabundance of single men in the Chesapeake ultimately led to the acceptance of a nascent bachelor lifestyle. With wives difficult to come by, several men cultivated a masculine domesticity in place of the traditional family. In their study of single men's estates in southern Maryland in the second half of the seventeenth century, Carr and Menard found that a third of the men who died unmarried (150 of 452) took up housekeeping without a wife. Among these single householders, about half appear to have lived alone by virtue of age or transitory status: thirty-six were sons, eleven were free immigrants, and thirteen were merchants. Most of the remaining householders were former servants who kept house by themselves, although at least four and perhaps as many as twenty died while living with a male partner. Such male partnerships were primarily practical. Early Americans believed domestic labors were the sole province of women and so men went to great lengths to avoid housewifery. Single men often contracted out their domestic duties to married women, widows, or even young men. When two men decided to live together, one of the primary objects may have been to pool resources for a housekeeper. Some male partnerships also had an emotional component. Many men purchased land together and worked it as partners. Some partnerships were apparently quite affectionate as was the case of Walter Gifford who left a deathbed missive to a household companion whom he addressed as his "Loving Mate."[119] To be sure, nuclear families were considered normative in the seventeenth-century Chesapeake regardless of how difficult it was to form and maintain them.[120] But there appears to have been no animosity directed at unmarried men and the alternative households they put together. Records of prosecutions for sex crimes reveal that apart from freemen who impregnated servant women, Virginia and Maryland authorities tended to look the other way when it came to sexual intimacy. Before 1670 there was only one prosecution for bestiality in Virginia and none in Maryland. Likewise, there was only one sodomy prosecution despite the number of men keeping house together.[121]

Even more impressive was how single men in the Chesapeake redefined the term bachelor in a way that predicted the future. In 1668 William Tomson surveyed a four-hundred-acre tract in Maryland and named it Batchelors Hope. Nor was

Tomson alone. Maryland rent rolls reveal at least a dozen plantations surveyed in the second half of the seventeenth century with a similar moniker including Batchellors Choyce, Bachelor's Chance, and Batchellors Delight. Such names conveyed a double meaning. They simultaneously announced that a man had acquired property and thus was able to marry and that he was content to remain single. Indeed, there was playfulness to the names, the most obvious being the inherent pun in the word hope, which also meant a small bay.[122] Yet there was also a sense that the men on these plantations were attempting to take ownership of their marital status, to proclaim their "choyce" to be single rather than admit that they were victims of demography. The use of bachelor in plantation names ultimately may have derived from maritime life—ships named *Batchelor's Delight*, *Batchelor's Club*, and *Bachelor's Hall* were common throughout the seventeenth century. In this context, the word bachelor evoked a world of independent men, unattached and in control of their own lives, masters of themselves.[123] Such connotations stood in sharp contrast to the inferiority and service of Chaucer's bacheleris.

Single men in the Chesapeake apparently even organized themselves into groups of bachelors. In a curious letter to Lieutenant Governor Francis Nicholson dated 1691, "the Bachelors of his Government in Virginia" thanked the governor for hosting Olympic-style games. The identity of the bachelors seems to have been connected to the masculine nature of athletics, or, as the bachelors put it, to "the manly exercises of youth and feats of activity." The bachelors in this context were self-proclaimed young men who saw the games as critical to their claim to manhood. Comparing their exercises to those of the "Grecians," the bachelors praised the governor's "Olympic games" for "setting edge upon our spirits, giving us the opportunity to antedate manhood, and to commence candidates for the prosperity of our native soil, in the minority of youth." Although their purpose was physical rather than spiritual or intellectual, the games gave the young men of Virginia common cause with those youthful Bostonians who organized the Friday Evening Association of Batchelors. At the same time, the group's moniker may have paid homage or even claimed a greater connection with Governor Nicholson who was himself a bachelor with a reputation as a ladies' man.[124]

At the same time, not all single men adjusted so well to living in the Chesapeake. In 1619 the Virginia Company raised subscriptions to send over "Maids young and vncorrupt to make wifes to the Inhabitnnts." Women would hopefully restrain the dangerous impulses of so many single men in the Chesapeake, or as company director Sir Edwin Sandys put it, "make the men there more setled & lesse moueable." If married, the colonists would hopefully be alleviated of the forces "wch will breed a dissolucon, and so an ouerthrow of the Plantacon."[125]

A half century later the words of Sandys sounded prophetic as Jamestown burned to the ground during the largest uprising in colonial American history. Bacon's Rebellion of 1675–76 was the culmination of increased tensions with Native Americans, charges of government corruption, and declining opportunity for former servants to transition to property ownership and full political rights.

Throughout the uprising, the voices and actions of men frustrated by a lack of eligible women seeped out. "Every thing here is now deplorable," Governor William Berkeley wrote at the height of the insurrection, "and three Young men that have not beene two Yeares in the Country absolutely Governe it."[126] Although the uprising's leader, Nathaniel Bacon, was married, at least one of the leaders hanged for the uprising was not. Moreover, the rebellion's rank and file was mostly single men. Of twenty-four rebels of Middlesex County identified in suits for damages, only nine were married at the time of the uprising.[127]

Moreover, the rebellion was filled with misogynist language and actions. Bacon and his followers rarely distinguished among Indians, indiscriminately murdering men, women, and children. As Bacon told the story of one such assault: "Wee fell upon the men woemen and children without, disarmed and destroid them all."[128] Although we might mark such actions as evidence of racial hatred rather than violence against women per se, Bacon's rebels also exhibited enmity toward the families loyal to Governor Berkeley. Colonel Edward Hill complained that the rebels took "my wife bigg w[i]th Child prisoner, beat he w[i]th my Cane, tare her Childbed linen out of her hands, and w[i]th her lead away my Children where they must live on corne and water and lye on the Ground."[129] Such treatment of women who were not marriageable may have been a violent expression of men frustrated by the inability to wed.

Although the official accounts of Bacon's Rebellion written by Virginians and the king's officials made little mention of the participants' marital status, such issues may not have been far from many people's minds. Upon reading accounts of the uprising, English playwright Aphra Behn penned *The Widow Ranter,* which was discovered among her papers after she died in 1689. Behn's fictionalized account tells the story of men driven violent by a lack of women, including Bacon himself who, upon killing the king of the Indians, rescues the queen and declares his love for her. When he inadvertently kills the object of his affection, Bacon exclaims: "Oh thou dear Prize, for which alone I toyl'd!" Although historical inaccuracies are obvious, the play suggests that contemporaries saw a clear connection between Virginia's single men and rebellion.[130]

It is difficult to draw a straight line between the presence of too many single men and Bacon's Rebellion. To be sure, historians have tried, most notably Edmund Morgan, who argued that the uprising was a result of too many idle and armed men for whom there was little hope for economic independence or a stable family life. "Bachelors are notoriously more reckless and rebellious than men surrounded by women and children," Morgan notes, adding "and these bachelors were a particularly wild lot."[131] Yet nowhere in seventeenth-century America was there anything approaching a collective bachelor identity. Social status and property ownership remained too great of a divide, especially in the Chesapeake. Although single men named their plantations things such as Batchelors Hope, it is doubtful that they saw themselves as having anything in common with the servants who raised their tobacco. In a curious twist, the fact that so many men in the Chesapeake were unmarried may have been a leveling factor in terms of the law but it did not bring together men without wives into a political movement. Bacon's Rebellion was certainly not a bachelor's rebellion.

At the same time, the effects of Bacon's Rebellion laid the groundwork for radical change a century later. As Kathleen Brown has argued, the uprising was essentially a struggle for manhood. The former servants and small landowners who followed Nathaniel Bacon demanded legitimacy in the eyes of the great planters. Ultimately, the colonial leaders obliged, sanctioning their claims to manhood and defining white men in opposition to all other dependents. Free white men might not have had much political power or chance at economic success but they were superior to women and African slaves, whose rights were increasingly constricted.[132] The emergence of the bachelor follows a very similar path. As unmarried men were singled out in the eighteenth century—becoming subject to increasingly intrusive laws and targets of character assassinations in the press—they knew that no matter how disempowered they were, they were different from other dependents.

Compared to New England, there was less of a discourse on the single state in the colonial Chesapeake. Be it labor laws, the prosecution of sex crimes, or uprisings among the dispossessed, the sources reveal a region largely uninterested in talking about marital status. In part, the fact that single men were such an ever-present part of everyday life explains the reticence. When the sex ratios balanced out in the early eighteenth century Virginia and Maryland quickly caught up with the northern colonies and began vigorously debating the role of bachelors in society. Yet the silence was also completely in keeping with how early modern Britons and the first two generations of Americans thought about single men. They were a permanent fixture of society that required little comment. Single men did not constitute a cohesive group and their existence did not elicit commentary from the vast majority of the population.

If we return to Stephen Hoppin and William Stoughton, we can see that there was more to their interaction than seemed evident at first. As Hoppin appeared before the Dorchester selectman to give an account of his life, both continuity and change in ideas about marital status were apparent. On the one hand, the distance between the young and propertyless single man and the older unmarried master spoke to the persistence of beliefs that linked the colonists to early modern England. Single people were a significant minority and widely accepted at all levels of society. There was nothing inherently problematic about being unmarried whether one was a master or a dependent. To be sure, people worried about the young and the propertyless, fearing that because of their liminal condition they might surrender to the temptations of idleness and immorality, and so laws were put in place to curtail such behavior. Unmarried men who were heads of households were not singled out by the law but were shielded by their mastery. In short, the differences between master and dependent overshadowed all other distinctions and kept men such as Hoppin and Stoughton worlds apart.

On the other hand, differences had begun to emerge between the English ideal and American practice by the time the two men met in 1672. Although the family government law in Massachusetts had made no distinction regarding gender, Stoughton and the other selectmen only enforced the placement of single men. Only single men sought special exemptions to the law and challenged the courts on fornication penalties. As a result, even though Puritan divines and governors taught that all young men should be reduced to a state of dependency, many colonists proved willing to grant them more independence. In the Chesapeake the overabundance of single men meant that issues of marital status were largely ignored. Throughout seventeenth-century America, a discourse on the bachelor was emerging.

The transatlantic exchange was not gone for good. By the fourth quarter of the seventeenth century American colonists were beginning to learn new ideas from England about the single state and to adopt versions of laws that singled out unmarried men and placed a larger civic responsibility on them. They were also beginning to read English pamphlets and periodicals that joked about bachelors, and not only about the young and propertyless ones. Such ideas filtered throughout the culture and soon single men were struggling with their identity as liminal creatures while enjoying a greater degree of freedom than John Winthrop or any of the first generation would have allowed. A new bachelor identity was emerging based on ideals of masculine autonomy. This transformation would wipe away the distance that separated Stephen Hoppin and William Stoughton, although, had they been attentive, these two men would have been aware that change was about to overtake them.

2

"If a Single Man and Able He Shall Make Satisfaction"

THE BACHELOR LAWS

In the summer of 1703 New Yorkers readied for another imperial conflict. England had declared war on France a year earlier in a struggle for control of the Spanish throne. Although Americans rarely fretted over dynastic intrigue, they had learned that wars that began in Europe rarely stayed in Europe. New Yorkers in particular worried that the struggle might embolden Indians on the frontier to attack or tempt a foreign army to seize their capital. New York City had twice fallen to invaders in the last forty years and colonists were anxious to avoid a third time. Thus in June 1703 the New York General Assembly voted to raise £1,500 to erect two batteries at the Narrows, the passage between Staten Island and Long Island. To fund the project, the assembly ordered taxes on a series of items not typically rated. Every assemblyman, member of the governor's council, and attorney was assessed a poll tax. So too was every slave, freeman over sixteen, and "every person wearing a Peruwigg." The act also called for a payment of three shillings from "every Batchelour being a Freeman of the Age of five and twenty Years and upwards."[1]

New York's tax on unmarried men signaled a sea change in the politics of marital status. It marked the first time Americans used the term *bachelor* in a law. Gone was the gender-neutral language of earlier legislation: this one applied only to men. It was also the first time that a law singled out unmarried men who were neither young nor propertyless. Men without wives by virtue of their age or social status were far more common in colonial America, yet New Yorkers taxed only those men who were at or past the average age at marriage and who could afford to pay their own taxes. The 1703 tax also marked a change in what aspects of the single state mattered most to lawmakers. Seventeenth-century statutes controlling labor and sexuality had existed to prevent idleness and immorality by reducing the masterless to dependence.

Legislators in New York expected bachelors to be independent, even if they did assess them a fee upon that independence. These differences between earlier laws and the New York tax of 1703 were vital to the emergence of the modern-day identity of the bachelor.

At the beginning of the eighteenth century new ideas emerged regarding the single state. Above all, unmarried men were a subject of increasing attention. Early-modern Britons had accepted the presence of single men rather passively, rarely exploring the meanings of the single state and only explicitly naming the unmarried in laws when they believed it was absolutely necessary. Seventeenth-century Americans had largely followed this practice with many colonists choosing to rescind even the minor control exerted by English law. By contrast, colonists in the eighteenth century were fascinated with bachelors. They agreed that the bachelor was a unique identity and that it embodied masculine autonomy, yet they could not agree on whether this was a positive development or not. Accordingly, a vibrant discourse accompanied the emergence of the bachelor, one that debated the role of single men in society, their obligations to the community, and whether the government should seek to decrease their numbers. The discourse found its way into the laws, literature, and lives of single men in ways that affected how Americans understood manhood, citizenship, and the relationship between the state and the individual.

Change appeared first and more definitively in the law. The idea of a bachelor tax was hardly confined to New York or to the early eighteenth century. It had roots on both sides of the Atlantic and gained adherents throughout the American colonies, appearing from New Hampshire to North Carolina. The idea was first mentioned more than fifty years earlier and retained popularity well after American independence. Additionally, the idea of placing heavier civic obligations on single men was not confined to fiscal policy. Lawmakers compelled unmarried men to military duty from which they excused married men, placed harsher fines on single men who committed crimes or became debtors, and offered bachelors fewer chances for clemency. Bachelors in the eighteenth century put up with an intrusive state apparatus that never seemed to tire of restricting their economic and personal freedoms. It also was of little consequence how wealthy or upstanding a bachelor was. In time, all unmarried men faced greater civic obligations.

Because the single state was increasingly burdensome in the eighteenth century, we might presume that the laws were evidence of a colonial distaste for the single state. Yet it is too simplistic to see these laws as either punishment for being unmarried or as attempts at social engineering. Few American lawmakers were prepared to deviate from the English tradition of allowing young men a liminal period of time to mature personally and professionally. Few people seriously believed that the state should be involved in directing the marital choices of individuals or that concerns about morality should trump the needs of farmers and planters for available labor. However, early American lawmakers did debate the basic responsibilities of the unmarried man. They asked whether the bachelor should be reduced to dependency and made the responsibility of his master or whether he should be treated as an autonomous individual and be made responsible for his own civic obligations. Ultimately, the colonial governments chose the latter, deciding to treat bachelors not as dependents but as men.

The origins of the bachelor laws are complex and multifaceted. Foreshadowed in the first decade of colonization, substantive change began in the 1670s when lawmakers reevaluated fatherhood. Over the course of the seventeenth century the affectionate patriarch gradually replaced the stern paterfamilias. Puritans and Quakers were at the forefront of this change, and by the 1730s few household heads retained absolute power over their dependents. Yet the father retained the responsibility to provide for his family and so the state granted him new rights to lessen the burden of mastery: exemption from the payment of certain taxes, release from military conscription, and immunity from prosecution for debts and some crimes. Lawmakers of the time defended such actions by citing the overwhelming cost of providing for a family and the patriotic duty of men who fathered many children. Because a married man fulfilled familial obligations, he was excused from certain civic ones. As a result, lawmakers shifted a greater share of the burden for funding and defending the colonies to men without families.[2]

This change had two important consequences. First, it legally divided men into different categories based on marital status rather than property. The master/dependent dichotomy that was critical to the statutes of laborers and artificers was replaced by a husband/bachelor dichotomy. Distinctions based on property and age declined and eventually fell away, creating the legal principle that all bachelors were the same. Second, the husband/bachelor dichotomy omitted women. To be sure, the law had subjected women to a married/single dichotomy for centuries, but the new statutes made little effort to forge a cohesive single female identity. There was only one spinster tax ever levied in colonial America and it lasted only two years. The ideal of the affectionate patriarch did not extend to women and thus lawmakers often ignored female householders when they granted exemptions to taxes or service for debts. Likewise, because women were not supposed to be autonomous, their legal status remained nebulous and contradictory while that of single men became uniform.

The fact that a husband/bachelor dichotomy emerged instead of a married/single one ultimately marks the masculinization of duty. In the seventeenth century gender only partially affected relations between masters and dependents, but in the eighteenth century manhood had become the sine qua non for all notions of responsibility. Married men had familial obligations that obviated certain taxes and penalties, while bachelors faced greater civic obligations because they lacked dependents. Married and unmarried men thus moved along parallel tracks of obligation. They coexisted as political identities defined in opposition to one another as well as by what they had in common. Both notions of duty excluded women, meaning that as much as the bachelor laws divided men they also united them. In time, the similarities between men would become more meaningful than the differences. By the American Revolution, the performance of obligation became the basis for single men to demand commensurate rights such as suffrage. Because women had been excluded from civic duty, they had little basis to demand the same rights as men.

In this chapter I explore the coming of the bachelor laws in America, examining how the laws came into being, the politics surrounding their adoption, and how they changed over time. I examine the origins of the bachelor laws in the early seventeenth century, the coming of the bachelor tax, the ways in which the laws spread from the northern colonies to the Chesapeake, and how the legal category of single men moved toward uniformity. Within this narrative, the adoption, implementation, and significance of three of the more important laws are explored in detail: the Pennsylvania tax on single freemen, the Virginia draft, and the Maryland bachelor tax. I demonstrate that the bachelor laws appeared as a result of practical considerations and intensified as the ideal of the affectionate patriarch took hold. Despite their variety and change over time, the laws evince the emergent identity of the bachelor as masculine and autonomous, far different from other dependents.

Origins of the Bachelor Laws

In the first half of the seventeenth century nearly all American laws that explicitly mentioned the unmarried closely followed English precedent. In New England and the Chesapeake colonial lawmakers placed restrictions on the labor and sexuality of propertyless singles, placing them in stable households and under the watchful eyes of a master. Yet the earliest settlers also had to contend with issues for which English law provided little guidance. Dividing the land and providing an adequate frontier defense forced Americans to devise creative solutions. Some early lawmakers placed these issues in the context of the family and sought to ensure stability by protecting the interests of those who had dependents. From these inauspicious beginnings bachelor laws originated.

In the fall of 1609 settlers headed for Virginia were shipwrecked on Bermuda. Although the settlers, under the capable leadership of Sir Thomas Gates, made it to the mainland the following spring, the discovery of Bermuda created new financial opportunities for the Virginia Company. Company officials claimed the right to settle the island and soon began devising schemes to attract people to this new colonial outpost. In 1612 Governor Thomas Moore authored a plan that gave settlers generous landholdings, enough for each male settler to erect his own house. Moore recommended that the company give out sufficient adjoining land for every colonist to start a garden although he specified that married men should receive two rods of land and single men only one.[3]

Two decades later the town of Dedham, Massachusetts, pursued a similar course of action. As Puritans migrated into the New England interior, they devised a scheme to place enough land in the hands of each male colonist for him to support a family. At a town meeting in August 1636 the selectmen ordered that "single men shall henceforth haue Eight Acres for an house lott and noe more for yer first sitting downe." The week before eight settlers had each received twelve-acre lots and thus the new policy decreased bachelor allotments by 50 percent. However, the select-men did recognize that the town's unmarried residents would probably not stay single forever. Accordingly, they approved a corollary provision whereby "as their [Families] increase," the men who had received only eight acres would be granted an "inlargemt as shalbe thought fitting."[4]

Although the actions of Governor Moore and the Dedham selectmen occurred without comment, it is clear that neither was aimed at punishing single men or discouraging their immigration. Instead, these early planners were simply making accommodations for men who had dependents to support. The logic was the same as the headright system of Virginia under which a landowner received fifty acres of land for every indentured servant he imported. The practice of advantaging those with many dependents persisted well into the eighteenth century and was especially popular in the southern colonies. It was also consistent with the idea of empowering the household head. Because masters played an important political role in early co-lonial societies, they received compensation in the form of more land. Although al-lotments in Bermuda and Dedham did not signal a new view of the unmarried, they did foreshadow future revisions. Both laws applied only to men and only to masters. The propertyless young singles subject to the family government laws were entirely excluded from land allocation decisions.[5]

The earliest colonists also deemed the lack of a family sufficient cause to take away the personal freedoms of bachelors. In 1631 Massachusetts formulated a plan for the defense of the colony against a potentially hostile aboriginal population. The colony demanded that all men be part of the militia and that each one own a firearm. In case a man was unable to afford a gun, the law decreed that the town was to buy one for him. A year later lawmakers amended the statute, adding "if any single p[er]son be not p[ro]vided of sufficient armes," then he "shalbe compelled to serue by the yeare with any maister that will retaine him for such wages as the Court shall thinke meet to appoynte."[6] Although frontier conditions demanded an armed populace, it would have been financially prohibitive for the towns to arm all their impoverished men. At the same time, the towns could not put married men to service without leaving a number of families destitute and so they had to buy them weapons. The Massachusetts militia law was subsequently adopted in Plymouth, Connecticut, New York, and New Hampshire. Practically, it was a variation on New England's family government law because it applied only to young men who did not live with a master or parent and thus had no one to provide them with arms. In Plymouth the connection between the two laws was explicit. In 1636 the colony's General Court ordered that no single man live alone or with other single men "till such time as hee or they be competently provided of Armes & municon."[7]

The idea of putting out single men to buy guns appeared only in the northern colonies. In the Chesapeake and the Carolinas, lawmakers simply placed the burden of providing arms on the masters.[8] The intervention of New England lawmakers was evidence of the region's earliest efforts to weaken the near absolute authority of the household head. This pattern of difference between the northern and southern colonies replicated a division already present in family government and fornication laws. Moreover, this different approach to mastery persisted well into the eighteenth century. As the singles' laws imported from England gradually ceased to be enforced and passed from existence, lawmakers in the Middle Atlantic and New England colonies continued to circumscribe the power of masters and detail the duties of economically dependent single men. Chesapeake lawmakers would not replicate such actions for another century.

In the last quarter of the seventeenth century the scope of the bachelor laws in the northern colonies expanded dramatically. In large part this shift correlated with emergent notions of the affectionate patriarch. Although New Englanders were particularly profamily, it was Middle Atlantic colonists who advanced a new legal understanding of fatherhood and the consequent body of new bachelor laws. As Barry Levy has demonstrated, the family was primary to the religious organization of the Society of Friends, or Quakers. The Friends who followed William Penn to the Delaware Valley in the 1680s sought to perpetuate their faith through the conscientious care of their offspring. They rejected sixteenth-century notions of fatherhood that encouraged autocratic control and brutal punishment in favor of tender instruction and gentle correction. They also sought to secure sufficient land for their children so that future generations would not have to leave the community and be corrupted by the moral and economic values of nonbelievers. The Quakers who founded Pennsylvania thus passed one set of laws that vigorously protected the ability of fathers to provide for their families and another that compassionately directed errant youths away from sin and toward affectionate fatherhood.[9] Both innovations had profound effects on the legal status of bachelors.

The idea of using the law to protect fathers surfaced in the writings of William Penn as early as 1681. In an early draft of "The Fundamentall Constitutions of Pennsilvania," Penn pondered the proper punishment for thievery and concluded that married men needed special protections:

> For the first offence if a Single man...and able he shall make Satisfaction; for the Second offense he shall if able make double Satisfaction; if not be kept in a work house till he h[ave] wrought out such a Satisfaction and for the 3d offenc[e] He shall if able pay a 3 fould Satisfaction, if not able, be a Perpetuall bondsman if married and has Children, then, unless the thing Stolen be found upon him or amongst his goods, he shall not be putt to make Satisfaction to the Prejudice of his Children that were Innocent of the fact, and which would only serve to encreas the Poor and so the Publique Charge.[10]

This was perhaps the clearest statement of the principle implicit in the land allocation and militia laws: the legal rights and responsibilities of men had to be correlated to marital status lest innocent family members and the community as a whole suffer. Although Penn removed the different punishments for thievery from the final draft of his constitution, the principle entered the province's legal codes in an early law against rape. Most American colonies classified rape as a capital crime, but the Quakers were more parsimonious in their application of the death penalty. The Pennsylvania law of 1700 ordered that convicted rapists face thirty-one lashes, seven years' imprisonment, and "if he be an unmarried person he shall forfeit all his estate; and if married, one-third part thereof."[11]

Rape was not the only sex crime for which Pennsylvania lawmakers drew a distinction between single and married men. The first generation of Quaker settlers paid close attention to marital status as they sought to prohibit nearly every type of nonmarital, nonprocreative intercourse. Like New Englanders, Pennsylvanians allowed magistrates to enjoin to marry couples guilty of fornication. They also demanded that any single person who knowingly wed a person already married be tried for bigamy. Yet the brunt of the Pennsylvania sex laws did not always fall on the shoulders of the unmarried. The ideal of the affectionate patriarch, which called for certain exemptions for fathers, also demanded that the law be compassionate toward errant youths particularly in matters of sexuality. Like a Quaker parent writ large, Pennsylvania shielded the province's "tender plants" lest they be unable to become responsible fathers. When lawmakers authorized punishment for adultery in 1682, they demanded a year of prison for any married person who "defileth the marriage bed," but added "if the party with whom the husband or wife shall defile themselves be unmarried, for the first offence they [the unmarried person] shall suffer half a year's imprisonment."[12] To be sure, if the young person did not learn his lesson the first time, the law demanded that he be punished the same as a married person for the second offense. Pennsylvania lawmakers also indulged the errors of youth when it came to the punishment of sodomy and bestiality. Once again, most colonies classified such actions as capital crimes, but the Quaker revulsion at death as a form of punishment led the Pennsylvania General Assembly to demand that these actions be punished with imprisonment for life and regular floggings. The sodomy and bestiality law of 1700 also ordered that if the offender "be a married man, he shall also suffer castration."[13] If such an irreversible punishment was applied to a man who was not married, there would be no hope that the offender could be rehabilitated; he could never go on to marry, father children, and become an affectionate patriarch. Interestingly, this was the sole example of a colonial American law connecting sodomy and marital status, but it did so in such a way that confounds modern-day suspicions that bachelors were seen as homosexuals. Early American lawmakers did not assume that single men were more likely to engage in sodomy than married men.

The body of Pennsylvania's sex crime laws was unique in the American colonies and quickly received the rebuke of the Crown because of its deviation from English law. Because of a clause in the province's charter, all laws passed by the Pennsylvania assembly were subject to the approval of the Privy Council. Beginning in 1693 the council persistently exercised its prerogative and struck down nearly all of the province's sex crime laws. In several cases the reason for doing so related to the province's special treatment of the unmarried. In 1706 the council abrogated the enjoin-to-marry provision of Pennsylvania's fornication law, because "for fornication, among single people, they are to marry which may be unreasonable, where young men may be drawn in by lewd women." The council likewise objected to the province's rape and sodomy laws and struck them down as well. The councilors were particularly incensed about the idea of castrating a man for sodomy or bestiality, noting that the penalty was "unreasonable, especially in case of a married man."[14] In the case of the fornication and sodomy laws, the Pennsylvania assembly acceded to the council's request and approved new statutes without reference to marital status. The unique language of the rape law was briefly revived, but after 1718 only the province's bigamy law made reference to marital status.[15]

Pennsylvania's attempt to translate the ideal of the affectionate patriarch into sex laws thus failed within a generation. Along with this failure died the idea that the state should serve in loco parentis for single men. Tellingly, single women saw their protection under the law diminish at the same time. In a replication of actions in New England, Pennsylvania reapportioned the punishment for fornication from people of both sexes to single women only. In 1706 the assembly decreed that birth itself "shall be sufficient proof to convict such single or unmarried woman of fornication."[16] The disappearance of protections for impetuous youths coincided with a change in the portrayal of the unmarried in popular literature and the experience of being a single person in the colonies. A larger cultural ethos had begun to emerge in which bachelors were no longer to be treated as a dependent class in need of parental supervision. They were full adults, responsible for their own actions and subject to the same treatment as any married man.

While young singles lost their legal protections, the exemptions for men with families to support began to increase. In 1698 the Massachusetts assembly took up the issue of impoverished debtors languishing in the province's jails. Like many American colonies, Massachusetts allowed creditors to imprison debtors and keep them incarcerated until restitution was made. If a debtor had no way of paying what he owed, theoretically he could be held indefinitely. In an attempt to grant some mercy to the poor as well as to clear out the province's jails, Massachusetts in 1698 allowed for the release of destitute debtors. Yet the law contained an exception. If the debtor was "a person formerly using any handicraft or day labour, and not having a wife or family," then the creditor could request the debtor be put to service.[17] The Massachusetts law was followed by a number of imitations in Pennsylvania, New York, and Delaware over the next half century. Not surprisingly, Pennsylvania's was the most complex. In 1706 the assembly ordered that all debtors be bound into service, adding that the length of service not exceed "seven years, if a single person and under the age of fifty-and-three years; or five years, if a married man and under the age of forty-and-six years."[18]

Over the course of the eighteenth century legislators grew increasingly uncomfortable with imprisoning debtors and moved toward ending the practice altogether. In 1730 the Pennsylvania assembly opted to free all poor debtors once their assets had been seized and remitted to their creditors. In this revision considerations of fatherhood persisted and thus married debtors were allowed to keep fifty shillings' worth of apparel but bachelors only twenty. Yet the matter of marital status apparently remained a contentious point for lawmakers. Less than a year after it had revised the debtors' relief law, the Pennsylvania legislature complained that the new provisions were being abused by "single or unmarried persons who were indebted in small sums of money which they could easily have paid by their labor." Accordingly, lawmakers rescinded their earlier debt forgiveness for "persons, being unmarried and under the age of forty years, having no charge of children" who owed less than £20. These bachelors continued to be imprisoned and were made to answer for their debts.[19]

The debtors' relief laws were noticeably vague in terms of gender. Some colonies seemed unable to decide whether relief should extend to women or not. The result was a curious usage of language such as Pennsylvania's 1706 relief act, which distinguished between a "single person" and a "married man." Others were more precise. Massachusetts's 1698 law applied only to men, made clear through its reference to debtors who had "a wife." Thirty-five years later the assembly made the provision gender-neutral by demanding that relief not extend to any debtor who was "able of body to labour, not having a husband, wife, or family."[20] In part, the inclusion of women may reflect Americans' growing perception that it was unseemly to confine a woman to prison for debts. Nevertheless, there was no consensus among lawmakers as to whether the exemptions granted to fathers should be extended to mothers.

As a body of law, there was remarkably little consensus among the bachelor statutes. Differences in religion and economics created a dissonance among the colonies as they approached laws relating to sexuality and debt. These in turn retarded colonial unity in the legal approach to the bachelor. But there were also broad lines of agreement. Between the middle of the seventeenth century and the middle of the eighteenth, American lawmakers largely abandoned the idea that single men were in need of special protection either from masters or the state. Instead, bachelors—regardless of age or rank—stood as individuals before the law. This is not to imply that young and propertyless single men were seen as equal to married men, since they would continue to be burdened with civic obligations but without commensurate rights until the American Revolution.

The Bachelor Tax

Of all the bachelor laws devised in the second half of the seventeenth century, none embodied the changing legal ethos as much as the bachelor tax. Ancient in origin, the practice of connecting taxation with marital status gained rapid popularity in America and found its way into the laws of ten American colonies. They varied widely from place to place, yet all of the bachelor taxes were built on the same premise as the bachelor laws before them: because a single man did not have a family to support, he could better afford to contribute money to the community. Like the militia laws, the bachelor tax singled out unmarried men from the rest of the population by placing an obligation on them that no single woman or married man was responsible for. The taxes also marked bachelors as economically independent individuals, a process by which propertyless single men emerged as a distinct group. As will be demonstrated in subsequent chapters, this dialogue was rarely confined to the statehouse. It spilled out into the streets and onto the pages of political and humorous tracts.[21]

The idea of connecting taxation to marital status dates back to antiquity when it was often touted as a means of punishing wealthy men who refused to marry. "He who at the age of thirty-five does not marry," decreed the Greek philosopher Plato, "is to pay a fine of such-and-such an amount every year—so that he won't be of the opinion that the bachelor's life is a source of gain and ease for him."[22] Four hundred years later Roman emperor Augustus Caesar put Plato's advice into effect. In a series of laws known as Lex Iulia et Papia, Rome limited the inheritances of people who neither married nor fathered children while cutting the taxes of those who fathered three or more legitimate children. The connection between taxation and marital status remained part of the Western legal tradition for the next fifteen hundred years, appearing, for example, in the writings of sixteenth-century French humanist Jacques de Cujas.[23] In early modern England, the idea received consideration in the court of King Henry VIII and was discussed in republican tracts during the English Civil War. Like the earlier writers, early modern advocates for the tax typically framed the issue as a penalty for nonprocreative men.[24]

Despite the rhetoric, the first bachelor tax to appear in England was not designed to punish but to make the tax burden more equitable. At the Restoration in 1660, King Charles II, finding the kingdom's treasury empty, called on Parliament to establish new sources of revenue. In response, lawmakers devised a scheme of levies including property taxes, a graduated poll tax on the nobility, and faculty taxes on clergymen, people in certain occupations, and royal officials. Parliament also went after those people who earned a living through more modest means but did not own land, placing a poll tax on subjects with estates worth less than £5. But not all heads were taxed the same. Whereas each person "not rated before in this present Act, nor receiving Alms, and being above sixteen yeares of age shall pay six pence," the act included a provision whereby "every person being a single person and above the age of sixteene yeares [shall pay] the summe of twelve pence."[25]

The 1660 tax may have reflected the growing value of workers. The Civil War had negatively affected population growth, which had consequently driven up wages, especially for the young and single. A supplemental act passed the following year ordered that "every Householder being Master or Mistris of a family shall ... deliver ... a true and perfect list of all persons above the age of sixteene yeares as shall be inhabiting or residing in their respective families."[26] In other words, the target of the 1660 tax was economic dependents, the same people subjected to the statutes of laborers and artificers. Consistent with its earlier laws, Parliament saw no need to draw a distinction between dependents based on gender. Masters were responsible for their servants' taxes and typically deducted them from servants' wages. The tax on singles thus did not imply masculine responsibility.

On the other side of the Atlantic, American colonists were simultaneously connecting marital status and taxation although to a much different effect. In 1653 the town of Marshfield in Plymouth Colony approved a special poll tax on its unmarried men. Like other New England towns, Marshfield enjoyed a degree of autonomy in financial matters including the right to decide which items should be rated. Previously, the bulk of the town's revenue had come from direct taxes on land and livestock, but in 1653 the selectmen went after a previously untapped resource: economically independent men who had neither property nor families to support. As the town records recall: "It is agreed upon that all young men who are in the township that are single persons, and are at their own hands, shall be liable to pay all the town's rates as the rest of the inhabitants do, after the value of ten pounds a head for every such person."[27] Marshfield's levy suggests that from the beginning Americans saw the relationship between taxation and marital status differently than the English did. Unlike England's double poll tax, the Marshfield rate applied only to men who could afford to pay their own taxes. Indeed, the Marshfield tax was not a variation on earlier singles' laws and thus serves as further evidence that the region's family government laws were not being enforced. Single men were asserting their independence and rather than trying to force them into households, Marshfield opted to profit economically from the situation.

Over the next thirty years Marshfield's actions were imitated by towns in New Hampshire, Rhode Island, and Plymouth colonies.[28] In each case the object of the law was to derive revenue from single men not otherwise taxed due to a lack of property. The town laws made no reference to age although economic independence appears to have been the main requirement. In a striking contrast to all previous laws, these New England taxes marked the first time that a government on either side of the Atlantic bestowed masculine responsibility on men without households. The new tax was surely an inconvenience for the propertyless single men who lived in these towns, but it was an inconvenience not extended to any other nonmasters.

Before lawmakers extended the application of the bachelor tax to an entire colony, Parliament acted again and altered the meaning of the levy. The revenue act of 1660 expired within a few years of passage and the tax on the unmarried was not renewed. In 1667, when England resumed war with the Netherlands, Parliament engineered a new tax scheme that demanded that "all and every person and persons shall pay unto His Majestie the summe of Twelve pence over and above the other Rates charged upon them by this Act."[29] The attempt to apply a poll tax equally to the population without regard to property or marital status soon raised complaints that the tax created a hardship for poor families. Accordingly, when war with France threatened a decade later, Parliament made some accommodation for the destitute. Like the 1667 law, the 1678 revenue act demanded that every person pay a one-shilling poll tax on top of all other taxes. This time, however, Parliament added a new exemption. In addition to the traditional immunities for people receiving alms and those under sixteen, the 1678 tax law granted a reprieve to "such who hath fower or more Children and is not worth in Lands Goods and Chattells the summe of Fifty pounds."[30] This provision immediately became a pillar of English revenue policy and appeared repeatedly in subsequent poll taxes as well as in the kingdom's first land tax twenty years later.

The actions of New England towns and the English Parliament appealed to lawmakers in Pennsylvania who saw the bachelor tax and exemptions for married men as part of a larger scheme to promote the ideal of the affectionate patriarch. From the start, Pennsylvanians preferred to derive the bulk of the province's revenue from a combination of poll and property taxes, although they did not initially factor marital status into the equation. In 1682 lawmakers ordered the province's first tax, "one half of the said tax to be paid, shall be raised upon the land, the other half by the poll, on the Male from Sixteen, to Sixty years of age."[31] However, in 1693 the assembly revisited the issue and began to make the province's tax scheme decidedly more profamily. First, in taxes collected for the support of the province, lawmakers added an exemption for men "who have a great charge of children & become indigent," indigence being defined as owning less than £30 worth of property. This exemption would persist as a part of the Pennsylvania county rates law until the Revolution.[32] Second, the assembly limited the application of the poll tax to single men. In 1693 the assembly ordered a tax of one penny per pound on all "reall, capital of and personal estates" and a six shillings poll tax on men "as are not otherwise Rated by this act." Three years later the assembly restricted the application of the poll tax at the county level to "freemen who have been out of their servitude for the space of six months, and all such who Come free into this government & have been therein resident for the space of fourty days, and are above the age of sixteen years, and have not families or charge to maintain, and are not under their parents tuition, and assisting to them on their plantations or trades, or are not otherwise Rated by this act."[33] With this revision, those with real and moveable estates paid the property tax and only single men who owned no property paid the poll tax.

In 1700 a modification of the colony's assessment law brought the provincial poll tax in line with the county rates, requiring that only those men not otherwise taxed and "not having families or charge to maintain" be liable for the tax. Over the next twenty years the language of the tax grew more explicit. Although the initial provincial tax fell on those "not having families," in 1711 the assembly changed the language to "single freeman." Like the New England rates, the Pennsylvania tax required economic independence on the part of taxed bachelors. By 1718 the legislature raised the minimum age from sixteen to twenty-one but also extended the tax to all single men whether they lived with their parents or not. With these adjustments, the Pennsylvania bachelor tax remained part of the provincial rates until the 1780s and part of the county levies until the twentieth century.[34]

The Pennsylvania bachelor tax is somewhat of an anomaly given its duration. Most English and American levies on the unmarried lasted just long enough to fund a war. In the case of Pennsylvania, the tax became an integral part of the province's annual tax schemes and remained so for nearly a century. Although the Pennsylvania levy may not be completely representative of bachelor taxes as a whole, its steady collection generated an incomparable amount of documentation and thus offers a unique insight into how this one tax worked. Specifically, important conclusions can be drawn from the eighteenth-century tax rolls of Chester County. One of the first three counties created in Pennsylvania, Chester County's religious and ethnic makeup and economy make it a microcosm for the province as a whole.[35] Because of this, Chester has attracted the attention of several historians including James Lemon, Gary Nash, Jack Marietta, and Lucy Simler. By carefully analyzing the county's tax rolls, these historians have offered new insights into the distribution of wealth, economic opportunity, and violence in early America. Although they often mention the tax on propertyless single men, these historians typically exclude bachelors from the final analysis.[36]

The records of Chester County reveal that the collection of the tax varied widely. At the county level, where the taxes were used to help fund the poor, the courts, and the local infrastructure, the decision of when to collect taxes and how much to charge was left up to county commissioners. The regularity of the county rates varied depending on the needs of the local government, although the counties collected them more often than not. In Chester County the commissioners ordered the tax collected about four out of every five years from 1718 to 1775. During this period single men paid between four and fifteen shillings per annum to the county in the years the tax was collected. At the provincial level the collection of the tax was far more irregular. The levies supported the assembly and governor although their most important function was to provide for the general defense. Accordingly, lawmakers typically kept provincial levies low unless and until war threatened, but when it did, taxes spiked. Pennsylvania collected provincial taxes through Queen Anne's War (War of Spanish Succession), although when the conflict ended in 1713 the legislature allowed the provincial bachelor tax to lapse along with the provincial property tax. When the Seven Years' War (French and Indian War) threatened forty years later, provincial taxes returned and became increasingly burdensome as wartime expenditures spiraled out of control. On the eve of the American Revolution, bachelors were paying fifteen to twenty shillings per year to the province. As a result, whether or not a bachelor was taxed and how much he owed varied greatly depending on when and where he lived.[37]

Despite fluctuations, the poll taxes on single men were consistently quite high. The county rates law of 1696 set the poll tax on single men at six shillings and the property tax at one penny per pound of an estate's value. Using this formula, a propertyless bachelor paid as much in county poll taxes as a landowner paid for an estate worth £72. Similarly, the provincial rate of fifteen shillings on single men in the 1760s was roughly equivalent to the taxes placed on a hundred-acre farm with a single dwelling in rural Chester County.[38] Such ratios meant that single men paid higher taxes than the vast majority of the province's taxable population. Before the American Revolution, county poll taxes on single freemen were higher than the property taxes on 80 to 90 percent of Chester County's landowners.[39] Nor was Chester County unique. Tax rolls reveal that single men in Lancaster and

Figure 3. "The Labourer Bathed in Sweat, Drops." The bachelor laws demanded greater obligations from single men such as special taxes, military service, and harsher penalties for crimes. The laws had the effect of uniting all unmarried men under a common political identity. With rare exceptions, the bachelor laws excluded women.

Source: James Hervey, *Meditations and Contemplations,* vol. 2 (Philadelphia: Kite, 1809), frontispiece. Reprinted with the permission of the American Antiquarian Society.

Bedford counties were paying more in taxes than 75 percent of property owners in the 1770s.[40]

In addition to being high, the Pennsylvania bachelor tax touched a considerable portion of the population. In Chester County single men consistently represented 10 to 20 percent of taxpayers. Moreover, their raw numbers and percentage of the taxpaying population steadily increased over the course of the eighteenth century. There were 90 single freemen rated in 1715, 582 in 1750, and 1,344 in 1788. Over this time the ratio of estates to single men dropped from eight to one in 1715 to three to one seventy years later. Incomplete census information makes it difficult to determine what percentage of the total population was unmarried, although if we apply the commonly accepted methodology of colonial historians that every house-holder and married wage laborer represented families of five to seven people each, then single taxpayers constituted between 2 and 5 percent of the total population.[41] Yet the financial importance of the province's bachelors was even greater than these numbers suggest. Given that single freemen paid higher rates than the vast majority of property owners, it is little surprise that they were responsible for a significant portion of the total taxes collected. In Chester County's Concord Township, single freemen at midcentury made up 27 percent of all taxpayers but paid 36 percent of the total sum of direct taxes collected in the township.[42]

In its 1696 formulation, Pennsylvania's system of property taxes and poll taxes reflected the expected life course of a male colonist. When he was young and single, a man paid a poll tax when he was working another's land. When he matured that same man married, bought land, and began paying property taxes. Although this pattern was followed by thousands of Pennsylvanians, there were also exceptions. By 1750 nearly all of Chester County had been subdivided into farms and the timely progression from single freeman to householder became more complicated. A number of bachelors left their parents' homes for the frontier to establish farms and others became artisans in the cities of Chester and Philadelphia. Still others remained close to home but extended their tenure as live-in servants, which par-tially explains the growing number of single freemen in the county. Others could not wait to marry but took a wife and began a family without first acquiring prop-erty. Termed inmates or cottagers, these men contracted employment with land-owners and typically lived in small cottages on their employers' land. As the number of inmates increased, some counties chose to assess a poll tax on them. Chester County tax rolls indicate that the number of inmates exploded from six in 1740 to 138 ten years later. By 1760 the numbers of inmates and single freemen were about equal.[43]

Despite an increase in propertyless married taxpayers, the tax burden on unmar-ried men remained disproportionately high. In the third quarter of the eighteenth century Chester County rated propertyless married men between nine pence and one shilling three pence at the same time that it was assessing single men eight to twelve times as much. As a result, single freemen continued to carry the heavier burden. In the 1771 county tax for Concord Township, propertyless bachelors constituted 15 percent of the taxable population but paid 26 percent of the taxes, while inmates who made up 25 percent of the population paid only 6 percent. Whether or not a married man owned property, he almost certainly could expect to pay lower taxes than a propertyless bachelor.

The bachelors who paid the Pennsylvania tax ultimately constituted a liminal category of men. Although they paid higher taxes than most property owners, their taxes did not entitle them to the rights of masters. Curiously, the political inferiority of propertyless bachelors had not always been part of Pennsylvania law. Before the first settlers sailed for America in 1682, William Penn and the other founders crafted a broad definition of political identity in which every "freeman" in the province would be entitled to equal rights. According to the "Laws Agreed upon in England," a freeman was any man who owned land and worked it as well as "every inhabitant, artificer, or other resident in the said province, that pays scot and lot to the government." Scot and lot was a medieval term for taxes, meaning that in Pennsylvania's first formulation of political identity, even a propertyless man "shall and may be capable of electing or being elected representatives of the people in Provincial Council or General Assembly in the said province."[44] In theory at least, the single men taxed in 1696 were entitled to the vote.

Restrictions on suffrage in Pennsylvania did not appear until 1700. As the Pennsylvania assembly attempted to wrest control of the colony from the proprietor at the turn of the eighteenth century, it seized control over both the franchise and election procedures.[45] As part of this struggle, the legislature approved a new suffrage law that severely restricted political participation. Although the law itself stated that it had been "enacted by the Proprietary and Governor, by and with the advice and consent of the freemen of this Province," it went on to state that only *freeholders* had the right to vote. Specifically, a man had to be native-born or naturalized, twenty-one years old, a resident of Pennsylvania for two years, and either possess fifty acres or be worth £50.[46] By the time this happened, the meaning of the word *freeman* had been curtailed from the franchise threshold to a set of basic civil rights. Between 1683 and 1719 the Pennsylvania assembly passed a series of laws guaranteeing that a freeman could not be imprisoned, dispossessed of freeholds or liberties, "Outlawed, or Exiled, or any other wise hurt, Damnified, or Destroyed" but "by the lawful Judgement of his equalls."[47] Although such laws protected a man's right to trial by jury, they narrowed suffrage to property owners. In effect, a two-tiered system of political participation appeared in Pennsylvania in 1700: one for freeholders and one for freemen.

Concurrent with the contraction of the number of voters was an expansion of the number of taxpayers and this is where marital status entered the equation. According to Pennsylvania's 1682 tax law, the poll tax fell evenly upon all men in the province aged sixteen to sixty, but when the assembly rewrote the tax law in 1696, it restricted the poll tax to propertyless single men. Only four years later the ability to stand for office and vote for a candidate was narrowed from being a right of all taxpayers and restricted to landowners. Thus at the same moment that the poll tax was made the unique responsibility of propertyless single men, the right to suffrage was divorced from taxation. In fact, had Pennsylvania not revoked the 1682 freeman law, the taxation of propertyless single men would have made them equal participants in the government of colonial Pennsylvania.

In time, the relationship between property ownership, marital status, and political participation grew in complexity. Propertyless married men were also taxed without the vote although their rates were only a fraction of what propertyless single men paid. The growing number of gradations of a person's relationship to the state was typical of citizenship in colonial America. James Kettner has detailed the varying rights and responsibilities of people in America before the Revolution, and indeed the picture sketched here only grows more complex when we factor in immigrants, debtors, and African Americans, or when we compare a person's local, colonial, and imperial rights and obligations.[48] Citizenship in the colonial period was rarely an either/or proposition as the example of propertyless single men in Pennsylvania demonstrates. Outcries about the unfairness of taxation without representation largely did not apply to everyday life before 1776. An exorbitant tax without commensurate rights of suffrage, office holding, and jury service were not incongruous because few thought they were supposed to be consistent.

At the same time, the unique levy on bachelors worked to bring more single men into contact with the polity. Because every propertyless bachelor—not just the lawless or the idle—had to face the taxman, a much larger number of single men assumed a unique relationship with the state than in places where there was no bachelor tax. This had been foretold by the New England militia laws that required single men be bound out for longer periods of time for no reason other than that they were single. However, it was not until the approval of the bachelor tax in 1696 that the principle became universal. A bachelor in seventeenth-century Massachusetts could avoid having a magistrate treat him differently simply by obeying the law: finding a family to live with and not impregnating an unmarried woman. In eighteenth-century Pennsylvania a propertyless bachelor could not avoid being singled out for higher taxes unless he either married before the age of twenty-one or never worked for wages, two things that the economy and social order of Pennsylvania made difficult for the vast majority of men. As a result, bachelorhood became a political category unlike anything that had come before.

Pennsylvania's bachelor tax was soon copied by the other middle colonies. In 1714 New Jersey altered its existing tax law to state "that every single Man, not a bound servant, the Value of whose rateable Estate does not amount to twenty four Pounds, shall pay six shillings per Annum." Initially, the colony collected the tax on single men along with a head tax of two shillings six pence on all freemen not otherwise taxed and not "maintained by Charity." However, in 1717 the poll tax was made the unique charge of propertyless single men. New Jersey renewed its bachelor tax several times until the assembly abolished all forms of direct taxation in 1739.[49] Delaware also adopted Pennsylvania's system of placing a poll tax on single men without sufficient estate to pay the property tax. A 1743 Delaware tax law for raising county levies noted "as to those single men who have no visible estates, they shall not be rated under Twelve Pounds, nor above Twenty-four Pounds."[50]

In all of the applications of the bachelor tax, it was men alone who bore the brunt of the revenue scheme. On only one occasion did single women face a special poll tax. In 1695 the Massachusetts General Court placed a poll tax of two shillings on "single women that live at their own hand."[51] In passing such a levy, lawmakers followed the same logic as the Marshfield selectmen of forty years earlier. Like Pennsylvania, Massachusetts derived the bulk of its revenue from direct taxes on property and people, rating land according to value and each adult man per head regardless of marital status or wealth. In this scheme, propertied single women faced taxes but propertyless ones did not. The onset of King William's War (Nine Years' War) had dramatically expanded the economic role of propertyless spinsters and widows in Boston. As a large portion of the male population enlisted to fight in the war, the traditional male world of business and finance fell largely on the women of the province. Massachusetts lawmakers no doubt hoped to profit from these women's work. However, the experiment with a single women's tax proved unpopular and was quickly abandoned. When the General Court renewed the province's poll tax two years later, it left the women out.[52] Although single women continued to make up an important segment of the Boston economy, it seemed out of place to charge them special taxes. As a result, although the bachelor tax served to distinguish single men from married ones, the more important distinction it drew was that between single men and women. Propertyless bachelors emerged as a distinct group of men and as men they were entitled to special obligations that affected no other group of dependents.

Bachelor Laws in the Chesapeake

In the first century of settlement those single men who faced higher taxes and other civic obligations lived exclusively in New England and Pennsylvania. Lawmakers in the southern colonies had been reluctant to interfere with the inner workings of the household, continuing the earlier practice of leaving marital status out of the laws regulating labor and sexuality. This regional isolation began to fade in the second decade of the eighteenth century as lawmakers in Maryland and Virginia adopted versions of the northern bachelor laws. In so doing, they promoted the independence and autonomy of propertyless single men much like their northern counterparts. Yet the transference of the bachelor laws to Maryland and Virginia also changed the laws as well. The Chesapeake colonies completed the process of entirely excluding women from exemptions for parents and greater obligations on singles. Their constituents also bristled more sharply at the new laws when they were imposed. Whereas the Pennsylvania bachelors dutifully paid their taxes with little complaint, single men in Virginia and Maryland resisted attempts to place greater civic obligations on them. In time, these modifications spread back to the northern colonies and helped to produce a coherent set of bachelor laws.

While the affectionate patriarch gained general acceptance in the northern colonies, Americans living south of Pennsylvania idealized a very different notion of fatherhood. In the seventeenth century there had been little place for sentimentality. The high death rates among parents and children created a world of broken families while the economics of tobacco created a system of powerless workers serving under the near absolute authority of a master. Accordingly, lawmakers had been largely reluctant to limit the powers of household heads, allowing them to punish minor crimes, apportion labor, and decide how best to provision the male members of their household for military service. These ideas began to change at the turn of the eighteenth century as the life expectancy increased, the sex ratios balanced, and natural increase came to the region for the first time. Likewise, the replacement of white indentured servitude with African slavery helped to raise the standard of living for the white population. These demographic changes allowed colonists throughout the region to indulge in an increasingly affectionate version of family life. By midcentury elaborate marriage celebrations were commonplace and childrearing included a great deal more affection and training for independence. As part of this transition, however, southern families did not abandon the stern patriarch of the seventeenth century. Instead, they embraced a system of what Allan Kulikoff has termed "domestic patriarchalism" that stressed gender inequality and confirmed the father's absolute authority in matters of property, political participation, and children's marriage decisions. The Chesapeake was thus far more family oriented in 1750 than it was in 1650, but this transition served to reinforce the centrality of fatherhood rather than displace it.[53]

The changing structure of family life in the eighteenth-century Chesapeake had two important consequences for bachelors: it encouraged the adoption of legal exemptions for married men and increased the tension between fathers and sons. The implementation of the former point is easy to observe in the context of the bachelor laws. Since 1698 Massachusetts had allowed impoverished debtors to be freed so long as they were not single. As this practice gained popularity in the Middle Atlantic over the next thirty-five years, it also attracted the interest of Maryland lawmakers. In 1725 the Maryland assembly first took up the issue, granting relief to "poor distressed Prisoners for debt" provided that the person had no "wife or Children of his own to maintain." Bachelor debtors, on the other hand, could be put to service for up to five years if the creditor requested it.[54]

The idea of freeing debtors proved quite controversial in Maryland. Between 1725 and 1765 the assembly twice repealed the law and twice renewed it. This was largely the result of bitter Maryland party politics and so the fate of single men soon became a weapon in the longstanding struggle between the two houses of the assembly. In 1765 the House of Delegates passed a version of the law that made no exception for single men and thus granted relief to all debtors regardless of marital status. However, the Governor's Council demanded the provision's reinsertion. The House conceded, once again barring bachelors from debtor relief, although it did add an exception for disabled bachelors. Eight years later the Council demanded that there be no exception for men who had married while in debtors' prison. The House allowed this proviso although it removed the unique treatment of single men the following year. By this point, the American Revolution was on the horizon and more substantive issues pushed the debate over debtor relief into the background, thus the assembly never renewed the bachelor clause.[55] As had been the case in Pennsylvania, Maryland's debtors' relief law unearthed a discourse over the place of the single man in society. Those lawmakers who attempted to remove the bachelor provision were asserting that marital status was not a meaningful division among men, while those who insisted on unequal treatment did so because of their distrust of the morality and honesty of bachelors. Those in the latter group insinuated that bachelors would go to any length, including marriage, to escape prison. This emulated the complaint in Pennsylvania that single men were abusing the benevolence of lawmakers by using the law to escape small debts.

None of the other southern colonies adopted a law relieving indebted husbands although this had more to do with the structure of the debtors' laws in these colonies than ideas about marital status. Of the Chesapeake and the Carolinas, Maryland alone imprisoned debtors.[56] It is also important to observe the gender-specific wording of Maryland's debtors' relief law. Whereas Pennsylvania left the language vague and Massachusetts went so far as to specifically include married women, Maryland's exemption extended only to husbands and fathers. Not once in the fifty years between the first and last relief laws did Maryland offer to include wives and mothers. This distinction marked the further masculinization of duty in the eighteenth century. In domestic patriarchalism, women were specifically excluded from all financial and legal matters. A woman was not supposed to be contracting debts anymore than was a child, a servant, or a slave. A single man, however, was free to engage in such matters. Although the law did not distinguish between bachelors with property and those without, any man imprisoned for debt had been reduced to propertyless status by virtue of his sentence. As a result, a propertyless bachelor stood before the law as an equal member of the polity, free to contract debts and face the consequences of his actions. Even though his punishment for debt was a return to the dependence of servitude, the process by which a propertyless single man got there set him apart from all other dependents.

The treatment of single men in Maryland's debtors' relief laws points to a second effect of changing ideas about the family in the eighteenth-century Chesapeake: a rise in father and son tensions. As part of the affectionate childrearing then gaining popularity, sons were socialized to be strongly independent and were prepared to assume the duties of mastery. Accordingly, young men were placed in a contradictory position exclusive to their gender: they felt contrary impulses to obey their fathers and to defy them. These tensions surfaced in the region's bachelor laws, in particular those governing taxation and military service.[57]

In large part, the bachelor tax was slow to penetrate the Chesapeake and the Carolinas because of the region's revenue system. New England and the middle colonies heavily taxed property and used poll taxes largely as a source of supplemental income. This allowed them a great deal of flexibility in the application of the poll tax and so several colonial and local governments could limit the head tax to property-less single men.[58] In the southern colonies the relationship between property and poll taxes was exactly the opposite: taxes on individuals were the core of southern fiscal policy and land taxes were added as an occasional supplement. Head taxes on propertyless single men thus would have been redundant.

Nevertheless, issues of marital status entered the tax system in the Chesapeake in terms of how the tax was collected. Since 1662 Maryland had collected an equal poll tax on free white men over age sixteen, white male servants, and "all Slaues whatsoever whether Male or female" over the age of ten.[59] In this system, all tax payments were the responsibility of the household head, and, whether the tax fell on a freeman, servant, or slave, it was the master's responsibility to see that all the taxes were paid. Yet this system only worked when every taxable individual was settled with a family. By 1719 the Maryland assembly began to complain "that there are many single Persons, (who are Free-men,) within this Province, who have not any settled Place of Residence." Because they were not "constant residents in their Families," single men "frequently escape paying any tax at all." To remedy the situation, the assembly ordered

> that it shall and may be lawful for any Constable... upon finding any such single Person or Free-man... who cannot procure some House-keeper... to give him in as a Taxable... the [Justice of the] Peace for such County... is hereby impowered and required to commit such Person, or Free-man, into the Sheriff's Custody, until he shall procure some House-keeper or return him as a Taxable, and be answerable for his Levy.[60]

Unlike Pennsylvania and the New England towns, Maryland did not lay a special tax on propertyless unmarried men. However, the 1719 law did place the onus of nonpayment on the single men themselves. In a deviation from the treatment of servants and slaves, only bachelors faced prison if they did not find masters for themselves. The law thus pointed to the growing autonomy of single men in the region, both by indicating their increasing mobility and by the assembly's refusal to treat them the same as other dependents.

The same pattern of young male autonomy and legislative acquiescence appeared again in Virginia at the start of the Seven Years' War. Before 1750 the only mention of marital status in the statutes of Virginia was the obscure sumptuary law of 1619. Yet as ideas about exemptions for fathers and greater obligations for single men gained acceptance throughout the Chesapeake, Virginia lawmakers began to look favorably on the precedents set by the northern colonies. Threats of war ultimately pushed the Virginia assembly to implement a bachelor law so that it could raise sufficient troops. In 1754 tensions over the Ohio country had risen to peak levels as both French and British forces attempted to lay claim to the valuable territory. Virginia governor Robert Dinwiddie took particular interest in the contest for the

Ohio country because he and several friends were heavily invested in frontier land schemes. As the French built forts along the Ohio River and cemented their relations with the local Indians, Dinwiddie took a proactive stance. He urged the legislature to raise troops and sent Lt. Col. George Washington to warn the French that they were encroaching on His Majesty's lands. However, these actions had the opposite effect of what Dinwiddie had hoped for. Washington was soundly defeated, leaving France and Britain on the brink of war.[61]

Anxious to defend his land claims and to deter an invasion, Dinwiddie implored the assembly to raise troops. The governor had wanted to draft every tenth men out of the militia and place them in the army, but in 1754 the assembly granted him a much less socially disruptive means of raising troops. It empowered him "to raise and levy such able bodied men, as do not follow or exercise any lawful calling or employment." An identical measure had been approved fifteen years earlier and ensured that only the poorest and least powerful members of society would face the draft. As the situation on the frontier became increasingly dire, the assembly revised its conscription laws so as to increase the number of recruits. In place of the poor and unemployed, the assembly ordered that propertyless bachelors be conscripted. In May 1755 the assembly granted the governor the right to order militia commanders in the frontier counties "to draft out of the militia ... such and so many young men of their militia who have not wives or children, as will make up the said number, to be employed in the said service." The defeat of British general Edward Braddock in the Pennsylvania backcountry two months later led the assembly to expand the bachelor draft to all counties. In 1756, when war was officially declared between Britain and France, the Virginia assembly redoubled its efforts to raise troops. Lawmakers demanded the conscription of "able-bodied single men" in March 1756 and "able-bodied men, not being freeholders or house-keepers qualified to vote at an election of burgesses" in April 1757.[62]

Concurrent with the appearance of laws drafting bachelors, leading Virginians made impassioned appeals to the men of the colony to fight for the defense of their families and their homes. In February 1754 Governor Dinwiddie told the assembly, "Think, You see the Infant torn from the unavailing Struggles of the distractd Mother, the Daughters ravish'd before the Eyes of their wretched Parents, and then, with Cruelty and Insult, butcher'd and scalp'd." He implored the body to raise an army "to drive away these cruel and treacherous Invaders of your Properties, and Destroyers of your Families."[63] Presbyterian minister Samuel Davies issued a similar call in his sermons, imploring young men to volunteer for the army. In a 1755 sermon Davies denounced the inaction of Virginia's bachelors, noting "sundry of you have nobly disengaged yourselves from the strong and tender Ties that twine about the Heart of a Father, or a Husband." Casting the war as a struggle between Catholicism and Protestantism, Davies called on Virginia's men "to keep from the cruel Hands of Papists, your Wives, your Children, your Parents, your Friends."[64] The appeals of Dinwiddie and Davies contained a curious irony given the conscription law. Although they appealed to men to defend their families and homes, the law specifically drafted men who had neither. Nevertheless, the call to protect families reiterated the now widely accepted idea that all men owed an obligation to the state. Married men performed their duty through fatherhood while bachelors did so through military service.

At the same time, Rev. Davies moved the discussion in a new direction. Unlike lawmakers, he spoke not only of the need to protect families but also of the unique obligation of young men. In a 1758 sermon, which also sought to encourage volunteers for the army, he reiterated his call for fathers to protect their dependents, but then he spoke directly to bachelors:

> Ye young and hardy Men, whose very Faces seem to speak that God and Nature formed you for Soldiers, who are free from the Incumbrance of Families depending upon you for Subsistence, and who are perhaps but of little Service to Society, while at Home, may I not speak for you, and declare as your Mouth, "Here we are, all ready to abandon our Ease, and rush into the glorious Dangers of the Field, in Defence of our Country?" Ye that love your Country, enlist: for Honour will follow you in Life or Death in such a Cause. You that love your Religion, enlist: for your Religion is in Danger. Can Protestant Christianity expect Quarters from Heathen Savages and French Papists? Sure in such an Alliance, the Powers of Hell make a third Party. Ye that love your Friends and Relations, enlist: lest ye see them enslaved or butchered before your Eyes. Ye that would catch at Money, here is a proper Bait for you; ten Pounds for a few Months Service, besides the usual Pay of Soldiers.[65]

Single men had neither wives nor children to fight for, so Davies implored them to fight for God and country. If this was inadequately persuasive, he asked them to fight for comrades and compensation. At one level, there was a resonance with Sir Francis Bacon's words in those of Davies. Single men were a unique constituency and their interests deviated from those of other men. Accordingly, his message had to be moderated and he had to take the concerns of the unmarried seriously. Davies did not speak to young men only as future husbands but as bachelors.

Davies also injected a challenge to the manhood of Virginia's "young and hardy men" that Bacon's *Essays* did not anticipate. In his 1755 sermon Davies rebuked the men who would not serve, citing them as evidence that all masculine vigor had gone out of the land. "You see Herds of Drunkards willing down their Cups, and drowning all the Man within them," he noted, adding, "you see the Prodigality squandering her Stores, Luxury spreading her Table, and unmanning her Guests." He continued this rhetoric in his 1758 address, again warning against the "sensual Pleasures and Debauchery" that could "unman" Virginia's inhabitants. Although Davies admitted that "Vice and Irreligion is perhaps no where stronger than in the Army," he called on Virginia's volunteers to resist the temptations of luxury and to inure themselves against immorality. Indeed, the vices of army life were nothing compared to the dishonor of resisting enlistment. It was a masculine obligation to volunteer for service and Davies looked down on those who had to be drafted into service: "If such unusual Encouragement does not prevail upon you to enlist as Volunteers, what remains but that you must be forced to it by Authority? For our Country must be defended: and if nothing but Force can constrain you to take up Arms in its Defence, then Force must be used: Persons of such a sordid unmanly Spirit, are not to expect the Usage of Freemen."[66] In essence, Davies was calling out bachelors who would not serve, questioning their very claim to manhood and insinuating that they preferred effeminate luxuries and vice. Yet in a curious twist, Davies was also providing a path to manhood that stood apart from marriage or family. In a development hinted at in the bachelor laws, Davies claimed that volunteer soldiers were full men, equal in virtue regardless of whether they married or not.

Despite the soaring rhetoric of Dinwiddie and Davies, volunteers were not forthcoming. Numerous letters from local militia officers describe the difficulty of raising troops, especially among the ranks of bachelors. Writing to George Washington in September 1756, Lt. William Fairfax noted how he had recently "held here a Council of War and had the single Men present drawn up in a Line and being askt if any inclined voluntarily to enter into his Majesty's Service." The result of his inquiry was "none offering." Accordingly, Fairfax began the process of conscripting unwilling soldiers. Fairfax's experience was not uncommon. The Seven Years' War was highly unpopular throughout Virginia, especially among men who faced conscription. "I am concerned to see a great Unwillingness in our young Men to enlist," Fairfax remarked.[67] He omitted the fact that a drafted man could opt out of conscription by paying a £10 fine or by providing a substitute and that many did so. "The Draught from the Militia [is] much short of my Expectations," Governor Dinwiddie complained to Washington. "The laying of the fine of ten Pounds on those that w'd not march out entirely defeated the Law."[68]

Ultimately, the Virginia conscription law elicited mixed responses from the population and left many torn between supporting the military and resisting intrusions on their freedom. When Butts Roberts appeared before George Washington to receive his orders, he carried with him a letter from Robert Carter Nicholas that appealed to Washington for "favour towards him." The letter explained that the young man had been in Maryland on business for his father at the time of the draft. "As he was a single Man upon the Muster Roll & did not appear at the Day appointed," Nicholas explained, Roberts was taken up by constables and forthwith sent to Washington. Although Nicholas had offered to pay the £10 fine, Roberts resisted his offer: "His Honr upon a somewhat similar Occasion having declared that he will not interfere with the Law, I am discouraged from the Attempt." In the end, however, the young man allowed Nicholas to pay for a substitute.[69]

Not every young bachelor was as fortunate as Butts Roberts. The fine of £10 was equal to half the annual income of most small planters and was completely out of reach for the colony's tenant farmers, poor artisans, and drifters. Such men had to join the army or face punishment.[70] Yet as the colony soon discovered, a policy of drafting bachelors too poor to pay their way out of the service had devastating effects on Virginia's army. Lt. Fairfax noted that the conscripts appeared "almost naked and in poor condition," and Washington informed Dinwiddie that a recent draft had turned up only seventy-five men, "many of them unarmed & all without ammunition or provision."[71] Worse, these men flouted military discipline and drank excessively, actions that imprisonment and the threat of hanging could not quell. The conscripts also used extralegal means of resisting the draft. Many simply did not show up for the muster or deserted the regiment after being impressed. "No man I conceive was ever worse plagu'd than I have been with the Draughts that were sent from the several counties," Washington lamented. "Out of 400 that were received at Fredericksburgh, and at this place, 114 have deserted, notwithstanding every precaution, except absolute confinement, has been used to prevent this infamous practice."[72]

In the end, the policy of drafting poor single men was an abysmal failure. For three years the Virginia Regiment remained sorely undermanned and ineffective, and so in the spring of 1758 the assembly changed the law. At the British ministry's assurance that it would pay for recruits, the colony shifted from conscripts to volunteers. Instead of demanding £10 from men unwilling to serve, Virginia began to pay men £10 bounties to enlist. By the summer of 1758 the Virginia Regiment swelled to near capacity and resistance to the war dissipated. In late 1758 a combined British and American force under Gen. John Forbes captured Fort Duquesne on the forks of the Ohio from the French and the southern part of the North American theater of the Seven Years' War came to a close.[73]

In retrospect, the Virginia draft law of 1755 reflects the problem of bachelors' liminal status. Having become subject to the obligations of manhood but having none of the rights, single men resisted their unique treatment and forced the assembly to rewrite the law. The experience in Virginia repeated the same problem Maryland tax collectors had identified in 1719. The father-son tensions were playing out in the attempt by Chesapeake lawmakers to pass bachelor laws: legislators were attempting to train young bachelors in the ways of manhood by taking them through a liminal stage of responsibilities without rights, but the young men rejected this inferior status. Although these tensions were more pronounced in the Chesapeake, they resonated throughout the colonies. They also grew more obvious as the American Revolution approached. In the wake of Britain's victory in the Seven Years' War, propertyless single men increasingly defied their unique obligations. This was the counterpoint to the fact that the bachelor laws separated single men from other dependents and treated them like men. Some bachelors had no interest in paying higher taxes, being attached to a household, or serving in the army. They preferred to define bachelorhood in terms of mobility and life outside the law.

Virginia was far from unique in its attempt to draft unmarried men. Instead, the connection between marital status and military service appeared throughout the American colonies in the 1750s, suggesting a growing consensus on the obligations of propertyless single men. Five months before Virginia approved its conscription law, Pennsylvania governor Robert Hunter Morris recommended to his province's assembly "that if the Exigency of Affairs should render it necessary to impress any, it might be only single Men, and such as have no Habitations or Settlements among us, whose Service may be wanted in the Course of this Expedition."[74] In 1757 and 1758 the Pennsylvania assembly twice resisted attempts by the governor to raise volunteers for the royal service, bemoaning that "the Province has been drained of its single Men by the King Officers in the Recruiting Service."[75] At the end of the war Governor Thomas Boone of South Carolina was optimistic about the prospect of bachelors serving in the military to fend off attacks by the Creek Indians. "Several settlers were come from the Northward and other parts," Boone told the assembly, "who, with many single men, seemed willing to make a stand, if they met with speedy and proper encouragement."[76] These ideas even spread back to Britain. In 1757 Parliament authorized a new militia law that exempted from duty those married men who had previously served in the militia and were presently engaged in a trade.[77] By the end of the Seven Years' War the bachelor laws were no longer confined to New England and Pennsylvania but had found a place throughout the British Empire.

"All Single Men . . . Shall Be Assessed"

With rare exceptions, the bachelor laws applied to the same group of men who had had their labor apportioned by England's statutes of laborers and artificers and their living arrangements directed by New England's family government laws: the young and the propertyless. Whether it was the absence of debtor relief in Massachusetts, the assessment of a special poll tax in Pennsylvania, or military conscription in Virginia, bachelors who were not masters faced the new laws alone. Time and again lawmakers ignored older bachelors and those who owned property. As the Pennsylvania legislature passed a flurry of bachelor laws from the 1690s to the 1730s, assemblyman and lifelong bachelor Jeremiah Langhorne saw little in the laws that concerned him. As one of the largest landowners in Bucks County and twice the Speaker of the House, Langhorne was not included in the group of men that he and the rest of the government denied debtors' relief to and taxed at rates higher than 90 percent of estates.[78] Yet the longer the bachelor laws remained in existence, the harder it was to limit them to the young and propertyless alone. In part, it was the logical conclusion of the ideology of the affectionate patriarch. If the purpose was to protect men with children, then it made little sense to limit tax exemptions to impoverished fathers or to require military service from only young and propertyless singles. By the middle of the eighteenth century, the husband/bachelor dichotomy became so great that legal considerations of wealth and age fell away altogether. All single men were bachelors and any differences among them were inconsequential.

The expansion of the category of men affected by the bachelor laws occurred primarily in the area of revenue collection. In a flurry of laws passed between the 1690s and 1760s, propertied single men found themselves obliged to pay a special bachelor tax. The practice of taxing propertied bachelors increased in popularity at the same time that several colonies, Pennsylvania among them, taxed propertyless ones. In time, several governments simply combined the two sets of laws into one that taxed all bachelors.

Lawmakers approved taxes on bachelors regardless of age or rank at the same time that political and humorous writers began touting a punitive bachelor tax. In pamphlets and periodicals writers schooled their readers in the history of the idea of using fiscal policy to penalize men for not marrying. They touted the words of Plato and recalled the stunning success of the Lex Iulia et Papia. Such laws were less about revenue, they opined, than about social engineering. Fearful about a decline in morals and population, English and American writers demanded that lawmakers adopt laws that would tax bachelors into marriage. It is important to recognize that bachelor taxes—especially on those with property—emerged in this atmosphere. However, a review of the laws, the events surrounding their passage, and their execution suggests that ideas of social engineering were not at the forefront of legislators' minds. Practical matters such as paying for a war or equalizing the tax burden took precedence, pushing a moral agenda into the background. Accordingly, although a notion of punishment was part of the larger cultural conversation about the bachelor tax, it was secondary to the decisions of lawmakers.

The new approach to the bachelor first appeared in England in 1695 when the kingdom was embroiled in the Nine Years' War. The first act in a century-and-a-half long struggle against France, the war was a particularly expensive matter. Seven years into the war, the English government found itself beset by a prolonged financial crisis. Searching for original and untapped sources of revenue, Parliament placed taxes on nearly everything in the kingdom from alcohol to salt. When King William III suggested taxing leather, legislators feared the encroachment of the excise and devised a revenue law that taxed births, marriages, and burials. As these rates necessarily left out those men who lacked familial commitments, the act also placed "certaine rates and duties... upon Batchelors."[79]

In part, the bachelor tax of 1695 was a continuation of the English fiscal policies of 1660 and 1678. Like the earlier laws, the 1695 tax was grounded in the belief that single men could better handle a heavier tax burden than married men because they did not have dependents to support. Indeed, Parliament made this idea pointedly clear when it placed the levies not only on men who had never married but also on any man "being a Widdower and haveing noe Child or Children." Also like earlier laws, the tax of 1695 was a means of deriving revenue from those people not otherwise rated. The comprehensive act assessed births, marriages, and burials, meaning that a householder had to pay at least two shillings every time his wife bore a child and four shillings every time a family member died. A man had to pay at least two shillings six pence to even become a husband. A bachelor faced no such levies.

At the same time, there was considerable divergence between the earlier levies and the 1695 tax. Foremost was the fact that the new levy was not directed solely at the young and propertyless nor was it an attempt to derive revenue from those who did not pay other taxes. "Every person," the law mandated, "being a Batchelor

above the age of Five and twenty yeares (except such as receive Alms) shall...soe
long time thereof as hee shall continue a Batchelor and noe longer pay unto his
Majesty his Heires and Successors the sum of One shilling yearely." In addition
to the base rate of one shilling, bachelors were assessed an additional tax based on
their personal wealth and rank. A single man who earned £50 a year or who had
an estate worth £600 was assessed an extra five shillings, while those with greater
landholdings or titles of nobility paid even higher sums. The maximum rates fell on
bachelor dukes who were rated £12 10s. above the base rate.

Although Parliament continued to affirm that being a bachelor made a man capable of paying higher taxes, it changed what kind of bachelors it sought to derive
money from. Given that 90 percent of English servants were under twenty-five, it
is clear that the *bachelor* in the 1695 law did not equate with the *single* in either the
1660 tax or the statutes of laborers and artificers. Indeed, before the 1695 tax, land
ownership and a title of nobility had always exempted bachelors from the bachelor
laws. The only exemption the tax allowed was for ones so desperately poor that they
received alms. As a result, the bachelor tax of 1695 decreed that marital status by
itself was sufficient grounds for the unequal treatment of men.

As revenue enhancement, the bachelor tax of 1695 was moderately successful.
The law was initially scheduled to last five years, and during that time Parliament
went to great lengths to enforce it. By 1700 the revenue act as a whole had brought in
more than a quarter of a million pounds sterling, and so a grateful Parliament renewed the act for another six years. By then, however, the war had ended and the
efficiency of collections declined considerably. When the extension expired, no one
felt the need to renew it a second time.[80]

It is unclear how much notions of social engineering effected the bachelor tax
of 1695, although lawmakers who hoped to encourage marriage ultimately failed to
make the single life financially prohibitive. For one, the larger revenue law placed
taxes on births, marriages, and burials, not just bachelors. This meant that men who
performed their requisite familial duties were penalized along with those who did
not. Worse, the rates on events that accompanied family life were far higher than
the penalties on bachelors. The levy on each birth was twice the yearly rate on a
single man and the tax on a marriage was two-and-a-half times as much. However,
the mere existence of a tax on bachelors did give advocates of punishment some
hope. It legitimized the principle of a levy on all single men and spawned several
imitations including the New York bachelor tax of 1703.

Discussions of a punitive bachelor tax flowered in America after New York began
rating wealthy single men, but no colonial assembly followed New York's lead until
another imperial conflict threatened. In 1756, as Virginia fretted about the prospect
of Indian attacks and began to build an army, neighboring Maryland took steps to
prepare itself for war by raising taxes. The Seven Years' War caused many American legislatures to reevaluate their revenue systems. Most colonies kept taxes low
during times of peace, but with a global struggle on the horizon, funds were suddenly needed to pay soldiers, build forts, and provide friendly Indians with gifts.

Accordingly, in late 1755 and early 1756 several assemblies raised existing taxes and implemented a series of new ones.[81] In Maryland lawmakers spent the first part of 1756 debating a £40,000 supply bill. Desperate to raise revenue by any means necessary, the legislature reversed its historical opposition to the land tax and increased poll taxes on imported slaves. It also added or increased taxes on alcohol, naval stores, court documents, and billiard tables. Finally, it approved the province's first tax on the unmarried. Specifically, the law required unmarried men "of the Age of Twenty-five Years or upwards, and have in Possession, in their own Right, an Estate of One Hundred Pounds, or upwards" to pay five shillings a year, and those who had £300 or more to pay twenty shillings.[82]

Although the Maryland legislature assumed most of the new taxes were self-explanatory, in the final version of the supply act it explained its reasons for the bachelor tax:

> Forasmuch as Divine Institutions ought to be strictly observed in every well-regulated Government, and as that in Regard to the entering into the holy Estate of Matrimony may tend to the more orderly Propagation of Mankind, it ought, not only in a religious, but political View, to be promoted, and the continuing in a State of Celibacy discountenanced, especially in every Infant Country: And as the Rank of Men called Batchelors are not burthened with the Charge and Expence that usually attends a Matrimonial Condition, they may be better enabled to contribute a larger Tax towards the Support of the Community.

The wording of the Maryland tax has attracted the attention of numerous historians who have often quoted it as definitive proof that early Americans sought to tax single men out of existence.[83] To be sure, the act was far more explicit in its intent than any other bachelor law passed up to that point, but the intent was clearly profamily rather than antibachelor. The law promoted the religious and political virtues of reproduction rather than denigrating the immorality of the single life. Similarly, the observation that single men could better afford a higher tax because they had no dependents resonates with the same logic of the affectionate patriarch as William Penn's commentary on laws against thievery. Bachelors were not paying a higher tax because they were particularly problematic but for the same reason that Maryland denied them clemency for debts.

The profamily intent can also be seen in the legislative debates surrounding the adoption of the supply act. The records of the House of Delegates reveal that most of the specific taxes in the 1756 supply bill were devised by the House's Committee of Ways and Means. In the committee's original version of the bill, there was no bachelor tax but there was a five-shilling fee on marriage licenses. The day after the committee presented the supply bill to the whole House, the body sent the bill to the Committee of Laws. While the second committee deliberated, the House entertained the question "whether the Tax mentioned in the Report, by the Committee of Ways and Means, to be laid on Marriage-Licenses, shall be altered, or

Not?" The House voted to retain the marriage license fees, although a number of members who voted against the provision sat on the Committee of Laws. It thus appears that after the House decided to continue taxing marriages, the Committee of Laws altered the language of the supply bill in such a way that would encourage the assembly to drop the license fee. The most effective way to do so would have been to include a tax on the unmarried. Tellingly, when the Committee of Laws returned the supply bill to the full house, the assembly again considered the marriage tax, and this time it jettisoned it.[84]

Despite the righteous rhetoric of the law, the Maryland bachelor tax only touched a small number of bachelors. Although England's 1695 bachelor tax exempted only those people receiving alms, Maryland's version applied to single men worth more than £100, thus excluding more than half the province's bachelors.[85] We might also consider the size of the tax and its effects on those called upon to pay it. As one historian has pointed out, five shillings on a £100 estate and twenty shillings on property worth more than £300 was hardly punitive.[86] To put the tax in perspective, five shillings was the same amount as the land tax on five hundred acres and twenty shillings was only one third of the assessment on a billiard table. Although the Maryland tax was the most harshly worded bachelor law in colonial America, its reach was circumscribed.

The execution of the Maryland bachelor tax was considerably more successful than that of the Virginia conscription law. Initially, there was some grumbling among the individual parishes that the law had designated to make lists of the taxable bachelors in their jurisdictions. The vestry of North Sassafras Parish in Cecil County refused to draw up a list until it received a copy of the law requiring them to do so.[87] Nevertheless, North Sassafras and the other parishes eventually complied with the law and made lists of local bachelors for 1756 and every year thereafter until the tax expired in 1763. Tax lists from four parishes scattered throughout the province reveal that between twenty and thirty-five bachelors were taxed per parish each year. Bachelors living in urban areas tended to be wealthier than those living in rural areas. In St. Anne's Parish, which included the capital city of Annapolis, men worth over £300 outnumbered those worth less by more than two to one, while the reverse was true in Worcester County's St. Martin's Parish on the Eastern Shore. In most parishes, the ratio of the two groups was about even.[88] Overall, there appears to have been little difficulty collecting the tax. According to committee reports, the levy brought in between £300 and £500 per year and accounted for 7 to 13 percent of the province's income from supply act taxes. The amount was significant since the Committee of Ways and Means had projected that the marriage tax would raise only about 1 percent of the £40,000 needed to defend the colony.[89]

The vestry records also reveal that taxed bachelors ran the gamut of respectability and social standing. According to Maryland's 1694 fornication law, cohabiting unmarried couples were required to face the admonition of the local minister and vestry. The idea was to encourage couples to legalize their unions and thus keep the matter out of the criminal courts.[90] In Cecil County's St. Mary Anne's Parish two different taxed bachelors were called to face the vestry while the bachelor tax was in effect, including Joseph Ellot who lived with a woman "big with Child."[91] At the same time, not all single men were reprobates. In several of the parishes, taxed bachelors served as churchwardens and vestrymen, the latter of which were charged with drawing up lists of bachelors for taxation.

The lives of bachelors in St. Anne's Parish in Annapolis demonstrate just how high up the economic and social ladder Maryland bachelors could climb. The parish's taxed bachelors included some of the province's wealthiest and most powerful men: the mayor of Annapolis, the master of King William's School, two militia officers, and a sheriff. Unmarried ratables also included several wealthy planters, merchants, attorneys, and two owners of public houses. Taxed single men served as vestrymen and churchwardens for the parish in all eight years that the tax was collected and these men were each rated accordingly. In addition to local men of stature, the St. Anne's Parish lists included provincial leaders. Three members of the House of Delegates from Annapolis and Anne Arundel County who lived in the parish were assessed as were three councilors, the governor's secretary, clerks for the assembly and the provincial court, and the province's attorney general.[92]

While bachelors were a vibrant part of Annapolis, they were hardly powerless in the rest of the province. During the collection of the tax, fourteen unmarried men served in the House of Delegates, representing seven counties on the Western Shore and the Eastern Shore, rural and urban areas, the colony's oldest settlements and its frontier. Four of these men served in the assembly when the bachelor tax was being considered, including a member of the Committee of Laws where the tax likely originated, as did a fifth man who married between the House's approval of the supply act in March 1756 and its implementation a few months later. However, it is difficult to determine whether marital status influenced any of these men's votes for or against the tax. Benjamin Mackall Jr., the bachelor assemblyman who married before he had to pay the levy, voted against the supply bill when it appeared before the House.[93]

Even though the Maryland bachelor tax applied to less than half the bachelor population in the province, it perpetuated a sense of inclusiveness among Maryland's single men. When St. Anne's vestry made up its first list of bachelors to be taxed, there was some disagreement as to who should be rated. The list submitted to provincial authorities included the observation that both the governor and the current pastor of St. Anne's "were both Batchelors, but did not take upon themselves to determine whether they came within the Act or not."[94] In the minds of the some vestrymen, all bachelors worth more than £100 were the same and should pay the requisite taxes. There were no exceptions for the proprietor's representative in Maryland or a man called to a religious vocation. Even more interesting is the fact that two wealthy bachelors, Robert Swan and James Maccubbin, sat on the vestry when the parish drew up the 1756 tax lists. Wealth and a religious duty had not exempted these men from the tax and perhaps they felt that no man should be above the law. Nevertheless, Governor Horatio Sharpe ignored the vestry's pointed comments, and even though his tenure and his bachelorhood continued for the duration of the supply act, he never once paid the tax. Rev. John MacPherson left the parish before the end of 1756 without being rated although his successors were less confrontational. Rev. Alexander Williamson and Rev. Samuel Keene both appeared in the parish tax rolls, apparently accepting the verdict of the parish that no single man worth over £100 should be excluded from "the Rank of Men called Batchelors."

The idea that all single men should be treated the same also appeared in efforts to enlarge the tax. In an effort to reduce the land tax, the Maryland House of Delegates in 1760 proposed a series of new taxes including one whereby "every single Man, whose Personal Estate is not valued at the Sum of One Hundred Pounds" would be "assessed the Sum of Ten Shillings in Bills of Credit, in Lieu of all Assessments to be made on his said Personal Estate."[95] This new levy, which resembled Pennsylvania's poll tax, was apparently an attempt to tax the bachelors whom the assembly had missed the first time around. Partisan wrangling prevented the bill from becoming law, although two years later the House of Delegates considered a proposal to place a five-shilling levy on untaxed bachelors and childless widowers between the ages of twenty-one and fifty. This too failed to make it out of the assembly. Had Governor Sharpe signed either bill into law, all bachelors in Maryland—regardless of property or rank—would have been taxed. The assembly also attempted to extend the existing levy on men worth £100 or more when the bachelor tax came to an end. Although there was no more fighting in the North American theater of the Seven Years' War, the House of Delegates in 1761 and 1763 proposed continuing the tax on wealthy bachelors to help fund a state college. Again, bitter party politics stalled both bills. When the Maryland bachelor tax finally expired in 1763, the threat of invasion was gone and the assembly moved in the direction of reducing taxes including those on bachelors.[96]

What Maryland attempted, Pennsylvania perfected. Like other American colonies, the financial cost of the Seven Years' War was intense for Pennsylvanians and required that the assembly continually seek new sources of provincial revenue. While the war continued, Pennsylvania used its existing formula of property taxes on landowners and poll taxes on propertyless single men to raise hundreds of thousands of pounds for His Majesty's service. Yet as the war costs reached new heights, the assembly extended the property tax to more Pennsylvanians by lowering the minimum amount of property required to qualify for the tax. In 1755 estates worth more than £30 were rated for the property tax, and this sum was cut in half four years later. For this reason, many bachelors who owned very little property—for instance, a horse—found themselves paying a property tax for the first time. Consequently, the number of single men paying the provincial poll tax began to decline and the burden of the bachelor tax became less than the rates on most estates. The end of the Seven Years' War brought little relief to taxpayers. Strapped with the war debts, the assembly continued to push for more revenue and once again it looked to its bachelors for help. Perhaps wanting to restore the burden of the poll tax or inspired by its neighbor to the south, Pennsylvania in 1764 issued the first American tax that fell equally on all bachelors. The law stated: "All single men residing in this province shall be assessed and pay fifteen shillings per head, and their property shall be rated in like manner as the same property belonging to other persons and in no other manner whatsoever."[97]

The revision in the tax code affected only the provincial rates and appears to have had no effect on the county levies. Nevertheless, as Pennsylvania worked to pay down its war debts, in the decade between the end of the Seven Years' War and the beginning of the American Revolution, all single men in Pennsylvania paid a poll tax to the colony whether they owned property or not. In the first year of the tax's revision, Jacob Taylor of Concord Township in Chester County paid the province nine shillings for eight acres of land "with buildings," one shilling for his horse, and fifteen shillings because he was a "singleman." Because most men who could afford to purchase land also married, only one other landowner in Concord Township was rated as a "singleman" in 1765 while twenty bachelors were rated for the poll tax because they owned no land. The experience of Concord Township was typical of Chester County as a whole. In the 1770 provincial tax for Chester County, 1,139 propertyless single men were rated compared to 176 propertied ones, a ratio of more than six to one. More important, the vast majority of propertied bachelors had estates of fifty acres or worth £50 and thus they had the right to vote, a privilege not accorded to their propertyless brethren.[98]

The end of the Seven Years' War was also the beginning of the end of America's connection to the British Empire. As the Revolution approached, Americans were beginning to reach a consensus on what in meant to be a bachelor in the eyes of the law. A single man had no dependents and thus was better able to contribute higher taxes, military service, and face harsher punishments than a man who did. It was a nascent notion of citizenship, one in which all men owed the community some obligation that could either be executed through paternity or through special services to the state. There was not yet the idea that equal obligations entitled men to equal rights although there was a certain leveling aspect to the apportioned responsibilities. In the eyes of the law, a bachelor was first and foremost a man and thus could be called upon to pay poll taxes or serve in the military. Such duties were inappropriate for women. A bachelor was no longer a dependent but a member of society, free to choose either marriage or higher taxes.

The bachelor laws thus mark a change in the way American society saw single men. It no longer lumped unmarried men together with unmarried women. Bachelors were a distinctly gendered subset of the population defined by unique obligations and separate from all other groups. Yet as the differences between bachelors and others sharpened, the differences among bachelors faded. Some single men had more money than others and thus wealthy bachelors were typically taxed at higher rates than propertyless ones but, because all single men lacked dependents, all single men owed the society greater obligations. In addition to creating a distinct identity, the bachelor laws also reflected a growing acceptance of the idea that single men could not be controlled. From the New England towns' poll taxes to the Virginia conscription act, legislators time and again acknowledged that it was nearly impossible to make bachelors live in certain households or even obey the law. There was something masculine in the way that bachelors claimed independence, and thus lawmakers, having already assigned single men the responsibilities of manhood, were unwilling to reduce them to dependence. A bachelor might make all the wrong decisions and devote himself to a life of luxury, but this was the bachelor's prerogative, which few Americans felt any compunction to hinder.

3

"Every One of Them Shall Be Chained about the Middle to a Post Like a Monkey"

LITERARY REPRESENTATIONS OF THE BACHELOR

By 1730 Great Britain had planted more than a dozen colonies on mainland North America and scattered many more among the islands of the West Indies. Yet in the opinion of one particularly vociferous member of Parliament, it was not too late for the king to carve one more settlement out of the wilderness. James Edward Oglethorpe envisioned a colony unlike any other, a colony where those Britons who had been jailed for debt could start anew. Oglethorpe's idea would eventually gain royal approval, and in February 1733 he led the first group of settlers to the province of Georgia. Before this happened, Oglethorpe drafted a statement of his goals and the potential benefits of the new colony. The treatise stated emphatically that success in Georgia would be contingent on the immigration of married men and the exclusion of bachelors.

Oglethorpe began with a review of history, specifically the lessons learned from previous colonies. The ancient Greeks illustrated how colonization opened up opportunities for those who went abroad as well as those who stayed home. "Waves embarked with their Wives and Familys," he noted of the Phoenicians, adding "the vacancys made by those who went off gave room for others to marry and beget Children." Consequently, the population of the colony and the motherland grew, bringing riches and power to both. Oglethorpe also considered recent French colonies, holding them up as an example of the failures that resulted from not promoting family life in the New World. He chided King Louis XIV for abandoning France's "old Soldiers" and speculated what might have happened had the monarch given his legions "leave to marry and Land to support their Familys in his new Conquests." Instead of an empty Canada, "it is demonstrable that from the many thousand Invalids who by a forced celibacy died Childless in the beginning of his

Reign might have proceeded Children sufficient to have formed mighty Armys in the latter end of it."

Oglethorpe applied these lessons to his plans for a new colony. Britain's prisons were bursting with poor debtors and such senseless incarceration was destroying families. "Want first reduces them to Sickness or to Prison," he wrote, "and when the Mans industry is useless the Wife and wretched Children must either perish or ask relief of their Parish." This suffering could be alleviated by sending married men and their families to the New World. Such a plan broke with the tradition of populating new settlements with bachelors. Single men had no familial responsibilities and were thus free to be idle and rebellious, qualities that could endanger a colony. On the other hand, men with families would ensure stability. "The first Colony should consist not of single Men but of Familys," Oglethorpe proclaimed, as "a Wife and Children are security for a Mans not abandoning the Settlement; and the presence of those dear pledges who will reap the advantage of it will the more strongly incite him to labour." With "laborious and honest people" working to support their families, Georgia's settlers "would not be apt to mutiny, since that would be destroying the end they aim at."

Oglethorpe then laid out a series of policies that would encourage the immigration of married men. The colony's trustees would provide clothing for wives and children. Those men who made it to America with families "shall during the time of their 3 Childrens being alive at once be exempted from the Rent of labour." To be sure, the trustees would have to be diligent in selecting immigrants because the proper male colonist would be "answerable for the behaviour of his Wife, Children and Servants." Such efforts might delay settlement but selectivity was paramount. The wheat had to be "whinnowed from the Chaff." It was "infinitely better to lose expence some Weeks than to carry over a mutinous or effeminate fellow." Once the venture had taken off, other measures would keep the bachelor population to a minimum. Land in Georgia was readily available and "as soon as there are 24 men who have no Land a new Village or Lath will be set out." Consequently, "no Man who is out of his Apprenticeship will remain unmarried, and as Males and Females are born in equal numbers if all the Men have Wives there can be no Woman without a Husband." Family life was also to be supported by legal strictures. "To encourage Marriage and make Children a profit instead of a burthen to their Parents," Oglethorpe speculated that fathers might be given full control over the labor of their sons until age twenty-one and of their daughters until marriage. He added: "Roman Law might be expedient exempting the Father of 3 Children from all Dutys whatsoever."[1]

The centrality of marital status to James Oglethorpe's plan for Georgia stood in sharp contrast to English colonization schemes of the sixteenth and seventeenth centuries. Previous writers had either ignored issues of marital status or promoted the immigration of masterless men as an attribute. But the context for understanding single men had changed drastically since Jamestown. By 1730 the bachelor had emerged as a distinct identity and was the subject of considerable attention. In part, Oglethorpe built on the paradigm introduced by lawmakers: bachelors were identifiable based on their lack of dependents to support, were distinguishable from other nonmasters because of their masculine autonomy, and were surprisingly uniform despite differences in age and social status. But whereas legislators had been relatively restrained in their attempts to affect the lives of unmarried men, writers such as Oglethorpe were more creative. Ideas only hinted at in actual laws were fully developed in eighteenth-century literature, further distinguishing the bachelor as a unique identity that attracted considerable controversy.

Oglethorpe's plan for Georgia illustrates the new literary identity of the bachelor that gained acceptance in the eighteenth century. It had roots in medieval and early modern depictions of single men, and like Chaucer's bacheleris or Shakespeare's Falstaff, it made light of single men for being sophomoric, lovelorn, and unmanly. Yet eighteenth-century writers contorted these images and rendered the bachelor far more troubling. He was a wild creature—"mutinous" in the words of Oglethorpe—rebellious and uncontrolled. He exuded immaturity and, like a child, was unconcerned with the consequences of his actions. He thought only of himself and this inherent selfishness was both a cause and an effect of his lack of familial attachments. The bachelor was unpatriotic because he did nothing to increase the size and power of the country through legitimate procreation. He was thoroughly immoral, devoted to a life of luxury and vice. His most destructive aspect was his sexuality. Some bachelors were emotionally unattached rakes who sired a brood of bastard offspring while others were attracted to the wrong sex—noted in Oglethorpe's scorn of the "effeminate fellow." Nearly all of the ideas about how to deal with this sinister creature rejected the sixteenth-century belief that a bachelor was best handled by placing him under household government. His vices were too great for any one man to control and thus only the full power of the state could effectively restrain him. Many writers, Oglethorpe among them, demanded harsh laws to circumscribe bachelors' actions and to encourage their marriage. Yet even the harshest critics of the single life acknowledged that true change could come only from within. The bachelor had to choose to abandon his wayward behaviors and accept the responsibilities of marriage and family.

This new and more severe portrayal of the bachelor began largely in the era of the English Restoration and reached a deafening crescendo in the early eighteenth century. Political writers led the charge, tracing a new relationship between marital status and political identity. Playwrights, essayists, and belletrists soon followed. The new literary attention to bachelors was in part a result of the growing popularity of the print media and the appearance of new forms of literature at the turn of the eighteenth century. The lapse of the English Licensing Act in 1695 encouraged a democratization of the print media and laid the groundwork for an increasing quantity and variety of literature.[2] The new obsession with bachelors was also a result of what Stephanie Coontz has termed "the love revolution." For five thousand years marriage had been a political and economic alliance between families. Although the individual possessed the right to choose whom to marry as well as whether to marry, affection rarely influenced one's choices. Indeed, moralists had long warned young people not to make lifelong connections based solely on love. Between 1650 and 1750 this understanding of marriage began to change.[3] The emergence of a new periodical literature brought a growing awareness to issues of the heart. Authors began to depict young people who searched their feelings to discover whether they really loved the person they were about to marry. These works in turn attracted an audience of young people who sought advice on love and relationships from knowing elders or who wrote their own verses and letters to capture their emotions. By the middle of the eighteenth century it was considered shameful to marry for any reason other than true love. This literary movement ultimately had a negative effect on the reputation of the bachelor. Because marriage was supposed to be based on love, authors concluded that the man who did not marry was either incapable of love or practiced an inappropriate type of affection. Like Oglethorpe, periodical writers and pamphleteers disparaged the single man as an unstable force in society who lived only for himself and who engaged in rakish or homosexual behavior. The bachelor deserved to be punished.

The literary treatment of single men followed a parallel track to the emergence of the bachelor laws. Like the bachelor tax, it was part of a transatlantic dialogue. Colonial discussions of the bachelor lagged about a half century behind England largely because of the late development of American printing. Before the 1720s colonists were largely confined to reading British periodicals and political tracts, meaning that many of the earliest American treatments of the bachelor were essentially identical to the British perspective. However, as the colonial press took off, a distinctive approach emerged that redefined the issues of marital status in an American context, although the colonists continued to consume the British treatments as well.[4] Also, the literature and the laws spoke to one another. Lawmakers and political thinkers both drew inspiration from ancient Roman laws and many authors closely followed the actions of Parliament and colonial legislatures. Oglethorpe's proposed bachelor laws in Georgia were merely an embellishment of statutes already in existence. Some legislators may have read pieces like Oglethorpe's plan for Georgia as they spelled out new civic responsibilities for unmarried men. The two were certainly mutually reinforcing.

At the same time, it is important not to overestimate the effect of literature. Historians have long cited the harsh rebuke of single men in colonial-era publications as definitive proof that bachelors were "a serious cause for concern."[5] There are two problems with this approach. First, it offers a one-dimensional reading of the material. Only rarely have scholars recognized the ironic humor of antibachelor tracts or their subversive potential. Many literary discussions of the bachelor tax actually made the case *against* using the law to punish men for being single. Second, accepting the literary depictions at face value ignores the dissonance between the text and reality. Although Oglethorpe served as governor of the colony for a dozen years, the government of Georgia implemented no bachelor laws before 1800. Moreover, Georgia filled with single men under Oglethorpe's leadership, leading to a situation in which men outnumbered women by more than two to one. In a 1743 letter to the trustees, Oglethorpe bemoaned the overabundance of bachelors in the colony, noting that "most of these would marry if they could get wives." Because "married soldiers live easiest, many of them having turned out very industrious planters," he proposed that the trustees fund the passage of "single women without families."[6] Most curious of all was the fact that Oglethorpe was himself a bachelor for all the time he lived in America. He did marry after he returned to England in 1744, but by then he was nearing fifty and was reluctant to give up the bachelor lifestyle he so harshly rebuked. Even though he took a bride half his age, Oglethorpe neither fathered children nor settled down. Instead, he maintained his reputation as a ladies' man until his death at nearly ninety years of age.[7]

Regardless of the limits of literary depictions, they were nonetheless critical to the development of the bachelor identity. They demonstrate the emergence of bachelorhood as a distinctly masculine identity defined by autonomy. Moreover, political and popular tracts offer a moral judgment of bachelorhood often missing from legislative debates. Not everyone accepted or even tolerated the emergence of bachelorhood. Many Britons and Americans tried to push back against the rising visibility of single men by promoting a profamily agenda. For such people, poll taxes and occasional military service were not sufficient to block the power of bachelors. The state had to take decisive action to encourage men to marry. Yet eighteenth-century writers were hardly unanimous in their support of punitive measures. Many essayists ridiculed the idea of the state directing the affairs of the heart. Although they disparaged bachelors, their devotion to the love revolution emboldened their conviction that marriage was a personal choice not to be directed by the government. Accordingly, a number of humorous writers took aim at those who wanted to use the law to punish bachelors by ridiculing the laws themselves. They advocated a gentler approach that appealed to the hearts of single men and consequently blunted the type of punitive laws that men such as Oglethorpe advocated.

In this chapter I explore the literary depictions of single men from the English Restoration to the eve of the American Revolution. Because of the voluminous production of the British press, many depictions come from the other side of the Atlantic. Much of this work was read widely in the colonies and inspired American imitations. Although several volumes could easily be devoted to all the writings on single men in the eighteenth century, for the sake of brevity I focus on the timely literature of the era, specifically pamphlets, periodicals, and newspapers. These works reached a wider audience than plays and novels, especially in the American colonies. They were also more politically oriented than other works and thus allow us to see the interplay between politics and literature. The chapter moves chronologically with particular emphasis on discussions of the bachelor tax in pamphlets, depictions of single men in the *Tatler* and the *Spectator*, and the uniquely American take on the unmarried in the serious and not-so-serious works of Benjamin Franklin.

"Fewness of People Is Real Poverty"

Authors were first drawn to the subject of single men as a result of changing ideas about population. Since the middle of the sixteenth century English writers and lawmakers had bemoaned the overabundance of people in the country. The poor laws, statutes of laborers and artificers, and the settlement of the American colonies had all been solutions to the surplus of people and the dearth of economic opportunities. A century later views on population had changed radically. As the number of English subjects leveled off and declined, political writers began to advocate measures to increase the population. Among the most popular solutions was the implementation of a harsh and punitive bachelor tax.

The second half of the seventeenth century was a period of demographic stagnation and decline in England. After growing steadily since the middle of the sixteenth century, the English population peaked at 5.3 million in the 1650s and then dropped over the next twenty-five years, dipping as low as 4.9 million in the late 1680s. The population remained depressed for the remainder of the century and did not surpass its 1650s heights until the second decade of the eighteenth century. Twentieth-century demographers have put forward various explanations for England's population decline, with some arguing it was the result of a dramatic increase in the number of deaths and others claiming that fertility declined. An analysis of English parishes by E. A. Wrigley and R. S. Schofield has demonstrated that both assertions have validity.[8]

Wrigley and Schofield have suggested that changes in marital patterns were partly to blame for the decline in population. Specifically, they argue that England in the second half of the seventeenth century had an abundance of single people. Using back projections, they estimate that 27 percent of the English population born during the Civil War was still unmarried at the age of forty. Although criticism of their methodology has caused Schofield to reduce these figures, even with revision it appears that in the second half of the seventeenth century perhaps a quarter of the English population who reached midlife never married. Historians have attempted to understand why so many English men and women remained single in this period but there are no conclusive answers. Wrigley and Schofield have correlated the overall growth of the English population to an increase in real wages. However, as wages grew steadily from 1650 to 1700, rates of marriage stumbled. David Weir has speculated that the rise in celibacy reflected sex-selective migration whereby the rapid growth of London attracted a large number of young women from the countryside seeking wage labor while their brothers stayed home. The effects of emigration to the colonies may also have served as a drain on the young male population of England although Wrigley and Schofield have found the effects of net migration to be largely negligible.[9]

English political and economic writers in the second half of the seventeenth century were keenly aware of the drop in population and the proliferation of singles.

In large part, this was due to a recent innovation in quantitative methods, or what one contemporary termed "Political Arithmetick."[10] In 1662 John Graunt published *Natural and Political Observations upon the Bills of Mortality* in which he examined the numbers of christenings and burials in England since 1628. Although parishes had collected vital records for some time, Graunt was one of the first writers to use the information to calculate the country's population, sex ratios, and rate of natural increase. Others soon followed Graunt's lead. They used increasingly sophisticated methodologies and began asking more complex questions, including Gregory King who calculated the ages, marital status, and potential wealth of the English population. In time, political arithmetic dramatically changed the political discourse in late seventeenth-century England, allowing political theorists and economists to contemplate the potential for population growth and its connection to the kingdom's wealth.[11]

One of the first writers to connect quantitative methods to a political agenda was Sir William Petty, who proclaimed in 1662 that "fewness of people is real poverty."[12] Petty argued that the strength of the country's labor force was as vital as land to its wealth and so he advocated that England facilitate its expansion. Sir William Temple concurred and wrote in 1685 "how much the number of inhabitants falls below what the extent of our territory and fertility of our soil, makes it capable of entertaining and supporting with all necessaries and conveniencies of life."[13] These and other writers bemoaned the loss of subjects to America as well as to foreign and domestic wars. Such missteps had caused the English to fall behind the French and the Dutch. A larger population could make England a stronger nation by supplying more warriors, workers, and taxpayers. "The people being the first matter of power and wealth," wrote Charles Davenant in 1699, "by whose labour and industry a nation must be gainers in the Balance, their encrease or decrease must be carefully observed by any government that designs to thrive."[14] These writers pondered several means of increasing England's population. Although Temple postulated that England should augment its numbers by any means necessary, including encouraging the immigration of foreign subjects, all believed that natural increase was the best way for England to repair its losses. They thus turned their attention to changing English laws. Graunt considered decriminalizing fornication and polygamy but ultimately rejected the idea.[15] The only acceptable form of procreation was the type that took place under the auspices of legal marriage. Such a formula would ensure that every child had parents to provide for him or her, resulting in a new generation of healthy and well-educated subjects.

Natural increase, and by extension the success of the nation, thus depended on the willingness of English men and women to marry early and have large numbers of children. However, it was this point that worried political and economic writers, as the current generation of young Britons were avoiding marriage in large numbers. "The first command of God was to encrease and multiply," asserted Petty in 1685, but the "way of marriage is now such, that of 100 capable women only 32 are maryed, and this 32 brought 11 children per annum."[16] If more people could be encouraged to marry, Petty believed that the population could double in twenty-five years and consequently the combined value of the kingdoms of England, Scotland, and Ireland would triple. Other writers concurred with Petty's findings. An anonymous pamphlet from 1690 claimed that "there are near one half of the People of England which die Single, and near a Third of those, which by many Years are not Married so early as they might."[17]

Although most authors did not speculate as to why so many Britons were growing old without entering the marriage covenant, some were not so taciturn. Temple charged that "the late humour" of "so many mens marrying late or never" had been "introduced by licentiousness," and Thomas Sheridan connected the fact that "England is already very much under-peopled" to "the Loosness and Debauchery of the present Age."[18] In other words, sexual deviance was to blame. Like Puritan moralists, proponents of political arithmetic did not distinguish between different types of nonprocreative sex. All were transgressions against God and the state. Although authors of this era were certainly aware of an increase in homosexual activity in London, for the purposes of advocating an expansion of the population it made little difference to them whether single men were engaging in intercourse with women, men, animals, or no one at all. As long as a man was not married, he was not producing legitimate children.[19]

With English men and women so imprudent regarding their duties to marry and procreate, writers looked to the past for inspiration. The ancient Roman Lex Iulia et Papia had retained currency in early modern England and reappeared periodically in political tracts. Thomas Starkey, chaplain to King Henry VIII, had speculated about the need for population growth in the 1530s, a time before fears of overpopulation changed the conversation. Advising that the government could "much entice men to marriage, specially if we gave unto them also certain privileges and prerogative, after the manner of the old and wise Romans," Starkey urged that "every bachelor, according to the portion of goods and lands, should yearly pay a certain sum."[20] More than a century later, as the Puritan commonwealth erected after the execution of King Charles I began to crumble, James Harrington sketched his 1656 vision for a republican England, *Oceana*. Harrington's plan placed the responsibilities of government with independent freeholders and recommended that magistrates be elected at militia musters. Yet these rights did not extend to unmarried men. "But for as much as the commonwealth demandeth as well the fruits of a man's body as of his mind," Harrington wrote, "he that hath not been married shall not be capable of these magistracies until he be married." Harrington also looked back toward the Roman model of punishing celibacy and rewarding procreation: "If a man have ten children living, he shall pay no taxes; if he have five living, he shall pay but half taxes, [but] if he have been married three years, or be above twenty-five years of age, and have no child or children lawfully begotten, he shall pay double taxes."[21]

Although Restoration-era political theorists had no love for Harrington's republican sympathies, they agreed with his assessment of the single state. Charles Davenant suggested that the English follow the Roman practice of "privileges and exemptions for such a number of children, and by denying certain offices of trust and dignities to all unmarried persons." Most writers, however, simply advocated punitive fines on singles.[22] "Let there be a tax upon all men of between 18 and 60, and upon all women between 15 and 45, to defray the said charges of lying in and nursing," demanded William Petty.[23] A number of writers concurred, although most limited the application of the tax to men. One scheme called for single men over the age of twenty-one to pay an eighth of their annual income to the state, another demanded a third of bachelors' yearly earnings, and a third suggested a tax graduated by rank and status. William Temple speculated that such revenues could be directed toward "the building of ships and public work-houses, and raising a stock for maintaining them."[24] Since bachelors were not producing workers and soldiers, they could at least aid the English economy and military financially.

In many ways the call for a bachelor tax was a reiteration of the principle that a single man should pay higher taxes because his lack of dependents made him better able to afford them. Yet there were other ideas involved as well. The bachelor tax was intended as an economic incentive to encourage men to marry. Although the writings of the political economist Thomas Malthus were still a hundred years in the offing, writers such as Petty, Temple, and Davenant implicitly invoked the Malthusian principle that the decision to marry involved an economic choice. If the costs of bachelorhood were increased, especially to as much as a third of a man's income, then the relative costs of marriage and childrearing would decrease. By taxing each bachelor's pocketbook, the writers hoped to make marriage a cost-effective proposition. The bachelor tax was also intended as a type of punishment. The political writers blamed single men for shirking their responsibility to produce a new generation of English subjects, for choosing an immoral lifestyle over patriotic duty. Unlike the statutes of laborers and artificers, the plans for a punitive bachelor tax were not about social control but about social engineering. In the reverse of all existent laws, political writers' plans for a bachelor tax emanated from an open hostility toward unmarried men and were designed to reduce the unmarried to an inferior status.

By indicting single men as morally deficient, proponents of the bachelor tax indiscriminately attacked all unmarried men in England, even those whose vocations demanded celibacy. In 1707 Nehemiah Grew advised that taxes should be increased fourfold on bachelors, including servants and celibate clergymen. He also recommended that fellowships at colleges be reduced because they prevented marriage. Such a stance challenged the long-standing English belief that certain professions were better suited to single men. Moreover, it elevated marriage from something a man could do for the society to the sine qua non of civic responsibility. According to men such as Grew, nothing justified the lack of a wife and children. Although Grew's ideas represented an extreme version of the type of proposals offered by political theorists, his position was the logical extension of the argument initiated by Petty, Temple, and Davenant. Indeed, for the rest of the eighteenth century writers continued to debate whether clergymen and college fellows were better off single or married.[25]

By the second decade of the eighteenth century it was clear that the kingdom's population was rebounding and that the percentage of singles was in decline. Nevertheless, calls for a bachelor tax persisted. Tax advocates writing at midcentury fleshed out many of the ideas implicit in earlier literature. For one, the tax became increasingly gender-specific in its aim. Although presumably single women were as much to blame for the country's decline in population, political writers laid the guilt solely at the feet of single men. Men were the ones who were expected to propose marriage and to take full economic responsibility for their families once the marriage began. Women thus increasingly faded to the background, becoming either expenses or victims in a world defined exclusively by selfish bachelors. For example, a 1748 pamphlet advocated a levy on single men as a means of bringing about tax equity. As the unnamed writer claimed, a husband paid higher taxes because he was responsible for rates "upon every Thing his Wife eats, drinks and wears that is taxable, and the same for every one of his Children" while the bachelor was only responsible for himself.[26]

Women's lack of agency in the politics of population was further demonstrated by the way that tax advocates increasingly equated lifelong celibacy with sexual incontinence. In 1726 the novelist Daniel Defoe pondered the number of prostitutes in London and concluded that "the main Cause is, that Neglect of Matrimony which the Morals of the present Age inspire Men with." With men preoccupied with their own sinful activities, many young women were "forced to become the Instruments of satisfying those Desires in Men which were given for a better Use, and which are the greatest Temptations to Matrimony." To help prevent women from being reduced to prostitution, Defoe argued that the British government should encourage marriage, recalling how the ancient Romans had "imposed a Fine upon every Man unmarried at a certain Age."[27] For other writers, the problem was not prostitution but women who fell victim to the "the natural Passion of the Sexes." Again, pamphleteers did not hold women responsible for their actions but laid the blame on unscrupulous bachelors. It was single men who were to the cause of "multitudes of Women, as well Ladies as others, who are forced to live in an uncomfortable State" of celibacy.[28]

Ultimately, arguments for the bachelor tax were arguments against luxury. Luxury was the great scourge of the eighteenth century, an enervating force that stripped men of their virtue and threatened to subject the populace to tyranny. The connections between luxury and gender were explicit in eighteenth-century writings, with authors claiming that luxury weakened men by effectively feminizing them.[29] The discussion of the bachelor tax was a subset of this larger discourse. The reluctance of men to marry and their preference for prostitutes were evidence of a moral plague on the land "greatly increased with our Infidelity and Contempt of Religion," according to a 1748 pamphlet. Such depravity was certainly not new but the manifestations of it were: "Celibacy or Single-Life, now growing into Fashion among us." The term *fashion* in this context was more than simply an expression meaning the current style. It was a culturally loaded signifier of all things ephemeral and ludicrous, diametrically opposed to the sober and serious duties of married men. When the bachelor and the husband faced the taxman together, the latter found himself burdened by the expenses of his family while the former was free to fritter his money away. "The rest he may bestow on his Pleasures," the pamphleteer surmised, adding "which are not always for the Good of the Community." The author wrote that the typical married man would find "that the Batchelor can outdo him in many Things, that he can appear in a more genteel way, with more Grandeur, and entertain his Friends with more Elegance, while he himself is rewarded with more Taxes." The only solution was a bachelor tax. The author concluded that rooting out evils was so paramount that even if the tax did not serve to increase population, "it would not be less reasonable, that Luxury and Vice should be discountenanced."[30]

"Every Batchelor...Should Pay Such a Tax to the Queen"

While political writers took an active interest in the bachelor, believing that changing his status was the key to increasing the size of the British population, a host of other writers found themselves similarly enchanted with unmarried men. In the theater and in novels, the bachelor garnered a devoted following.[31] Single men also appeared in less substantial works such as irreverent pamphlets, periodical essays, and ephemeral writings known as belles lettres. The discussion of bachelors in these pieces was typically as harsh as anything issued by Petty, Temple, or Davenant. Bachelors were immoral creatures who had become too numerous and thus were in need of harsh rebuke. Yet whereas political writers criticized single men in hopes of changing national policy, essayists and pamphleteers wrote send-ups of the unmarried for humorous effect. The emergence of the bachelor identity made it easier for humorists to caricaturize single men and they honed in on the distinctive features that defined them. A bachelor's masculine independence was not something attractive but was a vehicle for vice—what happened when a man went unchecked by a wife. Humorists also took on political issues, specifically the bachelor tax, although this too they ridiculed. In so doing, they questioned the legitimacy of using the state to interfere with matters of the heart. In the hands of humorists, the bachelor tax went from being a serious proposal to a transatlantic joke about desperate single women who used the law to force men to marry them.

In the light humor of periodicals and pamphlets, matrimony and courtship were favorite subjects. Writers raised questions about the people who sought marriage and also those who avoided it. As a general rule, they portrayed men as preferring the pleasures of the single life, loving to indulge in the excess of drink, sex, and gaming. In *The Batchelors Ballad*, published in 1677, a brokenhearted man cursed Cupid and declared that the next time he met an attractive woman he would get her drunk, take advantage of her, and then leave her.[32] Conversely, female writers complained about being single, although more often than not they blamed the poor quality of men for their situation. In *The Maids Answer to the Batchelors Ballad*, a single woman laughed at the bitter author of the *Batchelors Ballad* and assured him that no woman would fall for his pathetic advances.[33] Occasionally, female writers claimed that they preferred the single life, including one who decreed: "Tho Marriage is an Honour, house-keeping is chargeable, / And a Maidens life is free from strife, she likes it very well."[34] Such powerful and opinionated women stood in stark contrast to the hapless victims of political treatises, a theme that recurred repeatedly in pamphlets and periodicals.

Part of the playfulness of humorous pamphlets was their back and forth quality. A man or woman would decry the opposite sex and list his or her reasons, and shortly thereafter a person of the opposite sex would respond. In *The Maids Complaint against Batchelors* from 1675, an unnamed group of single women railed against the "insufferable Carriage of you, Barbarous Batchelers!" The maids contended that men were only interested in illicit sexual relations. "You count Fornication but a Venial Trifle, and yet think honest Marriage an unpardonable sin." When men married at all, the women charged, it was only for "the Price of our Portions." Ultimately, the maids appealed to the men for the sake of lawful issue as well as their own happiness. "And in this hope," they concluded, "for the future behave your selves more kindly, and prevent us from the necessity or running into Nunneries, or leading Apes in Hell," a reference to the allegorical fate of women who never married.[35] Later that year, the maids received their reply in *The Batchelors Answer* in which a group of single men rejected the women's accusation that they were wholly uninterested in marriage. Instead, they blamed single women. The bachelors inverted the women's argument and asserted that women pursued debauchery through wedlock. "The plain Truth is, you would not be so fond of Marriage, but to gain the greater Liberty, & make the Fopps your Husbands Cloaks for your wanton Sallies," the men complained, arguing that married women sought multiple sexual partners because their husbands had to provide for all offspring no matter who the father was. In the end, the bachelors made the same appeal to the maids that had been made to them: "If you will but be obliging and kind, wee'l free you from the dread of leading Apes in Hell" and "we may descend to the Folly of Wedlock with you."[36]

In the last decade of the seventeenth century, as political writers began to clamor for a bachelor tax, humorists followed suit. In 1693 an anonymous pamphlet appeared that decried men's unwillingness to marry titled *The Petition of the Ladies of London and Westminster to the Honourable House of Husbands*. Claiming to represent sixty thousand virgins, *The Petition of the Ladies* stood out in the way its format and its language imitated contemporary political tracts. The unnamed ladies began by marshaling religion and morality to their cause. "The Church men have been our surest & best Friends all along," they noted, particularly in the biblical commandment to "increase and multiply." They then proceeded to make an economic argument. Responding to charges that a family was too costly, the ladies noted of bachelors, "they pretend the Taxes run high, and that a Spouse is an expensive Animal, little considering that they throw away more upon their dearly beloved vanities"—namely, alcohol and prostitutes—"than would maintain a Wife, and half a dozen Children." Ultimately, the ladies invoked the laws of the ancient Greeks and Romans, and demanded that all men be obliged to marry by the age of twenty-one or "pay yearlie to the State." They suggested that the revenues from the tax could be used to support the army in foreign wars and "be distributed amongst poor House keepers, that have not sufficient to maintain their Wives and respective Families." However, the ladies did not stop there. They also advocated banning bachelors from taverns and ordering that all men who kept mistresses pay for "a Regiment of Foot for his Majesties Service."[37]

Later that year, the ladies received their response. In *An Humble Remonstrance of the Batchelors* unnamed single men refuted the ladies' charges one by one. The respondents defended wine and whores, claiming that the former was less harmful than marriage and that the latter were a necessity. They inverted the economic charges of the ladies and argued that the costs of the single life were nothing compared to the gifts demanded by women during courtship. The men did agree with the idea of a bachelor tax but demanded that the minimum age be increased to thirty. They also insisted that "all Virgins or reputed Virgins, who are passed the Age of One and Twenty" who had rejected the proposals of poor men "in expectation of a striking a Country-Squyer or Alderman's Son, shall be likewise amerced the same Summ for their Maiden-heads." They consented to ban bachelors from taverns "provided alwayes that none but married Women shall be licensed to appear at the Theatre, Chocolet-house, Whitehall or the Park."[38]

The repartee did not end there. A separate group of bachelors answered *The Petition of the Ladies* in the form of a ballad depicting single women as harlots and wives as shrews.[39] More curious was *The Petition of the Widows* in which previously married women joined the assault on bachelors. Mourning the death of their husbands in foreign wars, the widows demanded new ones, drawing on the examples of the ancients for laws to force marriage. Specifically, the widows asked that men under twenty-one years of age who were determined to marry but who had no sexual experience "shall be likewise obliged to take a Widow, as they do Pilots in difficult or unknown places." By providing sexual training to young men, the widows could do their part for England, as a union of two virgins "produce nothing but meer Butter Prints, addle-pated Fops, and dull senseless sleepy Boobies." The widows also called for a change in the revenue laws, although instead of a bachelor tax, they requested an exemption for themselves "for it is not hard, good Gentlemen, to pay four shilling in the Pound for empty Houses."[40]

The humorous treatment of the bachelor tax kept pace with the proliferation of political and economic tracts. Ten years after *The Petition of the Ladies* and its responses appeared, *The Levellers* was published in London. The equity to which the title of the pamphlet referred was "a Levelling of Mariages," a feat that was to be accomplished by forcing rich bachelors to take wives. The anonymously authored pamphlet was a dialogue between "two young Ladies of great Beauty and Wit" who complained about how difficult it was for them to find husbands. The first woman,

Politica, attacked the deficiencies of the 1695 bachelor tax and proposed instead that "every Batchelor, at the Age of twenty-four Years, should pay such a Tax to the Queen" for the military. Her companion, Sophia, disagreed. "Your Notions are very good and proper," she remarked, however "if this Act passeth, I do not find, that you and I shall be the better for it, for the Men are still left to the Liberty of Chusing." She argued that a better solution would be a law to compel men worth a thousand pounds to marry a "Gentlewoman of such Quality and Portion with our-selves" or else forfeit their estates to the public treasury. At length, the two debated the best methods of enticing men to propose, including forcing bachelors to wear yellow armbands, punishing their parents, and consigning them to an almshouse "wherein every one of them shall be chained about the Middle to a Post, like a Monkey."[41]

Pamphlets such as *The Petition of the Ladies* and *The Levellers* were intended to evoke laughter from readers through hyperbole and irony. On one level, the authors were merely updating the age-old battle of the sexes by placing it in the context of contemporary political debates. Of course, single men and single women would seize hold of something like a bachelor tax and wield it against the other side; such a weapon was too delicious to be ignored. As in any classic male-female battle, the bachelor tax presumably would be dispensed with once the opponents married and settled down. At that point, they would move their battle into a new arena and begin denouncing each other as cuckolds and shrews. In marriage, the sparring strategies of the single life would be but a pleasant memory.

At the same time, there were clear political implications in these wily pamphlets. They may have been timely humor but they also leave a record of incisive com-mentary on the laws of the day. In taking up the ideas of men such as Petty, Temple, and Davenant, the humorists implicitly criticized the idea of connecting marital status to revenue policy. They showed how silly the matter was by following the same logic of the political writers, citing the same evidence of demographics and ancient laws, and making an impassioned plea on behalf of patriotism. Yet the pam-phleteers reached a far different conclusion than the political writers did. For Petty and Temple, the bachelor tax was an instrument to help strengthen the nation; for Politica and Sophia it was an abusive tool of the government and little more than a state-sponsored matchmaker. Indeed, by comparing "a Tax to the Queen" with a plan to chain single men "to a Post, like a Monkey," the female debaters in *The Levellers* ridiculed all legal means to force bachelors to marry as exceeding the pur-view of the government. The caricature of the bachelor tax thus suggests that some Britons doubted the propriety of political and economic incentives to marry.

The most forceful part of the humorous pamphlets was that they used women to make their points. Because the authorship of these works was purposely con-cealed, it is impossible to know whether sixty thousand virgins actually signed on to *The Petition of the Ladies* or whether women even had a hand in composing any of the works.[42] Male writers often assumed female cognomens for effect. Often the point was to make light of the nature of women and this was certainly true of pamphlets that ridiculed the bachelor tax. Of course, women would demand government intervention to punish single men. According to the misogynistic logic of the era, the only thing that single women could think about was getting married. And being a particularly selfish and illogical sex, all women wanted rich husbands and would stop at nothing to have them. In assuming female personas, the humorists thus rendered the notion of a bachelor tax into a female issue unworthy of serious consideration. At the same time, the womanly pseudonyms may also have cut the other way. By giving women voice when it came to the topic of a bachelor tax, the pamphleteers empowered them to speak on the political issues of the day, at least so far as it related to love and marriage. But even then, the women who debated the bachelor tax betrayed any strength that their political commentary may have accorded them. They refused to contravene the age-old principle that men should propose marriage to women; instead of breaking with this tradition, they asked the state to come to their rescue. Although the identities of single men and women had always been more distinctive in literature than in the law, the increasing interest in courtship and marriage further polarized the two groups.

Bachelors in the *Tatler* and the *Spectator*

Where pamphleteers left off, the popular essayists began. Probably the most widely read and influential periodicals of the eighteenth century were the *Tatler* and the *Spectator.* Written in large part by Richard Steele, the *Tatler* first appeared in London in April 1709 and was published three times a week for three years. When the *Tatler* ended in 1711, Steele joined with Joseph Addison to begin publishing the *Spectator* six times a week for the next two years. The two periodicals were light-hearted works that made insightful observations on life in English society, including the conversations and activities inside London's coffeehouses, clubs, and salons. They presented their stories through the authors' observations and letters from readers. Love, courtship, and marriage were among the most popular topics of both works. In particular, the *Tatler* and the *Spectator* included extensive commentary on the deportment of young people seeking spouses, a discussion that inevitably led them to the issue of bachelors. The essayists had no love for single men, but unlike the pamphleteers, they warned against their ill effects on society. They also ridiculed the idea of a bachelor tax, although whereas pamphleteers stopped at satire, Addison and Steele offered an alternative solution. The best way to thin the ranks of bachelors was not through punitive legislation but through appeals to the manners, morals, and hearts of young men.[43]

As was the style of the day, the authorship of the two periodicals was disguised in the form of fictitious personalities. For the *Tatler,* Richard Steele became Isaac Bickerstaff, a man in his sixties who had spent his youth in the army. Although he had once been in love, he had never married. The narrator of the *Spectator* was a mysterious man named Mr. Spectator whose personal history and marital status were not much different from Bickerstaff's. "I have observed," Mr. Spectator began in the paper's first issue, "that a Reader seldom peruses a Book with Pleasure 'till he knows whether the Writer of it be a black or a fair Main, of a mild or choleric Disposition, Married or a Batchelor." Despite this caveat, Mr. Spectator was somewhat taciturn about his identity and only over the course of several issues did he reveal that he was an old bachelor who spent his time in books and coffeehouses. To keep him company in his celibacy, he had assembled a club full of old bachelors who had loved and lost as he once had himself. One of his clubmen was Sir Roger de Coverly of whom "it is said he keeps himself a Batchelour by reason he was crossed in Love, by a perverse beautiful Widow of the next County to him."[44]

The characterization of the authors as old bachelors was a literary device intended to render the narrators neutral observers. Although both had apparently been victims of the whims of Eros in their youth, they were far removed from the concerns of family and courtship at present. In this, Bickerstaff and Spectator were chaste observers of the human condition. "Thus I live in the World, rather as a Spectator of Mankind, than as one of the Species," noted Mr. Spectator. He added, "I am very well versed in the Theory of an Husband, or a Father," suggesting that by not having entangled himself in marriage or family he could offer objective opinions on both.[45]

In equating the single state with observation, Isaac Bickerstaff and Mr. Spectator were transitional figures in the history of the bachelor. The idea of the single man as a neutral witness of the human condition implicitly built on the medieval tradition of the man who forfeited marriage and family to devote his time and energy to helping the community as a whole, much like a religious celibate or an army officer. Indeed, Steele may have devised the military record of Bickerstaff to help explain why his narrator had never married. Yet the bachelor as a neutral observer was problematic in a world that was becoming increasingly sensitive to a man's marital status. Had Bickerstaff and Spectator been crafted a century earlier, their social status and age would have put them above suspicion. At the turn of the eighteenth century, however, such protections were fleeting. The only way that Addison and Steele could use the bachelor identity without eliciting attacks was by desexualizing it. In the political and humorous pamphlets, bachelors were being increasingly identified with uncontrolled sexuality, leading to bastard children or worse. Isaac Bickerstaff and Mr. Spectator were chaste observers, not dangerous because they were not sexual. These characterizations also suggest a nascent homophobia. Lest the readers think the narrators were unmarried due to deviant desires, the essayists continually repeated the fact that the men had loved women when they were young. Such disclaimers had not been necessary in earlier depictions of single men.

The fact that Bickerstaff and Spectator were bachelors occasionally put them into direct conversation with the political issues of the day. In one issue of the *Tatler,* the recent debate over whether or not England should adopt a Roman-style punishment for bachelors occasioned Isaac Bickerstaff to ponder the politics of the single state, his own and that of others. While contemplating "practical Schemes for the Good of Society," Bickerstaff noted "the Censors of Rome had Power vested in them to lay Taxes on the unmarried; and I think I cannot show my Impartiality better than in enquiring into the extravagant Privileges my Brother Batchelors enjoy, and fine them accordingly." Yet Bickerstaff did not think that all single men should be taxed. Instead, he suggested a two-tiered approach. In one category were those bachelors who "pretend an Aversion to the whole Sex, because they were ill treated by a particular Female, and cover their Sense of Disappointment in Women under a Contempt of their Favour." Bickerstaff labeled such men "Batchelors Convict" and advised they be "proceeded against" accordingly. In a completely separate category were those single men—presumably himself included—"who can plead Courtship, and were unjustly rejected, shall not be liable to the Pains and Penalties of Celibacy."[46] In short, there were two types of single men: those who rejected women and those who had been rejected by women. The former included those men who made only a vain attempt at love and subsequently had become woman haters. Only these bachelors were deserving of the harsh laws then being promoted by political theorists.

The division between bachelors who had tried to find love and those who had not informed much of the discussion of marriage and the single life in the *Tatler* and the *Spectator*. Addressing themselves to a population of young urbanites from well-to-do or middling families, Addison and Steele took it upon themselves to offer their readers a course in self-control. No longer could young people be left to the vagaries of the tavern and the bachelors' social round. Instead, they had to be taught the methods of refinement: perfecting polite manners, cultivating a gentlemanly appearance, and establishing a reputation for clever wit. A certain degree of youthful excess was to be expected, but for the man who hoped to join the ranks of the urban elite, even this liminal phase of life had to be closely monitored. Toward this end, the *Tatler* and the *Spectator* warned their audiences against becoming bachelors convict. Through satires of pitiful rakes and impotent misanthropes, Addison and Steele offered up cautionary tales against lovelessness. A young bachelor was to focus on finding genuine affection that would lead him to marriage, happiness, and success. He was to keep his heart open and earnestly pursue love as long as it took for him to find a wife. If he gave up on love, he would lose his morality and embark upon a steady descent into sin and disrepute, becoming an unfeeling rake, a sexual deviant, or a miser.[47]

The most common portrayal of the bachelors convict in the *Tatler* and the *Spectator* was the incontinent bachelor whose sexuality was so destructive that it obviated legitimate procreation. In one issue Mr. Spectator complained of "a loose Tribe of Men whom I have not yet taken Notice of, that ramble all the Corners of this great City, in order to seduce such unfortunate Females as fall into their Walks." These "several Batchelors who have raised up their whole stock of Children before Marriage" caused him to fear the effects of their sexuality on society at large. To prove his point, Mr. Spectator followed his tirade with a letter from an illegitimate son who had been "deprived of that endearing Tenderness and unparallel'd Satisfaction which a good Man finds in the Love and Conversation of a Parent."

Such unrestrained sexuality could only be dealt with through harsh laws. Like the political writers before him, Mr. Spectator recommended "the Privileges which were granted by the Roman Laws to all such as were Fathers of three Children" and that "this infamous Race of Propagators" be sent "into our American Colonies, in order to People those Parts of her Majesty's Dominions where there is a want of Inhabitants."[48]

The periodicals typically associated unrestrained sexuality with youth. Mr. Spectator claimed to "have heard of a Rake who was not quite Five and Twenty declare himself the Father of a Seventh Son" and a letter from a reader chided the "general Dissolution of Manners" that arose from "Libertinism without Shame or Reprehension in the Male Youth."[49] Yet Addison and Steele had a larger point to make. Fornication and bastardy in youth often led to misery and regret in old age. Accordingly, the *Tatler* and the *Spectator* were replete with stories of lonely and frustrated old bachelors who warned the young to learn from their mistakes. "I am now in the Sixty fifth Year of my Age," warned Jack Afterday in a letter to the *Spectator*, "and having been the greater Part of my Days a Man of Pleasure, the Decay of my Faculties is a Stagnation of my Life." He added: "I have lived a Batchelour to this Day; and instead of a numerous Offspring, with which, in the regular Ways of Life, I might possibly have delighted my self, I have only to amuse my self with the Repetition of old Stories and Intrigues which no one will believe." He urged his young readers not to squander their lives in the present, warning that "to those who live and pass away Life as they ought, all Parts of it are equally pleasant." Afterday ended his letter with the observation that within three years—"if I live"—his investments would have yielded him a great wealth and would make him worth fifty thousand pounds. In this, he suggested that the follies of youth were not simply sexual. Avarice also could turn a man's heart cold and leave him unable to marry.[50]

Yet not all bachelors who appeared in the *Tatler* and the *Spectator* were hopeless miscreants. He who lived a life of debauchery or avarice deserved legal and divine punishment, but most bachelors simply needed encouragement to reform themselves. When Isaac Bickerstaff separated single men into the unfortunate and the unfeeling, he hoped that the moral instruction of papers like his own would preclude legal mechanisms such as the bachelor tax. "I am not without Hopes," he wrote, "that from this slight Warning, all the unmarried Men of Fortune, Tast, and Refinement, will, without further Delay, become Lovers and humble Servants to such of their Acquaintance as are most agreeable to them, under Pain of my Censures."[51] No man who chose love was beyond redemption regardless of age. One of the most popular characters in the *Spectator* was Will Honeycomb. A man "who according to his Years should be in the Decline of his Life," Honeycomb pursued women with the eagerness of youth.[52] A recurring character, Honeycomb was often the butt of jokes because of his rakish adventures. Yet near the end of his paper's run, Mr. Spectator included a final letter from Honeycomb that he claimed "gives us the Picture of a converted Rake." In his missive, Honeycomb announced that he had married, retired to the countryside, and forever vowed "to live hereafter

Figure 4. "Will Honeycomb," by Cornelius Tiebout. The explosion of print media in eighteenth-century America increased awareness of bachelors. One of the most popular was Will Honeycomb, a character from the English periodical the *Spectator*. An old bachelor, Honeycomb pursued women with the abandon of a young man before reforming and taking a wife.

Source: The Spectator 4, no. 301 (Philadelphia, Bradford, 1803), facing page 228. Reprinted with the permission of the American Antiquarian Society.

suitable to a Man in my Station, as a prudent Head of a Family, a good Husband, a careful Father (when it shall so happen)."[53]

Because every bachelor possessed the ability to reform like Will Honeycomb, the *Tatler* and the *Spectator* opposed laws to punish men for being single. While they offered no quarter to bachelors convict, the essayists dismissed the notion of a bachelor tax as an abuse of government. To make their point, they employed misogynistic depictions of women to suggest that laws to encourage marriage were actually the ploys of desperate spinsters. The fullest discussion of the bachelor tax in either periodical came in the form of a letter written by Rachel Welladay, printed in a 1712 issue of the *Spectator*. "The Case of Celibacy is the great Evil of our Nation," Welladay asserted, "and the Indulgence of the vitious Conduct of Men in that State... is the Root of the greatest Irregularities of this Nation." Like the political writers, she quoted the ancient Roman denunciation of bachelors before calling for quantitative analysis. She even scolded Mr. Spectator for not employing the latest techniques of political arithmetic: "If you did your Duty as a SPECTATOR, you would carefully examine into the Number of Births, Marriages, and Burials" to determine "how many there are left unmarried." Ultimately, Welladay asserted that an improvement of the law was needed: "Such Calamities as these would not happen, if it could possibly be brought about, that by fineing Batchelors as Papists, Convicts, or the like, they were distinguished to their Disadvantage from the rest of the World." Despite her elevated rhetoric, Rachel Welladay betrayed her own argument by observing that she was not yet twenty-three but had received at least ten proposals for marriage, all of which were subsequently withdrawn.[54] Persuasion and example were far better tools for encouraging marriage than punitive laws because they appealed to the reasonable sensibilities of refined men. By contrast, bachelor taxes were hysterical machinations, the coarse and impractical methods of women and unsophisticated men.

By the time the last issue of the *Spectator* appeared in 1714, the ideas about bachelors pioneered by Addison and Steele were widely accepted. In the duo's next joint venture, the *Guardian,* Addison and Steele assumed the persona of Nestor Ironside, an old man "who has never entered into the state of marriage."[55] They also inspired other essayists to follow suit. For example, Henry Stonecastle of the *Universal Spectator* was an old single man as was the author of Dublin's 1766 the *Batchelor.*[56] Attacks on men who chose carnal pleasure over marriage also remained commonplace. An article from a 1732 issue of the *Gentleman's Magazine* titled "The Rake's Fortune" ridiculed a man who "grew old, without daring to think of Marriage," only to find himself poor and the pawn of a scheming young woman, "and he, who had made a Property of so many Females, became the Dupe of one in his old Age."[57] Humorous depictions of the bachelor tax as a scheme of desperate women also reappeared again and again. In February 1731 the *Universal Spectator* ran a petition from thirty thousand single women that demanded that bachelors propose to them or face an annual fine of ten pounds. The petition cited the precedent of the ancients and fretted about "Celebacy, which is at present so much in vogue amongst us, to the great Prejudice of the Kingdom."[58]

Bachelors in Early American Literature

As English writers in the second half of the seventeenth century worked to craft the literary identity of the bachelor, they did so without the help of the American colonists. Although the specific conditions of life in the New World before 1700 had led to a host of bachelor laws not present in England, colonial literary depictions of the unmarried state lagged far behind those of the mother country. In large part, this had to do with the late emergence of American printing. The Puritans in Massachusetts had begun printing books at Cambridge in 1638, but they had limited their production to religious works, official proclamations, primers, and a handful of rather dry almanacs. The two best sellers of the era—Michael Wigglesworth's *The Day of Doom* and the captivity narrative of Mary Rowlandson—were devoted to spiritual suffering and redemption, themes that allowed little room for subjects as light and worldly as marriage and the single life.

Change came in 1704 when John Campbell began printing America's first weekly newspaper, the *Boston News-Letter*. Thereafter secular presses appeared throughout the colonies. By 1740 there were twelve newspapers in five colonies, and there were thirty-six papers in ten colonies by 1775. The volume of colonial imprints exploded at the same time. Before 1689 fewer than five hundred works had been published in America. More than eleven hundred were published between 1689 and 1713, with the output doubling every twenty years until the Revolution. As this happened, the diversity of subject matter increased. History, drama, and verse became popular, and the coming of the love revolution turned Americans' thoughts to romance, courtship, and marriage. The earliest American authors mimicked their British brethren, devoting countless works to young people in pursuit of spouses as well as to those who failed in such matters.[59]

Before 1720 most of what Americans read about bachelors came in the form of reprinted English works. Those at the top of colonial society, especially those with established ties to Britain, managed to attain what the British public was reading. When he was governor of New York and New Jersey from 1728 to 1731, John Montgomerie possessed copies of those works by Harrington, Temple, and Davenant that advocated stiff penalties for bachelors including taxes. Likewise, at his death in 1744, wealthy Virginia planter William Byrd of Westover owned a copy of *Oceana* as well as works by Petty, Temple, and Davenant. Although the reach of such serious works was relatively limited, lighter discussions of single men filtered throughout colonial society, especially reprints of periodicals. Boston pastor Cotton Mather was reading the *Tatler* and the *Spectator* as early as 1713, and the libraries of Montgomerie and Byrd included multiple copies of each. By midcentury, multivolume collections of the two periodicals were circulating throughout the colonies, with fragments appearing regularly in American newspapers.[60]

In addition to the writings of Addison and Steele, American papers reprinted lesser-known treatments of single men from the British press. In 1732 and 1744 the *South Carolina Gazette* ran a petition from the Petticoat Club, a group of single women who decried "the unsufferable Stupidity and Obstinacy of a Sett of Men called Old Batchelors." Like Rachel Welladay, the Petticoat Club demanded "that all Batchelors above 26 Years of Age, may be obliged to pay a moderate Tax, which should yearly increase till they arrive to 40." A popular piece with transatlantic appeal, the petition had earlier appeared in Britain's *Grubstreet Journal* and subsequently appeared in the *New York Gazette* and the *Boston Evening-Post*.[61] Similarly, a letter that first appeared in the *Gentleman's Magazine* was reprinted in the *Boston Evening-Post* in 1746 in which Will Equitable demanded a levy on "old batchelors and old maids" because "they promise no help to the future generation." Playful in tone like the Petticoat Club, Equitable continued the back-and-forth quality of humorous pamphlets by blaming the rising number of single men on finicky women. "But for her who had, and without good occasion used the man ill, keeping him still a batchelor thro' pure love," he wrote, "I would have the duty levied upon her for both parties, and him excused."[62] Even a version of *The Levellers* appeared in the colonies. The names of the two women were changed to Eliza and Mariana but the result of their dialogue was the same. They demanded taxation or some other form of punishment to force wealthy bachelors to marry them.[63]

In the 1720s the more talented American writers began to try their hand at imitating British essayists. Over the next half century single men became one of the most popular topics in American literature, appearing in newspapers, pamphlets, and almanacs. Although the colonists were familiar with images of single men then appearing in British plays and novels, it was in the more ephemeral works that they contributed to the transatlantic discourse of bachelors. Because the works of Addison and Steele were far more popular in America than those of Petty, Temple, and Davenant, Americans largely experienced the discussion of the bachelor tax in reverse. In Britain, a serious discussion of punitive laws appeared first and satire followed, while Americans began with satire and then moved to a serious discussion of a punitive tax on bachelors.

The earliest mentions of bachelors in American literature were largely derivative of English sources, often repeating many of the same tropes and themes of the Old World press. In 1721 Boston printer James Franklin—the older brother of Benjamin—began printing the *New-England Courant,* which mimicked the tone and style of the *Spectator.* True to his British progenitors, Franklin assumed the persona of an aging bachelor. "As for my Age, I'm some odd Years and a few Days under twice twenty and three," he wrote in the first issue of the *Courant,* adding in a later issue, "I am contented to be call'd an old rusty Batchelor for Once, for fear of being call'd dishonest a Thousand Times." Although Franklin was unmarried when he began publishing the *Courant,* he was in his early twenties and thus hardly old and rusty.[64]

Other writers picked up on the British attack on rakish and coldhearted men. Misguided single men were a constant target of Proteus Echo, a pseudonym shared by three Harvard graduates in a series of letters printed in the *New-England Weekly Journal* from 1727 to 1728. Although Proteus's marital status was somewhat unclear, he jeered his friend Will Bitterly, noting "this Person had taken up a Resolution against Matrimony, by reason of several threatning Lines and Crosses in the Palms of his Hands, which he supposes portend domestick Jangles and Disasters." Like Mr. Spectator, Proteus urged a reformation of manners among his readers, especially when it came to courtship, noting that "some who maintain a bold and gallant Freedom with the Ladies" would never be ranked "in the number of polite Gentlemen." Marriage was the proper course for young men, and the man who chose a life of drink and whoring over marriage literally deluded himself. A reader named Sam Wildefare confirmed Proteus's admonitions when he wrote "as I am a Batchelour and lie alone, after my fancy is a little heated by a Debauch, I imagine

I am surrounded by your Ghosts and Apparitions, which almost scare me into Convulsions."[65]

Over time the depiction of bachelors in American literature became increasingly complex. Among the more popular pieces were those that savaged a man for being single. In 1768 the *Boston Chronicle* printed "A Bachelor's Will" in which a fictitious testator distributed not his material possessions but all the foibles of the single life: "a large treasure of whims, fancies, megrims, freaks, reveries, schemes, projects, and designs."[66] In 1775 the *Pennsylvania Gazette* ran the obituary of a life-long bachelor from Charleston, South Carolina, named James Macalpine. Although the eulogist championed the deceased's "unblemished character," the piece belied such an assessment. Macalpine's greatest foible was his credulity, "believing the most improbable stories, even of his most intimate friends, and tho' told by persons he scarcely knew." Macalpine, who "looked upon himself as the Champion of the Protestant religion," carried pistols wherever he went lest he fall victim to Jesuits whom he believed "were continually plotting his destruction." Moreover, the deceased was a man of questionable sexuality. Weakened early in life by consumption, he spent his career teaching music and "was remarkably abstemious." At the end, Macalpine was all alone as "it was remarked that six old bachelors as pallbearers could not be found in the whole town."[67]

Yet not all early American depictions of bachelors were character assassinations. For every searing attack on unmarried men there was another that treated his marital status as a matter of fact. The obituary of New Yorker Jacobus Rosevelt noted without irony that "he was a bachelor, bore an excellent character, was universally beloved and esteemed, and is as generally lamented by all his acquaintance."[68] Some writers even spoke to bachelors rather than about them, seeking to guide them through the treacheries of youth. One of the more popular genres of pamphlets in eighteenth-century New England was the advice sermon directed at young men and women. Leading divines such as Cotton Mather, Solomon Stoddard, and Charles Chauncy counseled youths to refrain from temptation and stay the course of righteousness. Detailing "what Sins they are, which Young Persons are more especially apt to indulge themselves in," Rev. Daniel Lewes listed pride, disobedience to parents, idleness, and sensual pleasures. Much like secular works such as the *Spectator,* religious authors took a great interest in the sexual incontinence of the young. Cotton Mather authored several pamphlets on sexual continence including one subtitled *Advice to a Young Man* in which he warned against the evils of "Self-Pollution."[69] But not all pieces directed at bachelors came in such moralizing tones. "Look out Bachelors for good warm Bedfellows," advised *The Loyal American's Almanack* in its entry for the chilly month of October 1715.[70]

On the eve of the American Revolution, the take on bachelors in colonial literature was becoming increasingly playful. Building on the widely accepted perception of single men as heartless loners and sexual deviants, some authors achieved humor by making the case *for* bachelorhood. In "The Batchelor's Soliloquy," printed simultaneously in the *Maryland Gazette* and *The Wilmington Almanack* in 1762, Hamlet's famous monologue became a forum to weigh the relative merits of marriage and the single life. The poem began:

> To wed, or not to wed—that's the Question:
> Whether 'tis better still to rove at large
> From Fair to Fair, amid the Wilds of Passion;
> Or plunge at once into a Sea of Marriage,
> And quench the Fires?—To marry,—take a Wife.

To be a husband was to put to rest "those restless Ardours," but a man could never predict what kind of wife his bride would become after marriage. "A Wife, Perchance a Devil:—Ay, there's the Rub," the author noted. Interestingly, the poem ended not in marriage but in Hamlet-like indecision and paralysis.[71] The following year, bachelorhood received a clear endorsement in Sir John Dillon's poem *The Pleasures of a Single Life.* Looking back from old age, Dillon sang an ode to solitude, especially the delights of uninterrupted reading during the day and "my bottle and my friend" at night. As a bachelor, he had been sexually chaste and moderate in his drinking, until one day "the curs'd fiend from hell's dire regions sent" flung a woman into his life. He fell in love and married only to discover that his new wife was unfaithful. The poem ended in divorce and the resounding bitterness of Dillon, who cursed not only women but God as well.[72] In both works the bachelor was a humorous figure, something to be rejected not idolized. But the idea of the single life as an alternative to marriage also was apparent. After the Revolution this theme would be further developed by a group of new American authors.

Benjamin Franklin, Polly Baker, and *Observations*

Of all the American literary interpretations of the bachelor, perhaps none were as innovative or as uniquely American as those of Benjamin Franklin. The Philadelphia printer and founding father authored dozens of short pieces on marriage and the single life, from wry newspaper articles to serious political tracts. His career, which stretched almost the entirety of the eighteenth century, was a microcosm of the American press writ large. Initially, his writing mimicked British works, but over time a distinctive voice emerged. By midcentury Franklin was a full partner in the transatlantic dialogue about bachelors, putting forth ideas that British authors imitated. Through it all, Franklin's approach was consistently antibachelor. Despite the complexities of his own marital status, he refused to associate himself with single men in print, rejecting them as indecisive, immature, and pathetically comical. Yet as a student of the *Spectator,* he rejected the idea of a tax to punish unmarried men, advocating moral persuasion instead. He also offered a new solution to the problem of bachelors, holding that the abundance of land in America was the best answer. Such ideas predicted a nascent American identity and set the stage for Americans to debate marital status in the new nation.

Benjamin Franklin was born in Boston in 1706, the younger son of a chandler. He excelled in grammar school, although his father "from a View of the Expence of a College Education which, having so large a Family, he could not well afford," apprenticed Franklin when he was twelve years to his brother James.[73] In his brother's print shop, young Franklin continued his education by reading a wide variety of British publications. As he later recounted in his autobiography, Franklin stumbled upon a volume of the *Spectator* when he was sixteen and immediately set about trying to imitate the paper with his own essays. The *Spectator* was to have a profound effect on Franklin's writing for the rest of his life, influencing several of his essays and even his autobiography. His first imitation of the *Spectator* was the Silence Dogood letters that first appeared in his brother's newspaper, the *New-England Courant*. Fearing that his brother James would not knowingly print anything written by his little brother, Franklin created the pseudonym of Silence Dogood to disguise his identity. Like the *Spectator,* the Dogood letters discussed manners and morals with an intelligent wit, and young Franklin's first literary endeavor met with great success.[74]

Despite Benjamin Franklin's debt to Addison and Steele, the Silence Dogood letters contained several features that set them apart from the British essays, particularly where bachelors were concerned. Franklin dispensed with the popular convention of making his narrator a single man, and, in striking contrast to Mr. Spectator, he styled Silence Dogood an old widow instead of an old bachelor. However, a single man was still integral to the story of Mrs. Dogood. In the first two letters Dogood explained how she had arrived in America as an infant and had been bound into the service of an unmarried country minister. Anything but a profligate, the minister was a bachelor for the same reasons as Mr. Spectator: he had been unlucky in love. As Dogood explained, the man had "made several unsuccessful fruitless Attempts on the more topping Sort of our Sex." As Dogood's master, the bachelor minister "labour'd with all his Might to instil vertuous and godly Principles" into the young woman. But when his young servant came of age, the minister "began unexpectedly to cast a loving Eye upon Me." An awkward courtship ensued and the couple elicited a variety of responses from the community, "some approving it, others disliking it." The two wed and remained together for seven years, producing three children before the minister died. "Whether it was Love, or Gratitude, or Pride, or all Three that made me consent, I know not," Dogood pondered, although she remembered her marriage fondly.[75] Superficially, Dogood's minister husband was an American version of Will Honeycomb. He was a faithful old bachelor whose patience and perseverance were rewarded. Yet the minister was neither a converted rake nor a coldhearted man who regretted his love of money late in life. Rather, he was a pathetic figure who lacked the sex drive of his British brethren—a non-threatening man who was further emasculated by a wife-servant half his age. This characterization of Mr. Dogood was the prototype for Franklin's later depictions of bachelors. Singleness was evidence of a lack of manliness, the exact opposite of the type of sexual incontinence that kept rakes such as Will Honeycomb unattached.

The minister's insignificance was further proven by the fact that he was dead and gone long before Silence Dogood began her correspondence. The Widow Dogood took center stage alone.

Franklin further established the distance between Silence Dogood and Mr. Spectator by making his character the complete antithesis of Addison and Steele's old bachelor. Where Mr. Spectator conducted his affairs in clubs, Mrs. Dogood confined her discussions to the household. Like Spectator, Dogood sought advice on her letters from those around her, but instead of convening a coterie at the coffeehouse, she sought advice from "my Reverend Boarder." While British periodicals contemplated Roman laws and a bachelor tax, the Dogood letters proposed a fund to provide for women without husbands. In one letter Dogood set forth a detailed plan for the relief of widows that worked like a mutual aid society: families would pay into a fund and widows would collect payments if their husbands died. Yet Dogood's compassion went far beyond widows. Upon the advice of an unmarried female reader, Dogood advocated the creation of a society "whereby every single Woman, upon full Proof given of her continuing a Virgin for the Space of Eighteen Years, (dating her Virginity from the Age of Twelve,) should be entitled to £500 in ready Cash." Mirroring Isaac Bickerstaff's sympathy for jilted bachelors, Silence Dogood took up the cause of women who had never received a proposal. Yet whereas British essayists contemplated a government policy to correct the economic imbalances of the single state, Dogood's insurance plans for widows and single women suggested the creation of private charitable associations. Even the name of Franklin's character signaled a difference. *Dogood* suggested action, in marked contrast to the passive *Spectator*. Compared to the Widow Dogood, Mr. Spectator looked weak, ineffectual, and unmanly.[76]

In rejecting the bachelor cognomen for that of a widow, Franklin was able to retain much of the humor and social commentary of Addison and Steele while divesting himself of the cultural implications that accompanied bachelorhood. In part, such a decision was calculated for effect. The more enfeebled and harmless Franklin could render his cognomen, the more outlandish and incendiary his letters could be. Such a consideration was critical in colonial Boston where criticism of the government could result in being thrown in jail as it did for his brother James in 1723.[77] A bachelor identity may also have seemed less than interesting to a sixteen-year-old youth for whom singleness was not a fantasy but an ever-present and confining reality. Despite his fascination with the *Spectator*, there was little opportunity for young Franklin to enjoy the coffeehouse culture that elite young Britons took for granted. Instead, bachelorhood to Franklin in Boston meant the same thing it had for the vast majority of young men in New England for the last hundred years: service, lack of freedom, and dependency. Perhaps for this reason, Franklin never warmed to the idea of posing as an unmarried man in his writings.

Franklin's contributions to the *Courant* were the beginning of a trend that characterized his writings for the next forty years. Time and again, Franklin refused to wear the mask of any bachelor, young or old. A decade after the Silence Dogood letters, Franklin moved to Philadelphia and began publishing the *Pennsylvania Gazette*. As a printer, he occasionally inserted his own writings in the paper. He never disguised himself as a single man but often played the part of a single woman. In 1732 Franklin ran two letters under the spinster pseudonyms Celia Single and Alice Addertongue. Celia Single's letter speculated about the connection between marriage and economics. "I have several times in your Paper seen severe Reflections upon us Women, for Idleness and Extravagance," she wrote, "but I do not remember to have once seen any such Animadversions upon the Men." She then rattled off a half dozen names of men whose gambling, idleness, or drunkenness would have sunk their families had it not been for the industry of their wives.[78] With this letter, Franklin indicated that marriage could be subjected to a cost-benefit analysis. Yet in linking matrimony and money, he inverted the point made by British political theorists. For Franklin, marriage did not diminish a man's earning power, it enhanced it. In this, Franklin inherently questioned the long-standing Anglo-American belief that a single man had more money than a married man and thus could afford greater financial obligations to the state. Such logic, while solidly promarriage, later allowed Franklin to refute the bachelor tax.

Despite his literary identity, Franklin had no qualms about wearing the mask of the bachelor in real life, especially when it suited his situation. When he fled his indenture and made his way to Philadelphia, Franklin sailed on a sloop whose captain agreed to give him passage because Franklin claimed that "had got a naughty Girl with Child, whose Friends would compel me to marry her." Once he was established as a printer in Philadelphia, Franklin surrounded himself with a club of other young tradesmen that he styled the Junto. Moreover, Franklin certainly lived the life of an incontinent rake, confessing in his autobiography "that hard-to-be-govern'd Passion of Youth, had hurried me frequently into Intrigues with low Women that fell in my Way." No doubt because of these exploits, he fathered an illegitimate son in late 1730 or early 1731. When Franklin did settle down, questions about the whereabouts of his fiancée's husband meant he had to opt for an informal union. Accordingly, although Benjamin Franklin and Deborah Read lived as husband and wife for more than forty years, they never obtained a marriage license.[79]

As Franklin's literary reputation and printing business expanded, he continued to avoid assuming a bachelor persona while increasing his vindictive attacks on single men. In 1733 Franklin assumed the identity of Richard Saunders to narrate one of the best-selling works in colonial America, *Poor Richard's Almanac.* Although Richard Saunders was the name of an actual seventeenth-century English astrologer, in Franklin's almanac he was recast as a cuckolded husband whose wife had ordered him to put his knowledge of the stars to good use.[80] As the fictitious Saunders explained in the first issue of his almanac: "The plain Truth of the Matter is, I am excessive poor, and my wife, good Woman, is, I tell her, excessive proud; she cannot bear, she says, to sit spinning in her Shift of Tow, while I do nothing but gaze at the Stars; and has threatned more than once to burn all my Books and Rattling-Traps (as she calls my instruments) if I do not make some profitable Use of them for the

good of my Family." Although he joked about a wife who wished to enjoy the material comforts of her husband's success, the *Almanac* was hardly a critique of marriage. In the first issue, right after the introductory letter, Franklin printed a poem
that ridiculed an old man who was still waiting for the perfect woman:

> Old Batchelor would have a Wife that's wise,
> Fair, rich, and young, a Maiden for his Bed;
> Not proud, nor churlish, but of faultless size;
> A Country Housewife in the City bred.
>> He's a nice Fool, and long in vain hath staid;
>> He should bespeak her, there's none ready made.

Nor was this the only bachelor to appear in *Poor Richard's Almanac*. Throughout
the almanac's twenty-six-year run, bachelors were constant objects of derision and
marriage was consistently encouraged. For the month of August in the 1733 issue,
the *Almanac* noted "a good Wife is God's gift lost." In the 1744 issue, it advised for
February, "He that has not got a Wife, is not yet a compleat Man," and for September declared: "All other Goods by Fortune's Hand are giv'n, / A Wife is the peculiar
Gift of Heav'n." Franklin even questioned the masculinity of bachelors, stating in
the 1755 issue that "a Man with out a Wife, is but half a Man."[81]

Two years after introducing Poor Richard, Benjamin Franklin again denigrated
bachelors in the *Pennsylvania Gazette*. The cause for the assault came in the form
of a poem submitted to the paper in which M.R. chided a close friend for his
decision to wed. "Let Fools in Life contend to wed," M.R. wrote, insisting that
through marriage a man lost liberty, friends, and money. Two weeks later, Franklin
responded under the pseudonym of A.A., claiming to be an old man who had been
widowed thrice. "So ill-natur'd a Thing must have been written," he wrote, "either
by some forlorn old Batchelor, or some cast-away Widower, that has got the Knack
of drowning all his softer Inclinations in his Bowl or his Bottle." He then proceeded
to disparage the single life while praising marriage as a means of achieving legitimate progeny and intimacy. He noted the expenses of bachelorhood, once again
inverting the traditional understanding of the economics of marriage. "A Man does
not act contrary to his Interest by Marrying," he contended. "What we get, the
Women save; a Man being fixt in Life minds his Business better and more steadily."
He added: "He that cannot thrive married, could never have throve better single;
for the Idleness and Negligence of Men is more frequently fatal to Families, than
the Extravagance of Women."[82]

Franklin's assault on bachelorhood reached its apogee in "The Speech of Miss
Polly Baker." First published in April 1747 in London's leading newspaper, the *General Advertiser*, "Polly Baker" was a short piece that purported to be a trial transcript
from a Connecticut courtroom. According to the story, Polly Baker faced charges for
giving birth to her fifth illegitimate child. Instead of meekly accepting the court's
rebuke, Baker defended herself vigorously and placed the blame for her condition

squarely on America's bachelors. From her testimony it was apparent that Baker was a good woman of high morals, the same type of economically wise woman that Franklin had praised under the pseudonyms of Celia Single and A.A. She supported herself and her children without a man's assistance by "having all the industry, frugality, fertility, and skill in oeconomy, appertaining to a good wife's character." Even though she survived on her own, it was not by choice. "I always was, and still am willing to enter into" marriage, Baker testified. The problem was deceitful men. "I readily consented to the only proposal of marriage that ever was made me, which was when I was a virgin," she noted, "but too easily confiding in the person's sincerity that made it, I unhappily lost my own honour, by trusting to his; for he got me with child, and then forsook me." Baker advised the court to look past her crime and confront "the great and growing number of batchelors in the country, many of whom, from the mean fear of the expences of family, have never sincerely and honourably courted a woman in their lives." Such men produced hundreds of illegitimate children and left the mothers to support them. The only solution was a bachelor tax: "Compel them, then, by the law, either to marriage, or to pay double the fine of fornication every year."[83]

With "The Speech of Miss Polly Baker," Franklin's attack on bachelors received its fullest expression. Once again Franklin assumed the persona of a strong and prudent single woman. Polly Baker was neither sister to *The Levellers'* Politica nor a member of the Petticoat Club. In sharp contrast to British literary depictions of women, Franklin rescued the gravity of a woman's voice and made her gender a reason to hear her plea rather than an excuse to dismiss it. Baker was no desperate single woman ready to misuse the machinery of the state to obtain a husband; she was more than capable of handling the responsibilities of raising five children on her own. Baker's call for a bachelor tax thus could not be dismissed as the hysterical ranting of a spinster who wanted a rich husband. Instead, she advocated the use of the law for the good of the community, especially its victimized women. In short, although "Polly Baker" was intended to elicit laughter, its mention of a bachelor tax was not. It was a serious commentary on the rakish behavior of single men and the need of the state to correct it.

The strength of the female lead in "Polly Baker" once again contrasted with the meekness of single men so typical of Franklin's writings. A preface to the speech noted that Baker's oratory was so successful that it caused the court to "dispense with her Punishment" and "induced one of her Judges to marry her the next Day, by whom she had fifteen Children." In this, Franklin inverted the meaning of feminine calls for a bachelor tax. While the women in *The Levellers* selfishly demanded fiscal penalties to bring them husbands, Polly Baker found a mate by recommending a bachelor tax for the good of the community. As in the Silence Dogood letters, the only person with a voice in "Polly Baker" was a single woman. Although she was surrounded by single men, Miss Baker overshadowed them all, their weakness complementing her strength. The five men who impregnated her were all disreputable and sexually incontinent bachelors convict. The judge who married her was weak and ineffectual, the type of man who did not marry until he was persuaded to do so by a woman. In both cases bachelorhood implied a lack of masculinity. In the case of the rakish fathers it was a lack of responsibility and self-control; in the case of the judge it was a lack of masculine vigor. Neither were candidates for reform nor good models for young men.

The setting of "Polly Baker" in a Connecticut courtroom is also noteworthy and is suggestive of Franklin's appeal to the profamily values of rural Americans. It is significant that the story does not take place in an urban coffeehouse where men were judged on their inner emotions instead of on how they cared for their families. Similarly, the story's setting in a Connecticut courtroom and Baker's call for "double the fine of fornication" may have been a criticism of the devaluation of the Puritan sex laws. By the end of the seventeenth century, New England magistrates no longer enjoined fornicating couples to wed. Instead, they placed hefty fines on the female offenders while the bachelors evaded punishment. In this, Franklin was possibly advocating a return to the days when the law could be effectively used to encourage men to marry.

Finally, "Polly Baker" allowed Benjamin Franklin to equate female fecundity with patriotic service. Franklin had been promoting a woman's reproductive talents since Celia Single, and as A.A. he had noted that children were one of the greatest gifts a wife could give a man. Yet both letters tied a woman's service to marriage and what she could offer her husband. In "Polly Baker" Franklin identified motherhood as a woman's most important asset. "Can it be a crime (in the nature of things I mean)," asked Baker, "to add to the king's subjects, in a new country, that really wants people? I own it, I should think it a praise-worthy, rather than a punishable action." In essence Baker asserted that a woman's capacity to produce children was so important to the strength of the country that it did not matter if she was married or not. Contained in this argument was the seed of an idea that Franklin would later develop in more detail: America needed its female population to be especially productive to fill the empty countryside.

"Polly Baker" was one of Franklin's last humorous works, published on the eve of a great transformation in his career. In the late 1740s Franklin turned away from the minutiae of the printing business and toward science and politics. Where Franklin had previously worked in ephemera, he began to concentrate more on serious issues.[84] Despite these changes, Franklin's negative opinion of the single life persisted. This can be most clearly seen in *Observations Concerning the Increase of Mankind*, which Franklin wrote in 1751 in reaction to British legislation prohibiting the erection of ironworks in the colonies. *Observations* was fundamentally an analysis of demography, specifically an attempt to understand the factors behind population increase. Franklin had dabbled in political arithmetic before, quoting Sir William Petty in the letters of Silence Dogood and discussing New Jersey censuses in *Poor Richard's Almanac*.[85] In neither case had he linked demography to bachelorhood, but he did so in *Observations*. "People increase in Proportion to the Number of Marriage, and that is greater in Proportion to the Ease and Convenience of supporting a

Family," he wrote, citing the economics of marriage. "When Families can be easily supported, more Persons marry, and earlier in Life." Unlike Europe, where land was scarce, America was full of fertile fields. Thus, while many Europeans were trapped in lifelong servitude and wage labor, "land being thus plenty in America, and so cheap as that a labouring Man, that understands Husbandry, can in a short Time save Money enough to purchase a Piece of new Land sufficient for a Plantation." Readily available land in turn removed the primary economic deterrent to marriage and procreation. "Marriages in America are more general, and more generally early, than in Europe," Franklin contended. Americans married at twice the rate of Europeans and produced twice as many children per marriage, leading him to speculate that "our People must at least be doubled every 20 Years."[86]

Integral to Franklin's praise of life in America was a glorification of rural life and a dismissal of urban life. The former he linked to fecundity and the latter to bachelorhood. "In Cities," he wrote, "many delay marrying, till they can see how to bear the Charges of a Family; which Charges are greater in Cities, as Luxury is more common." As a result, "many live single during Life" and "hence Cities do not by natural Generation supply themselves with Inhabitants; the Deaths are more than the Births." Although Franklin had foreshadowed a link between singleness and the corruption of urban life in his humorous works, in *Observations* he made the connection explicit. Moreover, he placed luxury at the center of the equation: "Home Luxury in the Great, increases the Nation's Manufacturers employ'd by it, who are many, and only tends to diminish the Families that indulge in it, who are few. The greater the common fashionable Expence of any Rank of People, the more cautious they are of Marriage. Therefore Luxury should never be suffer'd to become common." Luxury thus distracted people and diverted their attention from the virtues of marriage and family. In essence, luxury was again a critique of the type of men who remained single. According to contemporary British writers, prostitutes were the chief urban luxury that kept men from marriage. By speaking generally about luxury, Franklin enlarged the category to include a host of manufactured items responsible for weakening men. At the same time, luxury was associated with effeminacy, the supposition being that fancy clothes, china, and tea weakened a person's constitution, especially a man's. Once again, Franklin cast bachelors as men who lacked masculinity, although in this instance he identified the cause of men's enervation. By reason, a man who rejected the luxuries of urban life could regain his masculinity and marry.[87]

Franklin's dichotomization of the rural father and the urban celibate did not exist in the abstract but were fixed to locales, the former in America and the latter in Europe. In this, *Observations* was a critique of British luxury and a praise of American homespun balanced on the issue of marital status, written fifteen years before American patriots boycotted British manufactures in protest of parliamentary taxes. As Franklin had implied in "Polly Baker," female fecundity was an American trait not found in Europe. A Connecticut woman bearing five children was not unusual in a country where the average woman bore eight.[88] A woman's fruitfulness was made possible by a man's ability to labor for shorter periods of time before he could purchase land and set up a household. As a result, Franklin dismissed laws to encourage marriage as unnecessary in America. "As to Privileges granted to the married, (such as the Jus trium Liberorum among the Romans)," Franklin wrote, referring to Lex Iulia et Papia, "they may hasten the filling of a Country that has been thinned by War or Pestilence, or that has otherwise vacant Territory; but cannot increase a People beyond the Means for their Subsistence." In addition to rejecting exemptions for fertile men, Franklin also implied his opposition to a levy on bachelors, noting at one point that "heavy Taxes tend to diminish a People." Here, Franklin's earlier praise of the economic benefits of marriage to a man's earning potential came to its logical conclusion. Neither a three-child exemption nor a bachelor tax was necessary in America because of the availability of land. Legal efforts to encourage marriage were confined to Europe where the governments had no other method of expanding the population.

Franklin's *Observations* went on to achieve international acclaim, not the least of which came from the highly influential political economist and demographer Thomas Malthus. Yet even before Malthus, Franklin's dichotomy of rural fathers and urban bachelors as determined by land availability and luxury became standard fare for political thinkers in Europe. Ideas similar to Franklin's soon appeared in the works of David Hume, Robert Wallace, and Adam Smith.[89] Likewise, in *The Spirit of the Laws*, Baron de Montesquieu observed: "A rising people increase and multiply extremely. This is because with them it would be a great inconvenience to live in celibacy."[90] These writers abandoned the belief that economic sanctions on unmarried men could help increase the population, a view they may have also adopted from Franklin. Advocacy of a bachelor tax was conspicuously absent from the works of Montesquieu and Malthus. In time other American writers followed Franklin's logic and agreed that marriage and procreation could be better encouraged by positive incentives such as land rather than negative ones such as financial penalties.

From Graunt to Franklin to Malthus, the study of population served to further empower single men. Early modern British and colonial American demographers increasingly depicted men as the objects of study and the agents of change. It was men who could choose to strengthen the nation and thus it was men who were alternately presented with the option of marrying for the common good or paying a bachelor tax. By contrast, women were reduced to passive receptacles of male action. Their virtue and fecundity was necessary for national greatness, but they could not act on their own. A woman had to wait for a man to make her his wife. Political tracts thus followed a logic parallel to the bachelor laws. By the middle of the eighteenth century, bachelors were perceived as fully autonomous regardless of age or social status; their gender mattered more than their mastery or the lack thereof. This was the beginning of a path for single men to claim the moral authority associated with manhood and the respect that married men and masters received. This gendering of authority simultaneously isolated single women from political power or moral authority unless it was connected to motherhood.[91]

As his political offices demanded more and more of his attention, Benjamin Franklin had less time to devote to publications on bachelors. Nevertheless, he continued to vigorously advocate marriage and disparage single men in his personal writings. In 1760 Franklin wrote to his wife Deborah from London and complained "you cannot conceive how shamefully the Mode here is a single Life." As in *Observations*, Franklin blamed this condition on luxury: "One can scarce be in the Company of a Dozen Men of Circumstance and Fortune, but what it is odds that you find on Enquiry eleven of them are single."[92] It was also Franklin's perpetual wont to encourage marriage. Upon hearing of a young man's wedding, Franklin wrote to the beau: "You are now in the way of becoming a useful Citizen; and you have escap'd the unnatural State of Celibacy for Life, the Fate of many here who never intended it, but who having too long postpon'd the Change of their Condition, find at length 'tis too late to think of it, and So live all their Lives in a Situation that greatly lessens a Man's Value."[93] In another letter to a young man, Franklin improved upon Sir William Petty's political arithmetic and advised the man to employ "Moral Algebra" when making an important decision, that is, to make a list of pros and cons and then reach a conclusion logically. Still convinced of the superior value of a wife, Franklin commented on his scheme that "if you do not learn it, I apprehend you will never be married."[94]

Despite Franklin's ringing endorsement of conjugal bliss, his personal life continued to follow a different path. In the spring of 1757 Franklin sailed for London to represent the interests of the Pennsylvania assembly in Britain. He remained in London for five years and thereafter accepted appointments to represent other colonies and eventually the nascent United States. He returned to Philadelphia only briefly after his first appointment, meaning that his wife Deborah lived nearly all of the last eighteen years of her life without a husband. Moreover, Franklin lived out the rest of his life as a careless young rake. Franklin's affairs with the ladies of London and Paris became legendary and it is still a matter of some speculation as to whether these affairs were purely intellectual.[95] Although Franklin advised young men to avoid becoming old bachelors and profligates, he achieved the reputation, if not the identity, of both.

With Benjamin Franklin's *Observations Concerning the Increase of Mankind*, the literary discussions of single men that began in Restoration England came full circle. Single men were dangerous creatures who threatened the country because they chose selfish luxuries over the good of the nation. The greatest patriotic duty a man could perform was to marry and father children. The command to increase and multiply made no exceptions for men who had sincerely tried and failed. All single men were bachelors convict regardless of the reason. Yet the work of humorous pamphleteers and essayists had also largely discredited the idea of a law to force marriage. Instead, moral persuasion and the opportunities available in the New World emerged as more hopeful and more effective solutions. Yet this modification contained an inherent contradiction: if opportunities for land prevented any man from remaining single for more than a few years, then what was the point of worrying about single men at all? In this, Franklin's *Observations* coincided with literature's growing playfulness toward the bachelor and its move toward treating the unmarried state as a simple matter of fact. By the middle of the eighteenth century the bachelor had emerged as a unique identity, distinct from earlier portrayals and defined by masculine autonomy. As Americans grew familiar with the new identity, they gradually rejected the efforts of politicians and moralists to curtail it.

As the American Revolution approached, the diversity of opinions regarding single men became increasingly contradictory and complex. There was a particular disconnect between the legal and literary discussions of the bachelor. While Franklin and Mr. Spectator offered a path away from bachelor taxes, the subject began to gather serious political consideration in other sectors. Indeed, simultaneous with its printing of excerpts from the *Spectator,* the *Virginia Gazette* featured accounts of serious proposals to limit the number of bachelors. The paper featured stories on how Canadian officials "will give Encouragement of 10 l. [pounds] a Piece to such Women as are inclinable to go to be married and live at Cape Breton," that England had suspended fees on marriage in a law "for the Encouragement of Marriage," and in 1766 on Parliament resuming debate on "laying a tax on all bachelors past the age of 50."[96] The Maryland bachelor tax of 1756 was very much a product of this conflicting debate, suggesting punishment in its language but being ultimately restrained in its application. This tension would remain unresolved as the American Revolution approached.

There was also a conflicting notion of masculinity in literary depictions of the bachelor. For Franklin, the bachelor represented the antithesis of manhood: weak-willed, indecisive, and luxurious. Yet Franklin only attacked the coldhearted and effeminate bachelors. Nowhere in his writings did he impugn hypermasculine rakes such as Will Honeycomb or profligates who filled the countryside with bastards. Perhaps such a rebuke was too personal given his sexual proclivities. Whatever the reason, the significance was twofold. First, it suggested that Americans were growing increasingly comfortable with bachelor sexual activity so long as it was procreative. Like James Oglethorpe, Franklin's primary concern was populating an empty continent, and although he preferred legitimate procreation, the fathering of children even through illegitimate means was still better than having no children at all. In this, we can sense in the American works an acceptance of male heterosexuality not present in Restoration-era political tracts. This growing tolerance of bachelor heterosexuality had a profound impact on the lives of single men who lived in the middle of the eighteenth century. Second, although recognition of heterosexuality necessarily cast a dim light on nonheterosexual acts, American writers did not attack bachelors for being homosexuals. Throughout Franklin's writings, bachelors were called everything short of female but it is difficult to read homophobia in his words. Instead, those American writers who took up the issue of bachelor sexuality castigated all nonprocreative acts. There really was no meaningful difference between a religious celibate, a coldhearted miser, and a sodomite.

Much had changed in literary depictions of the single life between the plays of William Shakespeare and the ephemeral works of Benjamin Franklin. In place of humorous lampoons of superannuated rakes and rash young men, a far more complex depiction of the bachelor had emerged. Like their predecessors, bachelors who appeared in Anglo-American literature between 1650 and 1750 were defined by selfishness, immaturity, and problematic sexuality, but the consequences of such traits were far more sinister. In the eighteenth century a bachelor's foibles were associated with a lack of patriotism and morality as well as the presence of effeminacy and luxury. Renaissance audiences laughed heartily at harmless old Falstaff and knowingly winked at Romeo's juvenile behavior. In contrast, readers of Restoration political tracts worried about the destructive power of nonprocreative single men while devotees of the *Spectator* sought moral instruction from the examples of Will Honeycomb and Jack Afterday. Moreover, the suspicions that hung over the heads of single men persisted well into the second half of the eighteenth century, leaving it unclear whether the bachelor literary identity could be restored to its more innocuous earlier incarnation.

The development of a literary identity for bachelors in the late seventeenth and early eighteenth centuries stood apart from the simultaneous developments in the law and the personal lives of unmarried men. Although the works of Petty, Temple, and Davenant were read by lawmakers, they were extreme versions of what Parliament and the colonial assembly actually approved. The two harshest anti-bachelor laws of the era—and those closest in spirit to the demands of the political theorists—were the bachelor taxes passed in England in 1695 and in Maryland in 1756. Neither was punitive and neither drove herds of licentious bachelors to wed. Anglo-Americans had long been resistant to using the state to force people to marry, yet the efforts of humorous pamphleteers and essayists to discredit the tax as a scheme of desperate women no doubt helped to stymie social engineering. By ridiculing the idea of taxes to punish bachelors, these writers cleared the way for new ideas about the role of economic opportunity in encouraging marriage and family that Benjamin Franklin articulated. A similar dissonance was present between literature and the lives of actual single men. As I demonstrate in the next chapter, young and old bachelors alive at midcentury read the *Spectator* and other works that denigrated the unmarried state, but they did not always internalize the rebuke to the point of self-hatred.

Ultimately, this literary treatment of the bachelor had a fleeting existence, as did the bachelor laws. Nevertheless, it had a profound effect on the creation of the bachelor identity. Political and humorous works of the era dealt with the single man as a unique creature, one that could not be confused with a single woman or any other type of dependent. Moreover, nearly all of the attacks on the bachelor served to reinforce his reputation as an independent man. Behind the condemnation of the single man—whether as an incontinent rake or a coldhearted miser—was an attack upon the bachelor's selfishness. He was only thinking about himself and his own pleasure and this made him unpatriotic, immoral, and antisocial. In essence, all of the attacks on the bachelor were about him being *too* independent. Yet the censure of the unmarried man for being too independent was part of a value system that was on the way out. Although colonial planners such as James Oglethorpe and Benjamin Franklin fretted over what would become of a country in which men thought only of themselves, such a proposition seemed much less frightening in the age of revolution.

4

"I Resolve to Live a Batchelor
While I Remain in This Wicked Country"

LIVING SINGLE IN EARLY AMERICA

In 1755 Robert Treat Paine contemplated "whether the State of Matrimony be necessary for the Wellbeing or Benefit of the Common Wealth?" A friend had raised the question in a letter and Paine, then a twenty-four-year-old Harvard graduate and part-time minister, gave the matter serious thought. In response to the question Paine informed his friend that he had not yet married and preferred it that way. "I'm determined Never to loose that Freedom I brought into the world with me," he began, asking rhetorically "is it possible the aspiring Liberty of a Free born Soul should ever willingly Submit to be embarrassed with the perplexitys & cloggs of this fetter'd State"? Paine proceeded to dissect the issue with considerable detail. He noted the obvious attributes of the wedded state, how it brought stability to individuals, ensured virtue, and allowed for natural increase. Yet he held fast to the desirability of bachelorhood, citing selfish reasons for which he would not apologize. "Must I quit the gay assemblys, & concertos & forsake the fencing Room & Billiard Table & enter School to learn the Mistery of Rocking a Cradle," he asked. "Must I forsake a Masquerade where I represented an Eastern Monarch in power & Majesty & go home to learn patience of a Scolding Wife"? Living single meant the freedom to indulge in social pleasures and irreverent luxuries. Paine acknowledged that the laws of God and humanity required that people marry, but he preferred to be a bachelor.[1]

Paine was true to his word. He persisted in the ministry and later entered Massachusetts politics, all the while remaining single. As his fortieth birthday approached, Paine came under tremendous pressure to marry, brought about by friends and his own sexual appetite. Yet Paine favored celibacy, believing that it strengthened him. Because he considered "matrimony being really a high Seasoned flesh Diet," he dismissed the wedded state for "having a direct tendency to retard the operations of the mind & obliterate the last glimmerings of Reason." To stave off connubial connections, Paine surrounded himself with other bachelors and implored them to remain steadfast. Reflecting on a "New-Married Couple" in a letter to a fellow bachelor, Paine declared "mean while my freind you & I, like two Pillars of Celibacy, Stand it out to show the World what all might be. (that heroic!)." Ultimately, however, Paine lost his war against the flesh. Fifteen years after he first declared his independence from wedlock, he "heard Sally Cobb with child by me" and married her.[2]

The story of Robert Treat Paine is emblematic of the changing experience of single men in eighteenth-century America. Although bachelorhood emerged as an expression of masculine independence in politics and literature, it also affected the lived experience of being a single man. For the young and not-so-young unmarried men who lived in the fifty or so years before the American Revolution, bachelorhood was a vibrant personal identity and something to relish. Bachelorhood meant freedom, both from the obligations of childhood and the responsibilities of fatherhood. It was a liminal time, not to be cursed or feared but celebrated. Bachelorhood was about sociability, both for professional benefit and for pure entertainment. A bachelor studied those more knowledgeable than he was, but he was no man's servant. He assembled groups of peers of his class, race, gender, and marital status with whom he corresponded, traveled, and formed clubs. A bachelor also devoted considerable time and energy associating with the opposite sex, looking for romance and sexual encounters, although in the eighteenth century chastity was still considered a virtue. As had long been the case, most bachelors were young men and so these qualities of bachelorhood were associated with youth. However, the eighteenth century witnessed a number of older single men joining their younger compatriots in the new bachelor lifestyle. Robert Treat Paine continued to indulge in the pleasures of the single life even as he approached forty years of age.

Colonial bachelorhood as a lived experience is a far more difficult concept to encapsulate than its political and literary manifestations. Although it is possible to catalog laws and to trace literary trends, the diversity of the colonial population makes any assertion about a quintessential bachelor naïve at best. Differences in region, culture, religion, race, and ethnicity all conspired against a monolithic bachelor identity. Bachelorhood was often a luxury for the elite and educated, appearing first in urban areas among those men whose economic situation did not require extended service or economic dependence. Young New Englanders with backgrounds similar to Paine clearly experienced bachelorhood as did the young merchants and professionals in southern cities. Not surprisingly, it was these men who produced the richest record of their experience and whose sources leave the clearest expression of what it meant to be a bachelor. Yet bachelorhood had somewhat of a trickle-down effect in late colonial America. Single men in rural areas found their lives changed as well. For instance, the taxed bachelors of Pennsylvania became more mobile and experienced some of the material comforts that their wealthier neighbors touted. At the same time, there were segments of society that were not entitled to the masculinity and autonomy of the bachelor lifestyle. Thousands of single Americans, like African American slaves and recent immigrants, were left out. Their exclusion is not surprising given the lack of interest lawmakers and authors had for single men who were not free and white.

Perhaps the most important aspect of bachelorhood in the eighteenth century was just how conscious single men were of the fact that they were single. Paine's deep contemplation of his own bachelorhood would have been unheard of a century before. Of course, this introspection could arouse deeply conflicting emotions. Most bachelors worried about whether or not they would marry. Despite Paine's bravado, many wondered about the benefits of being a bachelor and whether their reputation had suffered because of it. This growing consciousness of single men led to an internal discourse that paralleled political and literary ones. Bachelors looked at themselves and wondered about their place in society, their claims to manhood, and whether or not their liberties were something to be proud of.

There were some essential interconnections between the laws, literary characterizations, and lives of colonial bachelors, but these should not be overemphasized. On the one hand, political and cultural changes dramatically influenced how bachelors thought about themselves. It was no coincidence that Robert Treat Paine framed his 1755 discourse around whether or not marriage was "necessary for the Wellbeing or Benefit of the Common Wealth." As a resident of Massachusetts, Paine did not pay a bachelor tax but he was aware of the political ramifications of his marital status. Likewise, Paine's missive repeated the same themes apparent in "The Batchelor's Soliloquy" where an unmarried man contrasted "the well-known, simple Path of single Life" to "the dark perplexed Ways of Wedlock."[3] Paine intended his discourse to be serious, but he also took his cues on what it meant to be a bachelor from popular literary fare. On the other hand, bachelor laws and the literary characterizations stood at some distance from the lived experience. Lawmakers who taxed single men did so because it was politically expedient while popular authors cast aspersions on bachelors because it made their readers laugh. They were not anthropologists studying the rise of a new identity. Thus, neither laws nor literature should be taken as authentic representations of what it meant to be a single man. The only place this can be found is in the lives and the writings of single men themselves.

In this chapter I explore further the creation of bachelorhood as an identity of masculine autonomy by focusing on the writings and lives of eighteenth-century bachelors. By the American Revolution bachelorhood had become an experience of sociability and autonomy and of homosocial and heterosexual pleasures. In contrast to the experience of the single man in the seventeenth century, the eighteenth-century bachelor no longer dreaded the time between childhood and fatherhood. Instead, he saw it as a necessary and formative stage, important to advancing his career and finding a woman whom he could truly love. Some even celebrated bachelorhood and sought to prolong it even while politicians and authors sought to encourage men to limit the time they spent unmarried. Although it is impossible to do justice to the breadth of bachelor experiences, three groups of bachelors are examined here that shed light on how living single in early American was changing. First, the diaries of two dozen unmarried New Englanders are examined to show how single men thought about themselves and how the experience of being a bachelor changed over time. Second, the lives of men from Concord Township, Pennsylvania, who paid the province's bachelor tax are explored as a means of probing how bachelorhood was changing the lives of men who were not elite, urbane, or highly educated. Third, the records of the Tuesday Club of Annapolis, Maryland, are dissected to investigate how a heightened awareness of marital status affected men's relationships with each other. The Tuesday Club also provides a way of charting the influences of political and cultural changes on the lives of actual men. Taken together, these case studies illustrate a bachelor experience in the eighteenth century that paralleled but rarely imitated the rise of singles' laws and recent literary depictions of bachelors.

Diaries of Single New Englanders

The best way to investigate how single men saw themselves is by perusing their diaries. Diary keeping was a popular activity for early Americans, especially educated New Englanders of middling and elite backgrounds. More than a hundred diaries have found their way into the collections of the American Antiquarian Society, providing significant insight into individuals' movements, accomplishments, and thoughts. Perhaps because most of these diaries were kept by married people or people for whom marital status cannot be determined, historians have largely ignored the perspective on the single life in these documents. Nevertheless, more than two dozen diaries survive that were kept by men who were unmarried when they made their first entry. The diarists came from elite backgrounds and nearly all attended Harvard College in preparation for a life in the ministry. All began their diaries in their late teens or early twenties and all later married—three quarters before they reached age thirty. Yet from this small sample some conclusions can be drawn about the experience of being a bachelor and how young men thought about themselves. Being an unmarried man changed dramatically over the course of the eighteenth century from an uncomfortable moment of liminality to a time full of heterosociability, self-awareness, and preparation for the rights and responsibilities of manhood.

Since the settlement of New England, men had kept journals to record observations of the world around them. Political leaders such as John Winthrop and William Bradford recorded the important events of their colonies while less notable New Englanders recorded their individual experiences as a means of charting spiritual regeneration. Others kept commonplace books in which they copied the truths of the ancients, transcribed sermons, or simply kept the financial records of a business. It is difficult to hear the voices of single men in such records. Many, like Winthrop and Bradford, began their records long after they had married and assumed positions of great authority, thus leaving them to comment on the state of young people from the vantage point of fathers and governors. Likewise, those concerned with spiritual or economic matters often ignored temporal or personal matters other than to note the day they married and when their children were born. To be sure, the silence on familial matters is more a result of the practice of seventeenth-century diary keeping than a commentary on whether or not people reflected on things such as courtship. Often mention of one's single life was included as a brief prologue to daily entries on more weighty matters. Massachusetts merchant John Hull disposed of his childhood, youth, and voyage to America in three paragraphs before noting: "In the year 1647, the 11th of the 3d month, Mr. John Winthrop married me and my wife Judith, in my own house, being the third day of the week." Hull felt no need to record how he met his wife or obtained property.[4]

The reflections of single men increased significantly in the eighteenth century. In part, this was a result of the diary's reevaluation. Logs of everyday events with little or no significance to people other than the diarist became common. Properly speaking, such "journals of personal memoranda" were a class of what Robert Fothergill has termed "proto-diaries."[5] Before the American Revolution, many diarists recorded only one line per day and even then they mostly wrote about the weather, daily excursions, or the text of a sermon. There was scarcely little personal reflection. Appropriately, most eighteenth-century New England journals were kept in the pages of almanacs. Scrawling in the tiniest of scripts, writers recorded the events of their day next to the almanac's prediction for the weather. After mid-century the space allotted for each entry grew as did the verbosity of the diarists. A few kept commonplace books, and by the Revolution many were recording their thoughts in blank books. Despite these limitations, these diaries provide an insight into the minds of single men.

In the prologue to his diary, John Hull noted that much of his early life, including his schooling and occupation, were directed by his father. Perhaps it was for this reason that Hull made no effort to record his youth since it was truly not his own. As Anne Lombard has argued, seventeenth-century New England boys typically did not stray far from the supervision of a paternal figure while he learned the self-mastery necessary to become a man from his father. If it was necessary for a boy to leave home, a master assumed paternal responsibilities over him. Only marriage and property ownership absolved a young man of filial duty. Nevertheless, many young men left their fathers' houses before attaining mastery. A Harvard graduate rarely returned home after matriculation, but ventured instead to a new town seeking work as a schoolmaster or a probationary minister. Other young men left home in search of new farmland because their fathers could not or would not provide an estate for them. Such men occupied an uncomfortable liminality in New England society as they were neither masters nor dependents, neither fathers nor sons. A number of these men reflected on their uncertain position by keeping diaries.[6]

The diaries of single men at the beginning of the eighteenth century typically depict youths torn between the expectations of a patriarchal society and their nebulous independence within it. Practically, they had masters to direct their actions, but within their diaries they had the opportunity to reflect on their thoughts and to initiate their own narrative. As Thomas Augst has observed, the very act of keeping a diary could be a declaration of masculine independence.[7] In 1710 twenty-four-year-old John May began keeping a journal shortly before he left his father's house in Brookline, Massachusetts, and began farming in Woodstock, Connecticut. The loneliness and boredom of his life that first winter comes through in the repeated entry, "I cleard swamp alone." Although May regularly mentioned the visits of friends, his entries exude a certain degree of comfort with the first-person singular. "I broke one of my axes," May lamented one December day.[8] Men like May were on their own for the first time, alone to make their own decisions and responsible for themselves alone. And they knew it.

The newfound independence was also somewhat unsettling for these young diarists. Out of the dominion of their fathers they cautiously maintained connections with their families and sought out new masters. Stephen Williams's diary, kept while he was a schoolmaster in Hadley, Massachusetts, in 1713–14, was little more than a catalog of correspondence to relatives back in Deerfield. "Wrote to my Father," reads Williams's entire entry for December 13, 1713. Before the end of the month, he had sent two more letters to his father and two to his sister.[9] John May went even further, making three trips to Roxbury to see his father during the first year he lived in Connecticut. That the journey took two days did not impede his duty to help his father chop wood. Of the early diarists, May was unique in that he had his own house. The rest took up residence under a master's roof, gravitating toward father figures with whom they had a previous affiliation. Recent Harvard graduate Thomas Robie began keeping a diary in February 1710 while teaching in Watertown, Massachusetts. A stranger in town, Robie relied on his college connections to secure parental guidance. "I came to live at Mr. Princes," he noted early in his diary, making reference to the father of a Harvard classmate.[10]

Diaries kept in the 1710s also suggest that newly transplanted men made little effort to engage in any sort of a bachelors' social round. Soon after he accepted the call to be settled as the minister at Weston, Massachusetts, in 1708, twenty-two-year-old William Williams began a diary that was particularly dry. Besides the weather and Sunday services, the only events that Williams recorded were his frequent trips to surrounding towns for Thursday evening lectures. Such events, especially away from Weston, would have given Williams opportunity to socialize with other young people, although lectures tended to be rather staid affairs. Only once did Williams not return home the same night. Likewise, the diaries give no indications that militia musters were much of an excuse for ribaldry. At the artillery election held in Weston on June 5, 1710, for the selection of militia officers, William Williams noted only: "Dr. Mather pr[eache]d. Minist[er]s at Mr. C.'s."[11] To be sure, it is clear that Williams was more sociable than his terse diary suggests because only one month after the artillery election he married Hannah Stoddard.

Williams also found it unimportant to make note of politics, gossip, or local events other than a public fast.

Several diarists relied heavily on their college friends for socialization. In addition to relying on the father of a Harvard friend to locate housing, Thomas Robie frequently entertained and visited former classmates. In his eight-month-long diary, Robie noted spending time with five recent Harvard graduates including John Cotton who "went for Cambridge" to receive his bachelor's degree that summer.[12] Commencement was an important event in the lives of these men and many returned annually to witness the matriculants' recitations. Yet these were sober events that the diarists did not describe. Beyond college friends, the diarists rarely mentioned any contact with other young people. There were no clubs or associations for bachelors in such places as Watertown, meaning that beyond Harvard alumni Thomas Robie had no forum to commune with other singles for either self-improvement or more sordid activities. Appropriately, by the time William Williams directed a sermon to "you that are Young" in 1721, he was speaking not as a fellow bachelor but as a man who had been married for more than a decade.[13]

A noticeable lack of sociability ultimately manifested itself in the lack of detail with which these bachelor diarists described the women they married. "A Great Days Work" was all John May wrote about his marriage to Elizabeth Child on December 18, 1711.[14] Neither before nor after his wedding day did he mention his wife by name in his diary. Samuel Sewall and Ebenezer Parkman—whose diaries are far more detailed and reflective than May's—omitted their wedding days altogether. In the early eighteenth century, men shied away from including the details of their courtship. As masculine objects, diaries were the record of important activities including work, weather, and notable visitors. There was no need to include trivialities such as the details of courtship, sexual desires, or even the name of one's wife. Although this was partly the convention of the day, the masculine asceticism may also reflect the extreme self-consciousness of young men filled with anxiety over their liminal position. They saw themselves as incomplete men because they lacked wives and households. With their own manhood brought into question, they could not risk including feminine trifles such as romance in their diaries. Perhaps this is why Sewall—who had nothing to say about his own marriage— filled page after page with the minutiae of his children's flirtations, courtships, and weddings.[15]

The reticence of the early bachelor diarists largely disappeared after 1720. Although May, Robie, and the Williams brothers avoided the intimate details of their existence, those who kept diaries at midcentury were far more explicit. The entries remained curt but they gave voice to men more fully aware of the world around them. These bachelors were not all that different from the diarists at the beginning of the century: most were Harvard graduates in their early twenties, away from the watchful supervision of their fathers for the first time. They were also liminal figures such as schoolmasters and probationary ministers, but they did not fear their liminality. They were at ease. By the mid-eighteenth century, lawmakers and authors had defined bachelorhood as a time of masculine independence and the young diarists were increasingly willing to accept this classification. To be sure, they all eventually married and became householders, fathers, and community leaders. Yet a mental change had taken place. To be a bachelor was to be temporarily free to pursue the types of frivolities and excitements that a married man had to denounce. Many recognized this transformation and made the most of it.

Most midcentury diarists retained an emotional connection to their fathers and families that earlier diarists would have found familiar. Young men on their own for the first time continued to write relatives frequently, visit parents whenever time allowed, and be closely attuned to the direction of their fathers. To be sure, a New Englander's sense of filial duty did not immediately evaporate as young men were not suddenly overtaken with antipatriarchal rage.[16] However, the diaries did express a growing sense of independence that set them apart from those of the previous generation. Among men who went to new towns to teach or preach, many did not take up residence with a fictive father but with someone they impersonally referred to as "my Landlord."[17] The move away from paternal supervision is perhaps best evidenced by the fact that many began boarding with women. When nineteen-year-old Elisha Odlin left his father's house in Exeter, New Hampshire, in 1729 and moved to Massachusetts, he took up residence with "the widow Boardman." Odlin paid the widow £5 per semester in rent, thus reducing his relationship with Mrs. Boardman to one of tenant and landlord instead of dependent and master. If there was any sense of filial duty on the part of Odlin, this no doubt evaporated once the widow pressed him for a series of loans that totaled eleven shillings and three pence.[18] A growing sense of independence can also be discerned by marking when the bachelors began keeping diaries. Although arrival in a new town or the start of a new position continued to be the time when most men began reflecting in the first-person singular, many did not wait for physical separation to begin a mental one. Odlin began keeping his diary when he was still living with his parents and continued it once he enrolled at Harvard. Although he had not married, acquired property, or begun his profession, Odlin had already proclaimed himself independent—at least within the confines of his journal.

A growing sense of independence is also evident in the homosocial interaction recorded in the midcentury diaries. Young men at midcentury looked to their peers to help them master self-improvement and to acquire legitimacy as men.[19] Occasionally this took place in the context of a club, but just as often connections among young bachelors were informal or flowed from circumstance. A college connection provided the basis for friendships as current and former classmates continued to regularly visit and correspond with one another. Yet Harvard offered more than a network of peers. By midcentury it had come to symbolize the freedoms and masculine pleasures of the single life. Twenty-year-old Nathan Fiske began keeping a diary in 1754 during his final year at Harvard, a record he would continue for the next forty-five years, charting his time as a schoolmaster, settled minister, husband, and father. Yet when he began his diary, he cherished his present situation. Placing his thoughts in an almanac amid formulaic poetry and weather predictions, Fiske recorded "Hail *Alma Mater!*" and noted:

> Happy the Man who void
> of Care & Strife
> Enjoys ye Pleasures of a
> College Life.

Curiously, Fiske placed this paean to masculine independence next to a poem the almanac addressed "To the Unmarried Ladies." The verse instructed young women to choose a man "who bears an honest Mind," although the juxtaposition of Fiske's poem suggests that he looked fondly on his time as a bachelor and was in no hurry to settle down.[20]

Fiske's praise of Harvard suggests that the college experience was becoming increasingly stimulating by the middle of the eighteenth century. Like their fathers, later diarists returned to Cambridge each summer to see the new graduates. However, the activities that followed the Latin recitations would have horrified earlier generations. Six years after he took his degree, Daniel Rogers remained at Harvard working as a tutor. Although he aspired to be a settled pastor, he was only able to find work filling in for ill or absent clergy in the towns surrounding Cambridge. When commencement arrived in June 1731, Rogers devoted the better part of a month to entertaining returning alumni and socializing. In his entry for commencement day Rogers recorded neither who graduated nor who gave the sermon, but noted instead "I was Exceedingly pleased with the Gambling Company."[21] Harvard student Stephen Peabody recorded similar adventures at the Harvard graduation of 1767, noting "we had not a great Commencement, but I had a good deal of Company of almost all Sorts." A particularly effusive diarist, Peabody noted that he attended the recitations of the graduates ("I heard their Performance which ware not Extraordinary"), although the activities that follow interested him more. "I had a fine Sing with Mssers Osgood & Adams," he wrote before noting that events turned more sinister as evening approached. "At Night we had a great Deal of Sport seeing three Negroes handle a Squaw."[22]

Bachelor sociability at midcentury also extended beyond classmates and often included young people of both sexes. Diarists writing after 1720 devoted their thoughts to lighthearted entertainments. More serious activities, such as muster days or Thursday evening lectures, were placed in an explicitly social context entirely missing from earlier diaries. When Benjamin Lynde Jr. began keeping a diary in 1721, he was reading law with his uncle and preparing for a life of public service. Accordingly, he was attuned to the political events swirling about him including town meetings and militia musters. Yet Lynde was often more interested in the social aspect of these affairs than the professional lessons they provided. "Training; cold weather; was at Prat's with a great company of young folks," is how Lynde recorded a militia muster in October 1721. Lynde remained unmarried for the next ten years and in the diaries that followed he repeatedly combined his observations of the workings of the law with heterosexual socialization. "Rainy," he wrote for July 14, 1730, adding "Inf[erio]r Court sat; at surveyrs; dance there; many couples; I did not dance; staid till 7 o'clock."[23]

For Lynde, gatherings of young people were a way to meet new friends and may have provided his introduction to the woman he eventually married. If their fathers' generation had felt uncomfortable discussing romance because it was too feminine, midcentury diarists indulged in it as a masculine pursuit full of adventure and conquest. John Burt was particularly enthusiastic about entertaining the ladies. A recent Harvard graduate, Burt was living in Boston in 1737 where he busied himself studying theology with the Reverend John Webb. Although his thoughts were on his own conversion and preaching his first sermons, he also took time to record his flirtations with the young women who came to visit. In April Nabby Allen arrived in Boston and the two began an intense if short-lived romance. Four days after Allen's appearance, Burt offered to escort her to the Thursday evening lecture in Cambridge. That night he "set up with her till 2 o't Clock next morning." The two were inseparable for the next week, often visiting until midnight. And then Nabby Allen left. Two months later, Burt had a rendezvous with Elizabeth Fulford, and in October he gave Hannah Carter a snuff box. It is unclear how serious Burt was about any of these women or if the relationships turned physical. It perhaps saddened him to record that "I heard yt Mrs. Eliz. Fulford of Marblehead was married last night," although none of Burt's heterosexual interactions were courtships. He remained single for another four years before marrying Abigail Viall in 1741. Unlike previous generations, wedded bliss was not the only object of Burt's amorous adventures.[24]

At the same time, courtship was becoming more sexual. In January 1745 Abner Bayley was finally ordained as pastor of the Congregational Church in Salem, New Hampshire. It had been nine years since Bayley had graduated from Harvard and he had waited patiently until he secured a proper position before proposing to his sweetheart, Mary Baldwin. Self-conscious about not yet being married, Bayley moved the courtship along as quickly as possible once he was ordained. Although "Mrs. Molly" lived in Woburn, Massachusetts, Bayley traveled to see her every other week until they wed in May. The two attended dinners with family and friends, but they also spent time alone. As winter dragged on, Bayley's impatience surfaced in his diary. In the almanac where Bayley recorded his thoughts, the following poem appeared:

> Now Virgins
>   will own, 'tis
> hard lying alone,
>   such weather as this.

In the blank leaf facing the almanac's adage, Bayley responded, "tedious cold weather for virgins to lodge alone." As Valentine's Day approached, Bayley's annoyance with "lying alone" may have gotten the better of him. The entry for February 14 reads: "Molly very well X' charmingly: returned." Although Bayley does not describe what he and Baldwin did that night, it would not have been unusual for a courting couple to engage in foreplay or even intercourse. He may have been uncomfortable describing his physical actions, yet he was far more forthcoming about his emotions than were diarists only twenty-five years earlier.[25]

In many ways, John Burt and Abner Bayley found themselves in the conundrum that was eighteenth-century bachelorhood. As young men aspired to become settled ministers, they did not marry until after they had received formal calls and thus had secured a steady income to support a household. Such had been the accepted pattern for young men for centuries: economic security came first, marriage and intercourse came later. However, the playful discussion of love and sex in the popular literature of the day complicated matters considerably. Many of the diarists recorded reading the *Spectator* and the *Rambler,* works that depicted bachelors as constantly wooing women and discussing their most intimate emotions with great ease. Heterosexual desire had itself become a dimension of the masculine independence that defined bachelorhood. Men who avoided courtship were effeminate or hypermasculine and thus the reticence of Samuel Sewall and Ebenezer Parkman to write about romantic matters was no longer evidence of masculine self-control.[26] Accordingly, Burt and Bayley found themselves torn between the economic practicalities and mounting social pressure. The two diarists resisted marrying before it was economically feasible to do so but they were clearly anxious to participate in the romance and sexual play then gaining popularity.

We might thus read young men's diaries as cathartic instruments that eased the bachelor's conundrum. In groups and letters single men could console each other as they faced rejection or worried that they would never marry, but in the privacy of a diary they were free to compensate for the lack of a sex life. While he was still a student at Harvard in the early 1750s, Nathan Fiske kept a series of commonplace books in which he transcribed the memorable writings he came across. One notebook was dedicated to history, another to religious treatises, and still another to sermons. In a fourth book, Fiske recorded his favorite poems and stories copied from periodicals, many of which dealt with women and romance. Some pieces are pedestrian, such as "The True Beauty," which praised the more enduring qualities of women such as intelligence. Others were more fully sexual such as "On the Sight of a Beautiful Young Lady" and "Upon a Rose in a Ladies Bosom." By copying these works, Fiske recorded in his own handwriting scenes that he was not experiencing and thus could not place in his diary. In one untitled poem, a newly married husband and wife joined each other in bed:

> How soft his Slumbers be, & how serene!
> While the past Joy employs his am'rous Dream.
> His roving Hand he stretches on her Bre'st
> And smiles & says, Now I'm compleat by blest.

Fiske also may have been daydreaming about himself when he copied the story of a "young Mahometan Persian" who went to India and became the object of affection of a Musti's "two Daughters of a very surpassing Beauty." Indeed, there was something voyeuristic if not erotic in a story about two women who competed for a man's affection until one killed the other in a jealous rage. That Fiske saw himself in such stories is evident in a recollection he provided about the night he strolled about Cambridge. He tantalizingly began the story by noting that "Night Walking particularly for Scholars & young Ladies is accounted a scandalous Practice." Unfortunately, the rest of the story, beyond an innocent description of the evening's weather, has been excised, removed either by Fiske or a prudish keeper of the Fiske family record. Assuming that the rest of the story is as overtly sexual as others in his record, we can surmise that such stories allowed bachelors to participate virtually in romance and sexual play at a time when they were unable to marry and unwilling to accept the risks of premarital sex.[27]

Sexuality was not the only thing tenuous in the lives of midcentury bachelors. Although they were more self-aware and independent than previous generations, single men remained insecure, trapped somewhere between masters and dependents. Some appropriated the term used to describe Harvard matriculants to loosely talk about their peers and the activities they engaged in. "The Batchelors Play Batt & Ball mightily now adays which Stirs our bloud greatly," noted Nicholas Gilman in 1729.[28] Tellingly, none of the diarists referred to themselves or their friends as bachelors. In the parlance of the day, they were "young men," but even that term evoked mixed responses as if the diarists did not know whether it pertained to them or not. While training for the ministry in Boston, John Burt recorded the time in February 1737 when he gave what was probably his first sermon, writing "at night I preach'd to a Society of Young men at Mr. Lasenby's from Matthew VI.33." The forum may have been a single men's group such as the Friday Evening Association of Batchelors then in existence in Boston, but Burt does not say. Although only twenty-one, it is unclear whether he saw himself as part of the group or only as one who ministered to it.[29]

Some bachelor diarists sought to distance themselves from any association with youth altogether by portraying themselves as masters even as they resided under another man's roof. While a schoolmaster in Roxbury, John Ballantine lived with Major Bowler, a man he described as "a very pious man and submissive to God." As a tenant, Ballantine would not have had the right to vote in Roxbury, but this did not keep him from following politics. He noted a session of the General Court of Massachusetts in August 1737 and detailed how the "Commissioners met to settle the line between this Province and New Hampshire." Three years later, while serving as an itinerant minister preaching in any pulpit he could find, Ballantine drew a distinction between himself and irresponsible youths. "At Plymouth two young men were scuffling," he wrote, "one having a hot iron in his hand, touched ye jugular vein of the other and burnt it through and he bled to death in 6 minutes." Although he was only twenty-three at the time, Ballantine did not count himself among such young men whose immature lack of self-control led to self-destruction. In describing these young men as an impartial spectator, Ballantine used his diary to assert his mastery even though he was not yet a master.[30]

As was the case with sexuality, some bachelor diarists used fantasy to assert themselves as masters. While keeping school at Medford, Connecticut, in the late 1760s, Asa Dunbar was frustrated repeatedly by the disrespect he received from his students. Accordingly, Dunbar used his commonplace book to sketch a semiautographical tale titled "The Book of Asa the Scribe" in which a particularly unruly student "set an evil example before the young men." Dunbar did not number himself among the young men but reserved this label for the teenage students. Perhaps as a way of working out his own angst, Dunbar's story described how "Asa the Scribe" assumed the role of a thunderous patriarch whose divine justice earned him the respect of his inferiors. "And when the children & the servants of the mistickites saw what was done, they were sore afraid; & all the young men did exceedingly quake & tremble for fear of Asa, for his fear fell on them all." Dunbar may have been only a schoolmaster, but he wanted the respect accorded a man.[31]

In the end, Anne Lombard may well be correct that "in the eyes of the majority of adults, bachelors were never really men."[32] Yet the status of bachelorhood was more dynamic than her work suggests. Over the course of the eighteenth century, unmarried men grew more comfortable with being single. Like their fathers, these late colonial New England diarists went on to marry, own property, and father children. None of them questioned matrimony as their ultimate destination. But unlike their fathers they learned to celebrate their friendships with other young men, to date women they would not marry, and to demand the respect accorded to masters. Bachelorhood remained a liminal time, although, as the practice of diary keeping reveals, men were more comfortable with asserting their independence and assuming the privileges of manhood. In the eyes of most adults, a single schoolmaster or probationary minister who lived under another man's roof probably was not a man. But the distance between a married master and a single man was narrowing.

It is also true that bachelorhood emerged as a unique identity in the middle of the eighteenth century. Notions of identity have attracted the attention of early American historians in recent years as a means of explaining how groups of previously disparate people united as one, especially along racial lines. It was not until the eve of the Revolution that colonists from various European countries began referring to themselves as *white* and diverse groups of Native Americans were referred to as *red*. At the same time, people from New Hampshire to Georgia began to try out the appellation of *American*.[33] In this surge of identity creation, the bachelor emerged as well. His was a broadly encompassing identity that made no distinction of age or social class. All free, white single men were bachelors. The bachelor stood on his own, separate from both single women and married men, although he was unquestionably closer to the latter than the former. Indeed, the uniqueness of his identity emanated from the fact that he was a man unchecked by the domestic control of a woman. He thus embodied masculinity in its most positive and negative light. The

Evn. now where Alpine solitudes ascend.
I sit me down a pensive hour to spend:
And plac'd on high, above the storm's career.

Figure 5. "The Traveller," by Richard Westall. Young men in the middle of the eighteenth century began to internalize the bachelor identity that had originated in literature and the law. They began to see themselves as increasingly independent even though they lacked the property requirements for mastery and marriage.

Source: The Poems of Oliver Goldsmith (Hartford, Conn.: Goodrich, 1819), facing page 30. Reprinted with the permission of the American Antiquarian Society.

bachelor at once represented freedom and strength, but also luxury and immorality. He thus benefited from his distance from femininity and suffered for it. It is not that bachelors were not men; they were a variation on normative manhood.

Spinsters and Old Bachelors

The yearning for independence in bachelors' diaries is even more apparent when they are compared to the journals of eighteenth-century single women. The surviving record is far more scant for single women than for single men although the diaries of three eighteenth-century spinsters survive at the American Antiquarian Society. These female diarists were demographically similar to the male ones: they came from middling families, were well educated, and occupied a liminal position between childhood and adulthood. Like the men, the women tended to record short entries that were primarily about the weather and religious matters. They also made note of their struggles to define themselves as individuals and their attempts to enjoy a burgeoning heterosexual lifestyle. But spinsterhood did not confer the type of independence and autonomy that bachelorhood did. Single women were bereft of the ability to assert mastery and thus they were closer to dependence than were the bachelor diarists.

All three single women began their diaries when they were still living in their fathers' houses. Although young men intent on a career in the ministry left their parents' houses before they acquired property, women of middling backgrounds usually remained in their natal homes until marriage. This meant that they lacked the physical independence that bachelor diarists enjoyed. Because she continued to live at home, Priscilla Holyoke found herself the subject of what must have been a rather humiliating ritual. Every January, her father insisted on weighing every member of the household and recording each person's weight in his diary as well as how many pounds the person had gained or lost in the previous year. The fact that Holyoke's father was president of Harvard College no doubt compounded the embarrassment. In 1760, the year she turned twenty-one, Holyoke's father weighed her along with her mother, unmarried sisters, two granddaughters, and several live-in servants, all but one of whom were female. This family activity continued for much of the next decade and included Priscilla Holyoke as long as she lived at home. In contrast, her brother Edward Augustus had left home some years before and thus avoided his father's interest in monitoring his dependents' weight.[34] Without physical distance from their fathers, single women may have relied more heavily than single men on their diaries as a way to cultivate emotional independence. Although Priscilla Holyoke refrained from commenting on her father's fascination with weight, Martha "Patty" Rogers was less reticent about the strain her father placed on her patience. An invalid, Rogers's father demanded constant attention, causing Rogers to complain more than once: "O when will my Papa get well & set me at liberty?"[35]

Because they had not yet left home, single women had fewer chances than single men to create networks of peers. Patty Rogers relied on her girlfriends to alleviate the stress of having to spend all day caring for her father yet her closest friends were not always her peers. Noting a visit in February 1785, Rogers commented that "Mrs. Adams, Mrs. Gilman, Mrs. Blodget, Mrs. Thurston came to see me, had a more agreeable time than I expected." Although she was equal in age and station to her friends, all were married and at least one was pregnant at the time. Sally Thurston, Rogers's most intimate confidante, was herself struggling with three small children, all of whom may have followed their mother to Rogers's house that night. Likewise, many single women supplemented their friendships with close contacts with their sisters, although this too had its perils, especially when the sisters were wives. "For some reason they wished to know my sentiments with regard to marage," Patty Rogers wrote after visiting her sisters. A twenty-four-year-old woman with no matrimonial prospects, Rogers bristled at her sisters' queries, writing in her diary, "I Frankly told them that I would not have a person whose education has been more contracted than my own that I was sensible of my own deficiencies but I had feelings which would prevent my marrying anybody at present."[36] To be sure, single men kept close contact with their brothers, but their college experience provided a rich forum for alterative friendships that single women were denied access to.

Despite the limits of living at home, single women managed to find ample opportunity for heterosexual interaction and amusement. Patty Rogers often attended balls and more than once recorded being hung over after a late night of tavern-going. She pursued several eligible bachelors the year she kept a diary and engaged at least one in sexual play. Memorializing an evening with Sam Tenney, Rogers noted that "in the course of the evening he took some liberties that would not have been strictly decent had they come to light."[37] The statelier Priscilla Holyoke also held the affections of several young gentlemen. During the year she kept a diary, Holyoke noted the several days she spent with her beau, Nathaniel Ward. She traveled with him from Cambridge to Salem in late August 1766, and a week later she noted her presence "at Sr Ward Chamber." The degree of Holyoke's relations with Ward is unclear, especially since, in October, she recorded being present in two other men's chambers. Holyoke was also more self-consciously chaste than Rogers, writing a preface to her journal in which she proclaimed how "My faculties & my time" were devoted to "the encouragement of Virtue and the suppression of Vice." Certainly, Holyoke was prepared to fend off any improper advances from Ward. The couple's extended courtship stretched out for another two years before it was interrupted by Ward's untimely death.[38]

In some instances, heterosexual interaction could be the source of great consternation for spinster diarists. In 1759 Mary Seccombe moved with her father, mother, and teenage siblings from Harvard, Massachusetts, to Chester, Nova Scotia. Isolated on the Canadian frontier, Seccombe began recording her occasional thoughts in a diary as she approached twenty-six years of age. Of particular interest to Seccombe was the presence of Ebenezer Fitch, who came to live with the family in the spring of 1769. She was clearly infatuated with the bachelor boarder and may have told him of her feelings. "A Sorrowfull Secret Revealed," wrote Seccombe in June, although she gave no indication what this secret was. Her contact with Fitch weighed heavily on her mind that summer and seems to have been linked to her confession in early July: "Delivered of a great affliction which I beg may never be forgotten by me." Ten days after Seccombe made this entry, she logged how her older sister Hannah accompanied Fitch to the neighbor's house. Shortly thereafter Hannah and Fitch began courting. This turn of events soured Seccombe's relationship first with Fitch and then with her sister. One night in late October she noted how she "Spent part of the Night in Conversation. & Plainly Saw mine own familiar friend in whom I trusted had lifted up his heel against me." The next day, "Eben went home." A year later when "Eben Fitch was Married to Hannah Seccombe," Mary marked the occasion by observing "I was very Ill."[39]

Immature romances and failed courtships were frustrating to both men and women and could easily leave a person embarrassed if not devastated. Yet as single men began to accept the vagaries of heterosexual interaction as a part of the texture of bachelorhood, single women found the new sexual order more challenging. Patty Rogers never married and there is no record that Mary Seccombe did either. After Priscilla Holyoke's courtship unexpectedly terminated with her fiancé's death, a new beau was slow to emerge and it was not until her forty-first year that she finally wed. To some extent, single women had always faced greater obstacles than single men. If a woman wanted to marry, she was dependent upon the man to propose; if she wanted to stay single, she faced either a life of chastity or a reputation as a whore. But the emergence of bachelorhood in the eighteenth century further complicated spinsterhood. Now single women found themselves pressured by men to engage in romance and sexual play long before the men were financially able to propose marriage. To make matters worse, single women had little of the autonomy that men achieved by leaving home and often lacked the network of peers that comforted single men. Mary Seccombe's journal was her only confidante. Perhaps for this reason, the diary became associated with women in the nineteenth century, creating a safe place for women trapped between childhood and adulthood akin to the type of safety that bachelorhood created for men in the eighteenth century. Indeed, as bachelors turned outward and began to assert their autonomy as men regardless of their age, property, or marital status, spinsters faced inward. As single men felt the pressure to embody the type of premarital sexual freedom heralded in literature, women were defined as passionless, passive creatures who were even more captive to the prerogatives of men.[40]

Although several diaries of the young and unmarried survive from the colonial era, evidence for those who never married is sparse. Records complied of New England matriculants indicate that nearly 10 percent of college graduates died without ever taking a wife.[41] To be sure, some died before they had the chance to establish themselves professionally and court a woman, but others refused to enter into wedlock despite vocational success and physical longevity. The latter group, termed "old bachelors" in the press, retained a presence in New England and typically led lives of quiet dignity. It is possible to examine such men by reviewing the experience of one who never married: John Pickering. Pickering was a member of a prominent Massachusetts family who held several offices in the Massachusetts government including a term as Speaker of the General Court. He was the older brother of early U.S. Secretary of State Timothy Pickering, and shared his thoughts and emotions with his brother through a correspondence that lasted nearly a quarter of a century. These letters allow some insight into the experience of being a man in early America who never married.[42]

Much like the young New Englanders who kept diaries, John Pickering was a man of considerable education who embarked on an independent life in his late teens. Born in Salem, Massachusetts, in 1740, Pickering attended Harvard where he forged deep friendships. Known affectionately by a classmate as "my old Chum Pickering," he enjoyed poetry while a student, and after graduating in 1759 he took a position as a schoolmaster in Manchester, Massachusetts.[43] Up until this point John Pickering's life was more or less conventional for his gender and status. Yet while other young men used their bachelorhood to pursue a profession and to begin dating, Pickering apparently squandered his youth. A contemporary recalled that for ten years after leaving college, Pickering's "prospects were very uncertain." As Salem minister William Bentley later told the story: "Being a modest man he could not determine himself to either of the learned professions & he became associated with some idle youth of his standing whose amusements led to gaming." Although the exact details of this portion of Pickering's life are unclear, his father "at length obliged his sons to Horticulture . . . & saved him from that perdition which seemed approaching." A decade after graduating from Harvard, John Pickering had not transitioned to mastery but had returned to his father's house.[44]

It is certainly possible that during his time in Manchester, John Pickering engaged in the types of activities that occupied his fellow Harvard alumni. In addition to gambling with his friends, he probably attended dances with young women. Yet he did not marry. Discerning why he chose not to wed is dangerous terrain because the reason a person stays single is rarely self-evident. In his study of contemporary men who have not married by age forty, psychologist Charles Waehler has observed that some bachelors seek isolation and some are alienated from their emotions, yet a majority are conflicted about their marital status—dissatisfied with their single state but reluctant to marry.[45] It is difficult to know whether John Pickering fell into one or another of these categories although he may well have hoped to marry and never found the opportunity to do so. Certainly none of the more conventional factors that inhibited marriage in colonial America kept him from wedlock: financial distress or a lack of eligible partners. As the eldest son, he received a sizeable inheritance and there was no shortage of young women in Salem. Physical ailments may have stymied the pursuit of a bride as Pickering spent much of his later years bedridden with what he termed "epilepsy."[46] Ultimately, he most likely remained single for the same reason that generations before him had: because he could. Despite the increasing attacks on men who never married, John Pickering only had to look to his Uncle Theophilus Pickering for a role model. This family member achieved notoriety and success as a settled minister in Massachusetts's Chebacco Parish despite never taking a wife.[47]

Having failed to achieve economic independence, John Pickering returned home and became a resident in the household of his father, Deacon Timothy Pickering. Yet unlike seventeenth-century families, Pickering's economic situation did not mean dependence. His father did not set him to work on the family farm but allowed him to follow his own pursuits. A century before, sons in their late twenties who lived at home had little political identity, but John Pickering joined the provincial leadership. He was elected to the Massachusetts General Court in 1769, and when the Coercive Acts pushed New England toward revolution, he joined the Salem Committee of Safety. Pickering was able to assume such positions despite the fact that his father maintained control of the family estate. Indeed, when Deacon Pickering died in 1778 his son was so flooded with sudden responsibilities that he griped to his brother, "I have been confined at home ever since by taking care of the business of his estate."[48] Young men maintained autonomy in the late eighteenth century even when they resided under their father's roof.

With the death of his father, John Pickering assumed full responsibility for the family's estate in Salem as well as for his ailing mother. At first Pickering viewed these duties as a nuisance and sought to delegate his responsibilities to others. Before his death, Deacon Pickering had hired a man to work the land and this gave his heir hope that "perhaps while he lives with us I may be able to attend the General Court except in hay time." Such hopes were soon dashed when the young worker ran away and Pickering had to abandon his seat in the assembly to devote his full attention to the estate. "You suppose I have more leasure to give you information respecting the measures taken by this state," he wrote his brother in 1781, adding "I expected more when I quitted publick life," but I "am there obliged to be much at my farming business."[49] Despite his initial displeasure with farming, Pickering eventually warmed to the experience as well as to the familial responsibilities that came with it. He cared for his mother while she was alive and administered her estate when she died. He also tended to his seven sisters when their husbands died as well as to their offspring. In return, Pickering's widowed sisters kept house for their brother. In 1792 William Bentley observed, "In Pickering's house were thirteen persons, & all females excepting a bedridden man."[50] In assuming his father's place at the head of the household, John Pickering achieved mastery and economic independence without marrying.

Like Patty Rogers, John Pickering looked to his siblings for strength, especially to his brother Timothy. A more vigorous individual than his brother, Timothy fought in Washington's army during the Revolution, built a home on the Pennsylvania frontier, and unabashedly pursued national power while his brother focused on matters in Salem. Timothy also married at age twenty-one and went on to father ten children. Through their correspondence, the two came to depend on each other for information and emotional support. During the war, when John was Speaker of the General Court, Timothy sent him a draft law to be "passed with all possible dispatch." When John responded, he opined that "the situation of the internal political state of this part of America may afford me an opportunities to give you some information."[51]

In their correspondence, the two brothers did not discuss matters of the heart and John never mentioned his marital status or any longing for a woman. Timothy was likewise reticent about his brother's personal life, although in letters to others he occasionally made note of bachelors that reflected contemporary perceptions. In a letter to his wife Timothy passed on advice about love to a nephew, hoping that the young man would listen to "these remarks from an old bachelor." Such a sobriquet may have been ironic or it may suggest Timothy's self-awareness of his previous single state even after his marriage. More revealing is a letter Timothy wrote to John Phillips who was planning an academy for Exeter, New Hampshire, in 1785. Timothy worried about the housing for students, writing "I have heard colleges compared to monasteries, as tending to produce, in a degree, the vices of monks." To prevent this type of sexual experimentation ("Be this as it may in respect to youth"), Timothy recommended that Phillips "place children to board but in the houses of married people, or of those who had been married, and of choice with those who were or had been parents." In these comments, Timothy touted old bachelors as comical spectators and sexual deviants, yet he never so much as alluded to such ideas in his letters to John. Perhaps he saw his brother as an embodiment of Isaac Bickerstaff or perhaps wondered whether John's desires did not include women. Yet such ideas were irrelevant. Timothy did not impugn John for being a bachelor; he accepted it as a simple matter of fact.[52]

Indeed, any connection between Timothy Pickering's fears about the "vices of monks" and his ideas about his brother ultimately was severed in 1786 when he sent his ten-year-old son John to live with his brother in Salem. The fraternal correspondence indicates that the situation was to be temporary, but the arrangement persisted for the next six years with John becoming a surrogate father to his nephew. Although he was only responsible for sending the nephew to class, John soon began instructing the boy. "I have taught him, myself, the first principles of Arithmetick, and intend the winter ensuing to carry him further in that science," John wrote his brother. Indeed, the presence of the boy revitalized John's vigor. When Timothy first broached the issue of sending his son to live in Salem, he was hesitant to do so because of his brother's declining health. A few months after his nephew's arrival, John's tone changed decidedly and the once ailing man could not contain his joy at his nephew's presence. "John is hearty & well and is I think taller of his age than almost any one of his associates," he proudly proclaimed to Timothy in September 1788, continuing "I have enjoyed my health very comfortably most of the year past."[53] It was as if the opportunity to be a father figure gave John a psychological and physical benefit he could not derive from his widowed sisters. The boy remained with his uncle until the summer of 1792 when, thanks to John's tutelage, he gained admission to Harvard. A few months later, Timothy sent a second son to live with his brother.

When John Pickering died in 1811 at the age of seventy-one, he concluded a rich life that stood in sharp contrast to the hyperbole of late colonial laws and periodicals. He had become a responsible landowner, statesman, master, and a patriarch, even though he had never married. Moreover, no one around him seemed particularly bothered by his marital status. Like the experience of the young bachelor diarists, John Pickering had a great deal more autonomy than single men at the beginning of the eighteenth century. He was free to waste his youth and was able to preserve an independent political identity while living in his father's house. A sense of familial duty was strong in Pickering but he was no captive of patriarchal control. However, gambling, much like a sexual indiscretion or commonplace book erotica, were child-ish things to be put away when a man matured. Once Pickering assumed his father's estate, he took on the same responsibilities as any other master, including a host of dependents. We might wonder about Pickering's sexual preference—perhaps he never married because he was not attracted to women—although such speculations are ultimately moot. When Pickering became an unmarried master he forfeited his sexuality. The sexual license granted to bachelors in the eighteenth century did not extend beyond youth. To achieve mastery, a man had to choose either marriage or chastity. In this, John Pickering was not that far removed from William Stoughton of a century earlier. A man could gain prominence without marriage, but manhood did not extend to anyone whose reputation matched the caricature of an old bachelor.

"Their Wages So High Doth Run"

Although Massachusetts diarists generally avoided referring to themselves as bach-elors, it is clear that they were assuming an identity that single men today would recognize as remarkably similar to their own. Although eighteenth-century New En-gland was still quite far from twentieth-century New York, many of the elements—independence, heterosociability, an interest in romance, and even erotica—meant that these men were closer to "the age of the bachelor" than they were to the single life of their fathers.[54] Throughout the colonies, young urban men were embracing the new bachelor ethos. In Philadelphia, single men built Batchellors Hall on the northern edge of the city, a meeting place that may have doubled as a boardinghouse. In a 1731 poem, George Webb commemorated the building, rhapsodizing, "Tir'd with the bus'ness of the noisy town, / The weary Batchelors their cares disown." The way Webb described the association it is not hard to imagine the aspiring min-isters of New England at home in its environs. According to Webb, Philadelphia's singles denounced "impious doctrines" associated with "a revel, or lascivious night." Instead, Batchellors Hall was a place "to mend the heart and cultivate the mind." The Hall proved quite popular, receiving numerous mentions in the *Pennsylvania Gazette* and inspiring imitations. When the structure was razed in 1776, it was not long before plans were made for a replacement.[55]

Yet the vast majority of the single male population in Pennsylvania had no ac-cess to places such as Batchellors Hall. Men in the rural areas and of modest means had little opportunity to leave home for a college education and the vocation they pursued was the same one that men in their families had followed for generations: farming. Such men continued the tradition of medieval England. They left their fathers' houses in their teens and went to work in another man's home. They typi-cally lived and worked for a number of years as a dependent with little of a Harvard graduate's independence. Indeed, they often married as soon as they had earned enough to buy land or came into their inheritance. There were thousands of these men in Pennsylvania and throughout the colonies, far outnumbering their urban counterparts.

Such men are difficult to study as few left diaries or letters and thus we cannot probe their inner thoughts for sexual longing or proof that they read the *Spectator.* We do not know whether they had a personal identity linked to marital status. Yet we do know that such men were not oblivious to the changes going on around them. They might not have attended Batchellors Hall, but they did pay taxes because of their lack of wives and estates. They stood apart from married and propertied men but also from other dependents such as servants, children, and women. A bachelor identity in such areas may have been nascent, but it was not unknown. Propertyless single men in Pennsylvania were gaining a growing sense of autonomy based on their employment and the responsibility of paying their own taxes. Like midcentury New England diarists, they were more mobile, more accustomed to the accoutrements of the bachelor life, and more economically independent than single men before them.

In Chapter 2 I looked at Chester County tax rolls to quantify the collection of the Pennsylvania bachelor tax. These records demonstrate that taxed bachelors constituted between 2 and 5 percent of the county's total population and were rated at levels higher than 90 percent of estates. In addition to demonstrating how much bachelors paid, the Chester County tax rolls also offer some perspective on who paid the taxes. We can glimpse the life of Pennsylvania's rural bachelors by looking at one part of Chester County: Concord Township. Concord was geographically and ethnically stable for much of the eighteenth century and thus provides an accurate microcosm of the rural Quaker population of the province. Records survive for thirty-four county rate assessments made in the township between 1715 and 1775. From these records it is possible to glean information about 267 men who paid the tax over that sixty-year span of time.[56]

As a group, the taxed bachelors of Concord Township were young, white, local, and highly mobile. Although there was no maximum age in the law, Pennsylvanians appear to have assumed that single meant young. The county officials who made up the lists typically termed the taxables "Freemen," and at other times referred to them as "Singlemen" and "Young Men." There appears to have been no attempt to tax widowers. Similarly, although there was no reference to race in any of the Pennsylvania tax laws, efforts to rate African Americans apparently were a rare exception. In the Concord rates for 1725, "Negro Sam" was rated the same as the other presumably white bachelors in the township, although Sam never reappeared in the Concord rolls nor was there another demarcation of race in that township for the next sixty years. In townships where blacks lived in larger numbers, assessors made no mention of race and thus it is unclear whether the intention was to treat all single men the same regardless of race or simply to exclude black workers altogether. In many ways, the odd reference in the Concord rolls is indicative of the connection between race and marital status more generally. Nearly all discussions of bachelors in colonial laws and literature omit reference to race. This omission appears to have been based on the assumption that no one counted African Americans as bachelors rather than a sense that the identity could be inclusive. Indeed, the masculine autonomy that so defined bachelorhood stood in stark contrast to the identity of servile nonwhites being crafted in eighteenth-century America.

Most of the taxed bachelors of Concord Township were native-born sons who grew up in the township. The Concord rolls reveal the presence of bachelor immigrants from England and Ireland, although a count of surnames reveals that more than half shared family names with other taxpayers in the township.[57] Numerous single freemen who did not hail from Concord came from nearby locales. For many, Concord Township was not the first place they were rated. About 7 percent of the bachelors assessed in Concord previously had been rated as single men in another Chester County township. One such mobile young man was Caleb James. Born in Westtown in 1736, James was rated for the poll tax in his hometown in 1757, in Concord in 1758, and in Birmingham in 1760. Two years later he returned to Concord where he married and became a freeholder.[58]

The story of Caleb James is typical of propertyless single men in Concord Township specifically and servants in husbandry generally. Mobility was common among English servants in the eighteenth century, with 70 to 80 percent not renewing their yearly contracts.[59] The same was true of Concord. Of 267 taxed bachelors, 171 (64.0%) appear only once and 55 (20.6%) appear twice. Moreover, mobility increased over time. In the first half of the eighteenth century, a bachelor was rarely rated for the poll tax in more than two townships, but after 1750 it became customary for single men rated in Concord also to be rated in three or more other townships. Although single men were a constant and important part of the population, they were hardly a static group.

Concord's taxed bachelors were quite well behaved. The population of Concord Township was overwhelmingly Quaker and many of the township's single workers fell under the watchful eyes of the Concord Monthly Meeting. Accordingly, these bachelors found their actions significantly circumscribed. Moses Mendenhall appeared before the Concord Monthly Meeting in 1765 for attending a marriage conducted by a priest, an action for which he was not forgiven until he acknowledged his transgression. A year later Mendenhall faced the elders again, this time "for fighting & attending where there was fiddling & dancing." Once more he made acknowledgment of his transgressions, although the elders had already grown skeptical of his sincerity. The meeting expressed concern with Mendenhall's residence, remarking that he lived "at considerable distance" from the congregation. In early 1769 Mendenhall appeared for the last time before the meeting. Again he was charged with drinking but now cursing and fighting were added to his list of sins. Abandoning all hope that Mendenhall could be reformed, the meeting promptly "disowned" Mendenhall. He apparently sought a living elsewhere because at this point he disappears from the meeting records and the Chester County tax lists.[60]

Despite the colorfulness of Moses Mendenhall's story, less than 10 percent of the township's taxed bachelors appeared before the Concord Monthly Meeting for moral offenses. Indeed, more than twice as many rated single men were received into membership upon confession of faith than were presented for drunkenness.

Likewise, only five out of 267 of the men rated for the poll tax in Concord Township faced charges for fornication. In all five instances, the men had already married before their case made it to the elders and thus they were being presented for premarital sex. It is possible that Concord's bachelors were particularly law-abiding or that those men who had no interest in abiding by the Friends' moral code sought employment in more tolerant locales. Nevertheless, Concord offers little support for Barry Levy's assertion that unmarried men were a "social curse for the Quaker discipline and for Quaker households."[61]

If the Concord bachelors were not particularly sinful, neither were they especially religious. Less than 10 percent of rated single men joined the Concord Monthly Meeting by either confession of faith or transfer of membership from other Quaker meetings. Moreover, many who did join the local church did so in anticipation of marriage. Of the nine taxed bachelors who made professions of faith, five were married before the meeting within a year. At the same time, the act of taking a wife could itself cause considerable discipline problems. Of the forty-five taxed bachelors whose marriages were recorded by the Concord Quakers, thirteen married without the blessing of the meeting. For some, this meant marrying a Quaker woman before a priest of another faith and for others it meant marrying a nonmember. Both breaches could result in excommunication. Richard Newlin was married in a Presbyterian church in 1777 "by priest to one not a member" and was thereafter disowned by the Concord Monthly Meeting.[62] Yet whether marriage brought a man closer to the faith or drove him from it, he who married had a spiritual independence that most Concord bachelors did not. On the whole, the rural bachelors of Pennsylvania remained spiritually undefined, a situation not surprising given their constant mobility. Having not yet established a household, most men likely attended a Quaker meeting with their parents or masters. From a spiritual vantage point, masculine independence continued to demand marriage for rural Pennsylvanians.

The subject of marriage also raises the question of how long the typical man remained single and what his prospects were for setting up a household when he did marry. Eighteenth-century Pennsylvanians tended to marry in their late twenties and Concord followed this trend. Although reliable vital statistics are sketchy for such a mobile population, the records of the Concord Monthly Meeting suggest that taxed bachelors men married between twenty-six and thirty-one years of age. Such men would have paid the Pennsylvania tax for five to ten years. Of course, not everyone married in such a timely fashion. Of all the single men taxed in Concord Township, Robert Bennett was rated more than any other, showing up twelve times in the county tax records between 1720 and 1740. Yet the most dramatic example of bachelorhood in the township was Richard Bates. Rated seven times in Concord between 1753 and 1775, Bates continued to pay taxes as a single man until 1785 when, at the age of sixty-four, he married Deborah Hibberd at the Concord Monthly Meeting. Although Bates is an extreme example, his case parallels the inclusion of older men among the ranks of bachelors.[63]

As had been true of sixteenth-century England, marriage accompanied the acquisition of property for most but not all rural Pennsylvanians. About a third of
all bachelors rated in Concord Township were later rated for property in Chester
County.[64] Many of these men owned land outright although a number were tenants. John Hall, rated as a single freeman in Concord from 1747 to 1750, rented a
250-acre farm in Concord in 1753 where he and his wife lived until he purchased
the land in 1778. At the same time, a handful of men obtained property without taking a wife. Some taxed bachelors acquired property with a family member, such as
John Rattew, who took up residence with his brother William in 1735. Others did so
by themselves. Daniel Trimble, born in 1745 as the youngest son in a family of eight,
began paying the poll tax at age twenty-four and by 1774 had become a landowner.
According to the county tax rolls, Trimble acquired a hundred acres of property, a
mill worth sixty pounds, eight horses, seven cows, and fifteen sheep. Trimble was
apparently still a bachelor when he died at the age of fifty-two in 1807. Such stories
were not unusual. In her study of inventoried estates in Chester County from the
first half of the eighteenth century, Mary Schweitzer finds that about one-sixth of
all inventories belonged to bachelor householders.[65]

Although it is likely that the single men who did not obtain property in Chester
County became landowners and tenants elsewhere, a sizable portion were unsuccessful in obtaining property. As land became scarce in Chester County, the traditional connection between marriage and the acquisition of property broke down.
Instead of marrying when land became available, many after midcentury married
and remained inmates long after their wedding day. Only one single freeman rated
in Concord Township before 1740 was a wage laborer after marriage, but twenty-
three single freemen rated after 1747 were later inmates in the township. After being
rated twice for the poll tax in Concord, William Norrey married in the mid-1750s
and was thereafter rated as an inmate for the next two decades, apparently never
obtaining ratable property in the county.

Whether the men obtained property, married, or both, the payments of Concord taxpayers became considerably less once they ceased to be bachelor workers.
John Hall paid lower taxes to the county in his first year as a tenant farmer than he
did in his last year as a single freeman. When John Rattew set up house with his
brother, his tax bill was cut in half. Among men who neither purchased land nor became tenants, marriage by itself became the determining factor in one's assessment.
Even though William Norrey did not obtain land, his taxes were reduced after he
married. As a single freeman Norrey paid six shillings a year, but as an inmate his
county rates averaged two shillings six pence.

Although most men in Concord Township were able to marry and acquire property, over time the prospects for doing both before age thirty became increasingly
uncertain. As available land grew scarcer, men were forced to delay marriage, marry
but remain a wage laborer, or leave Chester County. The man who remained single and stayed in Pennsylvania watched his bachelorhood grow longer and his tax
bill swell. In Concord the number of single freemen expanded at a far higher rate

than taxed estates: the number of bachelors almost tripled from eight to twenty-one between 1721 and 1750, while estates increased from forty-seven to fifty-seven over the same period. Barry Levy has connected this rise of freemanship to an increase in discipline problems among young Friends, especially those from poorer families whose parents could not guarantee them land. In a religious community held together by parents' ability to transmit property to their children, a short-age of land consequently induced offspring trapped in wage labor to abandon the faith. However, Levy's formulation ignores the fact that the experience of being a single man was undergoing tremendous change over the course of the eighteenth century and that even in rural Concord Township bachelorhood was becoming in-creasingly vibrant. Pennsylvania's taxed bachelors did not have to choose between filial obedience and renouncing their religion. As in the rest of America, there was another way.[66]

Although there was little mention of the Pennsylvania bachelor tax in the print media before 1760, the subject drew increased attention as the American Revo-lution approached. Specifically, Pennsylvania bachelors acquired a reputation for extravagance. In 1764 a householder bemoaned the province's high taxes in a broad-side. The anonymous author offered a pithy critique of each item rated including his workers. On the subject of single men, he wrote:

> No single Men have I at all,
> About my House living this Fall;
> If of them I'd an half a Thrave,
> There's not a Head of them I'd save
> 'Cause their Wages so high doth run,
> Few of them cares how little's done,
> At Noon or setting of the Sun.

Mention of "this Fall" was a reference to harvest season, the time when single men's labors were in high demand. Likewise, the author's charge "their Wages so high doth run" suggests the great expense of hiring bachelors, a charge the same author tellingly did not level against inmates. The charge of high wages is also especially revealing in light of the claim "Few of them cares how little's done." In other words, not only were single men overpaid, they were indolent.[67]

An analysis of wages in eighteenth-century Pennsylvania suggests that the pam-phleteer's grievances were grounded in fact. Single men in Pennsylvania received some of the highest wages in colonial America. Whereas lawmakers in New England and the Chesapeake set the workers' wages, Pennsylvania left the matter up to the vicissitudes of the market.[68] At the same time, there was a high demand for workers, to the point that by the 1760s landowners were advertising for workers in the local newspaper. "WANTED, TWO single Men, that understand the Farming and Garden-ing Business well," read one notice in a January 1766 issue of the *Pennsylvania Gazette*.[69] When combined, a lack of legal controls and a strong demand for labor

resulted in exceptionally high wages for farmhands. Indeed, James Lemon has estimated that wages for agricultural workers in Pennsylvania were 30 to 100 percent
higher than wages for similar workers in England. The high taxes on propertyless
single men thus correlated to their high wages. In 1775 the typical male farmworker
in Pennsylvania earned one shilling eight pence per day during harvest season and
two shillings six pence when harvesting grain or mowing. As a result, a single man's
tax burden might be as little as a week's pay during peacetime and as much as a
month's salary when the province was at war. Such taxes would hardly have been
an imposition on a man who lived under another man's roof and received room and
board in addition to wages.[70]

Although a scarcity of land in Pennsylvania forced more men to remain unmarried longer, many made the best of the situation. With generous wages, afford-
able taxes, and few of the expenses associated with a house or family, Pennsylvania
bachelors were free to indulge in the growing materialism of late colonial America's
consumer revolution. Lucy Simler has noted that young, single workers can be
distinguished from older, married ones by their spending habits. Husbands with
children were conservative in dispersing wages, but young men typically spent their
money freely on fine linen shirts, beaver hats, watches, and tobacco. Mary Schweitzer's survey of inventories likewise reveals that single youths held very little real
estate or livestock but owned proportionally greater amounts of personal property
than did older, married people. In the Concord rate for 1765, nearly one in four
landless single men were assessed an additional shilling for owning a horse. For men
who did not farm their own land, horses were the eighteenth-century equivalent of
automobiles, providing mobility and thus opportunities for socialization.[71] Such
materialism attracted the rebuke of the Quaker elders and secular moralists such
as Benjamin Franklin who wondered aloud about the connections between the
single state and luxury. Far from urban amusements, rural bachelors carved out a
niche to survive and even enjoy the growing gap between childish dependence and
the authority of being a married householder.

In addition to personal accoutrements, Pennsylvania's unmarried workers came
to bachelorhood through the process of paying their own taxes. Early American governments regularly placed taxes on the propertyless. Indeed, a significant portion
of the southern colonies' revenue came from poll taxes on indentured servants and
slaves. Yet no one expected them to pay their own taxes. Servants and slaves were
considered part of the master's household and it was the householder alone who
was responsible for all financial obligations to the colony. By contrast, Pennsylvania
demanded that its single freemen be accountable for their own assessments. On the
tax rolls, bachelor freemen were singled out from the rest of the taxables. The assessors listed each single freeman by name and how much he owed, but they gave
no indication as to who his master or father was. The same tax rolls enumerated indentured servants, but unlike bachelors, they went unnamed and were included in
their masters' estates like livestock. To be sure, a master or father may have paid a
bachelor's taxes by withholding a portion of his wages, but the responsibility for

making sure the tax was paid fell on the single man alone. The provincial tax law of 1711 demanded that the tax be paid "by himself or his friend" or by his "house-holder, master or employer." If no one paid the tax, then the constable was "to take such freeman...and bring him before any one of the said commissioners." The freeman would then remit his taxes or else the sheriff would "commit such a person to prison till he do pay the same."[72] Whether or not he faced the taxman himself, the bachelor alone faced the consequences if his civic obligation went unmet.

A single freeman thus stood at a considerable distance from servants, children, and women. Although he could not vote because he did not own property, he had a political identity as a taxpayer that the province denied to all other dependents. In this, we might see a broad correlation between the New England diarists and Pennsylvania's taxed bachelors. Even though the two groups were incomplete men because they were neither property owners nor husbands, both had begun to take on an economic and political independence that separated them from their single sisters and younger brothers. They occupied an intermediary political position between mastery and dependence. Moreover, much as recent Harvard graduates used fantasy and other means to cover the distance between themselves and propertied husbands, the taxed single freemen of Pennsylvania did likewise. Having attained the responsibilities of manhood through taxation, they sought the commensurate rights of manhood that such responsibilities entailed. Linda Kerber has argued that paying taxes politicized female landowners in the nineteenth century. Faced with the same financial obligations as men, women began to seek the right to vote.[73] A similar process may have been at work among Pennsylvania bachelors. At the American Revolution, Pennsylvania's single freemen asked why their taxes should not entitle them to the full political rights of manhood including that of suffrage.

The Tuesday Club of Annapolis

Ultimately, the experience of being a bachelor in early America proved changeable and contradictory. A man might relish his independence one day and curse it the next; his friends might praise his lack of a wife on Monday only to attack it on Tuesday. In part, this was a result of the inherently liminal nature of marital status. Unlike race or gender, a man changed his marital status in an instant, and when he did, his cultural, economic, and political identity was altered dramatically. Although marriage had long been a rite of passage, the emergence of bachelorhood as an intermediate life stage between dependent childhood and independent fatherhood complicated matters considerably. A man who prided himself on membership in Batchellors Hall had to leave his friends when he wed; after marriage, he befriended husbands and lost contact with those who remained single. Moreover, bachelorhood could be a precarious identity. In the seventeenth century marital status was subordinated to property: men with land were masters whether they were married or not, while all propertyless people were reduced to dependency regardless of age or gender. A century later, this equation was no longer necessarily true. Suddenly, young bachelors without property assumed political responsibilities and asserted sexual license while aging bachelors with considerable estates were attacked as rakes and misanthropes. As the American Revolution approached, the contradictions of bachelorhood helped to subvert the traditional order, contributing to a world turned upside down.

The contradictions and constant change of late colonial bachelorhood can perhaps best be seen in the Tuesday Club of Annapolis. Founded in 1745 by the noted belletrist Dr. Alexander Hamilton (not to be confused with the founding father), the club met regularly until 1756. Although hundreds of such clubs existed in early America, the Tuesday Club is remarkable for the record it left behind. Dr. Hamilton faithfully recorded the club's proceedings, poems, and music, and later wrote a mock history of the club that embellished the original record. These sources allow us to peek into an exclusive club and observe how its members thought about issues of marital status, their own and that of others. The Tuesday Club has attracted considerable attention from historians who have used it to observe late colonial ideas about luxury, polite letters, and politics. Wilson Somerville's study of the club includes a detailed analysis of gender including a look at marital status. He acknowledges "the differing status of married and unmarried men in the club," although he treats marital status as an unchanging identity when it was anything but static.[74]

The Tuesday Club is the story of a group of men who held deeply conflicted and constantly changing opinions about marital status. When the members convened the first year, single men outnumbered husbands and the club became a forum for raucous activities. As the members married, however, the jokes, songs, and activities of the club became increasingly less disorderly. Throughout this transition, the position of bachelors was unpredictable. Young bachelors without households could assert equal status with married members, but they were never certain they would receive it. Likewise, the club included a number of wealthy, older single gentlemen. Like old bachelors before them, these men claimed that mastery made their marital status irrelevant, but the club members did not always agree. In short, it was never completely obvious whether being a bachelor gave one better access to manhood or negated one's claim to it.

The Tuesday Club was never an exclusive preserve of the unmarried, but it was most certainly created as a bachelor refuge. Specifically, Dr. Alexander Hamilton needed a place where he could commiserate with other men who had also proven unfortunate in the marriage market. Born in Edinburgh in 1712, Hamilton was the fifth son of a professor of divinity. With little hope of receiving a landed estate from his father, Hamilton studied medicine with the eminent Dutch physician Dr. Herman Boerhaave and became a medical doctor. In the winter of 1738 Hamilton followed his brother to Annapolis, Maryland, where he quickly established a successful medical practice in a land desperate for doctors. However, Hamilton's professional success did not translate into a quick and profitable marriage. As he approached his thirtieth birthday, he began to obsess that he would never marry. In a letter to his brother written in 1742, Hamilton bemoaned that his indebtedness had rendered him celibate: "I resolve to live a batchellor while I remain in this wicked country, there being no moneyd wives to be had here."[75] A year later, he blamed his health, confiding to a friend, "I shall only say I am not well in health, and for that reason chiefly continue still a Batchellor."[76] Frustrated with women, Hamilton sought homosocial interaction. He had enjoyed the sociability of a men's club in Edinburgh, but as corollary institutions in Annapolis proved fleeting, he organized his own.

On May 14, 1745, Dr. Alexander Hamilton invited seven men to his house where they "erected themselves onto a Society or Club, under the name of Tuesday Club."[77] The men Hamilton chose to invite were comparable in stature to himself: white men of middling means such as merchants, professionals, and small planters. The club these men formed was typical for the era, combining the elements of an eating club with those of a coffeehouse or tavern association. The club convened at one of the members' houses and the hosting member, who wore the title of steward for the night, provided a meal for the members. After dinner the club turned its attention to taking tobacco, drinking alcohol, and conducting a meeting. As club secretary, Hamilton recorded all of the club's events in a minute book. His records indicate that the meetings were anything but serious. The club's gelastic law ordered that if any member began a serious discussion of politics or any matter that upset the members "no answer Shall be Given thereto, but after Such discourse is Ended, the Society Shall Laugh at the member offending, in order to divert the discourse."[78] In consequence, all of the club's proceedings, speeches, and laws were designed to be light and humorous.

Not all of the Tuesday Club's original members were bachelors. Of the first eight members, four were married and one was a widower. Yet the club had a distinctly bachelor flavor. At the fourth sederunt (as the club termed its meetings), the members approved the use of sandboxes to catch tobacco expectorations so as not to damage the floors of members' houses. However, sandbox rule was soon discontinued "because, it was thought, that the married men of the Club, were afraid of falling under the Ridicule of the Batchellors, by showing in this, a more than Common care and Sollicitude, about Incurring the displeasure of their wives." Bachelors also gained important concessions from the club when it came to meal preparation. According to the rules of the club, the evening's steward was to provide "a Gammon of Bacon, or one other dish of dress'd vittles for Supper." However, it was subsequently determined that this law imposed an undue hardship on "those batchelor members, who, not always having cooks at home" had "more trowble in providing, than such of the members as were matirmonized." Accordingly, at the fifth sederunt the members passed a law allowing unmarried stewards to serve "Batchellor's Cheese" instead.[79] Perhaps because of these accommodations for single members, the Tuesday Club attracted a number of new bachelor members during its first year in existence. Of the six members admitted in the summer of 1745, at least three and as many as five were unmarried. From among the new bachelor admissions, the club elected its one and only president: Charles Cole. The married members soon began to resent their minority status, and in August an unnamed member moved "that no more Batchellors Should be admitted into the Club."[80] Needless to say, the proposal was defeated.

Unlike New England diarists, the Tuesday Club members freely used the word bachelor to label themselves and each other. This may have been a regional variation that dated back to the seventeenth century when demographics forced many white men to live without wives at estates they named Batchelors Hope. As had been the case a century before, the Tuesday Club exploited the different connotations of the term. On the one hand, terming someone a bachelor suggested the type of masculine autonomy then gaining acceptance. It denoted men who sought homosocial interaction in place of heterosocial domesticity, mainly because they did not have homes of their own. Such men were shut out of power in the province because men without property could not vote or hold office in Maryland. In the confines of the Tuesday Club, however, they were full and equal members. Bachelorhood was also a line of demarcation that segregated two mutually exclusive groups that viewed each other with a degree of animosity or at least distrust. Although single and married men both joined the Tuesday Club, bachelors clearly had the upper hand and they used their power to ridicule and marginalize the married minority. On the other hand, neither in Hamilton's letters nor in his history of the club did the term bachelor appear without dubious connotations. Hamilton cursed his bachelor status as a personal failing, while the term bachelor in the context of the club denoted men with inadequacies. The single members not only lacked wives and households of their own, they lacked the poise and manners then gaining acceptance as the mark of civility. That the single members were content not only to spit on the floor but to ridicule their married counterparts for their gentility suggests they possessed a rough-hewn immaturity contrary to the responsibilities of manhood. Yet being in the majority, the club's single members were not answerable for these shortcomings.

With bachelors in control, the Tuesday Club embraced a decidedly heterosocial agenda. At an early sederunt, the members voted "that Immediatly after Supper, the Ladies Shall be toasted, before any other toasts or healths go round." Only on rare and extraordinary occasions were women actually allowed in club meetings, yet the club often sought to create forums for the single members to socialize with eligible women. In December 1745 the members voted "there shall be a ball at the Stadt house for the entertainment of the Ladies, at the common expence of the Club" and an elaborate New Year's Eve celebration ensued.[81] Not all venues for entertaining the opposite sex took on such formality. One evening during the club's first year, honorary member Edward Lloyd burst in on the proceedings and announced "that he had Just now left the Company of the Ladies, those dear angelical creatures!" Lloyd's speech consequently "put the members of the Club into an amorous vein" and each one "resolved to have his Girl that very night." The meeting was immediately adjourned and four of the members without wives ventured in search of female companionship. Hamilton later remembered that for at least one bachelor, the evening's adventures included full exercise of sexual license. Edward

Dorsey "resolved not to return, till he had blunted the edge of his desires, with some Gentle and kind Nymph." However, "the Sight of a Superannuated female" quickly changed his mind.[82]

Bachelor members also affected the club's sense of humor. Cuckolded husbands were a popular topic of ridicule in the club's songs and poetry. In late 1745 John Gordon sang a version of "The Drunken Wife of Gallowa," a humorous tale in which a husband complained about his wife's immoderate appetite for alcohol. Some time later bachelor member and Chief Musician William Thornton sang "Orpheus and Euridice" in which Pluto punished Orpheus for visiting hell by giving him back his wife.[83] The single members also led the Tuesday Club into a battle of wits with another club that Hamilton dubbed "the Baltimore Bards." An extracurricular event in the life of the club, the battle did not occur during an official meeting but "at a place called Batchellor's Hall." Imbibing "a large Tankard of Lamb's wool, a reviving liquor," five Tuesday Club members who styled themselves "the Junto of Bards and Critics at Batchellors hall," penned a verse that ridiculed the writings of the Baltimore Bards. The Junto accused the Bards of depending upon an errant muse much like a cuckolded husband who took orders from an unfaithful wife. In the last verse, the Junto declared: "As Cuckolds are hooted and scoff'd in the Streets / For their horns, so may you for your wit." The harshest insult that the bachelor wits could muster was to call their opponents husbands.[84]

The bachelor revelries and humor that characterized the Tuesday Club's first year dissipated in the second. The attention of the meetings began to focus on the internal activities while those unmarried members who sought "to dance with the Girls in the State house" went alone.[85] Contemporaneous with the decline of bachelor revelries was a shift in the club's membership. When the club celebrated its third anniversary in May 1748, several of the single members had either married or left the group, while among new initiates, husbands outnumbered bachelors two to one. By the end of 1748 married men had gained the majority. Among the ranks of husbands were several eloquent members who set the tone for the club as a whole, including *Maryland Gazette* printer and club poet Jonas Green. Most important, Dr. Alexander Hamilton made the switch from bachelor to husband in May 1747 when he married Margaret Dulany, the daughter of Maryland's attorney general. In so doing, Hamilton finally found the economic and political success he had long craved as his new father-in-law provided him with a thousand acres of land and secured for him a seat in the Maryland House of Delegates. It was no coincidence that Hamilton's new brother-in-law, Walter Dulany, had been a longstanding member of the Tuesday Club since 1745 and that two of Walter's brothers were frequent visitors. As Wilson Somerville has noted, the history of the club ultimately follows a romance plot, since from the start Hamilton organized the club to aid his pursuit of a wife. Having found one, Hamilton's interests and the club's activities generally turned away from the bachelor pursuits of the early days.[86]

Tuesday Club members generally welcomed Hamilton's marriage. On the sederunt following Hamilton's wedding, John Gordon delivered a speech "which contained a congratulation of the Secretary upon the late event of his marriage, which Speech the Club approved of."[87] However, some bachelor attendees feared that Hamilton's marriage might put a damper on the group's frivolities. "I am now obliged to hold out alone against that numerous and powerful host we... formerly provoked by our united hostilities,—for poor Hamilton is gone!—not dead, but married," wrote occasional visitor Stephen Bordley to a former member. Two days after the wedding Bordley noted an immediate change, writing that Hamilton "is already become what you would from your knowledge of the lady now suppose him to be, a very grave sober fellow."[88]

Bordley's fears were well founded. As husbands began to outnumber single men, the tone of the meetings changed, especially its humor. In 1751 Jonas Green entertained the club with his first singing of "Robin and Jeck," a favorite that he performed at least four more times. The song was a dialogue between two brothers, one of whom feared marriage. Although the song poked fun at the woman Robin was to marry, it also made light of Robin's ineptitude at winning the woman's affections and how she returned his advances with physical abuse.[89] In presenting such a piece, Green turned the tables on the bachelors, and made them the butt of the club's humor. A change was also noticeable in Green's introduction of the conundrum to the meetings. First appearing in February 1750, a conundrum was a riddle that had to be answered with a pun. Over the course of sixteen sederunts, Green and Hamilton each presented conundrums of varying degrees of vulgarity. Women were a popular topic, such as: "Why is a wanton Lass in bed like a book Just printed?" "Because She is in Sheets and want Stitching." Whorish women were not the only females in the conundrums; there were also pregnant women, widows, and housewives. The most revealing conundrums were those that dealt with marriage. In place of accusations of cuckoldry in the club's early humor, the conundrums approached marriage with a gentle teasing, such as: "Why are dried apples like married people?" Because "they are pair'd—pared."[90]

The shift in sensibilities also affected informal gatherings outside the club. In January 1749 the club met at Batchellor's Hall and engaged in more ribald humor than was typically permitted. Specifically, John Bullen took advantage of the fact that the president was absent to "drink the first toast, expressly contrary to the Rules of the Club." Yet Bullen's usurpation of presidential prerogative did not offend the membership nearly so much as his "nauseous fowl mouthd and beastly toast." In his toast, Bullen repeated a running gag that the letters "S.S.C." on coins minted by the South Seas Company did not stand for the name of the company, but for "to the pious memory of Sally Salisbury's C—t." Outraged by Bullen's actions, Dr. Hamilton introduced two indictments against Bullen at a club meeting a month later.[91] The denunciation of Bullen proved an indirect hit on the club's single members. Bullen was a founding member of the group and had been one of the husbands marginalized when bachelors were in the majority. By giving a vulgar toast at Batchellor's Hall, he essentially associated single men with a misogyny that went beyond the limits of acceptable Tuesday Club innuendo. Bullen thus used a subversive tactic to retaliate against the bachelor minority, not by attacking the single members openly but by impugning the reputation of bachelors generally. After the incident, the club never again convened at Batchellor's Hall.

The practice of assailing bachelorhood ultimately caused some single members to internalize a sense of shame about their marital status. In August 1749 recent initiate John Beale Bordley was selected to host a meeting. A single man who lived under another man's roof, Bordley had to use the residence of another member to perform his duties as steward. When President Cole did not attend that night, Bordley feared he had offended him and immediately resigned. In a reversal of the accommodations made for bachelors in the club's first year, when Bordley confessed that it was of "great inconvenience and trowble" to host a meeting because he was "a Single man, who had no house of his own," the club "willingly, and Chearfully" accepted his resignation. About a year later, John Beale Bordley was readmitted to the Tuesday Club. Soon after, he married and joined the group's majority. Once he was in the majority, Bordley delighted in attacking the members of the bachelor minority. In January 1755, when the club was debating how to help fund the British forces in their renewed hostilities with the French, a member moved that the club should raise a sum. Bordley seconded the motion "and observed, that it would be very proper for that purpose, to lay a tax upon the batchellors of the Club."[92]

The examples of John Bullen and John Beale Bordley suggest just how precarious claims of bachelorhood could be in the eighteenth century. A young man might assert his equality with other men, but there was no guarantee that anyone would honor his claims. Sometimes property ownership was irrelevant, while at other times it could define the limits of manhood. Indeed, Bordley's humiliation suggests a parallel to the contradictions contemporaneously being faced by single freemen in Pennsylvania. Such men had civic responsibilities because they were men, yet they were denied the manly act of suffrage because they lacked property. A bachelor's manhood was tenuous, constantly dependent on the shifting opinions of those around him. Similarly, reputation and sexual license could prove both an avenue to the full exercise of manhood and be an impediment to it. While Edward Dorsey's pursuit of a "Gentle and kind Nymph" put him on equal footing with married men, bachelors could also be demonized with a rumor of rakish reputation that delegitimized their sexuality. In this, the Tuesday Club was a microcosm for late colonial society: little was stable or assured for the bachelor who asserted manhood.

Although many of the bachelors associated with the Tuesday Club were young and propertyless, not all were. A few months after the Tuesday Club met for the last time in February 1756, the Maryland assembly approved a levy on unmarried men over age twenty-five who were worth at least £100. That year four members and four regular visitors appeared on the bachelor tax rolls for St. Anne's Parish, Annapolis.[93] Most of these wealthy older men appeared in the records of the club without incident. For instance, the marital status of Stephen Bordley received no comment from the club's secretary and chief historian. Yet when Bordley joined the club, he was fifty years old and a confirmed bachelor. His correspondence indicates that he had pursued an Annapolis socialite in his twenties, but that the woman spurned his advances, leaving him brokenhearted. "I am likewise single," he informed his relatives as he approached his thirtieth birthday, "and at present continue so as well as to avoid the noise and uneasiness of a large family & the continual labor and fatigue of providing fortunes to be left them at my death."[94] Much like John Pickering of Massachusetts, Bordley took up housekeeping with an unmarried sister and served as a paternal figure to several younger siblings including his half-brother John Beale Bordley. He also pursued an active career in the law and politics, serving in the Maryland House of Delegates, on the Governor's Council, and as attorney general. In his mock history, Hamilton depicted Bordley as churlish and pedantic, but fully heterosexual. He recounted a night in 1751 when Bordley, serving as steward, deemed the evening's attendance so inadequate that he invited several ladies of the town to join the members for the evening.[95]

When it came to the club's president, however, bachelorhood was indicative of deep character flaws. Of the actual man, little is known. Born in England, Charles Cole migrated to Annapolis in the 1710s and became a successful merchant. He served one term on the vestry at St. Anne's Church, and in 1740 stood as godfather at the baptism of one of Jonas Green's daughters. Having no relations in Annapolis, Cole lived with a servant, a young man named John Charlotte who occasionally appeared at Tuesday Club meetings. When he joined the club in 1745, Cole was already in his seventies and it is likely that he was named president because of his advanced age. Over the course of the club's eleven-year history, Cole was frequently absent because he suffered from a debilitating case of gout. He died a little more than a year after the group disbanded, although even in death his marital status defined him. As his 1757 obituary noted, "This Gentleman was a Batchelor, who, it is said, Repented of nothing in his latter Years, so much as that he had not Married while he was Young."[96] Charles Cole was not all that different from Stephen Bordley as a single master whose social standing and advanced age commanded the respect of his community regardless of his marital status.

In the records of the Tuesday Club, however, Cole's marital status was neither inconsequential nor benign. In the club's history, Hamilton dubbed the president Nasifer Jole because of his long nose and recorded a detailed character sketch of Cole that centered on his bachelorhood. In his youth Cole had served in the military and the bachelor lifestyle that this experience forced upon him had stuck with him through the years. Cole's "education on board a man of war" had taught him culinary skills and now he cooked extremely elaborate dishes. Likewise, he reveled in the decorative arts, knowing how to set a table "in the neatest and most showy order," arrange flowers, hang pictures, and cut valences for beds. "Jole had a very elegant taste, in most things relative to household affairs, which he acquired by long and painful experience and application, during the many years that he spent in a Single life." At the same time, because Cole had lived without a wife for so long, his personal hygiene had become obnoxious. He preferred cats to people, but his feline companions produced "a perfume of a Ranker nature" that infested Cole's clothes, forcing him to wear strong perfumes and carry flowers wherever he went. This practice attracted attention at church where because of the constant flower twirling "some suspected, as Mr Jole was a Batchellor, that he Intended thus to lay traps, or attract the Regards of the fair Sex." Yet as any single woman quickly discovered, Charles Cole had absolutely no interest in women.[97]

Above all, it was Cole's lack of interest in the opposite sex that Hamilton and the other members found the most disturbing. In many ways, Cole was a stock figure who would have been at home in the *Spectator*. In his youth he chose money over love and thus he became a miserly misanthrope. "He has lived always Single, having been, as it is thought, ever averse to the Clog of a wife, and a man of too much prudence and Solitary ever to keep a concubine," Hamilton wrote, adding "the world is not likely to be much entertained with his amours, and the transactions of his life would therefore afford very unfit materials for a novel." He kept women at arm's length and "tho' he never showed any affection to the Sex," he was no woman hater. Instead, "he would deign to converse with them as rational Creatures," essentially treating attractive women the same as he treated anyone else. "He would behave himself with the same Indifferent coldness, as one man does to another, or as one maid would accost another." Effete, obtuse, and passionless, Cole possessed an identity that was in direct opposition to late colonial manhood.[98]

Dr. Hamilton was not the only member of the Tuesday Club befuddled by Charles Cole's bachelorhood. During the bachelors' majority, Cole took no part in the activities of socializing with ladies. When Edward Lloyd inspired the members to seek female companionship, Cole went home by himself. When the club hosted a ball for the ladies on New Year's Eve in 1745, Hamilton noted that "nothing being wanting to compleat all, but the presence of his honor the president, who, by his absenting that night, showed that he was not altogether pleased, with this piece of Gallantry." It was disappointing that Cole did not attend these events, but not a cause of great concern. Through the eyes of young bachelors, a loveless old bachelor seemed odd, but not problematic. As control of the club shifted to husbands, however, Cole's bachelorhood began to arouse suspicions. Some of the married initiates perceived the president to be a rake and teased him for his licentiousness. At the club's fourth anniversary, Jonas Green presented "An Anniversary Ode on the Tuesday Club" in which he paid tribute to Cole, proclaiming:

> The Ladies too, with whom the President,
> Their Constant friend and hero first begins,
> In bumpers round the Spacious room are sent,
> But no one yet his Sole affection wins.

Later that year the club received a petition from "the Single Ladies of Annapolis," which cited how Cole's toasts to specific women had led to their marriages. Claiming that Cole was an effective intercessor, the petitioners asked the president to drink to all ladies in the town so that the "benevolent Condescention of your honor, will have a tendency to multiply the Inhabitants of this City, as well as to better our present forlorn Situation." The request aped the mock petitions then appearing in newspapers and was likely intended to inspire laughter. Stoic as ever, "the honorable the president was pleased to declare that he would grant this petition as far as lay in his power." The issue was never raised again.[99]

In time the gentle joshing waned. As Cole failed to live up to the code of heterosexual desire that bachelorhood required, the members grew increasingly hostile toward him. His lack of a wife was not evidence of rakishness but of an absence of masculinity. When Jonas Green presented an acrostic to Cole in February 1750, Hamilton sarcastically noted that such a piece of poetry "is most commonly exercised upon the fair Sex, and I cannot say, I ever knew it applied to any male Subject but one, which was upon the honorable Mr President Jole." A year later Hamilton told the story of a mythical female pontiff whose sex was not revealed until she gave birth. A member responded by demanding a search of President Cole's body, claiming "since his Lordship has given no proofs of his virility as yet, I move, that it may be Scrutinized, whether we have not now, a Pope Joan, in the Chair."[100] Ultimately, the growing disdain for Cole resulted in a "great Clubical Civil war." In December 1751, during a moment of sophomoric humor, one member hid the "Great Seal" of the club on another member's person. Attempting to identify the culprit, the club's chancellor demanded that all members be searched. When Cole refused this invasion of his person, the chancellor flew into a rage and cursed him, which in turn caused Cole to resign the presidency. For the next few months the club continued without a leader until the members grew bored with their experiment in republicanism and invited Cole back.[101]

The treatment of Charles Cole ultimately raises the question of Cole's sexuality as well as perceptions of homosexuality more generally. Cole's depiction conforms closely to the effeminate bachelors that Thomas Foster has observed in eighteenth-century Massachusetts. Like such men, Cole was tagged with the attributes of idle boys and women: luxury, physical and moral weakness, and a complete lack of interest in procreative sex.[102] Such deviance had no place in late colonial bachelorhood. Much as the New England diarists found, late colonial masculinity was exclusively heterosexual and the bachelor ethos demanded that unmarried men be constantly pursuing eligible ladies. John Pickering had escaped the type of rumor and intrigue that haunted Cole, although Pickering did not place himself in the midst of young men obsessed with marital status. Clubs in the eighteenth century jealously guarded their reputation and they cast out any member who threatened the integrity of the group. Rumors of sexual deviance threatened all members and thus Cole's bachelorhood had to be problematized and defined as unusual within the group. In his study of early-twentieth-century New York, George Chauncey has argued that a vibrant bachelor subculture helped to give rise to a homosexual community. With single men filling boardinghouses, cafeterias, and saloons, there were plenty of places for men who loved men to congregate.[103] In contrast, colonial bachelor spaces such as the Tuesday Club, Batchellors Hall, and Harvard commencements seem to have allowed little opportunity for single men to engage in homosexual activity.

Nevertheless, the volatile nature of late colonial bachelorhood could also be forgiving of unusual single men. Throughout his presidency Charles Cole lived with a servant named John Charlotte. Although the relationship between the two may have been strictly platonic, Cole repeatedly brought Charlotte to the meetings, leading the other members to vote him "Clerk of the Kitchen." Both Hamilton's history and evidence in the *Maryland Gazette* indicates that the relationship between the two men was particularly contentious, with Charlotte constantly running away and even physically assaulting Cole on one occasion. Tellingly, Hamilton depicted the battles between the president and his servant as a marital dispute. When the club charged Charlotte with "several violent assaults" on Cole, Hamilton noted how the servant had "taken the Command of the house and the keys into his own hands, and Called his honor by several Scurrilous and oprobrious names, as dam'd old Son of a Bitch & the like."[104] From Hamilton's vantage, Charlotte was acting the role of a shrewish wife and Cole the cuckolded husband. The men's connection ended in 1757 with Cole's death, and five years later Charlotte married. He also garnered material success that may have come from Cole's generosity. Although he was a servant in 1756, Charlotte was rated as possessing over one hundred pounds when St. Anne's vestry drew up the schedules for the first bachelor tax.[105] If Hamilton's insinuations and Charlotte's wealth are indicative of an intimate connection, it is curious that the club made no attempt to disrupt the relationship. It was simply part of who Cole was.

Whether Charles Cole was homosexual or simply chaste, the members ultimately forgave his lack of heterosexuality. Despite all the hostility directed at Cole's inappropriate bachelorhood, the members were not prepared to exclude him from the club forever. In many ways, the club's civil war of 1751 was the culmination of building hostility directed at Cole. Having ousted their leader, the members could have elected a new president in his absence. But to do so would have given sanction to faction and eliminated the affable ethos of the group. In the end, the gelastic law endured. Members did not convene on Tuesday nights to debate actual politics or to seek economic advantage; they were there to devote themselves to things light and inconsequential. Nothing was more comical or more disdainful of history than a "great Clubical Civil war." Indeed, Hamilton's history of the club was itself a belles lettres that mocked serious history by suggesting there was some great relevance to this small provincial club. In this, we might interpret Hamilton's preoccupation with Cole's sexuality as utterly meaningless. Indeed, this may be the greatest lesson to take from the story of Charles Cole. Unlike later eras in American history when homosexuality and gender inversion were deemed dangerous and subversive, the Tuesday Club found Cole's lack of masculinity to be humorous and the subject of great sport. The members might wonder about their unusual president, but he was a member of the group and they had no intention of permanently excluding him.

Unfortunately, we can do no more than speculate as to the experience of men who preferred same-sex affections in the late colonial era. At a time when even men who fully embraced the emerging heterosexual ethos were reluctant to disclose the details of their intimate lives in their diaries, reliable accounts of men who engaged in sexual relations with other men are practically nonexistent. Nonetheless, the Tuesday Club provides some clues as to the evolving dimensions of single sexuality in the eighteenth century. First, no longer did the absence of a wife necessarily mean the absence of sexuality. Through innuendo, humor, and carousing, bachelors freely acknowledged their lack of chastity. Second, while bachelorhood was a fully heterosexual identity, there was room within it for men who did not fit the mold. Stephen Bordley's sexuality drew no suspicions and Cole's perceived deviance proved moot. As bachelorhood increased in complexity, it became increasingly diverse and allowed more opportunities for men to claim sexualities that were previously dismissed as simply deviant. Third, from the perspective of the early twenty-first century, when sexuality is an instrumental aspect of identity, sexuality in the eighteenth century proved far less important than gender, race, social status, and age. Charles Cole's uncertain sexuality was trumped by his reputation, wealth, and the fact that he was twice as old as many of the members. Cole was at no greater risk for losing his cultural legitimacy because he was unmarried than was William Stoughton. However, being surrounded by men obsessed with marital status made being a bachelor in the eighteenth century far different than being single in the seventeenth.

In the end, it is probably wise that we not take Hamilton's depiction of Cole at face value. Like the descriptions of bachelors contemporaneously being published in American newspapers and pamphlets, Hamilton's depiction of Cole played off a late colonial stereotype. However, it would be a mistake to assume that such a characterization necessarily affected how people thought about men who were single or reflected how bachelors saw themselves. As with any stereotype, there was a dissonance between the cultural representation and the lived experience. We might thus question the assumptions made by Thomas Foster and Mark Kann that the virulent antibachelor tracts of the eighteenth century actually mirrored the experience of the single life. Despite aspersions cast on him by the club, Cole was not excluded from the group even though his bachelorhood was linked to deviant sexuality. Nor was the experience as one dimensional as these historians suggest. In the eleven-year history of one club, bachelorhood was both praised and condemned, a source of pride and a source of shame. The literary denigration of the bachelor may have gone unquestioned throughout much of the era, but the experience of being a bachelor was never stable. It varied from colony to colony, from year to year, and from person to person. Moreover, the place of unmarried men in the Tuesday Club suggests how bachelorhood could be both monumentally important and completely meaningless. Being single when the club was commanded by husbands and vice versa ultimately did not result in expulsions, because from beginning to end the club welcomed both married and single men. There was a great deal of distance between William Stoughton and Charles Cole and yet none at all. Early Americans, even the most profamily among them, neither negated the right of people not to marry nor sought to keep them out of power even when their singleness was associated with effeminacy, luxury, and deviant sexuality.[106]

The experience of being a bachelor underwent significant change over the course of the eighteenth century. Although it is difficult to speak definitively about all single men, those for whom sources exist suggest that unmarried men had a great deal more independence at midcentury than those of earlier generations. Bachelors adopted increasingly heterosexual personae, acquired more material comforts, and spent more time with other single men. Behind all of these changes lay an emergent ethos of independence and masculine autonomy. Being unmarried did not only mean an uncomfortable liminality or even a time of uncertain dependence, it had also become a time to benefit from and even celebrate the temporary absence of familial responsibilities. Like single men in the sixteenth and seventeenth centuries, late colonial singles tended to be young men without property who lived with their fathers or masters. Yet their ranks also included older and propertied men, some of whom joined their younger and poorer brethren for the first time. The difference between master and dependent was blurring among men as property ownership was becoming less important to manhood. In short, bachelorhood had become an identity that stood apart from age, property, or rank.

Yet as the distance between master and dependent shrank, the space between single men and all other dependents widened. In a move that paralleled the laws and literature of the eighteenth century, bachelors in the late colonial era stood on their own as men. Bachelor diaries embodied a freedom that spinster diaries only hoped to achieve. Similarly, the act of paying taxes entitled rural farmhands to political responsibilities that no servants, slaves, or women had access to. Yet perhaps it was in men's clubs where single men most forcefully asserted their separation from those others who lacked land and economic independence. In the confines of a selective club, members could set the rules and allow all attendees to participate equally regardless of property or age. Moreover, by focusing on conflicts between single and married members, the clubs actually placed both groups on the same plane. Even at its most contentiously antibachelor, the Tuesday Club never suggested that men who did not have property and wives were the servants of those who did. With the emergence of a bachelor identity, then, it became less plausible to set masters apart from the populace as a whole and bestow upon them alone the full privileges of political participation. Membership in the category of men was expanding and citizenship in the republic would have to be adjusted accordingly.

5

"The Bachelor Is the Only Free Man"

THE SINGLE MAN AND THE AMERICAN REVOLUTION

In 1767 Stephen Salisbury set up shop in Worcester, Massachusetts. Only twenty-one years old, Salisbury had ventured west from Boston to establish a branch of the family's dry goods business in the New England interior. Salisbury was the junior partner to his older brother and so he kept in constant contact with his relatives on matters both professional and personal. The family worried about young Stephen being on his own although Salisbury tried to ease their worries. "I like my Situation Very well," he wrote, "the Old Lady [that?] I abode with, her way of Living, & having Busyness enough to do I am pretty well Contented wth a Country Life." Yet Salisbury's family, especially his aging mother, worried that his independence might lead to idleness and immorality. When rumors of Salisbury's activities reached Boston, his brother chided that "mother has heard you left the Old Lady's & now board at Bigelow's which makes her very uneasy, she has also heard you lay a bed very late Sabbath day mornings & Absent yourself from meeting in the morning, it gives her a great deal of uneasiness." In essence, Salisbury's family feared that he was living the life of a bachelor. The letter so alarmed Salisbury that he responded with a detailed reply refuting the charges against him one by one. Of particular annoyance to Salisbury was that people were gossiping about his personal life. As he asked his brother, what "right has anybody to know our Business or my private affairs"?[1]

Stephen Salisbury's experience was not unusual for a single man living on the eve of the American Revolution. In essence, he was caught between the expectation that he be a dutiful son and the desire to be his own man. Salisbury's mother and brother constantly goaded him to put his familial responsibilities before personal desires. As had been the case for centuries, they worried about a young man left to his own devices. There were even shadows of the old New England family government law in the family's insistence that Salisbury board with a trustworthy mistress. Changes over the last hundred years had only compounded these fears. Once families only worried about the young, now there was a whole culture of bachelorhood to contend with. The well-read Salisburys were no doubt familiar with the tales of bachelor excesses, of selfish rakes and defiant drunkards. From personal experience, they probably knew that young men who moved away from home were becoming more sexually free. If Salisbury became one of those bachelors who lived outside of household government and slept in on Sunday mornings instead of going to church—no doubt because he was up late the previous night drinking and whoring—then the family business would suffer. The family needed its youngest member to ignore the temptations of the single life and make dry goods his singular focus.

From his perspective, Stephen Salisbury knew his familial obligations but he had hardly gone west to be a glorified servant. As his reply to his brother suggests, he bristled at the idea that his personal life was open to scrutiny. Salisbury also knew the laws and the literature of the era and had learned from his peers that leaving home meant independence. In Boston he was an economic dependent, but in Worcester he was a business owner. Less than two months after he was accused of sleeping in on the Sabbath, he hired an apprentice, a young man named William Maccarty. Salisbury no doubt appreciated that Maccarty's indenture stated "he shall not commit Fornication, nor contract Matrimony within the said Term" and that it forbid him to play "at Cards, Dice or any other unlawful Game...nor haunt Alehouses, Taverns, or Playhouses."[2] All of these were things that a bachelor such as Salisbury was free to engage in. Moreover, Salisbury's standing in the community gave him a voice in politics, especially as the tensions between Great Britain and the American colonies heated up. As a merchant, he was particularly interested in the nonimportation agreements. As he and his brother discussed how to balance patriotism and business, Salisbury gained a sense of how powerful his bachelorhood made him. When sales declined in early 1770, Stephen heard his married brother lament "I having a family stand in more need of the Proffitts of Goods we might import than your self."[3] In some sense, Salisbury found virtue in the vices that worried his family, but it was more than that. Bachelorhood had entitled him to a masculine independence not available to a child or a husband and he refused to let anyone impinge on it.

By 1750 bachelorhood stood as a distinct identity and unique cultural category. It had emerged slowly over the previous hundred years, a combination of changes in the laws, literature, and lives of early Americans. Since the middle of the seventeenth century colonial lawmakers had gone from protecting the social order by placing young and propertyless singles with masters to assigning greater civic obligations to bachelors regardless of age or wealth. A fascination with the bachelor had become a central theme in periodicals and political tracts, inspiring a discourse on the character of the single man and his place in society. The experience of bachelorhood had also changed from an undefined and uncomfortable transitional period to a purposely liminal time of self-definition and autonomy. These political, literary, and social changes produced bachelorhood: a masculine independence distinct from other cultural identities that encompassed more and more unmarried men.

The emergence of the bachelor had not been without controversy. Although young single men such as Stephen Salisbury seized the new freedom that bachelorhood promised, the view of bachelorhood from America writ large was more complex. Some, like Salisbury's brother and mother, saw bachelorhood as a celebration of vices long associated with masterless men. Such people had a favorable view of laws designed to encourage marriage and they welcomed the writings of Benjamin Franklin that portrayed the single life as pathetic, immature, and effeminate. Some unmarried men even internalized these negative views or, as was the case with Salisbury, were at least sensitive to the fact that others disapproved of bachelorhood. Other Americans had a more neutral opinion about single men and their new celebrity. Although they did not approve of rakish men fathering bastards, they were also uncomfortable using the law to punish an individual's choice not to marry, and they favored more lighthearted depictions of the unmarried. Such people tended to look the other way as young men became more independent and sexually adventurous.

The great American conversation about the meaning of bachelorhood reached its apex in the era of the American Revolution. With the Stamp Act crisis of 1765, Americans began a twenty-five-year-long process of breaking with Great Britain, fighting a war of independence, and creating a new nation. The politics of bachelorhood appeared at every stage of this process, from anti-British propaganda to the logistics of raising troops and funding the war. While the bachelor's critics conflated being single with Anglophilia, his defenders asked whether the obligations placed on the single man to fight the war and pay for it did not entitle him to commensurate rights. The debate also raged after the war had been won and the United States had been created. As a new government came into being and a new national identity began to awaken, lawmakers, authors, and single men themselves asked whether the bachelor had a role in American society. The stunning denunciations of the single man surpassed the spleen vented over the previous century, yet they were matched time and again by vigorous defenses of the single life.

In many ways, the debate over bachelorhood continues to this day. We continue to wonder about the morality of the bachelor and to use unflattering portrayals of single men to assail political enemies. Yet the parameters of this conversation were permanently changed by the American Revolution. Most important, the assignation of unique legal obligations to unmarried men ended with the creation of the United States. By 1800 most states either had or were on the verge of adopting a notion of citizenship that demanded equal rights and obligations for all citizens. Because bachelors had been separated out from other dependents, such as women, children, and servants, and then classified along with husbands, they were men.

All men were created equal and thus all men—at least all white men—stood equal before the law. This legal framework made it difficult to continue special bachelor taxes and separate punishments for crimes. As a result, the bachelor laws all but disappeared within a few years of the creation of the United States. Any legal distinctions that persist today are but a shell of the treatment bachelors received in the seventeenth and eighteenth centuries.

The end of the bachelor laws hastened a greater acceptance of the single man in literature and in everyday life. Marked as the married man's equal, the bachelor began to defend himself in print. He asserted that bachelorhood was a positive good and other writers picked up on this theme. In the new American literature that followed in the early nineteenth century, the bachelor became an endearing figure of independence and strength instead of persona to be feared. Individual bachelors also became much more self-aware and less subservient than their fathers had been. Sexual experimentation became increasingly commonplace while the young and propertyless bachelor embraced a mobility and sense of individuality that made him practically indistinguishable for all other men. A discussion of laws to punish the unmarried continued to appear in the press, but by 1800 they stood slim chance of being implemented. Authors embraced such tracts only in jest, and single men knew that such laws would never be approved.

In this chapter I examine the apex of the discourse on the single life and its resolution. First, I explore the role of single men in the lead up to and the fighting of the American War of Independence. Bachelors were a popular target for propagandists who wanted to contrast effete and luxurious Britons with manly and virtuous Americans. Yet while they denigrated bachelors in the press, Revolutionary leaders viewed single men—especially the young and propertyless—quite favorably when it came to finding soldiers to fight the war and taxpayers to fund it. Second, I explore the changing status of the bachelor by briefly looking at source materials explored in detail in the previous three chapters: laws, literature, and lives. The Pennsylvania bachelor tax serves as an excellent example to demonstrate how the obligations of unmarried men became the basis for their commensurate rights. Having collected a special poll tax on young and propertyless single men for longer than any other colony, Pennsylvania became the first state to enfranchise men who paid taxes regardless of marital status. The actions of Pennsylvania are placed in a larger context of citizenship and compared to the legal changes in the other twelve states. I then turn to literature, especially the flurry of periodicals that appeared in the 1780s and 1790s, to demonstrate the vibrancy of discussions of bachelors and how single men were beginning to defend themselves as well as to find advocates. Finally, I explore several diaries kept by single men in the last quarter of the eighteenth century. These intimate portraits reveal that bachelors had gained a degree of independence that single men a generation earlier had only dreamed of. They also indicate that the single life was becoming an increasingly diverse experience.

Single Soldiers and Virtuous Americans

When Benjamin Franklin wrote *Observations Concerning the Increase of Mankind* in 1751, he could not foresee the eventual division between Great Britain and the American colonies. A proud subject of King George II, Franklin saw North America as an integral part of the powerful British Empire. Yet with the conclusion of the Seven Years' War in 1763 and Parliament's attempt to pay for its war debt by taxing the colonists, relations between Britain and America worsened. For ten years, the colonists and the king's ministers sought a way to balance the financial needs of the kingdom with the constitutional rights of Americans. Following the skirmishes at Lexington and Concord in April 1775, the hope of reconciliation waned and Americans prepared for a long and bloody war of independence. As they did so, they resurrected the ideas Franklin had floated in his *Observations*. Patriots claimed that the broad expanse of land made it easy for American men to marry young and father many children. In contrast, they claimed that Britons were deprived of such opportunities and thus persisted in the luxurious bachelorhood of urban life or became professional soldiers. Such ideas became popular as Americans began to define the differences between themselves and Britons in preparation for independence. As numerous historians have noted, ideas of manhood were key to the rhetoric of the American Revolution.[4] While Americans defined themselves in terms of normative and productive manhood, they stressed the abnormality and vice of their English brethren. Given the criticisms of bachelorhood that had emerged over the previous hundred years, it was not surprising that ardent patriots connected Anglophilia to the single state.

In the earliest days of the imperial crisis, a dichotomy of luxurious Britons and virtuous Americans coincided with ideas about marital status. Massachusetts lawyer and future U.S. president John Adams observed such a connection in the person of Anthony Wibird, his pastor in Braintree, Massachusetts. Adams saw Wibird as an old bachelor, noting how he "had his mind stuffed with Remarks and stories of human Virtues, and Vices, Wisdom and folly." As a result, Wibird's "soul is lost, in a dronish effeminacy," wrote Adams, noting that the parson's lack of manly fortitude left him with "not Resolution enough to court a Woman." With the Stamp Act crisis, Adams's distaste for Wibird's missing masculinity took on political overtones. At a service in December 1765 Wibird took for his text "I have nourished and brought up Children and they have rebelled against me," which caused Adams to note "I began to fear a Tory Sermon on the Times from the Text." Although Wibird "confined himself to the Spirituals," to Adams it made sense to expect a defense of the corrupt policies of the Crown from a man with a "want of Resolution to Court."[5]

While John Adams saw unmarried Anglophiles as effeminate, other patriots impugned the aggressive tendencies of British regular soldiers. Redcoats had long suffered a torrent of criticism for being "the scum of the earth," and this reputation only worsened after British troops began arriving in Boston in October 1768.[6]

Patriot leader Samuel Adams complained that soldiers "make laws for themselves, and enforce them by the power of the sword!" He reasoned that the ruthlessness and immorality of British troops was due to the fact that they lacked homes of their own and thus were absent the restraints of domesticity. As a remedy, the Boston brewer urged officers to remember "that when quartered in cities they are to consider themselves and their soldiers in no other light than as a family in the community,— numerous, indeed, but like all other families and individuals, under the direction of the civil magistrate."[7] Boston merchant John Hancock likewise dismissed the British regular as "an unfeeling ruffian" whose "idleness and luxury...were used to betray our youth of one sex into extravagance and effeminacy, and of the other into infamy and ruin." He also cited the regulars' lack of homes, although for him this meant the troops had no allegiance and could be bought by tyrants. He charged that standing armies were "composed of persons who have rendered themselves unfit to live in civil society; who have no property in any country; men who have given up their own liberties, and envy those who enjoy liberty." Hancock preferred American militiaman to British "parricides" because the former fought "for their houses, their lands, for their wives, their children, they fight pro aris et focis [in defense of our altars and our fires]."[8]

As the standing army controversy morphed into war, the connection between bachelorhood and British regulars became explicit. In a 1777 letter printed in the *New-Jersey Gazette*, Trenton resident Monsieur de Lisle expounded on the advantages of employing militiamen to fight the British. "You must know that nine-tenths of the freemen of America are farmers," he opined, "who are either married men, or connected in such a manner with families, that they will not forego the sweets of domestic life for three, four, or seven years service." As such, married men could not become drones of despots but remained faithful defenders of liberty and property. He contrasted this with British regulars, observing "the armies of Europe are composed chiefly of single men, and this is the reason why they are now employed so successfully in supporting the thrones of tyrants." By relying on married militiamen, Monsieur de Lisle predicted that Americans would ultimately be successful in defeating the British.[9]

Faulted for being effete spectators and heartless warriors, bachelors thus were associated with the British because they were weak and dependent. Whether he was a pawn of womanly luxuries or a drone to tyrants, the single man did not have the independence and virtue necessary to be trusted with the liberties and privileges of republican citizenship. To some degree, the rhetoric of marital status in the Revolution found a willing reception in the minds of the war's participants. When Selleck Silliman of Fairfield, Connecticut, left his family to join the Continental Army in 1777, he explained to his wife Mary that "the Safety of our Country requires this Sacrifice of our domestick Delights" and noted that the Americans were fighting for "the Defence of the Dear Wives of Bosoms, and our Dear Children."[10] Likewise, when young Israel Keith marched off with the Continentals in late 1776 his lack of a family caused him to question why he was fighting. "What am I engaged in this war for?" he asked a friend. "Is it to defend my wife and children or farm? No—I have neither."[11] By the same token, a number of men without familial attachments identified with the Tories and fled the country when the war turned against the British. Apparently none of the four loyalists known to have left Charles County, Maryland, in the fall of 1775 had wives or children.[12] In Massachusetts five bachelor assemblymen chose to side with the British and resettled in England or Canada, and two South Carolina bachelor assemblymen fled as Tories.[13] Most of these men left considerable property behind and they went to great lengths to be compensated for it after the war ended.[14] Such men may have found it easier to leave because they did not have wives and children in their care.

Of course, it was not always this simple. Although a number of bachelor assemblymen fled the country, many more swore allegiance to the United States and assumed leadership roles in the Revolution. Five bachelor assemblymen in Massachusetts took positions in the interim state government as did two in South Carolina. In Maryland forty-three out of the 252 (17%) men elected to the nine conventions that governed the state between 1774 and 1776 were unmarried. After new state governments were formed, bachelors continued to play integral roles in the assemblies. Sixty-three bachelors served in the South Carolina assembly between 1775 and 1790, as did fifty-nine single men in Maryland in the 1780s. Four governors who served from 1775 to 1789 never married, and three single men signed the Declaration of Independence. Seven bachelors placed their names on the U.S. Constitution including the document's "father," James Madison.[15]

Such contradictions existed not only at the level of Revolutionary leadership. In spite of the deep suspicion some held of single men as unpatriotic, others resurrected Samuel Davies's lessons from the Seven Years' War that military service could provide an alternative path for the unmarried to achieve manhood. A letter printed in Massachusetts's *Essex Gazette* in 1773 proclaimed that war would cause men to put country above personal allegiances: "That bubble honour will excite many a good husband to take their last adieu of loving wives; many a fond father must bid farewell to their tender prattlers, and many an honest bachelor must leave endearing friends and obliging mistresses."[16] Similarly, the popular Revolutionary song "Collinet and Phebe" told the story of a maiden who broke off her romance with a young shepherd to send him off to war:

> Our country's call, arouses all,
> Who dare be brave and free!
> My love alone shall crown the youth alone,
> Who saves himself and me.[17]

In the end, martial duty made no exception for marital status.

In terms of who actually fought the American War of Independence, single men were an important contingent if not the central constituency. More than 80 percent of native-born soldiers recruited in Maryland were younger than twenty-five, the average age at first marriage in the state. Not surprisingly, few of the recruits were heads of a household in the 1783 tax lists.[18] The Maryland recruits were typical of American soldiers in general. One study of the Continental Army reveals that the bulk of the fighting fell to African Americans, recent non-English immigrants, and "free white men on the move," despite rhetoric to the contrary. Although incomplete records make it difficult to determine the marital status of soldiers, most recruits possessed the attributes that coincided with bachelorhood: they were young men of meager backgrounds who lacked artisans' skills and significant landholdings. For young men, military service could be an adventurous alternative to the toil of farm life as well as a means of acquiring money with which to purchase property and later marry. Older recruits also tended toward bachelorhood, as most were foreign-born, vagrant, and lacking land or other property.[19]

The military service laws authorized by the states during the Revolution reflected these contradictions. Lawmakers idealized the notion of married men fighting in defense of property and families while recognizing that it was necessary to compel the service of men who had neither. They thus offered aid to the families of men who joined the military while inducing the service of propertyless single men. This approach followed the logic of colonial laws. The governments knew that if they drafted a married man and he was killed in a war, then the state would be responsible for his dependents. Single men, especially those without property, offered no such complications.

Since the seventeenth century, English and American lawmakers had made provisions for the widows and orphans of soldiers killed in the line of duty. Typically, such support was limited to families who could not provide for themselves and thus were a means for governments to cope with the burden of impoverished widows and orphans.[20] With the start of the Revolution, lawmakers in the northern states looked beyond supporting only the families of the deceased and attempted to address the needs of the families of soldiers then engaged in battle. In 1778 Massachusetts granted towns the right to collect taxes "for the supply of the families of the soldiers, in such manner as shall appear most elig[a][i]ble and convenient to the majority of voters present at any town meeting."[21] The right to raise such funds was part of a town's duties to support the poor and thus, like pension laws, the provisioning of soldiers' families was a way of aiding the indigent.

Support for poor families of soldiers was also a concern for Pennsylvania lawmakers. Because pacifist Quakers controlled the province from its founding until the Seven Years' War, Pennsylvania was bereft of a military establishment when the Revolution began. Desperate to raise as many troops as quickly as possible, the Pennsylvania assembly approved a series of laws that placed exorbitant fines on men who chose not to take up arms. In September 1776 Pennsylvania fined nonassociators—men who refused take up arms in defense of the country—twenty shillings in poll taxes and four shillings for every pound worth of property they owned per month. The proceeds of the fines were directed toward "the relief and support of the families of poor associators of this state while out in the service" as

Figure 6. "The Patriotic Lover," by Joseph H. Seymour. During the American Revolution patriot leaders idealized American men fighting in defense of their homes and families. However, laws and recruitment techniques tended to favor the enlistment of young and propertyless bachelors.

Source: The Gentlemen and Ladies Town and Country Magazine (Boston), December 1789, frontispiece, facing page 563. Reprinted with the permission of the American Antiquarian Society.

well as to help maimed soldiers and the widows and orphans of soldiers killed in battle. The logic of family influenced not only support of the impoverished soldiers' families, it also affected who was counted as a nonassociator. Although men over fifty were not expected to join the army, the 1776 law ordered such men to contribute to the defense of the commonwealth unless they "have one or more sons who are associators, unmarried and residing with his or their father."[22]

Although Pennsylvania laws hinted at an inclination toward bachelor soldiers, laws in the Chesapeake made the preference for single recruits explicit. Virginia, which had tried unsuccessfully to draft single men during the Seven Years' War, was once again unable to raise enough troops when the American War of Independence began. Remembering the success of offering handsome bounties to induce recruits, the assembly voted lucrative payments to men who joined a Virginia regiment or the Continental Army. In late 1775 Virginia offered bounties of twenty shillings, but when men proved unwilling to enlist, the government began offering recruits tax abatements for life, one hundred acres of land, and a signing bonus of up to $750. These also proved unsuccessful, and so in October 1777 the assembly authorized a law whereby "a number of men shall be draughted from the single men of the militia of the several counties, and the city of Williamsburg, whether officers or privates, above eighteen years of age, who have no child."[23] Unfortunately, the Revolutionary draft proved no more successful than the one twenty years earlier had. The men called to serve responded with riots or by failing to attend musters. When only 1,242 of the 3,500 troops recruited from Virginia reached Gen. George Washington in the spring of 1778, the situation must have seemed all too familiar to the commander in chief. Perhaps because of the apathetic response from bachelors, the assembly deleted all mention of marital status from the Virginia draft law in May 1779.[24]

Despite Virginia's troubles, its neighbor to the north followed its lead. In March 1778 the Maryland assembly approved a law ordering "that every idle person, who is able bodied, and has no fixed habitation nor family, nor any visible method of getting a livelihood, ought to go as a soldier."[25] Yet this draft of single men in Maryland was no more popular than it had been in Virginia. In a 1781 accounting of enlistments in Prince George's County, Lt. Josias Beall complained to the governor about his trouble drafting recruits out of the militia. "It was a fixt rule with me," he wrote, "where a maryed and single man was drafted in the same Class to send the single man." However, the single men incessantly questioned the legality of conscription and Beall ended up drafting husbands. "I indeavourd to put an Equal Number of single men in Each Class, yet in many of the class None but Marryed men were Drafted." Beall advised that if the state wanted to raise more single recruits, it would have to raise taxes and induce volunteers with large bounties.[26] In the end, Maryland was forced to change tactics. In 1780 the assembly replaced the singles draft with public support for families of men recruited for the Continental Army.[27]

Both northern and southern states also looked to propertyless single men to do their patriotic duty when it came to funding the military. Pennsylvania, which had been collecting taxes on propertyless single men since 1696, continued to collect the poll taxes at the county level throughout the war. As had been the case during Queen Anne's War and the Seven Years' War, the assembly authorized poll taxes on bachelors who paid no property taxes to support the commonwealth during the Revolution. Reflecting the dire need for soldiers, the statewide poll taxes granted exemptions to those single men who enlisted in the military. Unlike the previous wars, the Revolution caused other states to imitate Pennsylvania's actions. Before the Treaty of Paris officially ended the American War of Independence in 1783, New Jersey, Maryland, and North Carolina had all approved nearly identical poll taxes on their propertyless bachelors. Unlike the taxes of the colonial era, those of the Revolutionary era were largely uniform. Although Americans were only beginning to learn to work together as a country, their bachelor taxes were already beginning to reflect a spirit of national cooperation.

Most of the Revolutionary-era bachelor taxes were short-lived, driven more by expediency than by a desire to rewrite the entire tax code in the middle of a war. Yet the widespread application of the bachelor tax forced a discussion that Americans had ignored for nearly a century: Were single men to receive any political benefit in exchange for their taxes? Some states, such as Pennsylvania, finally agreed that they should and granted propertyless single men the right to vote. However, this sentiment was far from universal. Nevertheless, events in Pennsylvania initiated a national dialogue that ultimately reversed the unique legal treatment of bachelors throughout the country. By 1800 most of the single laws passed during the colonial period had either ceased to exist or had been mitigated by the extension of commensurate rights.

Taxation and Representation in Pennsylvania

The American Revolution opened up a debate on the very notion of citizenship. In the colonial era a person's rights and responsibilities had varied widely among locales and were determined by a series of factors such as church membership, race, and sex. Among white men, political participation was often graduated. At one end of the spectrum were slaves and foreign-born people who had not been naturalized, both of whom enjoyed no political rights and were prevented from even owning property. A little higher up were native-born dependents—such as children and servants—who had no rights in the present but who could acquire property and enjoy political benefits once they attained the age of majority or gained their freedom. Higher still were free native-born adult white men, although even among this group there were gradations. All white men were obliged to follow gainful employment, pay their taxes, and serve in the militia. Those who owned property had the added obligations of paying property taxes and caring for dependents, although they also enjoyed rights denied to propertyless men such as suffrage and the opportunity to hold office. Wealthy property owners also could avoid basic obligations by hiring others to work for them and paying for substitutes to serve in the military.

There were exceptions to this formulation. Although typically women were excluded from the polity, a single woman who owned property faced taxation on her wealth and could occasionally claim limited rights such as speaking in a New England town meeting when the selectmen considered an issue that affected her land. African Americans likewise were excluded, although free black men could claim rights including suffrage depending on where they lived. Among free native-born adult white men, the formulation reflected an evolution of a man's political identity from dependent son to youthful propertyless worker to mature property owner. As we have seen, a man's marital status could complicate his position in the polity. Propertyless single men faced greater obligations to the state than married laborers in the form of special poll taxes, military service, and harsher punishments for crimes. Propertied single men were not without increased responsibilities such as higher taxes.

With the American Revolution, this formulation of political participation was thrown open to debate. As the states wrote their first constitutions in 1776–77, they radically revised the rights and responsibilities required of members of the polity. Massachusetts and Vermont chipped away at slavery while New Jersey opened suffrage to all propertied persons regardless of race or gender. Among free native-born adult white men, there was an examination of the usefulness of the distinction between the propertied and the propertyless. As James Kettner has argued, the Revolution ushered in the notion that republican citizenship ought to be without gradations. One either had the full rights of a citizen or none at all. To accomplish this, some Americans, including Thomas Jefferson, floated the idea that citizens should be guaranteed fifty acres of land. Ultimately, a more moderate solution was agreed upon. In addition to owning property, a person earned the right to vote and hold elective office by paying taxes or serving in the military. As revolutionary as this was, it was predicated on the conservative notion that the propertyless had to make a public demonstration of their commitment to the state before they could gain the same rights as property owners. Propertyless single men were among the first Americans to benefit from this formulation of citizenship. For over a century they had been required by law to pay taxes and serve in the military, and now they received the right to vote in exchange for these very obligations.[28]

The demands of single men for equal treatment began in Pennsylvania. It was fitting that change should come first to Pennsylvania because the province had had more singles laws than any other American colony. The process of change began less than a week after American minutemen faced British regulars at Lexington and Concord. As news of the shot heard 'round the world made its way to Pennsylvania, men took it upon themselves to prepare for war. On April 25, 1775, nearly eight thousand men met in Philadelphia and began drilling. Because Pennsylvania lacked a militia, these men formed a voluntary association for the defense of the colony and took the title associators. Within a week of forming military companies, the associators elected officers. The militia elections were probably the first time many of these men had ever voted. The elective franchise had been off limits to most associators because they did not meet the property requirements for suffrage or because they were not native born.[29]

Despite being politically inexperienced, the associators had no problem finding a collective voice and they soon began to make formal entreaties to the Pennsylvania assembly. They demanded pay for men training for service, provisions for families of soldiers killed in battle, and laws to make militia service compulsory. When the assembly gave a lukewarm response to these demands, the associators devised their own representative body. In September 1775 the General Committee of Associators met for the first time. Made up of three representatives from each militia company, the group was soon renamed the Committee of Privates to reflect the fact that it represented the interests of common soldiers. By January 1776 the Committee of Privates had begun to lobby the assembly for greater voting rights. Among their petitions was one they submitted to the assembly in March 1776 that demanded "that all Persons, (not being Mercenaries) who expose their Lives in Defence of a Country, should be admitted to the Enjoyment of all the Rights and Privileges of a Citizen of that Country which they have defended and protected."[30] Throughout the spring of 1776 calls increased for "a fair and equal representation" for soldiers denied the vote due to foreign birth or lack of property.[31]

At the same moment that the associators began to demand the vote, a corollary movement arose in Pennsylvania that insisted on suffrage for all taxpayers. Similar to the soldiers' request, appeals for taxpayer suffrage emanated from the logic that all who helped fund the government ought to have a say in choosing its leaders. Since 1700 suffrage in Pennsylvania had been limited to men who owned fifty acres or fifty pounds of moveable property, and for seventy-five years men who labored for a living paid taxes without the vote. The imperial crisis drew new attention to the link between taxation and representation and soon Pennsylvanians began to see the connection between taxes and the vote in their own lives. In 1770 an opponent of slavery asked whether "those brought amongst us against their Wills" should be "taxed without their Consent, and without being represented?"[32] As independence approached, advocates for enfranchising associators and taxpayers coalesced into one movement. In April 1776 a letter in the *Pennsylvania Packet* asserted "every man who pays his shot and bears his lot [pays taxes] is naturally and constitutionally an Elector," adding "more especially I will affirm, that every citizen who has armed and associated to defend the Commonwealth is, and should be an Elector."[33]

In May 1776 the Second Continental Congress advised the colonies to draw up their own constitutions. The call for a state constitution was met with enthusiasm in Pennsylvania, especially among those men who had taken up arms. With an opportunity to discard the privileges of rank and wealth guaranteed by the provincial charter, a state constitution would allow the implementation of real democratic reforms including an expanded electorate. Yet even before the delegates met to write the constitution, change had taken place. In a conference convened to decide how to choose representatives to the constitutional convention, German American soldiers from Philadelphia presented a petition "praying that all associators who are taxables may be entitled to vote." The conference agreed and admitted every volunteer soldier to vote for delegates to the constitutional convention, with three caveats. In addition to being an associator, an elector with little or no property had to be twenty-one years of age, had to have lived in Pennsylvania for at least one year, and had to have "contributed at any time before the passing of this resolve to the payment of either provincial or county taxes, or shall have been rated or assessed towards the same."[34]

When the delegates to the Pennsylvania constitutional convention met in Philadelphia in June, the dramatic reforms continued. The result was the Pennsylvania Constitution of 1776, which one historian has aptly termed "the most radically democratic frame of government that the world had ever seen."[35] Indeed, the new constitution was a significant departure from anything attempted in colonial America. It placed unchecked power in the hands of the assembly, reduced the executive to an advisory council, and required annual elections. In terms of suffrage, the Pennsylvania Constitution of 1776 swept away property requirements altogether. The document stated emphatically: "Every freeman of the full age of twenty-one years, having resided in this State for the space of one whole year next before the day of the election for representatives, and paid public taxes during that time, shall enjoy the right of an elector."[36] By this act, Pennsylvania became the first state to abandon property requirements for suffrage.

The impact of the Pennsylvania Constitution of 1776 was impressive and immediate. Overnight, the electorate rose from half of the adult white male population to 75 percent in rural areas and 90 percent in Philadelphia.[37] Although the new requirements brought in a variety of new voters, propertyless single men were the key beneficiaries of the new suffrage provisions. Tax records from the 1770s and 1780s indicate that propertyless single men made up 13 percent of taxpayers and about 3 percent of the total population.[38] To be sure, taxed bachelors were not the only newly enfranchised group. Married men who owned less than fifty acres or fifty pounds' worth of property also gained the right to vote for the first time. So too did the rapidly expanding group of married laborers known as inmates. However, tax records reveal that propertyless unmarried men made up a larger percentage of the newly enfranchised than any of these other groups. More than 40 percent of new voters in Chester County were taxed bachelors. In neighboring Lancaster County, about 25 percent of those who received the vote under the new constitution were propertyless single men, although they did outnumber inmates. More important, bachelors paid far higher taxes than married men who owned little or no property. In these two counties, taxes on inmates varied from one shilling to four shillings six pence while single men paid fifteen shillings—three to fifteen times as much. Because the taxes were disproportionately higher on bachelors than on other groups, their enfranchisement was necessarily costlier than it was for any other newly enfranchised citizens.[39]

In addition to suffrage, there were other benefits granted to propertyless single men by the Pennsylvania Constitution of 1776. The constitution used, with very few exceptions, the term *freemen* to describe the citizenry. This meant that not only did all taxpayers have the right to vote but all taxpayers also gained the right to stand for elective office. The constitution also stated "taxes can never be burthens" and insisted that any new tax be proved "of more service to the community than the money would be, if not collected."[40] Although this restraint on taxation gave no specifics, it insinuated that taxes were not to become exorbitant. Especially since suffrage was tied to the payment of taxes, such a provision meant that the assembly could not disfranchise its citizens by raising taxes so high that men, such as propertyless bachelors, could not pay them. The constitution also limited the punishment of debtors, stating that a person "shall not be continued in prison, after delivering up, bona fide, all his estate, real and personal, for the use of his creditors."[41] Although this provision did not explicitly mention bachelors, it effectively voided the 1731 law that forbade single men from being freed from debtors' prison even after they had forfeited all their possessions. As a result, the Pennsylvania Constitution of 1776 extinguished the last American law that tied debtor relief to marital status.

Curiously, the enfranchisement of propertyless single men in Pennsylvania elicited little comment from contemporaries. None of the four men believed to be the principal authors of the constitution left any evidence of their thoughts on bachelors. Certainly none of them were single or propertyless when the convention met in the summer of 1776.[42] Nor did opponents of the document necessarily fault it for extending suffrage to the unmarried. Benjamin Rush, a Philadelphia physician and delegate to the Second Continental Congress, denounced the constitution's unicameral legislature as "mob government," claiming that "a single legislature is big with tyranny."[43] Fellow congressional delegate and later U.S. Supreme Court Justice James Wilson agreed, and both he and Rush immediately began campaigning for a new constitution. Yet neither man found fault with taxpayer suffrage. It was almost as if no one noticed that thousands of propertyless single men were suddenly enfranchised for the first time.

Yet the absence of commentary on bachelors speaks volumes. In the eyes of Pennsylvanians, marriage and property ownership were inconsequential qualifications for citizenship and thus irrelevant to determining suffrage. To be sure, both proponents and critics of the constitution continued to view bachelorhood with distrust. On the eve of the Revolution, constitutional convention president Benjamin Franklin advised a young man that "becoming a useful Citizen" required escaping "the unnatural State of Celibacy."[44] Likewise, Benjamin Rush opined in 1788 that "matrimony in all ranks of people lessens the temptation to vice and furnishes fresh motives to just conduct." Three years later the good doctor advised a bachelor to wed for his own health "for your disorder is seldom met with in married life."[45] Yet such sentiments had no place in constitutional law. Instead, citizenship was to be determined solely by a man's contributions to the state and his independence. James Wilson captured this sentiment when he wrote:

> A momentous question now occurs—who shall be entitled to suffrage? This dar-ling privilege of freemen should certainly be extended as far as considerations of safety and order will possibly admit. The correct theory and the true principles of liberty require, that every citizen, whose circumstances do not render him neces-sarily dependent on the will of another, should possess a vote in electing those, by whose conduct his property, his reputation, his liberty, and his life, may be all most materially affected.[46]

In other words, every freeman who paid his own taxes or served in the military should have the right to vote.

Although this radical idea made sense to Pennsylvanians, some outside observers called into question the legitimacy of extending suffrage to every freeman. They could not believe that a man who lived under another man's roof had the requisite independence to render an impartial decision in selecting his leaders. The French philosopher Gabriel Bonnot de Mably, also known as Abbé de Mably, warned that "the inevitable result" of the state's liberal franchise "would be that a crowd of young men who did not enjoy the rights of citizenship in the other states would flock to Pennsylvania." Because such men did not "have the simple morals which democracy demands," they would soon sell their votes to the highest bidder.[47] Likewise, John Adams saw no difference between live-in single workers and other household dependents, warning that "the same reasoning which will induce you to admit all men who have no property, to vote, with those who have, for those laws which affect the person, will prove that you ought to admit women and children."[48] But such criticisms did not fully comprehend the lessons learned through a century of bachelor laws. Propertyless single men had been recognized as independent and autonomous by Pennsylvania since the assembly first made them responsible for their own taxes. In so doing, lawmakers had already drawn a distinction between single men and other economic dependents such as women and children. The ex-tension of the vote to taxed bachelors moved a process begun in the era of William Penn toward completion. Propertyless bachelors who paid their taxes were full citi-zens; it mattered not that they resided in other men's houses.

The process moved *toward* completion, but the framers still harbored some reser-vations about the abilities of the single and propertyless. The Pennsylvania Consti-tution of 1776 was replete with warnings aimed at keeping the newly enfranchised independent. The attached Declaration of Rights announced that "government is, or ought to be, instituted for the common benefit, protection and security of the people, nation or community," adding, lest anyone act purely out of self-interest, "and not for the particular emolument or advantage of any single man, family or set of men who are a part only of that community." The framers also prohibited the creation of patronage positions, claiming that sinecures would make property-less men economic and political dependents. "As every freeman, to preserve his independence (if without a sufficient estate), ought to have some profession, call-ing, trade or farm, whereby he may honestly subsist," the constitution proclaimed, "there can be no necessity for, nor use in establishing offices of profit, the usual effects of which are dependence and servility, unbecoming freemen."[49]

Single men were not only kept independent by the moralizing tone of the con-stitution. The Pennsylvania assembly presented propertyless bachelors plenty of opportunities to prove their allegiance to the commonwealth. As the American War of Independence dragged on, the government became increasingly dependent on single men's military service, loyalty, and taxes. As we have seen, Pennsylvania ex-pected young bachelors to come to its defense and fined men who did not serve. Moreover, suffrage was an effective way of ensuring the allegiance of young bache-lors because men had to swear to defend the government before they were allowed to cast a vote.[50] Yet perhaps more than anything else, single men continued to dem-onstrate their devotion to the commonwealth by the politically independent act of paying taxes. In 1779 the assembly reaffirmed the county rates tax scheme with its special poll tax on propertyless single men. It also approved four new singles taxes for the support of the commonwealth and four more to help fund the Continental Army and to pay down the debts of the United States.[51] Had it voted to end the bachelor tax, the legislature would have closed the primary method by which most propertyless bachelors proved their citizenship and thus would have prevented thousands of men from becoming voters. That the assembly repeatedly renewed the levy is the best evidence that Pennsylvanians realized they were enfranchising thou-sands of propertyless single men and did so willingly.[52]

The Pennsylvania Constitution of 1776 also moved toward completing the pro-cess of completely excluding women from the political sphere. As Ruth Bloch and Linda Kerber have argued, the creation of citizenship in the Revolution was predi-cated on a notion that all *men* were created equal. Women were specifically excluded.[53] The enfranchisement of taxed bachelors certainly supported this concept because it placed propertyless men ahead of propertied women. Indeed, nearly a hundred and fifty single women owned property in Chester County on the eve of the Revolution and they were all assessed for taxes. These women were not enfranchised despite the fact that they were independent and helped support the government. In this, single men quietly joined the universal manhood that became the basis of the Revolution-ary innovation of universal manhood suffrage. Historians have also noted the differ-ences drawn between groups of men at the Revolution, with Mark Kann detailing the way bachelors were vilified as disorderly men to help justify the citizenship of other men.[54] The Pennsylvania Constitution of 1776 and subsequent actions of the state assembly both conformed to and contradicted this formulation as they treated all taxpaying men the same but continued to require single men to pay special poll taxes. Issues of race eventually entered the equation as well, although before 1838 Pennsylvania made no mention of race in its requirements for suffrage.[55]

The End of the Bachelor Laws

Pennsylvania pointed the direction for the country as a whole. Although property ownership had been the sine qua non of suffrage before the Revolution, by 1792 half of the states in the union had granted the vote for at least some statewide offices to men who paid taxes.[56] In this transition, taxes on propertyless single men occupied an important middle ground in the emergence of universal suffrage in the United States, often constituting the vanguard of the newly enfranchised. The same arguments used to justify their inclusion in the polity—that they paid taxes and served in the military—would later be used by women and African Americans to justify their own inclusion. Yet in the era of the American Revolution, such a development was far from assured. Although Pennsylvania did so, not all the states that rated propertyless bachelors drew the same connection between taxation and representation.

The radical spirit of the Pennsylvania Constitution of 1776 trickled throughout the nation as a whole and helped convince North Carolina to adopt one of the more radical constitutions of the era. Warnings from John Adams ensured that the state did not go as far as Pennsylvania and thus North Carolina's 1776 constitution included a bicameral legislature and a governor. When it came to voting, however, the framers proved progressive. Before the Revolution North Carolina had restricted voting at the provincial level to freeholders, but the new constitution guaranteed suffrage for representatives to the House of Commons—the lower house of the General Assembly—to all white men who "have paid public taxes." To be sure, taxed men who owned no property were barred from voting for senators and were prohibited from holding office.[57]

This provision had no immediate impact on the rights of propertyless single men. Like other colonies south of the Chesapeake, North Carolina had avoided adopting bachelor laws—including taxes—during the colonial era. However, as North Carolina set about restructuring its tax policy in 1776, it sought a means to reduce the burden of the provincial poll tax. The legislature adopted ad valorem property rates although this left a considerable hole in the budget and meant that a number of men paid no taxes. To restore equity to the tax system, the assembly passed a revenue law in 1778 by which "every freeman in this State of the age of twenty-one years and upwards" who did not have at least "four hundred pounds in taxable property shall pay annually, in lieu of assessment on property, a poll tax equal to the tax for that year on four hundred pounds taxable property." The law then added "that married men who are not possessed of one hundred pounds of taxable property shall pay annually in lieu of assessment a poll tax equal to the tax for that year on one hundred pounds."[58] The North Carolina poll tax thus ensured that all men paid some taxes, although a landless bachelor owed four times more than a landless married man. As in Pennsylvania, the logic behind the North Carolina bachelor tax was not punitive but was an effort to spread the tax burden to those men without families to support. Yet the addition of the new tax effectively enfranchised propertyless single men. In a curious reversal of what happened in Pennsylvania, in North Carolina rights preceded obligations.

The North Carolina bachelor tax persisted for the duration of the American War of Independence and served to enfranchise thousands of single men.[59] Records from several counties suggest that propertyless bachelors constituted between 6 and 13 percent of the total number of taxables.[60] The levy proved to be a product of wartime exigencies, and in 1784 the assembly repealed the bachelor tax. However, the principle of taxpayer suffrage was not easily shaken. In place of the poll tax on propertyless single men, the assembly placed a poll tax "equal to the public tax on three hundred acres of land" on all freemen who possessed less than three hundred acres.[61] In so doing, North Carolina extinguished all divisions of marital status for suffrage and made qualifications for citizenship the same for all white men.

Propertyless bachelors in Maryland proved far less fortunate than those in Pennsylvania and North Carolina. In 1781, with the war entering a costly seventh year, the Maryland assembly ordered "that all able bodied male inhabitants of this state, being free persons, who have no families, and are above the age of twenty-one years and under fifty, and whose property is not valued above thirty pounds" pay "the sum of seven shillings and six-pence current money, in lieu of all other taxes."[62] Tax rolls reveal that about the same percentage of men were affected by the tax as in Pennsylvania and North Carolina although they received little for their troubles.[63] The Maryland Constitution of 1776 limited suffrage to men who held a fifty-acre freehold or "property in this state above the value of thirty pounds current money," and despite the protests of militiamen, the state refused to enfranchise the propertyless. Perhaps most humiliating for Maryland's taxed bachelors was the constitution's declaration "that the levying the taxes by poll is grievous and oppressive, and ought to be abolished" and that every "person in the state ought to contribute his proportion of public taxes for the support of government according to his actual worth in real or personal property within this state." Fortunately for Maryland's single men, the state's bachelor tax ended soon after the war, and in 1801 the assembly granted all free white men the right to vote.[64]

Nowhere was the treatment of single men more egregious than in New Jersey. Like Maryland, New Jersey approved a bachelor tax on propertyless single men in 1778 even though its 1776 constitution limited the franchise to "all Inhabitants of this Colony of full Age, who are worth Fifty Pounds proclamation Money clear Estate in the same."[65] The New Jersey bachelor tax persisted well into the nineteenth century but propertyless men were not enfranchised until 1844.[66] Worse, the state seemed almost cavalier in its disregard for the rights of bachelor taxpayers. Writing on New Jersey tax policies in a 1792 letter to the *Pennsylvania Gazette*, A Freeman noted that "because poll taxes are so generally disapproved . . . they are always made very light in this country, and are seldom or never imposed on any but single men."[67] More curious is the fact that when the New Jersey framers wrote the state's 1776 constitution, they decided to include the gender-neutral term *inhabitant* instead of the more specific *freeman*. Such wording enfranchised single women who possessed fifty pounds' worth of property. It is unclear whether the inclusion of women was inadvertent or not, but some women did vote before the state limited the electorate to propertied white men in 1807.[68] As a result, New Jersey was the one place in Revolutionary America where propertied single women fared better than propertyless single men.

No other states adopted bachelor taxes before the end of the eighteenth century, although the idea was widely considered. In New England, a region that had not adopted a new bachelor law since the seventeenth century, the idea of taxing bachelors suddenly gained adherents. In Massachusetts an assemblyman recommended a levy on single men because he "set down old bachelors and dogs upon a par."[69] The unique legal treatment of the unmarried had been unheard of in the Carolinas and Georgia before the Revolution, but according to German visitor Johann Schoepf, South Carolina lawmakers considered a bachelor tax in the early 1780s.[70] Virginia almost did New Jersey one better. In 1777 the assembly contemplated a plan whereby "every bachelor above the age of 30 years, worth an estate real or personal, of 500l. [pounds] currency, shall enter into the service of the United States, procure an able bodied man" in his stead, or pay an annual sum of money to the commonwealth "so long as he remains a bachelor."[71] The previous year conventioneers considered a state constitution drawn up by George Mason that limited suffrage "to every housekeeper who hath resided for one year last past in the county, and hath been the father of three children in this country."[72] Both ideas were rejected, but had they been approved Virginia would have been the first state to tax propertied bachelors *and* exclude them from voting.

Bachelor taxes even followed Americans across the Appalachians as they settled the Midwest. In 1795 the governor of the Northwest Territory, Arthur St. Clair, approved a law for raising county rates, the title of which stated it was "adopted from the Pennsylvanian code." In keeping with the tax's origins, the territory collected fifty cents on "those single men whose estates shall not be rated at one hundred dollars."[73] When the Northwest Territory was later subdivided, its revenue policies followed the new polities and the bachelor tax found new life in the territories of Indiana, Louisiana, Missouri, and Arkansas. Nearly a half century after American independence, the state of Missouri was collecting one dollar on "every unmarried free white male" between twenty-one and fifty years of age.[74] By this point, however, Pennsylvania's innovations in taxpayer suffrage already seemed dated as most western states guaranteed all white men the right to vote regardless of service to the community.

The extension of the bachelor tax to the Midwest masked a larger trend away from the principle of legally distinguishing between married and single men. Over the last quarter of the eighteenth century, as the states wrote and rewrote their constitutions, lawmakers reviewed the statutes of the colonial era and weeded out those that had fallen into disuse and no longer seemed relevant. As part of this process, they abolished nearly all of the colonial bachelor laws.

Since the seventeenth century militia laws in Massachusetts and New Hampshire had differentiated between men based on their marital status. The statutes ordered the towns to provide arms for impoverished married men but allowed magistrates to put out to service single men who were unable to afford a gun. When the two states rewrote their militia laws in 1776, they ordered that all unarmed men to have weapons provided for them at public expense.[75] The same two states also voided the last remnants of the family government laws not long after the war ended. In 1789 and 1791 Massachusetts and New Hampshire, respectively, removed the provision of the poor law that forbade single people under twenty-one from living at their own hand.[76] In both the militia and poor laws the distinction between married and single had been important because the unmarried were to be reduced to unfree labor. The Revolution largely ended the practice of indenturing native-born whites, making differences of marital status moot.

The Revolution also put an end to the separate treatment of single and married people for sex crimes. Although lawmakers in New England and Pennsylvania had removed the singles provisions in fornication, adultery, and rape laws by the second decade of the eighteenth century, it was not until 1790 that Pennsylvania began to prosecute all bigamists equally regardless of marital status.[77] Of course, it remained technically illegal for unmarried people to engage in sexual intercourse, but the prosecution of fornication had been on the decline for most of the eighteenth century. Research by Richard Godbeer, Cornelia Hughes Dayton, and Clare Lyons shows that penalties for fornication became lighter over time, suggesting that this once grave crime had largely ceased to concern the courts.[78]

By 1800 nearly all of the bachelor laws approved in the colonial era had disappeared. The one exception, appropriately, was Pennsylvania. In a 1718 supplement to its poor law, Pennsylvania ordered that for the purposes of determining which locality was responsible for a destitute person's support, "where any unmarried person, not having child or children, is or shall be lawfully hired as a servant . . . during the space of one whole year, such service shall be adjudged and deemed a good settlement therein."[79] Although the poor law was revised considerably over the next two centuries, this provision was not removed until 1913.[80] Even more impressive was the resiliency of the Pennsylvania bachelor tax. Pennsylvania continued to collect the tax after the Revolution much as it had since 1696. When the assembly rewrote the law on county rates in 1799, it modified but did not abolish the poll tax on propertyless single men. Instead, it changed the tax from one on all bachelors without property to "all single freemen, above the age of twenty-one years; who shall not follow any occupation or calling" and who did not pay property taxes.[81] The tax remained on the books in this form until 1919.[82] Interestingly, this revision belied the 1776 constitution's protection against dependent men gaining the vote as it turned men without work into taxpayers, and by extension, voters.

As the bachelor laws faded from existence, there was little or no discussion of how the changes advantaged single men. It may have been that most lawmakers, like Benjamin Franklin and Benjamin Rush, held a low opinion of bachelors and had no interest in advantaging the single state. Yet as was true of the Pennsylvania Constitution of 1776, the new formulation of citizenship made issues of marital status irrelevant. During the Revolution, the performance of civic obligations became the justification for admission into full membership in the polity and to concomitant rights. Before long this principle gave way to the belief that all white men were equal, meaning that all efforts to distinguish between their rights and responsibilities, whether on the basis of property or anything else, were simply un-American. After having been distinguished from other nonmasters by colonial laws, bachelors in the early republic could rest assured that the law no longer saw them as anything but free white men.

Immutable Miscreants and Citizen Bachelors

Bachelors were a popular topic in American literature during the last quarter of the eighteenth century. They seemed to be everywhere in the press, attracting the attention of serious patriots and humorists alike. Much like their British and colonial predecessors, American writers in the Revolutionary era detailed the foibles of bachelors and addressed them with an invectiveness that was hardly new. Single men were loveless, overly choosy, lazy, sick, and weak. These were ultimately cautionary tales intended to frighten the young. Bachelors brimmed with abnormal sexuality, both as homosexual fops and heartless rakes. Such vile qualities made unmarried men unsuitable candidates for citizenship; they were, instead, pathetic creatures fit only to stand outside the polity. As historians and literary scholars have aptly noted, the Revolution was a true low point for literary depictions of the bachelor.[83]

As dominant as the attacks on bachelors in the press were, there were also important countercurrents at work. In the colonial era there had been retorts to the most severe antibachelor writings in the form of humorous petitions and paeans to the promise of reform. As the relationship between Great Britain and the colonies began to deteriorate in the 1760s, a new strain of works emerged, such as "The Bachelor's Soliloquy" and *The Pleasures of a Single Life*, that defended the solitary state. These trends escalated in the era of the American Revolution. Accordingly, as the literary attacks on the bachelor increased in the 1780s and 1790s, so too did humorous treatments of single men and optimistic appraisals of the bachelor as capable of being reformed and integrated into republican society. At the same time, the increasing popularity of seduction stories forced a reevaluation of manhood and led many to wonder whether immoral bachelors could be so easily brought to domestic felicity. Yet this notion of the bachelor as an immutable miscreant also worked to the advantage of single men because it led some authors to accept the bachelor with all his flaws as simply another segment of society. Still others defended the single state or sought to locate impediments to marriage in society rather than within the bachelors themselves. Most important, a number of single men began to speak for themselves and to defend their bachelorhood as an acceptable alternative to married life. In short, the negative portrayal of single men was only part of the story.

Lampoons of single men were perhaps strongest in the weekly and monthly magazines that were published in the 1770s and 1780s. Appearing in most northern cities and a considerable number of southern ones, these periodicals aspired to rival the *Spectator* in terms of subject matter, humor, and insight to the human condition. Not surprisingly, a number took a dim view of bachelors.[84] A number of essayists dismissed single men as unnatural miscreants, treating the bachelor as a sort of specimen to be examined in order to discover what was wrong with him. A prime example of this is "Character of a Bachelor," which was first published in 1787 in Matthew Carey's Philadelphia monthly, the *American Museum,* and later reprinted in a number of New England periodicals. "A bachelor is a sort of whimsical being, which nature never intended to create," wrote an anonymous author. "He was formed out of the odds and ends of what materials were left after the great work was over." The article went on to describe the single man as self-absorbed, passionless, unaffected by women, and doomed to spend his life in coffeehouses where "he solitarily sits down to his unsocial meal." Two years later the same magazine published "Distresses and Complaints of a Bachelor" in which a self-proclaimed single man explained, "I am engaged in no kind of business" despite "having had a liberal education." In addition to being idle, the man was "troubled with weak nerves, and suffer under a thousand evils, which the unfeeling neither comprehend nor know how to pity." In these pieces loveless bachelors deserved no sympathy.[85]

Other writers took a less clinical approach to bachelors. Instead, they depicted bachelors as either asexual or sexually deviant for humorous effect. Readers in Pennsylvania and Vermont were amused to read "The Pitiable Case of an Old Bachelor," the narrative of a thirty-eight-year-old man who was "one of the oddest and most unhappy fellows extant." The bachelor told of how he had courted a woman for six years. When the couple disagreed on a wedding date, the man took his sword and "pricked my breast to make it bleed" with "a determination to put an end to my wretched life, unless she would recede from her cruel resolution." In response, the man's paramour "requested me to walk to the fire-place, before I stabbed myself, for blood was the worst thing in the world to stain a floor, and hers was newly washed." Emasculated by his lover's indifference, the man ran home and resolved to remain an old bachelor "till the day of my death."[86] In 1784 the *Georgia Gazette* likewise took pleasure in lampooning aged celibates as useless, printing a mock tombstone that read:

> Here lies an Old Bachelor,
> Who died childless
> And worthless.
> Oh! that it had been written upon his father's grave,
> "Here lies an Old Bachelor
> Who died childless."[87]

Such attacks continued the character assassinations typical of the colonial period.

In addition to these psychological and sociological attacks, the American War of Independence also inspired a number of authors to criticize single men for not being patriotic citizens. In the opening years of the Revolution, Americans looked back to the writings of republican theorists from the English Civil War such as James Harrington who advocated financial penalties on bachelors.[88] Such ideas gained new life as Americans sought to define citizenship in the new republic. As he consulted with George Mason on the Virginia Constitution of 1776, Thomas Jefferson opined that domestic attachments might be a better gauge of a man's commitment to the polity than property ownership, writing "I can never doubt an attachment to his country in any man who has his family ... in it."[89] Although Jefferson was ultimately unwilling to exclude unmarried men from the full rights and responsibilities of citizenship, many Revolutionary-era Americans were not. Having acquired a reputation as selfish and addicted to luxury over the course of the eighteenth century, bachelors lacked the requisite self-control and self-sacrifice necessary for citizenship.

These ideas filtered into the periodical literature of the era. *The New-England Almanack* for 1780 ran a poem titled "The Old Bachelor's Lamentation" that told the story of an old man who pined for the pleasures of his youth. "Say, can you imagine a state worse than this?" the author asked, adding:

> Ye bachelor drones, who intrude on the hive,
> You most insignificant creatures alive!
> Go—quit you like men—that no more it be said,
> You are useless alive, and dispis'd when dead.

The poet then turned the bachelor's failings into a lesson for the nation's young citizens: "Hear this! and be wise, oh ye nymphs and ye swains! / Ye youths and ye virgins, Columba's first pride." Youth was not a time of mere merriment but a time to "join hearts, and join hands."[90]

In the last quarter of the eighteenth century it seemed as though everywhere one looked, one saw a negative depiction of bachelors. Dismissed as immoral and unpatriotic, single men's reputation reached a nadir, the confluence of a century of literary attacks and the fears of a new nation obsessed with virtue and stability. Yet it would be a mistake to take these portrayals at face value. As had been the case since the turn of the eighteenth century, some Revolutionary-era authors lightened their attacks on bachelors by poking fun at single women. In 1787 the *American Museum* ran a petition from a group of young women from several eastern cities. Addressed to the members of Congress then meeting in New York City, the ladies had heard that many marriages "have taken place in New-York, since your residence in that city" and demanded that "delegates in congress ought to be all bachelors, and a new election ordered in consequence of marriage, domestic duty being a good excuse from public service."[91]

Moreover, the strong current of condemnation was occasionally disrupted by appeals to single men to reform themselves. In *Hymen's Recruiting Serjeant* Mason Locke "Parson" Weems appealed "to all the singles, whether masculines or feminines, throughout the United States" and encouraged them to marry for the sake of the new country:

> May the children of Columbia hearken to thy counsel! that there be no more old Bachelors in our land, like scrubby oaks standing selfishly alone, while our maidens, like tender vines lacking support, sink to the ground; but that, united in wedlock's blest embraces, they may grow up together as the trees of the Lord, whose summits reach the skies, and their branches overspread the nations, making their country the pride and glory of the earth!

Although Weems addressed both sexes, it was mainly single men who received his attention. Terming them "citizen Bachelors," Weems spoke hopefully to young men, believing they were all "true-hearted republicans" who could be called upon to wed as a form of patriotic duty. He detailed the "pleasures of the married state" such as friendship, children, "defraying family expences," and because "it excites the noblest virtues." He also championed marriage for saving men from the horrors of bachelorhood: "the harlot's clutches," "hateful passions," and dueling. Weems then spoke at length about how matrimony served the nation. "If you love your country," he declared, "you ought to marry, to raise up soldiers to defend it." Repeating the advice of Mr. Spectator and Benjamin Franklin, Weems heralded the path of gentle persuasion to bring more men to the altar. He warned single men that the ancients had "jeered and jested, taxed and tormented" their bachelors, but ultimately Weems foresaw no such laws being necessary in the United States.[92]

A more poignant presentation of the same message appeared in a series of letters that the *Pennsylvania Magazine* printed in 1775. The author of the letters was George sanby, a sixty-five-year-old Philadelphian who signed himself the Old Bachelor. A superannuated fop, Sanby toyed with self-deprecating humor, complaining about living with servants who constantly stole from him. He anticipated death, printing his will in one issue that bequeathed to his fellow bachelors the advice that they not to imitate his lonely life. Like an updated Mr. Spectator, Sanby was uninvolved with love and this made him a passive observer of affairs of the heart. He decried cuckolds, distressed over people who married for money, and reflected on the unpleasantness of both marriage and the single life. Above all, Sanby harshly judged the unmarried and called on the state to stamp out their kind. "I'd give my vote to make it felony for any man to remain a bachelor after forty," he proclaimed. The fact that such a penalty might result in his imprisonment or the loss of his life troubled Sanby little. "I ought to be hanged for not being married before; but I ought to be hung in chains if I get married now."[93]

Yet antiquated bachelorhood was not the static mask for Sanby that it was for Addison and Steele. Instead, Sanby's Old Bachelor was a man of remarkable transformation. In his first letter Sanby explained that he had chosen a life of gaiety in his youth, "but ever since I reformed, which is now two years, I have pondered very seriously thereon" the choice not to wed. His thoughts about being single grew darker as the pleasures of the single life began to crumble around him. A regular frequenter of Batchellors Hall, Sanby claimed he felt the sting of divine retribution when the Philadelphia club was consumed in flames, noting that "Jove highly displeased at such riotous doings, / Sent TIME to reduce the whole building to ruins." In the end, Sanby's Old Bachelor brought a message of hope. In his eighth and final letter he told of how he had been out for a walk one day when two women passed him in a carriage. He began to notice the younger one when suddenly the horse upset the vehicle and the young woman fainted. Sanby rushed to her rescue and escorted her home. After this incident he became obsessed with the young woman. He debated whether or not to contact her and turned to the Bible for guidance before finally deciding to call on her. The rendezvous went well and thereafter George Sanby was a changed man. "I amused myself next day with writing this letter," he told his readers, "but, if ever you expect to hear from me again, I must insist upon it, that you do not intitle this, or any subsequent letter, The old Bachelor; but only, The Bachelor." The incident with the young woman had reinvigorated Sanby, causing him to note that "a man as hearty and ruddy as I am, cannot with any propriety, be called old." The moral of the story was that no man, not even one in his sixties, was ever too old to find love. In a postscript Sanby noted, "know that it is not impossible but I may yet marry."[94]

Although the letters of George Sanby repeated the negative depiction of bachelors in Revolutionary-era periodicals, they also worked against contemporary assaults. Readers no doubt delighted in hearing another single man bemoan his bachelorhood, but the story proved that it was never too late for a bachelor to reform. With such a message, Sanby put the final nail in the coffin of the idea of a financial penalty to encourage marriage. Borrowing a page from the *Spectator*, George Sanby proved that bachelors only needed gentle guidance, and not legal pressure, to marry. Had a law been in place such as the one Sanby proposed, whereby all bachelors would be put to death at age forty, he would have never married. It was better to encourage single men to open their hearts, whatever their age. As a result of the approach favored by Weems and Sanby, the literature of the last quarter of the eighteenth century was largely absent of the calls to tax bachelors into marriage that had been ubiquitous a century earlier. Ultimately, the idea that bachelors had to choose to reform themselves coincided with James Kettner's claim that the Revolution introduced volitional allegiance: the idea that citizens willingly joined the polity and acted out of a sense of duty.[95]

The idea of reform was a powerful one and caused some writers to take a more sympathetic look at bachelors. If all single men were potentially virtuous husbands, then society had to be changed to make marriage more palatable. Accordingly, some writers directed their criticism at American society and how its addiction to luxury was thwarting marriage. In a letter from Stephen Sorrowful, printed in the *New*

York Weekly Magazine in 1797, an old bachelor recalled that when he was a young man he had feared marrying a woman he could not afford and thus decided "to lose myself in the recesses of counting-houses, and the accumulation of money." Now that he was old and rich, he retained his distaste for courtship because he was afraid of attracting gold diggers. In essence, this story of a miserly old bachelor was an exaggeration of Malthusian worries that the expenses of marriage and a family were keeping men from the altar. Other writers blamed not the cost of marriage but the lure of luxuries then multiplying in the country. In a nation born out of fears of British corruption, the single life was not a cause of the enervating effects of luxury but a symptom of it.[96] In a "Letter on Marriage" printed in the *American Museum* in 1788, a married man looked back on his transition from the single life to marriage five years earlier and offered his observations on matrimony. "Luxury tends to discourage early marriages," he wrote, noting that this had become a particularly American problem. "It has been the misfortune of the united states, that a passion for expensive living has increased faster than the means of supporting it. . . . Although I regret that this is the prevailing taste of my countrymen, I lament still more the unhappy effects of it in multiplying the number of bachelors and maids."[97]

Not everyone believed that bachelors could be counted on to change their wicked ways. This message was particularly clear in the seduction stories that were popular in this era. In the years before independence, Americans had been avid readers of Samuel Richardson's novels *Pamela* and *Clarissa*, and in the 1790s they began writing their own seduction stories. Among the most popular such American stories were Susanna Rowson's *Charlotte Temple* and Hannah Foster's *The Coquette*. In these thinly veiled morality tales, innocent young women were abused by heartless rakes, pressured into marriage by selfish clods, or abandoned by otherwise upstanding young men because of insufficient dowries. As Rodney Hessinger and Richard Godbeer have argued, such stories taught young women to be vigilant in the protection of their virtue while offering little hope that men could be redeemed. These historians have concluded that the Revolution marked a time when Americans began to see manhood as debased and immutable. Women, be they virtuous daughters or republican mothers, were thus critical to preserving America's morality. By extension, bachelors were to be feared because they possessed manhood unleavened by a woman's love.[98] Although the perception of manhood as immutable coincided with the negative depictions of bachelors and further denigrated the single state, it also had some positive if somewhat subtle consequences for bachelors. Because all men were naturally corrupt, bachelors could be forgiven for their actions.

The idea of manhood as unchangeable led some authors simply to concede the presence of bachelors and treat them as a legitimate constituency. Dr. Benjamin Rush certainly had no love for single men as his private writings can attest. In the press, however, he was more conciliatory toward single men and recommended that bachelors not be pressured to change their ways. In his *Plan for the Establishment of Public Schools*, published in the *Pennsylvania Gazette* in 1786, Rush sought to allay fears that a taxpayer-financed system of education would be prohibitively expensive.

Although the cost would be high initially, Rush argued that by creating a society of well-educated and industrious citizens, public schools would "lessen our taxes" in the long run. Still, Rush anticipated criticisms of his plan especially from those who would not benefit directly from it. "But, shall the estates of orphans, bachelors, and persons who have no children be taxed to pay for support of schools from which they can derive no benefit?" he asked. He argued that all citizens, whether parents or not, would benefit from a better-educated populace: "The bachelor will in time save his tax for this purpose, by being able to sleep with fewer bolts and locks to his doors." Although he had no love for bachelors, Rush did not dismiss their concerns out of hand as his colonial predecessors had.[99]

Whether men could be changed ultimately became a moot point as bachelors began to defend the single state. For every George Sanby or Stephen Sorrowful who mourned his unmarried life, there was another bachelor who reveled in the fact that he had no family. "I am an advocate for celibacy," wrote "An Old Bachelor" in a letter to the *Columbian Magazine* in 1789, "having, from an early introduction on the theatre of life, taken disgust at the married state, from the intolerable noise and petulance of about a baker's dozen of squalling brats."[100] A year later the *Universal Asylum* ran a "Geographical Description of Bachelor's Island" that told how "Bachelor's Island is situated on the burning sands of the deserts of Folly, where even the savage inhabitants of the forest seldom venture to tread." However, this attack did not go unanswered. A reader provided the magazine with a "Geographical Description of the Isle of Matrimony" where "the men grow fretful and surly, and the women loquacious, and scold immoderately."[101] Beyond these isolated articles, entire magazines committed themselves to a bachelor clientele through a hearty embrace of the single life. Under bachelor Charles Brockden Brown's editorship of the *Monthly Magazine and American Review*, young men found both a safe haven from vilification. They were encouraged to use the time other men devoted to their wives to study science and math, build public improvements, and help their fellow men, all for the glory of the new nation.[102]

As bachelors took up their own defense, they inverted the arguments of Parson Weems and others that American citizenship demanded that single men marry by calling bachelors patriotic and claiming that they were imbued with republican values. In "Arguments in Favour of Celibacy," printed in the *American Universal Magazine* in 1797, an old bachelor wrote an extended treatise condemning women for being ignorant, irrational, and wasters of money. The article's author signed himself Misogamos and his virulent attacks on women approached homosexual fantasy. He yearned for "any thing to marry but women," adding "if we could make it convenient, or by any means bring it about to answer the purpose, to marry one another, perhaps the married state might be less tormenting." Although the article was probably written to inspire laughter, its language of patriotism makes it difficult to completely dismiss the work as ironic humor. "The batchelor is the only free man," Misogamos asserted, adding, "'Liberty or death!' is re-echoed by a thousand ghosts of Columbian heroes who have sealed their testimony with the richest blood of America." He then charged that marriage "extinguishes ambition, stupi-fies youth, and gives a check to every species of mental improvement," qualities he equated with slavery. If a man wanted to retain his mental faculties and preserve his ambition, the author recommended that he choose celibacy, noting that "most emi-nent characters, generals, magistrates, or legislators, are or have been Old Bache-lors." This piece thus employed the Revolutionary dichotomy of liberty and slavery to imply that single men were more American than married ones.[103]

An even more interesting defense of bachelors came from James Stuart in a 1790 commencement address delivered at his graduation from the University of Pennsyl-vania and later printed in the *Universal Asylum*. "The character which I would, at present, wish to recommend to your good opinion, or imitation," Stuart began, "is that of the deliberate batchelor." Although Stuart clarified that he was not an "advo-cate for final celibacy," he argued that men who were prudent in their pursuit of mar-riage exhibited qualities every man should aspire to. In so doing, Stuart made positive attributes out of the traits contemporary writers had decried as fatal flaws. He praised the man who had suffered a failed courtship because "he bears disappointment with fortitude." Whereas others insinuated that a bachelor's lack of passion was the sign he was a woman hater or a homosexual, Stuart found this to be evidence of "the most difficult of human virtues—a power over his passions." Even Malthusian consider-ations, which some writers claimed made misers into old bachelors and others asso-ciated with luxury, Stuart praised as evidence of the bachelor's reason and foresight: "If he finds his present circumstances inadequate to the probable expences of a fam-ily, he will prudently wait till better circumstances may enable him to undertake that charge." Ultimately, the man who refused to rush into marriage was a better judge of women and "always makes the best of husbands." If there was any cause for criticism, Stuart reserved blame for women's "rage for extravagance, in dress and amusements," which deterred men from marriage. "If therefore celibacy be thought an evil," he concluded, "and perhaps it is peculiarly so, in a country like this, the only radical cure lies with the ladies" who should convince men of their "frugality and economy."[104]

If George Sanby's letters were a testament to the fact that no old bachelor was beyond reform, then James Stuart's oration suggested that there was no reason for any bachelor to be ashamed. In this, we might read Stuart's oration as portending things to come. Lee Virginia Chambers-Schiller has argued that single women began to celebrate their liberty as unmarried people immediately after the Revolution as they inverted the colonial notion that spinsterhood was a fate worse than death.[105] Appar-ently, the same was true for bachelors.

Although many writings on bachelors in the last quarter of the eighteenth cen-tury ridiculed single men, it would be a mistake to ignore the countercurrents at work. As had been true of attacks on bachelors going back to the *Tatler* and the *Spectator*, humor often lightened the accounts, whether it was directed at desperate single women or at single men themselves. Faith in the power of gentle persuasion to bring single men to the altar also remained an effective trope. At the same time, the Revolution witnessed the beginning of an opportunity for single men to reclaim some legitimacy. Some seized on the perception that no man could be reformed to excuse his single state while others defended bachelorhood as virtuous. In this, literary depictions of single men in the era of the American Revolution paralleled political developments. Although bachelors were not warmly embraced by all, they began to claim cultural legitimacy for the first time.

Single Diarists and Sexual Freedom

Changes in political and literary treatments of single men ultimately paralleled a change in the lives of single men themselves. Although evidence is scant for understanding how propertyless single men reacted to being enfranchised, some bachelors, George Sanby and James Stuart among them, expressed their opinions of bachelorhood in print. Yet the experience of being single remained an intrinsically personal one perhaps best understood through diaries. As we saw in chapter 4, young bachelor New England diarists in the middle of the eighteenth century embraced the psychological freedom of being unmarried and reveled in a masculine independence denied to single women. A look at bachelors' diaries kept in the last quarter of the eighteenth century reveals that these trends continued and expanded, adding more freedoms including a vibrant single sexuality. To be sure, some single men continued to internalize self-hatred for being unmarried and sought to wed as quickly as possible. Yet more and more young bachelors were becoming less self-conscious about being unattached. The midcentury yearning for autonomy ultimately gave way to a late-century embrace of the single life and its freedoms.

A handful of diaries kept by single New Englanders during the last quarter of the eighteenth century survives at the American Antiquarian Society. Although it is difficult to generalize based on such a small sample, the diaries allow us to judge anecdotally the cleavage between colonial bachelors and their Revolutionary-era successors. Most significantly, the entries do not share space with astrological predictions. Instead of being sewn into almanacs, the diaries of men in the 1780s and 1790s were written in blank books. This change allowed for more personal reflection and more details of everyday life. Symbolically, we might see this transition as a centering of the self. No longer did the diarists feel the need to place their lives in the context of some external reality; now everything was subjective. Such a development suggests that the yearning for greater personal freedom and self-awareness evident in New England bachelors' diaries of the 1750s had become acute by the end of the century.

As a group, the diarists of the Revolutionary era were socially similar to the diarists of the previous generation. All were native-born white men in their early twenties and all had received an extensive education, most having matriculated at a New England college. All were self-employed in a profession or trade and, as had been the case before the war, several taught school in anticipation of a career in the ministry. Yet there were also important differences. Several diarists did not aspire to become clergymen, and among those who did, not all were Congregationalists.

The vocational diversity, in turn, led many to locations far from home. The diarists were firmly committed to self-improvement, constantly reading the Bible, classical tomes, and popular periodicals. Most had an eye on the young women around them, with some courting and even marrying before their journals concluded.

For some diarists, the path of the previous generation still held considerable attraction. The experience of Jonathan Fisher suggests that, at a basic level, the thoughts of young single men continued to be dominated by career concerns and hopes of marriage. Born in New Braintree, Massachusetts, in 1768, Fisher graduated from Harvard College in 1788 and aspired to a career in the ministry. He began keeping a diary in his midtwenties as he traversed the New England countryside looking for available pulpits. The diary details his travels as well as his eclectic intellectual interests, suggesting he was a young man intent on improving himself in every way possible. For example, Fisher described a week in May 1795: "Heard Mr. Holmes. Read in the Koran. Copied & painted figures from George Edwards, & read in British Encyclopedia. Went to Boston & returned."[106] In June 1794 Fisher journeyed to the frontier village of Blue Hill, Maine, where he preached for the next three months in exchange for $80. Fisher liked the parishioners in Blue Hill, and the following year he accepted an offer to settle as pastor at the town's Congregational church.

Jonathan Fisher had patiently deferred marriage until he received a formal call from a congregation, but once this happened his interest in taking a wife increased precipitously. For most of 1795 Fisher had courted Bridget Reubins, a young woman who suffered from consumption. When Fisher received his call to Blue Hill, Reubins's condition took a turn for the worse and it became apparent that she would not survive a trip to the Maine frontier. As Fisher puzzled over his commitment to Reubins, he met Dolly Battle, a woman in excellent health who welcomed the opportunity to be a minister's wife. In late 1795 Fisher ended his relationship with Reubins to pursue Battle. Reflecting on his actions twenty-five years later, Fisher noted: "Thus closes one more busy year ... Have resigned at her request one whom I had in view as a partner for life, & have commenced an acquaintance with another, whose manner of life may be more congenial to the place in which God may please to station me." Bridget Reubins passed away in January 1796 with Jonathan Fisher by her side the day she died. A month later Fisher engaged Dolly Battle in a serious conversation and "the question of our future connection this evening settled." For the next three months, the two conducted a hurried courtship before Fisher left for Blue Hill. In November he briefly returned to Massachusetts to marry Battle. Twenty-eight years old before he achieved occupational stability, Fisher had no interest in persisting in the single life once he could afford a wife.[107]

The experiences of Moses Bond Wheelock were also largely consistent with his father's generation. When he began keeping a diary in late 1788, Wheelock was a twenty-year-old schoolteacher in Templeton, Massachusetts. Although the details of his education are uncertain, Wheelock was an avid learner, constantly perusing the *American Museum* and purchasing books from Worcester printer Isaiah

Thomas. He also enjoyed socializing with other young people in the area, attending balls, singing, dancing, and even playing cards on occasion. Although he lived with a landlord and had no immediate hopes for marriage, Wheelock kept his eye on a number of young women, especially Miss Mindwell Grant who kept a school for girls. Intelligent and independent, Wheelock was free to enjoy the pleasures of the single life.

However, Moses Bond Wheelock's diary also reveals a young man beset with depression due in part to the isolation he felt as a single man. When he began keeping the diary, Wheelock's tone was upbeat and hopeful, but then sickness and death invaded the narrative. He repeatedly mentioned the declining health of Lydia Warren, a young woman whom he apparently had more than a casual interest in. "PM went to see LW who is very low indeed," he noted in February 1789, "she is all pin'd to a Skeleton." Then, when Wheelock's own health took a turn for the worse, his thoughts grew increasingly pessimistic. In early March he recorded the story of a man killed in a farming accident. Three weeks later he noted how "a young man ... cut his throat yesterday & Dyd instantly," adding, perhaps to reflect on his own condition, "he had been Sick." As the diary drew to a close in May 1789, Wheelock was hopeless and abandoned. Although his own health improved and he took a teaching position in a new town, death seemed to stalk him. He learned that the previous schoolmaster had died of consumption, and perhaps most disappointing of all, that the object of his affection, Miss Grant, had died as well.[108] Perhaps this young man internalized the spate of sermons and stories then circulating throughout New England that pitied the death of young people struck down in their prime. As Thomas Foster has noted, such tales were a rebuke of the immaturity of bachelors as well as morality tales designed to discourage young men from choosing the vanities of the single life over matrimony.[109] Although Wheelock's perspective appears to have been partially colored by his own health problems, his pessimistic outlook may have been an identification with the negative portrayal of bachelors or a manifestation of the guilt he felt for enjoying his independence.

Not all New England bachelors were torn between the pleasures of the single life and the obligation to marry. Indeed, several diarists from the Revolutionary era embraced the freedoms offered by bachelorhood to improve themselves spiritually and economically. Although aspiring Congregational ministers such as Fisher continued to connect being a settled pastor with settling down, those outside the Puritan tradition took a more ascetic approach. James Tufts was one of the more conservative single diarists of eighteenth-century New England and his writings chart not the parallel paths of career and courtship, but a spiritual journey. A recent graduate of Brown and a Baptist, Tufts's bachelorhood was not unusual. He began his diary in December 1789 when he received an offer to teach school in Bowentown, New Jersey, and continued with intermittent entries until he was licensed as a minister in Brookfield, Massachusetts, two years later. However, he made no mention of reading material, social events, or young women. Instead, he focused on regeneration and spiritual discipline. After attending a funeral, he prayed that

"God my creator mortfy every lust & sin [and] make greater advances in holiness and every christian Grace." During his travels of 1791 Tufts did not socialize with young people but sought lodging with "a respectable and cleaver family." Even the chore of teaching did not elicit venom or drive Tufts to drink. Instead, he patiently commented: "Feel some uneasy as to my situation and employment in this place &c May God direct me to chuse that profession & calling which shall be most for his glory for which end I desire to live."[110] Bachelorhood clearly meant freedom to James Tufts but it was a freedom that harkened back to medieval notions of chaste celibacy rather than eighteenth-century expectations of secular pleasure.

Unmarried diarist Stephen Peabody Jr. also saw bachelorhood as a time of personal freedom that did not necessarily include either a career or courtship. The son of a New Hampshire minister, Peabody was a 1794 Harvard graduate who had no interest in following in his father's footsteps. Two years after graduation, he headed for Buckston (later Bucksport), Maine, where he and a partner opened a dry goods business. There was apparently little excitement for a single man in Buckston, not that this seemed to matter to Peabody. He had at least one bachelor pal in town, although he spent most of his time with his newly married business partner, Asa. Indeed, for most of his diary Peabody lived with Asa and his wife. Peabody took notice of a daughter of the town's namesake, noting on several occasions "Esqr B[uck]'s daughter spent the evening here," but he made no effort to court her. He apparently had no interest in settling down and seemed conflicted about how much responsibility he wanted to assume. His education and position as a businessman earned him the respect of the town and led to the day in March 1797 when "I found myself chosen a select man."[111] However, he skipped the town meeting where the town voted on candidates for the U.S. House of Representatives, and when it came time to debate Maine's separation from Massachusetts, Peabody seemed relieved to serve as an impartial moderator. After almost ten months living in Buckston, Peabody's thoughts turned back to Cambridge and he began corresponding with Harvard president Joseph Willard about obtaining his master's degree. His entries end abruptly in the summer of 1797 during a trip to Massachusetts to attend commencement. When he began a new journal two years later, Peabody was still single and trying his hand as a captain in the U.S. Army, raising recruits in Haverhill, Massachusetts. Not marrying until 1810, Stephen Peabody had a single life that was less spiritual than James Tufts, but the two shared a sense of self-discovery. For both, bachelorhood was less monolithic than it had been for the previous generation. The pleasures of the single life were not specifically secular, short-lived, or even focused on the pursuit of a wife.

To a man, the New England single diarists were closed-mouth about sexuality. Although much changed in the lives of young bachelors, those alive in the Revolutionary era were as reticent about sex as their fathers had been. Yet it has long been accepted that Americans in the last quarter of the eighteenth century were far more willing to engage in premarital sex than any of the preceding generations of Americans. Daniel Scott Smith and Michael S. Hindus estimate that 30 percent of births in the era of the Revolution were conceived before marriage, a figure three times greater than rates a century earlier.[112] Commenting on this development, Susan Klepp has argued for a greater degree of female agency and Richard Godbeer has labeled the development a "sexual revolution." Nearly all traditional restraints to single sex—be it parental control or prosecution for fornication—broke down as American independence coincided with an increase of personal sexual freedom.[113] To what extent the New England diarists took advantage of this development is uncertain, although Stephen Peabody Jr.'s wife did give birth eight months after the couple married. Fortunately, not all bachelors were as taciturn about sex as New Englanders.

Diaries kept by two Virginia bachelors in the 1790s suggest that some single men of the late eighteenth century were quite comfortable with sex outside of marriage. Only a few unmarried colonial Virginians left diaries, commonplace books, or reminiscences, and these offer little insight into the experience of being single.[114] Bachelors writing after American independence were far more eloquent. They describe a world charged with sexual opportunity and activity in which single men *and* single women took advantage of the general lack of parental supervision to make their own decisions about their morality. Independent and autonomous, neither age nor occupation constrained their sexual ardors.

Sixteen-year-old William Bolling filled the better part of his two-year diary with stories of trying to seduce young women. Ostensibly, the overarching plot of Bolling's diary is his pursuit of Mary "Polly" Randolph, a cousin who eventually became his wife. Early in the diary, Bolling noted Randolph's presence at family dinners with little enthusiasm, but then a fortuitous turn of events changed his opinion of Randolph markedly. One day in June 1794 Bolling called on Randolph's family and found Polly alone. When a thunderstorm prevented his return home that night, the two engaged in intimacies. "Nous avions un peu de la Conversation privée [We had a little private Conversation]," he wrote coyly. Although what transpired at this meeting is unclear, it marks the moment when Bolling earnestly began to pursue his cousin. Whenever he dined with her family or saw her in church, he noted her presence in his diary, always recording these incidents in French. On one occasion, he pressured Randolph to make promises of affection and was jubilant when "et ayant été invité demeurer toute la Nuit [and having been invited to remain all the Night]" he had a chance for further intimacies.[115]

It was hardly unheard of for a courting couple to engage in sexual relations, but Bolling's diary suggests that he was hardly ready for marriage. Indeed, the couple did not wed until February 1798, more than two years after Bolling's diary concluded. In the meantime, Bolling pursued more than a half dozen other women, all while he was chasing Randolph. At a wedding in June 1795 Bolling met Eliza Duncan. Love struck by "la belle Eliza," Bolling traveled to Petersburg a week later to call on her and made several visits thereafter. By December he was obsessed. "Instead of going to my Studies which I generally did, after Breakfast," he wrote, "I went again to see Miss Eliza, she, running so much in my head." A self-perceived rake, Bolling qualified his fixation by noting parenthetically "as would have been the case with almost any other Girl." He continually looked for opportunities to see Duncan until she finally received his company. However, the meeting did not live up to expectations but proceeded "dans une manière non pas le plus agreeable parce que Je n'avait pas une Opportuniti avour une entretun[?] privée avec lui [in a manner not the most pleasing because I had not an Opportunity to have a private meeting with her]." Duncan's rejection sufficiently cooled Bolling's passions and he never mentioned her again.[116]

For William Bolling, bachelorhood was a time of asserting manhood. Practically, he was still a man-in-training when the diary ended, only eighteen years old and still living on his father's plantation. His diary often revealed him playing the dutiful son: attending family dinners, acting as his father's legal representative, and helping to manage the harvest. Constrained by economic and familial obligations, the one avenue Bolling had available to him was demonstrative sexuality. In playing the part of the seducer and the rake, he tapped into male power denied to women and children and thus set himself apart from other dependents. The diary was crucial to this process as it provided Bolling with a space to perform his manhood, even if only for himself. In some sense, Bolling was part of a longer tradition of Virginian diarists and we might see him as a pedestrian William Byrd.[117] Bolling also tapped into the negative depiction of bachelorhood then popular in the press, but he embraced it rather than rejecting or apologizing for it. In the characterization he drew of himself, Bolling was selfish, irresponsible, and utterly unchaste. Of course, such depictions existed only as part of an elaborate fantasy. His actions did not disqualify him from respectability and his pretended rakishness was no impediment to marrying his sweetheart, settling down, and raising a family.

The carefree tenor of William Bolling's diary stands in sharp contrast to the more sober reflections of Richard N. Venable. Twenty-seven years old when he began keeping a diary in January 1791, Venable was already established in his career as an attorney. Unlike Bolling, he lived on his own and seriously pursued marriage. Indeed, by the time he made his first diary entry, Venable was already infatuated with Elizabeth "Betsy" Williams. Her very presence made Venable "sever the Cords of duty" and led him to take certain liberties that he was not able to fully describe in cursive. Whereas Bolling recorded his moments of great intimacy in French, Venable did so in stilted and verbose English. Upon visiting Williams in February 1791, he noted "an Artificial Cloud is seen," explaining only "in familiar chat we should avoid the Commencement of a subject wch is improper to be disclosed." Early in their relationship, Venable tried the honorable route and proposed marriage, but Williams turned him down.[118]

Despite the fact that she would not marry him, Betsy Williams continued to see Richard Venable on a regular basis. By January 1792, nearly a year after she had rejected his marriage proposal, Venable's connection with Williams reached its climax. Calling on Williams one night, the relationship suddenly became physical. In his diary, Venable wrote "here I will have a full blank page that imagination may fill it with the description of a man in and yet is bound by the firmest resolution never to reveal it." When he resumed his narrative a page later, his description of the evening's events was equally opaque. "What pain, cramp, & Spasm was produced by this unfortunate warfare, between the Caput & Cors [head and heart] upon the Cortial and Liguatious nerves," he asserted, implying that Williams was ultimately able to resist his advances, much to Venable's chagrin. "It was a Sore victory," he concluded, adding, "it was late at night & I went to bed tho: not to sleep," perhaps intimating that he followed the incident with masturbation. The next day's entry finds Venable sullen, as he described himself as "a hungry bear driven from his prey" and near death. He returned home but by noon his ardors already had arisen again and he found himself "simpathising rather with the vanquished than the Victor." Lost in a fog of sexual obsession, Venable spent the evening at home alone, noting coyly, "I arrived at home & know not how I spent the evening."[119]

After this encounter, Richard Venable attempted to meet other women but he continued to visit with Elizabeth Williams and spend the night with her. In May 1792 he recorded without explanation: "spend the evening & morning with Miss E.W.—&c &c &c &c." When the diary concluded in November 1792, Venable was still pursuing Williams. He never did change her mind and it was apparently a number of years before he was able to completely sever all ties with her. It was more than four years after Venable's last entry that he finally wed Polly Morton.[120]

Bachelorhood was also about asserting manhood for Richard Venable although it did not have the fantastic element that William Bolling's did. Venable was established in his career and independent of his father's control and thus he did not have to imagine himself as a rake to assert masculine power. Instead, bachelorhood for Venable was about male entitlement. He might not be married, but he had the same sexual urges as any man and he believed himself free to act on them. Despite his reticence to provide the details of his sexual encounters, Venable expressed little guilt or remorse for his actions. Indeed, he was only casually interested in demonstrating self-control. Like Bolling, Venable's sexual activities did not mitigate his respectability or impede his marriage. The fully sexual bachelor was no longer the problem he once had been.

Taken as a whole, the diaries of single men who lived during the last quarter of the eighteenth century suggest that bachelors were increasingly free in the era of the American Revolution. Their experiences as single men were becoming richer. Bachelorhood evoked greater personal reflection and spiritual searching for some, and it permitted sexual experimentation for others. It was also much less of a prelude to marriage. Although some single men continued to use their bachelorhood to patiently court women while they waited for the economic stability that would make marriage possible, others were content to date casually or drift from one occupation to another. As was true of diarists at midcentury, we have very little self-reflection by the men most affected by the bachelor laws and thus it is difficult to gauge how changing political ideas affected the experience of being single. Certainly the lack of a wife was no impediment to Stephen Peabody's election as a selectman or to Richard Venable's admission to the bar, although neither man was an economic dependent. More important, the equality of all free white men implicit in the Revolutionary construction of citizenship was borne out in the lives of these bachelors. The diarists assumed all the privileges of manhood without regard to age, social standing, or marital status. There was also a parallel development between lives and literary developments. Nearly all of the diarists mentioned here recorded reading newspapers and periodicals such as the *American Museum* and the *Spectator*. If the experiences of Moses Bond Wheelock and William Bolling are representative, some internalized the negative depiction of the single life while others buoyantly embraced it. The majority, however, were clearly able to separate themselves from literary constructions of the bachelor.

In 1771 Stephen Salisbury purchased a farm in Worcester, Massachusetts, and began building a mansion for himself. He operated his dry goods business from the first floor of his new house and took up residence in the upper story. When the American Revolution enveloped the Massachusetts countryside, Salisbury declared himself for the American cause and joined the local Committee of Correspondence. Although a property owner, Salisbury resisted marrying and lived by himself in his mansion until 1775 when his mother and brother fled British-occupied Boston and moved in with him. The master of his own estate, Salisbury was in a far different position than when his brother had once chided him for his bachelor idleness and immorality. His brother returned to Boston after the war but Salisbury's mother continued to live with him in Worcester until she died in 1792. All the while, Salisbury remained single, living as a bachelor until 1797 when he married Elizabeth Tuckerman at the age of fifty-one.[121]

Having made it through the American War of Independence and the creation of the United States as a single man, Stephen Salisbury witnessed the dramatic culmination of the emergence of bachelorhood. Arising simultaneously in the law, literature, and lived experience, bachelorhood was a mark of masculine independence and autonomy. Building on a process that had begun in the middle of the seventeenth century, bachelorhood at the end of the eighteenth century was a permanent part of American life and would remain so for years to come. That is not to say that the fate of single men was without controversy in the Revolutionary era. They were disparaged as unpatriotic fops and British sympathizers, forced to pay for and serve in the cause of American independence, and ultimately were the subject of ridicule in periodicals. In many ways, the last quarter of the eighteenth century was the nadir for single men in American history, far worse than the Puritans' treatment of the unmarried.

But to simply leave it at that fails to take into account the broader cultural trends set in motion during the American Revolution. The taxing and drafting of single men became the basis for them to claim equal rights and further advanced the notion that there was no meaningful legal difference between the rights and obligations of free white men because of marital status. Similarly, the literary assaults on unmarried men retained humor and the message of hope. Some authors criticized society instead of bachelors and a number of single men spoke up for the pleasures of the single life. Perhaps most important, the experience of being a single man enveloped even more freedom. There was less pressure to marry quickly and more time for self-discovery than fifty years earlier, with some bachelors enjoying the benefits of greater sexual liberty. These developments ultimately placed bachelorhood on a firm foundation and guaranteed its persistence for the next two hundred years.

Epilogue

In 1856 lifelong bachelor James Buchanan was elected the fifteenth president of the United States. The election turned on slavery and fears of disunion, with Buchanan's Democrats predicting a civil war if the newly formed Republican Party succeeded at the polls. Amid these great issues of the day, Buchanan's marital status became part of the debate. America had had widowed presidents before but never one who was a confirmed bachelor. Was the country ready for this? For his part, Buchanan knew that his lack of a wife would raise questions and so he arranged for his operatives to release an explanation. In the popular *Harper's Magazine* Buchanan was quoted at length telling the story of how he had courted "the affections of a lovely girl, alike graced with beauty of person and high social position" when he was a young lawyer in Philadelphia. However, in a story befitting a Victorian novel, Buchanan's efforts at love were thwarted at every turn, by the woman's devious mother, an untrustworthy stead, and idle gossip. These difficulties kept the two apart and ultimately caused the woman such grief that she died. Buchanan never recovered from this heartbreak and resolved thereafter to live as a bachelor. In an epilogue to Buchanan's story, a supporter reflected on how "the country strangely becomes intrigued" that "the 'White House' may possibly have a bachelor for its occupant." Yet he assured the American public that Buchanan remained unmarried "not so because of indifference to woman, but really from the highest appreciation of one of the loveliest of the sex."

Buchanan's explanation did not end the debate over his marital status. Republicans rejected the maudlin tale and connected questions about Buchanan's moral character to his qualifications for office. A pamphlet claimed the candidate favored the acquisition of Cuba for a slave state and raised fears of miscegenation by claiming

"Buchanan the choice of Virginia Slave-breeders." The *New York Herald* attacked Buchanan's explanation of his marital status that had appeared in *Harper's*. Instead of being a story about love and loss, Buchanan's bachelorhood was the result of far more sinister causes. "One of two things: either Mr. Buchanan shows that he had no taste for matrimony, which plainly implies a lack of some essential quality," that is, he lacked either the ability to love or the desire for women, "or Mr. Buchanan has signified by his conduct that there was not in Pennsylvania or in Washington a lady fit to be his bride." We might read a thinly veiled charge of homosexuality in the latter explanation because the author found it unbelievable that any normal man could remain a bachelor in the midst of such beautiful women. Regardless of cause, Buchanan's marital status was hardly inconsequential. The article concluded that "if he is elected, he will be the first President who shall carry into the White House, the crude and possibly the gross tastes and experiences of a bachelor."[1]

The debate over James Buchanan's bachelorhood serves as a fitting portrait for the status of bachelorhood in America after 1800. Much had changed since the first English colonists had settled in America. Back in the early seventeenth century, the marital status of a law-abiding man with his own estate would have been irrelevant. Indeed, it is doubtful that the earliest colonists would even have considered Buchanan a bachelor; such an appellation—along with its reputation for immorality—was saved for the young and masterless. Since then a series of political, cultural, and social changes had caused Americans to reconsider the single man. Attempts to ease the burden on men with families to support had led to new civic obligations on single men, while the unprecedented growth of print media and a new fascination with love led authors to ponder the character of the single man and his place in society. These developments had the dual effect of separating young and propertyless bachelors from other dependents, such as women, children, and servants, and classifying all unmarried men together regardless of wealth or age. These developments created the bachelor as a legal identity, a cultural ideal, and a lived experience. It also ensured that the bachelor was a permanent fixture of American society. Whether one loved him or hated him, no one could deny the existence of the bachelor.

In this, James Buchanan lived in a society where the rules of bachelorhood had been fixed. In the colonial era Americans had heartily debated the role of the single man in society, and by the Revolution they had reached several important conclusions that remain with us today. First, gender was more important than mastery in the marital status of whites. As a man, Buchanan was not classed with spinsters. Because Americans believed that all *men* are created equal, he was entitled to the same rights and responsibilities of any married man. Second, as part of the emerging importance of gender, legal distinctions between men based on marital status largely melted away. Not only could Buchanan vote and stand for elective office, he did not have to pay special taxes and he never would have faced harsher sentencing if he had been convicted of a crime. Third, while the legal assault on the unmarried state had long since passed away, the moral attacks were as vicious as anything seen in the colonial era. Yet there were rules here as well. Taking a page from the *Spectator*, Buchanan assured voters that he was no loveless bachelors convict, but had courted a woman only to be denied marriage by cruel circumstance. Fourth, there were some vagaries when it came to issues of sexuality. Whereas earlier generations had condemned all single sexuality as problematic, the attacks on Buchanan demonstrate that there were increasing opportunities for bachelors to engage in intercourse. Although Buchanan intimated that he had had no carnal thoughts since his beloved died, the attacks on him suggest that his explanation was becoming untenable. Americans expected single men to be unchaste even if such activities were immoral.

The debate over James Buchanan's bachelorhood suggests that the experience of the single man in 1856 was far closer to our own time than to the colonial past. Then as now Americans wondered about the bachelor and argued whether he was the embodiment of freedom or an example of immorality. But everyone accepted that the bachelor was an intrinsic part of society and agreed on the basic elements of his existence. A full century before the age of the bachelor, the bachelor had already emerged as a unique identity in America.

Since 1800 the laws, literature, and lives of bachelors have continued to evolve. The idea of connecting marital status and tax policy began to wane in the first years of the nineteenth century, but it has never completely gone away. In 1835 Maine proposed a special tax on bachelors, as did New Mexico in 1903. More recently, the idea has appeared at the federal level in the debates surrounding the so-called marriage-penalty tax. Opponents have claimed that the heavier tax burden on married couples with nearly equal incomes has the effect of discouraging marriage. Although numerous commentators have questioned whether making it less expensive for couples to file their taxes together would strengthen the family, the idea of a financial incentive for marriage would have fit in well in the colonial era.[2] However, the similarities between the bachelor laws of the seventeenth and twenty-first centuries are largely rhetorical. Attempts to revise the marriage-penalty tax do not seek to deprive the unmarried of their political rights or even to require them to submit to obligations not required of married people. Indeed, the idea of ending the marriage-penalty tax originally emanated from a desire to equalize the tax burden among all Americans regardless of marital status. In short, Americans will probably always debate the best way to balance one's financial obligations to the state and one's financial obligations to the family, but we have never returned to the colonial practice of directing where the unmarried should live, requiring bachelors to pay taxes while denying them the vote, or meting out separate punishments based solely on one's marital status.

Literary treatments of the bachelor have changed less radically than the laws. For example, humorous depictions of the bachelor tax have remained popular, with few authors seriously promoting the idea for adoption. In 1839 the Philadelphia periodical *Lady's Book* published an editorial occasioned by the fact that "a number of ladies lately petitioned the legislature to pass a bill laying a tax on Old Bachelors."

The editors used the opportunity to take a few swipes at single men: "All commodities taxed should have some specific value, else how should the rate of duty be determined? If bachelors be taxed ad valorem, the tax will amount to little or nothing." In the end, however, the magazine opposed the ladies' scheme as unworthy of serious consideration. Similar send-ups continue to this day. Carolyn Davidson's 2000 Harlequin romance, *The Bachelor Tax*, tells of a single man living in the Old West who, in an effort to avoid paying a fine on his marital status, makes a marriage of convenience. In the end, of course, the reluctant man falls in love with his wife.[3]

The bachelor cognomen has also remained a popular literary conceit. The idea of an old bachelor proffering advice on affairs of the heart and youthful deportment— á là Mr. Spectator—was repeatedly employed by the first generation of great American novelists. Washington Irving posed as old bachelor Diedrich Knickerbocker to narrate his wildly popular *History of New York*, while James Fenimore Cooper used the single life to feign objectivity in his *Notions of the Americans: Picked up by a Travelling Bachelor*. Nor was the popularity limited to novelists. In 1814 future U.S. attorney general William Wirt published observations on life in Virginia in a series of letters that he signed "The Old Bachelor," while in the 1840s Henry David Thoreau embraced his title as "America's bachelor uncle" in order to dispense advice on the solitary life.[4]

Probably the greatest changes have come in the lives of individual bachelors. Since 1800 single men have continued the trend of demanding more freedom and respect. In the first half of the nineteenth century, bachelor clubs seemed to pop up everywhere. When Daniel Haynes addressed the Society of Bachelors of Natick, Massachusetts, in 1824, he gave his own reasons for deciding against marriage, saying that "because I had so good a regard for the happiness of the ladies, and my own happiness." He expected to marry eventually, but in the meantime he devoted his life to reading and deep reflection, having "learnt that happiness depended mostly on the mind." Other bachelor clubs appeared in New York, Philadelphia, and Virginia, each hosting elaborate balls and producing a voluminous written record. Single men in Boston published newspapers titled *Bachelors' Journal* in 1828 and *Old Bachelor* in 1843. The authors of the latter even included a bachelors' Declaration of Independence, proclaiming: "When, in the sincerity of certain Feelings, it becomes convenient for one Class of People to refuse the domestic Bonds which are prepared for them by another."[5] As this piece suggests, bachelors' clubs were both ironic and deadly serious, self-depreciating and self-indulgent. They did not take themselves seriously but they did demand that their marital status be taken with sincerity. Of course, all of this was merely a prelude to the age of the bachelor at the turn of the twentieth century when the number of single men skyrocketed and a nationally recognized bachelor subculture emerged. This trend continued after World War II with the appearance of *Playboy* and singles' bars.

As this book has demonstrated, correctly placing the emergence of the bachelor in early America is no minor historical fact. It sheds new light on the complexities and importance of gender in the creation of the United States. In the end, the bachelor gained his political privileges and sexual license by successfully asserting that he was no different from other men. Having paid taxes and served in the military, he demanded the commensurate rights of citizenship. Despite James Stuart's valorization of bachelorhood, few bachelors gained their rights by disputing the negative depiction of their marital status. They simply asserted that one's marital status did not matter to manhood. In this, they followed a path to citizenship that necessarily excluded women. In the short run, the bachelor's attainment of manhood meant that he gained citizenship by distinguishing himself from other nonmasters. In the long run, however, the pattern that the bachelor followed to gain suffrage proved the model for women and African Americans to join the free white bachelor at the polls. The connection of civic obligation and political privileges would resonate throughout American history and become one of the most cherished bedrocks of American freedom.

The process by which the bachelor gained manhood also challenged and changed the very ethos of American manhood. Manhood had long been connected with mastery, self-control, and marriage. Through claiming masculine privileges, bachelors helped start a social revolution. By the middle of the eighteenth century bachelors were asserting independence from their fathers. Through such actions, young men dared society to treat them like servants or children and reduce them to dependence. It did not. Instead, America allowed these men to carve a new avenue to the full privileges of manhood, one by which a man did not prove himself through internal qualities or fatherhood. It would take another century for manly self-control to be completely displaced by the aggressiveness, brute strength, and virility of masculinity, yet the origins of this change were already in place a hundred years earlier.

Ultimately, the history of the bachelor suggests that historians may have overstated the importance of the family in early America. To be sure, it was the central institution, but there were constant exceptions. Marriage and family were not assumed or even expected for all. For reasons of status, vocation, or simply personal taste, Americans accepted that some portion of the population would always be unmarried. They resisted using the state to coerce the individual to marry. Long before the Bill of Rights, Americans granted that there were certain individual rights that should not be subjected to the will of the majority.

Appendix

Sources for Appendix: Singles' Laws, 1550–1800

Connecticut
The Public Records of the Colony of Connecticut, ed. J. Hammond Trumbull et al., 15 vols. (Hartford: Case, Lockwood, and Brainard, et al., 1859–90), 1:8, 527, 542; 4:411; 5:73.

Delaware
Anno Regni Georgii II Regis Magnae Britanniae, Franciae, & Hiberniae, Septimo: At a General Assembly of the Counties of New-Castle, Kent and Sussex upon Delaware, Begun and Holden at New-Castle, the Twentieth Day of October, Anno Dom. 1733 (Philadelphia: Franklin, 1734), 14; *Laws of the State of Delaware*, 4 vols. (New Castle: Adams et al., 1797–1816), 1:261.

Maryland
Archives of Maryland, ed. W. H. Browne et al., 72 vols. (Baltimore: Maryland Historical Society, 1883–1972), 1:373–74; 36:596–97; 38:371; 39:135–36, 299–300; 52:503–4; 59:282; 64:414–19; *Votes and Proceedings of the House of Delegates of the State of Maryland, March Session 1778, Being the Second Session of the Assembly* (Annapolis: [Green], 1778), 80; *Laws of Maryland, Made and Passed at a Session of Assembly, Begun and Held at the City of Annapolis, on Monday the Eighth of November, in the Year of Our Lord One Thousand Seven Hundred and Seventy-Nine* (Annapolis: Green, [1780]), chap. 36; *Laws of Maryland, Made and Passed at a Session of Assembly, Begun and Held at the City of Annapolis, on Thursday the Tenth of May, in the Year of Our Lord One Thousand Seven Hundred and Eighty-One* (Annapolis, Md.: Green, [1781]), chap. 24, § 17; *Laws of Maryland, Made and Passed at a Session of Assembly, Begun and Held at the City of Annapolis, on Monday the Fifth of November, in the Year of Our Lord One Thousand Seven Hundred and Eighty-One* (Annapolis: Green, [1782]), chap. 4, § 66; *Laws of Maryland, Made and Passed at a Session of Assembly, Begun and Held at the City of*

Annapolis, on Monday the Fourth of November, in the Year of Our Lord One Thousand Seven Hundred and Eighty-Two (Annapolis: Green, [1783]), chap. 6, § 47–48; *Laws of Maryland, Made and Passed at a Session of Assembly, Begun and Held at the City of Annapolis, on Monday the Third of November, in the Year of Our Lord One Thousand Seven Hundred and Eighty-Three* (Annapolis: Green, [1784]), chap. 17, § 35; *Laws of Maryland, Made and Passed, at a Session of Assembly, Begun and Held at the City of Annapolis, on Monday the First of November, in the Year of Our Lord One Thousand Seven Hundred and Eighty-Four* (Annapolis: Green, [1785]), chap. 56, § 38–39; chap. 83, § 16.

Massachusetts
Records of the Governor and Company of the Massachusetts Bay in New England, ed. Nathaniel B. Shurtleff, 5 vols. (Boston: White, 1853–54), 1:93, 186; 2:22; *The Acts and Resolves, Public and Private, of the Province of the Massachusetts Bay*, 21 vols. (Boston: Wright and Potter, 1869–1922), 1:52, 213, 278, 332, 538; 2:831–33; 5:448; *Acts and Laws of the Commonwealth of Massachusetts* (Boston: Adams and Nourse, 1788), 99.

New Hampshire
Laws of New Hampshire Including Public and Private Acts and Resolves and the Royal Commissions and Instructions, ed. Albert Stillman Batchellor et al., 10 vols. (Manchester: Clarke et al., 1904–22), 1:16, 60, 222; 3:391; 6:442, 693.

New Haven
New Haven's Settling in New-England and Some Lawes for Government: Published for the Use of that Colony (London: M.S., 1656), 32, 50.

New Jersey
Laws of the Royal Colony of New Jersey, 1703–45, ed. Bernard Bush, in *New Jersey Archives* 3d ser., vol. 2 (Trenton: Archives and History Bureau of the New Jersey State Library, 1977), 119, 215, 232, 498–502; *Acts of the General Assembly of the State of New-Jersey, at a Session Begun at Trenton on the 28th Day of October 1777 and Continued by Adjournments, Being the Second Sitting of the Second Session* (Trenton: Collins, 1777), 57; *Acts of the General Assembly of the State of New-Jersey, at a Session Begun at Trenton on the 27th Day of October 1778, and Continued by Adjournments, Being the First Sitting of Their Third Session* (Trenton: Collins, 1779), 9, 71; *Acts of the General Assembly of the State of New-Jersey, at a Session Begun at Trenton on the 26th Day of October, 1779, and Continued by Adjournments, Being the First Sitting of the Fourth Assembly* (Trenton: Collins, 1780), 4; *Acts of the General Assembly of the State of New-Jersey, at a Session Begun at Trenton on the 24th Day of October, 1780, and Continued by Adjournments, Being the Second Sitting* (Trenton: Collins, 1781), 85; *Acts of the General Assembly of the State of New-Jersey, at a Session Begun at Trenton on the 23d Day of October, 1781, and Continued by Adjournments, Being the First Sitting* (Trenton: Collins, 1782), 34, 83; *Acts of the Seventh General Assembly of the State of New-Jersey, at a Session Begun at Trenton on the 22d Day of October, 1782, and Continued by Adjournments, Being the Second Sitting* (Trenton: Collins, 1783), 32; *Acts of the Eighth General Assembly of the State of New-Jersey, at a Session Begun at Trenton on the 28th Day of October, 1783, and Continued until the 24th Day of December Following* (Trenton: Collins, 1784), 45–46, 60; *Acts of the Ninth General Assembly of the State of New-Jersey, at a Session Begun at Trenton on the 26th Day of October, 1784, and*

Continued by Adjournments, Being the First Sitting (Trenton: Collins, 1784), 158, 161; *Acts of the Tenth General Assembly of the State of New-Jersey, at a Session Begun at Trenton on the 25th Day of October, 1785, and Continued by Adjournments, Being the First Sitting* (Trenton: Collins, 1785), 218; *Acts of the Eleventh General Assembly of the State of New-Jersey, at a Session Begun at Trenton on the 24th Day of October, 1786, and Continued by Adjournments, Being the Second Session* (Trenton: Collins, 1787), 406–9, 430; *Acts of the Twelfth General Assembly of the State of New-Jersey, at a Session Begun at Trenton on the 23d Day of October, 1787, and Continued by Adjournment* (Trenton: Collins, 1787), 446–47; *Acts of the Thirteenth General Assembly of the State of New-Jersey, at a Session Begun at Trenton on the 28th Day of October, 1788, and Continued by Adjournments, Being the First Sitting* (Trenton: Collins, 1788), 492–95; *Acts of the Fourteenth General Assembly of the State of New-Jersey, at a Session Begun at Perth-Amboy on the 27th Day of October 1789, and Continued by Adjournments, Being the First Sitting* (New Brunswick: Blawelt, 1789), 570–73, 615; *Acts of the Fifteenth General Assembly of the State of New-Jersey, at a Session Begun at Burlington the 26th Day of October, 1790, and Continued by Adjournments, Being the First Sitting* (Burlington: Neale and Lawrence, 1790), 704–6; *Acts of the Sixteenth General Assembly of the State of New-Jersey, at a Session Begun at Trenton the 25th Day of October, 1791, and Continued by Adjournments, Being the First Sitting* (Burlington: Neale, 1791), 728–29; *Acts of the Seventeenth General Assembly of the State of New-Jersey, at a Session Begun at Trenton the 23d Day of October 1792, and Continued by Adjournments, Being the First Sitting* (Trenton: Collins, 1793), 791–93; *Acts of the Eighteenth General Assembly of the State of New-Jersey, at a Session Begun at Trenton on the 22d Day of October 1793, and Continued by Adjournments, Being the First and Second Sittings* (Trenton: Collins, 1794), 899; *Acts of the Nineteenth General Assembly of the State of New-Jersey, at a Session Begun at Trenton on the 28th Day of October, 1794, and Continued by Adjournments, Being the First Sitting* (Trenton: Day, 1795), 962–63; *Acts of the Twentieth General Assembly of the State of New-Jersey, at a Session Begun at Trenton on the 27th Day of October, 1795, and Continued by Adjournments, Being the First Sitting* (Trenton: Day, 1795), 4–5.

New York
The Colonial Laws of New York From the Year 1664 to the Revolution, 5 vols. (Albany, N.Y.: Lyon, 1894), 1:21, 35, 161–62, 550; 2:675, 753–56; *Charter to William Penn, and Laws of the Province of Pennsylvania, Passed Between the Years 1682 and 1700*, ed. Staughton George, Benjamin M. Nead, and Thomas McCamant (Harrisburg: Hart, 1879), 42.

North Carolina
The State Records of North Carolina, ed. William L. Saunders et al., 26 vols. (Raleigh, N.C.: Hale et al., 1886–1907), 24: 202, 258, 260, 390–91, 432, 435–36, 438, 498, 594.

Pennsylvania
Charter to William Penn, and Laws of the Province of Pennsylvania, Passed Between the Years 1682 and 1700, ed. Staughton George, Benjamin M. Nead, and Thomas McCamant (Harrisburg: Hart, 1879), 109–11, 145, 222, 257; *The Statutes at Large of Pennsylvania from 1682 to 1801*, ed. James T. Mitchell and Henry Flanders, 17 vols. (Harrisburg: Busch et al., 1896–1915), 2:6–8, 35, 115, 180, 250, 374, 389; 3:83–84, 128–29, 180–81, 202, 221–22, 296; 4:14, 178–79, 212; 5:202, 295–96, 339, 380; 6:8, 358; 9:5–8, 102, 153, 232–33, 363–64, 403, 447; 10:240, 330–31; 11:90; 16:379; *Laws of the Commonwealth of Pennsylvania, from the*

Fourteenth Day of October, One Thousand Seven Hundred, to the Twentieth Day of March, One Thousand Eight Hundred and Ten, vol. 2 (Philadelphia: Bioren, 1810), 533; *Supplement to Purdon's Digest: A Digest of the Statute Law of the State of Pennsylvania for the Years 1917–21,* 13th ed. (Philadelphia: Bisel, 1923), 8920–37, 9176–77.

Plymouth
Records of the Colony of New Plymouth in New England, ed. Nathaniel B. Shurtleff et al., 11 vols. (Boston: White, 1855–61), 11:17, 46.

Rhode Island
Records of the Colony of Rhode Island and Providence Plantations, ed. John Russell Bartlett, 10 vols. (Providence: Greene, 1856–65), 1:332.

Virginia
"Proceedings of the Virginia Assembly, 1619," in *Narratives of Early Virginia, 1606–25,* ed. Lyon Gardiner Tyler (New York: Scribner's Sons, 1907), 263; *The Statutes at Large; Being a Collection of All the Laws of Virginia, from the First Session of the Legislature in the Year 1619,* ed. William Waller Hening, 13 vols. (New York: Bartow, 1819–23), 6:465, 527; 7:163–69; 9:339; 10:82–83.

Great Britain
Statutes of the Realm, Printed by Command of His Majesty King George the Third, in Pursuance of an Address of the House of Commons of Great Britain; from Original Records and Authentic Manuscripts, 9 vols. (London: Eyre and Strahan, 1810–22), 3 & 4 Edw. VI, c. 22; 5 Eliz. I, c. 4; 12 Car. II, c. 9; 29 & 30 Car. II, c. 1; 1 Gul. & Mar., c. 13; 2 Gul. & Mar., st. 2, c. 7; 3 Gul. & Mar., cc. 6, 11; 5 & 6 Gul. & Mar., c. 14; 6 & 7 Gul. & Mar., c. 6; 9 Gul. III, c. 38; 1 Ann., c. 6; 30 Geo. II, c. 25.

Colony	Type of Law	Passed	Specifics	Expired
Connecticut	Family Government	1636	Young single man without servant or office not to live alone (20s. fine)	unclear
	Fornication	1647	Unmarried partners can be enjoined to marry, fined, or whipped	1703
	Militia	1650	Magistrate can put to service a single man unable to afford arms	1708
Delaware	Debtor Relief	1733	Person under 40 years, without children, and debts less than £20 put to service	1740
	County Tax	1743	£12 to £24 on single man with no visible estate	unclear
Maryland	Fornication	1658	Single freeman who promised marriage required to wed or compensate partner	1715?
	Constable Duties	1719	Take into custody unsettled single freeman until he is placed in a household	unclear
	Debtor Relief	1725	Man without wife or children can be put to service for up to five years	1726
	Debtor Relief	1733	Man without wife or children can be put to service for up to five years	1737
	Province Tax	1756	5s. per year on bachelor aged 25 years worth £100; 20s. on £300 or more	1763
	Debtor Relief	1765	Man without wife or children can be put to service for up to five years	1774
	Military Draft	1778	Draft man over 18 years who has no family, habitation, or occupation	1779
	State Tax	1781	7s.6d. on freeman aged 21 to 50 without family and worth less than £30	1781
	State Tax	1782	15s. on freeman aged 21 to 50 without family and not otherwise rated	1782
	State Tax	1783	Single man to give security; tax relief to married man with many small children	1783
	State Tax	1784	15s. on single man aged 21 to 50 without family and worth less than £100	1784
	State Tax	1785	Single man to give security; tax relief to married man with many small children	1785
	State Tax	1786	15s. on single man aged 21 to 50 without family and worth less than £50	1786
Massachusetts	Militia	1632	Magistrate can put to service a single man unable to afford arms	1776
	Family Government	1636	Towns to place single person in service or in a household	1692
	Fornication	1642	Unmarried partners can be enjoined to marry, fined, or whipped	1692
	Province Tax	1695	2s. per year on single woman who lives at her own hand	1697
	Debtor Relief	1698	Man without wife or family can be put to service in payment of debt	1737
	Poor Law	1703	Single person under 21 years not to live at his or her own hand	1789

(continued)

Colony	Type of Law	Passed	Specifics	Expired
New Hampshire	Fornication	1680	Unmarried partners can be enjoined to marry, fined, or whipped	1682
	Militia	1688	Magistrate can put to service a single man unable to afford arms	1776
	Poor Law	1766	Single person under 21 years not to live at his or her own hand	1791
New Haven	Fornication	1656	Unmarried partners can be enjoined to marry, fined, or whipped	1662
	Family Government	1656	Single person not to live apart from family unless approved by the Court	1662
New Jersey	Colony Tax	1714	6s. per year on free single man worth less than £24	1717
	Colony Tax	1717	6s. per 18 months on single man who works for hire	1719
	Colony Tax	1719	4s. per year on single man who works for hire	1739
	State Tax	1778	15–30s. on single man not otherswise rated; 25–50s. if he owns a horse	1778
	State Tax	1778	15–25s. on single man not otherwise rated; 25–40s. if he owns a horse	1779
	State Tax	1779	£7 10s.–£20 on single man not otherwise rated; £10–25 if he owns a horse	1779
	State Tax	1779	Up to £20 on single man not otherwise rated; up to £30 if he owns a horse	1780
	State Tax	1781	Up to 30s. on single man not otherwise rated; up to 40s. if he owns a horse	1781
	State Tax	1781	Up to 20s. on single man not otherwise rated; up to 30s. if he owns a horse	1782
	State Tax	1782	Up to 15s. on single man not otherwise rated; up to £1 2s.6d. if he owns a horse	1782
	State Tax	1783	Up to 20s. on single man not otherwise rated; up to £2 if he owns a horse	1783
	Tax for USA	1783	Up to 15s. on single man not otherwise rated; up to 25s. if he owns a horse	1784
	State Tax	1783	Up to 5s. per year on single man not otherswise rated; up to 10s. if owns horse	1787
	State Tax	1787	Up to 6s.3d. per year on single man not otherwise rated; up to 12s.6d. if horse	1790
	State Tax	1790	5–15s. per year on single man not otherwise rated; 10–25s. if he owns a horse	1794
	State Tax	1794	3–8s. per year on single man not otherwise rated; 5–14s. if he owns a horse	1802
New York	Adultery	1665	Single person having sex with married person to be fined	1684
	Fornication	1665	Unmarried partners can be enjoined to marry, fined, or whipped	1684

Militia	1665	Magistrate can put to service a single man unable to afford arms	1684
Province Tax	1703	3s. on free bachelor aged 25 years	1704
Debtor Relief	1730	Single person allowed to keep 20s. in apparel (married person allowed 50s.)	1732
North Carolina			
Assessment Rule	1778	Single freeman aged 21 years, not a soldier and not worth £400, rated for £400	1782
County Tax	1779	Single freeman aged 21 years, not a soldier and not worth £400, rated for £400	1784
Poor Law	1779	Single freeman aged 21 years, not a soldier and not worth £400, rated for £400	1783
State Tax	1781	£150 on single man not worth £1000	1781
Assessment Rule	1782	Single freeman aged 21 years, not a soldier and not worth £100, rated for £100	1784
State Tax	1782	8s.4d. on single man aged 20–50, not a soldier and not worth £100	1782
Tax for USA	1782	Single freeman aged 21 years, not a soldier and not worth £100, rated for £100	1782
Pennsylvania			
Adultery	1682	Single person to face half year in prison for first offense, life in prison for second	1700
Bigamy	1682	Single person who knowingly weds a married person to be charged as bigamist	1790
Fornication	1683	Unmarried partners can be enjoined to marry, fined, or whipped	1706
Province Tax	1693	Exemption for married person with many children and worth less than £30	1694
County Tax	1696	Exemption for married person with many children and worth less than £30	1799
County Tax	1696	6s. per year on freeman aged 16 years without a family to maintain	1700
Rape	1700	Single man to forfeit entire estate (married man to forfeit a third)	1718
Sodomy/Bestiality	1700	Married man to suffer castration	1706
County Tax	1700	4s. per year on freeman aged 16 years without a family to maintain	1718
Province Tax	1700	Exemption for married person with many children and worth less than £30	1706
Debtor Relief	1706	Single person under 53 years can be bound out up to seven years	1730
Province Tax	1711	8s. per year on single freeman aged 21 years worth less than £50	1715
Tax for the Queen	1711	20s. per year on single freeman aged 21 years worth less than £50	1717
Province Tax	1715	Exemption for married person with many children and worth less than £30	1755
County Tax	1718	4–12s. per year on single freeman aged 21 years worth less than £50	1725

(continued)

Colony	Type of Law	Passed	Specifics	Expired
	Poor Law	1718	Unmarried person without children to receive relief where s/he was a servant	1913
	County Tax	1722	Propertyless single freeman not to be rated more than 3s. in county taxes	1725
	County Tax	1725	3-9s. per year on single freeman aged 21 years worth less than £50	1799
	Debtor Relief	1730	Single person allowed to keep 20s. in apparel (married person allowed 50s.)	1776
	Debtor Relief	1731	No relief for single person without children and under 40 years	1776
	Tax for the King	1755	10s. per year on single freeman aged 21 years worth less than £30	1763
	Tax for the King	1757	Additional 10s. per year on single freeman aged 21 years worth less than £30	1763
	Tax for the King	1759	20s. per year on single freeman aged 21, worth less than £15, and not a soldier	1770
	Tax for the King	1764	15s. per year on single freeman aged 21 years in addition to property taxes	1772
	State Tax	1777	10s. on every single freeman aged 21 years and not a soldier	1778
	State Tax	1777	Additional 20s. on every single freeman aged 21 years and not a soldier	1778
	Tax for USA	1778	£3 on every single freeman aged 21 years and not a soldier	1778
	State Tax	1779	£5-30 on single freeman aged 21 years and not otherwise rated	1779
	County Tax	1779	Propertyless single freeman not to be rated more than £5 in county taxes	1799
	Tax for USA	1779	£5-30 on every single freeman aged 21 years	1779
	Tax for USA	1780	£1-3 on every single freeman aged 21 years	1780
	State Tax	1781	45s.-£6 on every single freeman aged 21 years	1781
	Tax for USA	1783	20s.-£4 on every single freeman aged 21 years in addition to property taxes	1783
	County Tax	1799	Up to $10 per year on single freemen without occupation or calling	1919
Plymouth	Family Government	1636	Single person not to keep house for himself unless he be able to afford arms	1692
	Fornication	1645	Unmarried partners can be enjoined to marry, fined, or whipped	1692
Rhode Island	Family Government	1656	Young man aged 21 years who is disorderly to be scattered or fined £5	unclear

Virginia	Sumptuary	1619	Unmarried man to be fined if wearing apparel above his station	unclear
	Military Draft	1755	Draft young man without wife or children from the militia in frontier counties	1756
	Military Draft	1756	Draft able-bodied man without wife or children from the militia in all counties	1758
	Military Draft	1777	Draft single man who has no children from the militia	1779
Great Britain	Labor	1549	Unmarried journeyman to serve by quarter year, single worker to serve yearly	1834
	Labor	1562	Unemployed unmarried person not worth 40s. to serve by the year	1834
	Kingdom Tax	1660	12d. per year on single person aged 16 years and not otherwise rated	1660s
	Kingdom Tax	1678	Exemption for person with four of more children and worth less than £50	1698
	Poor Law	1691	Unmarried person without children to receive relief where s/he was a servant	1834
	Kingdom Tax	1695	1s.-£12 10s. on bachelors aged 25 years, graduated by rank	1706
	Land Tax	1702	Exemption for person with four of more children and worth less than £50	unclear
	Militia	1757	Married men who already served may practice trade in place of service	unclear

Notes

Introduction: Bachelors in Early America

1 *The Papers of James Madison: The Congressional Series*, ed. William T. Hutchinson and William M. E. Rachal et al., 17 vols. (Chicago: University of Chicago Press et al., 1962–91), 1:75–76. Also see Jack N. Rakove, *James Madison and the Creation of the American Republic* (New York: HarperCollins, 1990).

2 *Papers of James Madison*, 1:109, 87.

3 Peter Nicholas, "Uncle Sam to Needy: Why Not Try Marriage?" *Philadelphia Inquirer,* March 2, 2003; Robert J. Sampson, John H. Laub, and Christopher Wimer, "Does Marriage Reduce Crime? A Counterfactual Approach to Within-Individual Causal Effects," *Criminology* 44 (2006): 465–508; Robert Fisk, "What Drives a Bomber to Kill the Innocent Child?" *Independent,* August 11, 2001; Philip Shenon, "A Chinese Bias against Girls Creates Surplus of Bachelors," *New York Times,* August 16, 1994. Also see Bella DePaulo, *Singled Out: How Singles Are Stereotyped, Stigmatized, and Ignored, and Still Live Happily Ever After* (New York: St. Martin's Press, 2006); Linda J. Waite and Maggie Gallagher, *The Case for Marriage: Why Married People Are Happier, Healthier, and Better Off Financially* (New York: Doubleday, 2000).

4 Howard P. Chudacoff, *The Age of the Bachelor: Creating an American Subculture* (Princeton: Princeton University Press, 1999). Also see David T. Courtwright, *Violent Land: Single Men and Social Disorder from the Frontier to the Inner City* (Cambridge: Harvard University Press, 1996); George Chauncey, *Gay New York: Gender, Urban Culture, and the Making of the Gay Male World, 1890–1940* (New York: Basic Books, 1994), 76–86.

5 Arthur W. Calhoun, *A Social History of the American Family*, 3 vols. (Cleveland: Clark, 1917–19), 1:67; also see 1:245–46.

6 Edmund S. Morgan, *American Slavery—American Freedom: The Ordeal of Colonial Virginia* (New York: Norton, 1975), 163, 221, 235–42; John Demos, *Entertaining Satan: Witchcraft and the Culture of Early New England* (New York: Oxford University Press, 1982), 50–52; Mark E. Kann, *A Republic of Men: The American Founders, Gendered Language, and*

Patriarchal Politics (New York: New York University Press, 1998), 52–62; Thomas A. Foster, *Sex and the Eighteenth-Century Man: Massachusetts and the History of Sexuality in America* (Boston: Beacon Press, 2006).

[7] Scott Slawinski, *Validating Bachelorhood: Audience, Patriarchy, and Charles Brockden Brown's Editorship of the* Monthly Magazine and American Review (New York: Routledge, 2005); Karin Wulf, *Not All Wives: Women of Colonial Philadelphia* (Ithaca: Cornell University Press, 2000). Also see Lee Virginia Chambers-Schiller, *Liberty, a Better Husband: The Generations of 1780–1840* (New Haven: Yale University Press, 1984).

[8] Anne S. Lombard, *Making Manhood: Growing Up Male in Colonial New England* (Cambridge: Harvard University Press, 2003), 97. Also see Lisa Wilson, *Ye Heart of a Man: The Domestic Life of Men in Colonial New England* (New Haven: Yale University Press, 1999).

[9] Kann, *Republic of Men,* 52. Also see Foster, *Sex and Eighteenth-Century Man,* 101–27.

[10] R. W. Connell, *Masculinities,* 2nd ed. (Berkeley: University of California Press, 2005).

[11] Ruth Mazo Karras, *From Boys to Men: Formations of Masculinity in Late Medieval Europe* (Philadelphia: University of Pennsylvania Press, 2003).

[12] Linda K. Kerber, *No Constitutional Right to Be Ladies: Women and the Obligations of Citizenship* (New York: Hill and Wang, 1998). Also see James H. Kettner, *The Development of American Citizenship, 1608–1870* (Chapel Hill: University of North Carolina Press, 1978); Linda Kerber, *Women of the Republic: Intellect and Ideology in Revolutionary America* (Chapel Hill: University of North Carolina Press, 1980).

[13] The language used to express male traits and the quality of being male is imprecise. As Gail Bederman has argued, *masculinity* encapsulated the aggression and physical prowess that came to be associated with men at the end of the nineteenth century, while *manly*—a word that implied control and self-discipline—was more characteristic of the Victorian era. Neither term was particularly popular in the colonial era and so readers should be aware that I am using anachronistic terms for much of my discussion of manhood since a more precise vocabulary is simply not available. See Gail Bederman, *Manliness and Civilization: A Cultural History of Gender and Race in the United States, 1880–1917* (Chicago: University of Chicago Press, 1995), 18–19; Lombard, *Making Manhood,* 183n18.

[14] Michel Foucault, *The History of Sexuality,* vol. 1: *An Introduction,* trans. Robert Huxley (New York, Vintage, 1990); David M. Halperin, *One Hundred Years of Homosexuality: And Other Essays on Greek Love* (New York: Routledge, 1990); Jonathan Ned Katz, *The Invention of Heterosexuality,* new ed. (Chicago: University of Chicago Press, 2007).

[15] Randolph Trumbach, "The Birth of the Queen: Sodomy and the Emergence of Gender Equality in Modern Culture, 1660–1750," in *Hidden from History: Reclaiming the Gay and Lesbian Past,* ed. Martin Duberman, Martha Vicinus, and George Chauncey Jr. (New York: Meridian, 1989), 129–40; Richard Godbeer, "'The Cry of Sodom': Discourse, Intercourse, and Desire in Colonial New England," *William and Mary Quarterly,* 3rd ser., 52 (1995): 259–86; Thomas A. Foster, "Antimasonic Satire, Sodomy, and Eighteenth-Century Masculinity in the *Boston Evening-Post,*" *William and Mary Quarterly,* 3rd ser., 60 (2003): 171–84.

[16] John D'Emilio and Estelle Freedman, *Intimate Matters: A History of Sexuality in America,* 2nd ed. (Chicago: University of Chicago Press, 1998).

[17] For example, see Jonathan Katz, *Gay American History: Lesbians and Gay Men in the U.S.A.* (New York: Discus, 1976).

1. Singles in Early Colonial America

[1] *At a General Court Held at Boston, in the Year [1668]: Order to Dispose of Single Persons, Stubborn Children, and Servants to Houses of Correction* (Cambridge, Mass.: Green, 1668); *Whereas the Lawes Published by the Honoured General Court, Lib. 1, Pag. 76, Sect. 3,*

Do Require All Towns from Time to Time to Dispose of Single Persons and Inmates within Their Towns to Service (Cambridge, Mass.: Green, 1668).

[2] *History of the Town of Dorchester, Massachusetts, by a Committee of the Dorchester Antiquarian and Historical Society* (Boston: Clapp, 1859), 223–24.

[3] Clifford K. Shipton et al., *Sibley's Harvard Graduates,* 17 vols. (Cambridge, Mass.: Sever et al., 1873–1975), 1:206. Also see Enders A. Robinson, *The Devil Discovered: Salem Witchcraft 1692* (New York: Hippocrene Books, 1991), 19–36; Mary Beth Norton, *In the Devil's Snare: The Salem Witchcraft Crisis of 1692* (New York: Knopf, 2002), 197–99.

[4] E. A. Wrigley and R. S. Schofield, *The Population History of England, 1541–1871: A Reconstruction* (Cambridge: Harvard University Press, 1981), 424. Also see Ralph A. Houlbrooke, *The English Family, 1450–1700* (London: Longman, 1984), 64; T. H. Hollingsworth, "The Demography of the British Peerage," *Population Studies* 18 supplement (1964): 17.

[5] K. J. Allison, "An Elizabethan Village 'Census,'" *Bulletin of the Institute of Historical Research* 36 (1963): 91–103; Marjorie J. McIntosh, "Servants and the Household Unit in an Elizabethan English Community," *Journal of Family History* 9 (1984): 11n4, 12n6.

[6] On single women in medieval and early modern Europe, see Judith M. Bennett and Amy M. Froide, eds., *Singlewomen in the European Past, 1250–1800* (Philadelphia: University of Pennsylvania Press, 1999); Amy M. Froide, *Never Married: Singlewomen in Early Modern England* (New York: Oxford University Press, 2005); Bridget Hill, *Women Alone: Spinsters in England, 1660–1850* (New Haven: Yale University Press, 2001).

[7] Mary Beth Norton, *Founding Mothers and Fathers: Gendered Power and the Forming of American Society* (New York: Knopf, 1996), 97–101; Carole Shammas, *A History of Household Government in America* (Charlottesville: University of Virginia Press, 2002), 24–27; Robert J. Steinfeld, *The Invention of Free Labor: The Employment Relation in English and American Law and Culture, 1350–1870* (Chapel Hill: University of North Carolina Press, 1991), 55–60, 70–72; Ann Kussmaul, *Servants in Husbandry in Early Modern England* (Cambridge: Cambridge University Press, 1981), 7–10, 31–34, 79–82; Rosemary O'Day, *The Family and Family Relationships, 1500–1900: England, France, and the United States of America* (New York: St. Martin's Press, 1994), 29–63. Also see Barbara A. Hanawalt, *The Ties That Bound: Peasant Families in Medieval England* (New York: Oxford University Press, 1986), 188–204; Diana O'Hara, *Courtship and Constraint: Rethinking the Making of Marriage in Tudor England* (Manchester: Manchester University Press, 2000); Susan Dwyer Amussen, *An Ordered Society: Gender and Class in Early Modern England* (Oxford: Basil Blackwell, 1988); David I. Kertzewr and Marzio Barbagli, eds., *The History of the European Family,* vol. 1, *Family Life in Early Modern Times, 1500–1789* (New Haven: Yale University Press, 2001); Holly Brewer, *By Birth or Consent: Children, Law, and the Anglo-American Revolution in Authority* (Chapel Hill: University of North Carolina Press, 2005).

[8] Stephanie Coontz, *Marriage, a History: From Obedience to Intimacy or How Love Conquered Marriage* (New York: Viking, 2005), 123–32; Alan Macfarlane, *Marriage and Love in England: Modes of Reproduction, 1300–1840* (Oxford: Basil Blackwell, 1986), 20–27; J. Hajnal, "European Marriage Patterns in Perspective," in *Population in History: Essays in Historical Demography,* ed. D. V. Glass and D. E. C. Eversley (London: Arnold, 1965), 101–46; J. Hajnal, "Two Kinds of Preindustrial Household Formation System," *Population and Development Review* 8 (1982): 449–94; Herbert S. Klein, *A Population History of the United States* (Cambridge: Cambridge University Press, 2004), 26–27n27.

[9] Paul Griffiths, *Youth and Authority: Formative Experiences in England, 1560–1640* (Oxford: Clarendon Press, 1996), 30–31; Kussmaul, *Servants in Husbandry,* 80; Steinfeld, *Invention of Free Labor,* 11, 19, 27–28. As Robert Steinfeld points out, "servant" could mean a domestic, a wage worker who was unmarried and lived with his master, or any worker who

served another for wages. Like Steinfeld, I use the second definition. Steinfeld, *Invention of Free Labor,* 17–22.

[10] There is considerable debate among historians on the incidence of service. See Peter Laslett, *The World We Have Lost, Further Explored: England before the Industrial Age,* 3rd ed. (New York: Scribner's Sons, 1983), 13–16; Graham Mayhew, "Life-Cycle and the Family Unit in Early Modern Rye," *Continuity and Change* 6 (1991): 201–26; Richard Wall, "Leaving Home and the Process of Household Formation in Pre-Industrial England," *Continuity and Change* 2 (1987): 77–101; Griffiths, *Youth and Authority,* 7.

[11] William Gouge, *Of Domesticall Duties: Eight Treatises* (1622, repr., Amsterdam: Johnson, 1976), 184. On singles and religion, see Eric Josef Carlson, *Marriage and the English Reformation* (Oxford: Blackwell, 1994), 3–8; John Witte Jr., *From Sacrament to Contract: Marriage, Religion, and Law in the Western Tradition* (Louisville, Ky.: Westminster John Knox Press, 1997), 43–56; Thomas Wilson, *The Art of Rhetoric (1560),* ed. Peter E. Medine (University Park: Pennsylvania State University Press, 1994), 89.

[12] William Perkins, *Christian Oeconomie, or, a Short Survey of the Right Manner of Erecting and Ordering a Families, According to the Scriptures* (London: Kyngston, 1609), 671.

[13] Gouge, *Of Domesticall Duties,* 211. Also see Matthew Griffith, *Bethel: Or, A Forme for Families in Which All Sorts, of Both Sexes, Are So Squared, and Framed by the Word of God, as They May Best Serve in Their Severall Places, for Usefull Pieces in God's Building* (London: Badger, 1633).

[14] "Articles of Religion," in Edward Cardwell, *Synodalia: A Collection of Articles of Religion, Canons, and Proceedings of Convocations in the Province of Canterbury, from the Year 1547 to the Year 1717,* vol. 1 (Oxford: Oxford University Press, 1842), 29–30.

[15] Francis Bacon, *The Essays or Counsels Civill and Morall of Francis Bacon, Baron of Verulam, Viscount Saint Alban* (New York: Heritage, 1944), 23–24.

[16] Carlson, *Marriage and the Reformation,* 52–65.

[17] *Calvin: Institutes of the Christian Religion,* ed. John T. McNeill, trans. Ford Lewis Battles, 2 vols. (Philadelphia: Westminster Press, 1960), 1:405–7.

[18] Perkins, *Christian Oeconomie,* 671. Also see Griffith, *Bethel,* 20–22; Gouge, *Of Domesticall Duties,* 182, 212.

[19] William Smith, "Universal Love," in *Balm from Gilead: A Collection of the Living Divine Testimonies* (London: n.p., 1675), 88.

[20] Lawrence Stone, *The Family, Sex, and Marriage in England, 1500–1800* (New York: Harper and Row, 1977), 377–78; A. L. Beier, *Masterless Men: The Vagrancy Problem in England, 1560–1640* (London: Metheun, 1985), 93–95, 516–18; Bernard Bailyn, "Introduction: Europeans on the Move, 1500–1800," in *Europeans on the Move: Studies in European Migration, 1500–1800,* ed. Nicholas Canny (Oxford: Clarendon Press, 1994), 4; Sylvia R. Frey, *The British Soldier in America: A Social History of Military Life in the Revolutionary Period* (Austin: University of Texas Press, 1981), 6–7, 25, 59–61; Jackson Turner Main, *The Social Structure of Revolutionary America* (Princeton: Princeton University Press, 1965), 91–95, 141–44.

[21] Bacon, *Essays,* 23.

[22] John Mayer, *The English Catechisme Explained: Or, A Comentarie on the Short Catechime Set Forth in the Booke of Common Prayer* (London: Mathewes, 1623), 359–60.

[23] Peter Fleming, *Family and Household in Medieval England* (Houndsmill: Palgrave, 2001), 6–18; Stone, *Family, Sex, and Marriage,* 10–20; Macfarlane, *Marriage and Love;* George Elliott Howard, *A History of Matrimonial Institutions Chiefly in England and the United States with an Introductory Analysis of the Literature and the Theories of Primitive Marriage and the Family,* 3 vols. (Chicago: University of Chicago Press, 1904), 2:152–69; Lawrence Stone,

Road to Divorce: England, 1530–1987 (Oxford: Oxford University Press, 1990); Martin Ingram, *Church Courts, Sex and Marriage in England, 1570–1640* (Cambridge: Cambridge University Press, 1987), 125–218; William Blackstone, *Commentaries on the Laws of England,* 4 vols. (Philadelphia: Lippincott, 1888), 1:345–66; 4:122–23.

[24] Stephen Parker, *Informal Marriage, Cohabitation, and the Law 1750–1989* (New York: St. Martin's Press, 1990), 29–47.

[25] Shammas, *History of Household Government,* 83–107; David Cressy, *Birth, Marriage, and Death: Ritual, Religion, and the Life-Cycle in Tudor and Stuart England* (Oxford: Oxford University Press, 1997). Also see Michael M. Sheehan, *Marriage, Family, and the Law in Medieval Europe: Collected Studies,* ed. James K. Farge (Toronto: University of Toronto Press, 1996); Georges Duby, *Love and Marriage in the Middle Ages,* trans. Jane Dunnett (Chicago: University of Chicago Press, 1994).

[26] *Oxford English Dictionary,* 2nd ed. (Oxford: Clarendon Press, 1989), s.vv. "bachelor," "maiden," "single," "virgin." For earlier uses of bachelor, see *Statutes of the Realm, Printed by Command of His Majesty King George the Third, in Pursuance of an Address of the House of Commons of Great Britain; from Original Records and Authentic Manuscripts,* 9 vols. (London: Eyre and Strahan, 1810–22), 3 Edw. IV, c. 5; Terence O'Brien, "The London Livery Company and the Virginia Company," *Virginia Magazine of History and Biography* 68 (1960): 137–55.

[27] "The Merchant's Tale," IV (E), lines 1274–85. For alternate uses, see "Prologue," I (A), line 80; "The Manciple's Tale," IX (H), lines 107, 125; "The Knyghtes Tale," I (A), line 3085; "The Franklin's Tale," V (F), line 1126.

[28] Shakespeare, *Romeo and Juliet,* 1.5.112.

[29] Shakespeare, *1 Henry VI,* 5.4.13. Also see Shakespeare, *3 Henry VI,* 3.2.103.

[30] Shakespeare, *Much Ado about Nothing,* 1.1.216, 2.3.227–28.

[31] Hilda L. Smith, *All Men and Both Sexes: Gender, Politics, and the False Universal in England, 1640–1832* (University Park: Pennsylvania State University Press, 2002), 1–38; Griffiths, *Youth and Authority,* 200–13.

[32] Griffiths, *Youth and Authority,* 207; Elizabeth A. Foyster, *Manhood in Early Modern England: Honour, Sex and Marriage* (London: Longman, 1999), 39–48.

[33] Thomas Gouge, *The Young Man's Guide, Through the Wilderness of this World, to the Heavenly Canaan* (Boston: Draper, 1742), 107, 111; Mayer, *English Catechisme Explained,* 359.

[34] Gouge, *Young Man's Guide,* 104–5.

[35] The idea of same-sex toleration promoted by Richard Godbeer and Thomas Foster is not without considerable qualifications. It ultimately revises but does not displace Foucault's argument that Europeans in the sixteenth and seventeenth century did not draw considerable meaning from the different types of nonmarital sex. See Richard Godbeer, "'The Cry of Sodom': Discourse, Intercourse, and Desire in Colonial New England," *Maryland Historical Magazine* 52 (1995): 259–86; Thomas Foster, *Sex and the Eighteenth-Century Man: Massachusetts and the History of Sexuality in America* (Boston: Beacon, 2006); Michel Foucault, *The History of Sexuality,* vol. 1, *An Introduction,* trans. Robert Hurley (New York: Pantheon, 1978).

[36] Falstaff appears in both parts of *Henry IV, Henry V,* and *The Merry Wives of Windsor.* James C. Humes, *Citizen Shakespeare: A Social and Political Portrait* (Westport, Conn.: Praeger, 1993), 65–71; Tim Spiekerman, *Shakespeare's Political Realism: The English History Plays* (Albany: State University of New York Press, 2001), 105–17.

[37] Ruth Mazo Karras, *From Boys to Men: Formations of Masculinity in Late Medieval Europe* (Philadelphia: University of Pennsylvania Press, 2003); Alexandra Shepard, *Meanings of Manhood in Early Modern England* (Oxford: Oxford University Press, 2003); D. M. Hadley, ed., *Masculinity in Medieval Europe* (London: Longman, 1999).

[38] Bacon, *Essays*, 23.

[39] Beier, *Masterless Men*, 19–22. Also see James Horn, *Adapting to a New World: English Society in the Seventeenth-Century Chesapeake* (Chapel Hill: University of North Carolina Press, 1994), 48–52; John Pound, *Poverty and Vagrancy in Tudor England*, 2nd ed. (London: Longman, 1986).

[40] *Statutes of the Realm*, 23 Edw. III, cc. 1–8; 25 Edw. III, cc. 1–8; 12 Ric. II, c. 3–10. Also see Eli F. Heckscher, *Mercantilism*, trans. Mendel Shapiro, vol. 1 (London: Allen and Unwin, 1935), 226–27; W. Cunningham, *The Growth of English Industry and Commerce in Modern Times*, vol. 2 (Cambridge: Cambridge University Press, 1910), 25–26; Susan Brigden, "Youth and the English Reformation," *Past and Present* 95 (1982): 46; Bertha Haven Putnam, *The Enforcement of the Statutes of Laborers: During the First Decade after the Black Death, 1349–1359* (New York: Columbia University, 1908), 71, 175–76, 179–82, 212–13.

[41] *Statutes of the Realm*, 43 Eliz. I, c. 2. Also see *Statutes of the Realm*, 22 Hen. VIII, cc. 12, 27; Hen. VIII, c. 25; 14 Eliz. I, c. 5; Blackstone, *Commentaries*, 1:275–77.

[42] In 1691 Parliament revised the kingdom's poor law to recognize the labor of the unmarried, ordering that "if any Unmarried person not having Child or Children shall be lawfully hired into any Parish or Towne for one yeare such Service shall be deemed a good Settlement." Pennsylvania adopted a nearly verbatim provision in its poor law in 1718, something that the assembly did not remove until 1913. *Statutes of the Realm*, 3 Gul. & Mar., c. 11; *The Statutes at Large of Pennsylvania from 1682 to 1801*, ed. James T. Mitchell and Henry Flanders, 17 vols. (Harrisburg: Busch et al., 1896–1915), 3:221–22; 4:266–77; 5:79–86; 7:75–79, 159–61, 310; 8:75–96, 474; 9:228–29; George Wharton Pepper and William Draper Lewis, *A Digest of the Laws of Pennsylvania, 1700–1907*, 2nd ed. (Philadelphia: Johnson, 1910), 5742.

[43] McIntosh, "Servants and Household Unit," 12–18.

[44] Beier, *Masterless Men*, 16–17, 51–57, 216–17.

[45] *Statutes of the Realm*, 3 & 4 Edw. VI, c. 22.

[46] *Statutes of the Realm*, 5 Eliz. I, c. 4. For contemporary commentary, see Thomas Smith, *De Republica Anglorum*, ed. Mary Dewar (Cambridge: Cambridge University Press, 1982), 135–42; Blackstone, *Commentaries*, 1:336. For historical perspective, see Steinfeld, *Invention of Free Labor*, 22–41, 60–66, 98; Griffiths, *Youth and Authority*, 33, 76; Kussmaul, *Servants in Husbandry*, 78–80; Donald Woodward, "The Background to the Statute of Artificers: The Genesis of Labour Policy, 1558–63," *Economic History Review*, 2nd ser., 33 (1980): 32–44; Heckscher, *Mercantilism*, 227–32; Cunningham, *Growth of English Industry*, 25–37; S. T. Bindoff, "The Making of The Statute of Artificers," in *Elizabethan Government and Society: Essays Presented to Sir John Neale*, ed. S. T. Bindoff, J. Hurstfield, and C. H. Williams (London: University of London, Athlone Press, 1961), 56–94; David W. Galenson, "The Rise of Free Labor: Economic Change and the Enforcement of Service Contracts in England, 1351–1875," in *Capitalism in Context: Essays on Economic Development and Cultural Change in Honor of R. M. Hartwell*, ed. John A. James and Mark Thomas (Chicago: University of Chicago Press, 1994), 116–18.

[47] John Hostettler and Brian P. Block, *Voting in Britain: A History of the Parliamentary Franchise* (Chichester: Rose, 2001), 10–14.

[48] It was not until after 1780 that a majority of single people began to contract as daily laborers rather than by the year. See Cunningham, *Growth of English Industry*, 633–60, 754–55; K. D. M. Snell, *Annals of the Labouring Poor: Social Change and Agrarian England, 1660–1900* (Cambridge: Cambridge University Press, 1985), 24, 73–75; Beier, *Masterless Men*, 23.

[49] Margaret Gay Davies, *The Enforcement of English Apprenticeship: A Study in Applied Mercantilism* (Cambridge: Harvard University Press, 1956), 193. Davies misreads section 3 of the Statute of Artificers as *only* applying to single men under thirty.

[50] Court records quoted in Davies, *Enforcement of English Apprenticeship,* 193–94; F. G. Emmison, *Elizabethan Life: Disorder, Mainly from Essex Sessions and Assize Records* (Chelmsford: Essex County Council, 1970), 33.

[51] Griffiths, *Youth and Authority,* 358; Emmison, *Elizabethan Life,* 210. Also see "Presentments in Yorkshire Under the States of Artificers Etc. (1605–8)," in *Tudor Economic Documents: Being Select Documents Illustrating the Economic and Social History of Tudor England,* ed. R. H. Tawney and Eileen Power, vol. 1 (London: Longmans, 1953).

[52] *Statutes of the Realm,* 3 Hen. VII, c. 3; 4 & 5 Phil. & Mar., c. 8; 39 Eliz. I, c. 9; Blackstone, *Commentaries,* 3:139–40; 4:208–16. Also see Howard, *History of Matrimonial Institutions,* 1:291–316; Stone, *Road to Divorce,* 51–54, 67–74, 96–106; Carlson, *Marriage and the Reformation,* 18–29; Ralph Houlbrooke, *Church Courts and the People during the English Reformation, 1520–70* (Oxford: Oxford University Press, 1979), 55–67; Ingram, *Church Courts,* 132–34, 210–11; Ronald A. Marchant, *The Church under the Law: Justice, Administration and Discipline in the Diocese of York, 1560–1640* (Cambridge: Cambridge University Press, 1969), 224–25.

[53] *Statutes of the Realm,* 25 Hen. VIII, c. 6. On Puritan criticism of the church courts, see W. H. Frere and C. E. Douglas, eds., *Puritan Manifestoes: A Study of the Origin of the Puritan Revolt* (London: Society for Promoting Christian Knowledge, 1907), 17, 27; Marchant, *Church under the Law,* 138, 215–22; R. H. Helmholz, *Canon Law and the Law of England* (London: Hambledon Press, 1987), 145–55; Ingram, *Church Courts,* 210–11, 221, 225.

[54] *Statutes of the Realm,* 18 Eliz. I, c. 3. This provision appears in Michael Dalton, *The Countrey Justice, Containing the Practice of the Justices of the Peace out of Their Sessions* (London: Societie of Stationers, 1622), 32. Also see Houlbrooke, *Church Courts,* 64, 78; Carlson, *Marriage and the Reformation,* 142; Keith Thomas, "The Puritans and Adultery: The Act of 1650 Reconsidered," in *Puritans and Revolutionaries: Essays in Seventeenth-Century History Presented to Christopher Hill,* ed. Donald Pennington and Keith Thomas (Oxford: Clarendon Press, 1978), 269; Ingram, *Church Courts,* 210–37, 276; Helmholz, *Canon Law,* 145–55.

[55] Robert Beverley, *The History and Present State of Virginia,* ed. Louis B. Wright (Chapel Hill: University of North Carolina Press, 1947), 286–87.

[56] Richard Middleton, *Colonial America: A History, 1585–1776,* 2nd ed. (Oxford: Blackwell, 1996), 251; U.S. Bureau of the Census, *A Century of Population Growth: From the First Census of the United States to the Twelfth, 1700–1900* (Washington, D.C.: Government Printing Office, 1909), 149–51, 166–69.

[57] James Horn, "Servant Emigration to the Chesapeake in the Seventeenth Century," in *The Chesapeake in the Seventeenth Century: Essays on Anglo-American Society,* ed. Thad W. Tate and David L. Ammerman (Chapel Hill: University of North Carolina Press, 1979), 54; Herbert Moller, "Sex Composition and Correlated Culture Patterns of Colonial America," *William and Mary Quarterly,* 3rd ser., 2 (1945): 115–18; Lois Green Carr and Russell R. Menard, "Immigration and Opportunity: The Freedman in Early Colonial Maryland," in *Chesapeake in Seventeenth Century,* 211; David Cressy, *Coming Over: Migration and Communication between England and New England in the Seventeenth Century* (Cambridge: Cambridge University Press, 1987), 52–68; Robert V. Wells, *The Population of the British Colonies in America before 1776: A Survey of Census Data* (Princeton: Princeton University Press, 1975), 72, 74, 81, 85, 90, 93, 100, 103, 112, 122, 135, 139, 147, 154. Also see Horn, *Adapting to New World,* 32–38; David Souden, "'Rogues, Whores and Vagabonds'? Indentured Servant Emigrants to North America, and the Case of Mid-Seventeenth-Century Bristol," *Social History* 3 (1978): 23–41; Anthony Salerno, "The Social Background of Seventeenth-Century Emigration to America," *Journal of British Studies* 19 (1979): 31–52; Christopher L. Tomlins, "Reconsidering Indentured Servitude: European Migration and the Early American Labor Force, 1600–1775," American Bar Foundation Working Paper #9920, 1999.

[58] Irene W. D. Hecht, "The Virginia Muster of 1624/5 as a Source for Demographic History," *William and Mary Quarterly*, 3rd ser., 30 (1973): 65–92; Moller, "Sex Composition," 115–18, 121; Rodger C. Henderson, *Community Development and the Revolutionary Transition in Eighteenth-Century Lancaster County, Pennsylvania* (New York: Garland, 1989), 52, 109; Bernard Bailyn, *Voyagers to the West: A Passage in the Peopling of America on the Eve of the Revolution* (New York: Knopf, 1986), 131–33, 206–7.

[59] Robert V. Wells, "Quaker Marriage Patterns in a Colonial Perspective," *William and Mary Quarterly*, 3rd ser., 39 (1972): 415–42; Barry Levy, *Quakers and the American Family: British Settlement in the Delaware Valley* (New York: Oxford University Press, 1988), 273–76; Susan E. Klepp, "Fragmented Knowledge: Questions in Regional Demographic History," *Proceedings of the American Philosophical Society* 133 (1989): 223–33; Karin Wulf, *Not All Wives: Women of Colonial Philadelphia* (Ithaca: Cornell University Press, 2000), 65–70; Christine Leigh Heyrman, *Commerce and Culture: The Maritime Communities of Colonial Massachusetts, 1690–1750* (New York: Norton, 1984), 213, 215–18; Wells, *Population of British Colonies*, 131–33; William B. Bailey, "A Statistical Study of Yale Graduates, 1701–92," *Yale Review* 16 (1907–8): 400–26. Also see Daniel Vickers, *Farmers and Fishermen: Two Centuries of Work in Essex County, Massachusetts, 1630–1850* (Chapel Hill: University of North Carolina Press, 1994), 86–89; Daniel Vickers and Vince Walsh, *Young Men and the Sea: Yankee Seafarers in the Age of Sail* (New Haven: Yale University Press, 2005), 112–18, 267, 295n36, 295n38.

[60] Henry A. Gemery, "The White Population of the Colonial United States, 1607–1790," in *A Population History of North America*, ed. Michael R. Haines and Richard H. Steckel (Cambridge: Cambridge University Press, 2000), 143–90; Robert V. Wells, "The Population of England's Colonies in America: Old English or New Americans?" *Population Studies* 46 (1992): 85–102; Daniel Scott Smith, "The Demographic History of Colonial New England," in *The American Family in Social-Historical Perspective*, ed. Michael Gordon (New York: St. Martin's Press, 1973), 406.

[61] On the family in early New England, see Arthur W. Calhoun, *A Social History of the American Family*, 3 vols. (Cleveland: Clark, 1917–19); Edmund S. Morgan, *The Puritan Family: Religion and Domestic Relations in Seventeenth-Century New England*, new ed. (New York: Harper and Row, 1966); John Demos, *A Little Commonwealth: Family Life in Plymouth Colony* (New York: Oxford University Press, 1970); Laurel Thatcher Ulrich, *Good Wives: Image and Reality in Northern New England, 1650–1750* (New York: Knopf, 1982); Gloria L. Main, *Peoples of a Spacious Land: Families and Cultures in Colonial New England* (Cambridge: Harvard University Press, 2001); Norton, *Founding Mothers and Fathers*, 27–137; Shammas, *History of Household Government*, 24–52.

[62] Robert E. Wall, *The Membership of the Massachusetts Bay General Court, 1630–86* (New York: Garland, 1990), 134–35; *Records of the Governor and Company of the Massachusetts Bay in New England*, ed. Nathaniel B. Shurtleff, 5 vols. (Boston: White, 1853–54), 1:179–374; *Early Records of the Town of Dedham, Massachusetts*, 6 vols. (Dedham: Dedham Historical Society, 1886–1936), 3:3–88; 4:287; *A Plan of Dedham Village, Mass., 1636–1876: With Descriptions of the Grants of Lots to the Original Owners, Transcribed From the Town Records* (Dedham: Dedham Historical Society, 1883), 7, 11; Kenneth A. Lockridge, *A New England Town: The First Hundred Years, Dedham, Massachusetts, 1636–1736*, expanded ed. (New York: Norton, 1985), 28–29, 60–61.

[63] *The Journal of John Winthrop, 1630–49*, ed. Richard S. Dunn, James Savage, and Laetitia Yeandle (Cambridge: Harvard University Press, 1996), 18. Also see *Journal of John Winthrop*, 8, 417, 500–502, 510, 669–70, 687–88.

[64] Anne S. Lombard, *Making Manhood: Growing Up Male in Colonial New England* (Cambridge: Harvard University Press, 2003), 18–45. Also see Lisa Wilson, *Ye Heart of a*

Man: The Domestic Life of Men in Colonial New England (New Haven: Yale University Press, 1999), 13–36; Steven Mintz, *Huck's Raft: A History of American Childhood* (Cambridge: Harvard University Press, 2004), 7–31.

[65] *Records of Massachusetts,* 2:6; 3:101.

[66] *Records of Massachusetts,* 1:186. Also see *The Book of the General Lauues and Libertyes Concerning the Inhabitants of the Massachusets Collected Out of the Records of the General Court For the Several Years Wherin They Were Made and Established, and Now Revised by the Same Court and Dispersed into an Alphabetical Order and Published by the Same Authoritie in the General Court Held at Boston, the Fourteenth of the First Month, Anno 1647* (Cambridge: General Court, 1648), 51.

[67] *The Public Records of the Colony of Connecticut,* ed. J. Hammond Trumbull et al., 15 vols. (Hartford: Case, Lockwood, and Brainard, et al., 1859–90), 1:8; *Records of the Colony of New Plymouth in New England,* ed. Nathaniel B. Shurtleff et al., 11 vols. (Boston: White, 1855–61), 11:17; *New Haven's Settling in New-England and Some Lawes for Government: Published for the Use of that Colony* (London: M.S., 1656), 50–51; *Records of the Colony of Rhode Island and Providence Plantations,* ed. John Russell Bartlett, 10 vols. (Providence: Greene, 1856–65), 1:333. New Hampshire did not institute a family government law.

[68] William B. Weeden, *Economic and Social History of New England, 1620–1789,* vol. 1 (Boston: Houghton Mifflin, 1894), 230; Alice Morse Earle, *Customs and Fashions in Old New England* (New York: Scribner, 1893), 36–38; Howard, *History of Matrimonial Institutions,* 2:152–61; Calhoun, *American Family,* 1:67, 165; Morgan, *Puritan Family,* 27, 144–46; Demos, *Little Commonwealth,* 77–79; Norton, *Founding Mothers and Fathers,* 41–42, 250–52; Mark E. Kann, *A Republic of Men: The American Founders, Gendered Language, and Patriarchal Politics* (New York: New York University Press, 1998), 61; Main, *Peoples of Spacious Land,* 70–71. The continuity between the New England family government laws and the English statutes of laborers and artificers has been noted in Steinfeld, *Invention of Free Labor,* 49, 58, 120, 132; Lawrence W. Towner, "'A Fondness for Freedom': Servant Protest in Puritan Society," *William and Mary Quarterly,* 3rd ser., 19 (1962): 204; Lawrence William Towner, *A Good Master Well Served: Masters and Servants in Colonial Massachusetts, 1620–1750* (New York: Garland, 1998), 56–57; Eric Guest Nellis, "Labor and Community in Massachusetts Bay: 1630–60," *Labor History* 18 (1977): 530–31; David Hackett Fischer, *Albion's Seed: Four British Folkways in America* (New York: Oxford University Press, 1989), 73.

[69] David Grayson Allen, *In English Ways: The Movement of Societies and Transferal of English Local Law and Custom to Massachusetts Bay in the Seventeenth Century* (Chapel Hill: University of North Carolina Press, 1981); Jack P. Greene, *Pursuits of Happiness: The Social Development of Early Modern British Colonies and the Formation of American Culture* (Chapel Hill: University of North Carolina Press, 1988); Fischer, *Albion's Seed,* 68–111, 274–326; Norton, *Founding Mothers and Fathers,* 415n23; David W. Galenson, "Labor Market Behavior in Colonial America: Servitude, Slavery and Free Labor," in *Markets in History: Economic Studies of the Past,* ed. David W. Galenson (Cambridge: Cambridge University Press, 1989), 84–88; Vickers, *Farmers and Fishermen,* 59–60, 64–77; Ross W. Beales Jr., "Boys' Work on an Eighteenth-Century New England Farm," in *The American Family: Historical Perspectives,* ed. Jean E. Hunter and Paul T. Mason, 75–89 (Pittsburgh: Duquesne University Press, 1991). The only exception was Rhode Island where dairy and livestock plantations were worked by slaves.

[70] *Records and Files of the Quarterly Courts of Essex County, Massachusetts,* ed. George Francis Dow, 8 vols. (Salem, Mass.: Essex Institute, 1911–21), 5:104. On Littlehale, see *Records of Essex County,* 5:421–22; 6:32–33, 54–55, 79–80, 118; George Madison Bodge, *Soldiers in King Philip's War: Being a Critical Account of That War with a Concise History of the Indian*

Wars of New England from 1620–77 (Leominster, Mass.: Bodge, 1896), 138; Stephan Thernstrom, *Poverty and Progress: Social Mobility in a Nineteenth Century City* (Cambridge: Harvard University Press, 1964), 35–36; Richard Godbeer, *Sexual Revolution in Early America* (Baltimore: Johns Hopkins University Press, 2002), 100–101. For other prosecutions, see *Records of the Court of Assistants of the Colony of the Massachusetts Bay, 1630–92*, ed. John Noble, 3 vols. (Boston: County of Suffolk, 1901–28), 1:70; *Records of the Suffolk County Court, 1671–80*, ed. Samuel Eliot Morison and Zechariah Chafee, 2 vols. (Boston: Colonial Society of Massachusetts, 1933), 1:82–83, 89, 231, 255, 258, 306, 436; 2:597, 717, 719, 721, 751, 753–54, 835, 844, 846, 870–71, 915, 957; *Records of Essex County*, 2:180; 5:104, 166.

[71] *Records of Plymouth*, 2:148. Also see Demos, *Little Commonwealth*, 78; *Records of Plymouth*, 1:68; 2:146–48; 3:37; *Records of the Town of Plymouth, Published by Order of the Town*, ed. William T. Davis, vol. 1, *1636 to 1705* (Plymouth: Avery and Doten, 1889), 138–39.

[72] *Early Records of Dedham*, 4:52. Dorchester selectmen also took no action against single men before the late 1660s. See *History of Dorchester*, 157–210.

[73] *New Haven Town Records, 1649–1769*, ed. Franklin Bowditch Dexter et al., 3 vols. (New Haven: New Haven Colony Historical Society, 1917–62), 3:33.

[74] Henry R. Stiles, *The History and Genealogies of Ancient Windsor, Connecticut; Including East Windsor, South Windsor, Bloomfield, Windsor Locks, and Ellington, 1635–1891*, rev. ed., vol. 1, *History* (Hartford, Conn.: Case, Lockwood and Brainard, 1891), 1:81; Weeden, *Economic and Social History*, 2:230. Also see *Records of Plymouth*, 1:135–36.

[75] "General Court in Boston" (1668). Also see Albert Matthews, "Hired Man and Help," *Publications of the Colonial Society of Massachusetts*, vol. 5, *Transactions, 1897, 1898* (Boston: Colonial Society of Massachusetts, 1902), 234.

[76] *History of Dorchester*, 211.

[77] *Early Records of Dedham*, 4:170.

[78] *Records of Essex County*, 5:425. Also see Howard, *History of Matrimonial Institutions*, 2:155–56.

[79] *History of Dorchester*, 223–26; *Early Records of Dedham*, 5:5, 40, 53–54.

[80] *Records of Connecticut*, 1:538–39; *Records of Plymouth*, 11:223.

[81] *Early Records of Dedham*, 5:53.

[82] *The Acts and Resolves, Public and Private, of the Province of the Massachusetts Bay*, 21 vols. (Boston: Wright and Potter, 1869–1922), 1:538. Also see Towner, *Good Master Well Served*, 56; *Acts of Massachusetts*, 1:587, 654; 2:73–74, 182–83, 243–44, 579–80, 1053–54; 3:488; 4:324; 5:39, 258, 903; *Acts and Laws, Passed by the Great and General Court or Assembly of the Commonwealth of Massachusetts: Begun and Held at Boston, in the County of Suffolk, on Wednesday the Twenty-Ninth Day of May, 1782; and from Thence Continued by Adjournment to Wednesday the Eighteenth Day of September Following, and Then Met* (Boston: Edes and Sons, 1782), 105–6; *Acts and Laws of the Commonwealth of Massachusetts* (Boston: Adams and Nourse, 1788), 99–100. New Hampshire adopted a similar provision in its poor law of 1766, which remained in force until 1791. *Laws of New Hampshire Including Public and Private Acts and Resolves and the Royal Commissions and Instructions*, ed. Albert Stillman Batchellor et al., 10 vols. (Manchester: Clarke et al., 1904–22), 3:391; 4:16; 6:693.

[83] Stiles, *History of Windsor*, 81. The fate of Rhode Island's family government law is equally muddled while laws in New Haven and Plymouth ceased to exist when the colonies were absorbed by Connecticut and Massachusetts, respectively. Neither Connecticut nor Rhode Island added language regarding marital status to their poor laws.

[84] *The Autobiography of Benjamin Franklin*, ed. Leonard W. Labaree et al. (New Haven: Yale University Press, 1964), 63.

[85] Roger Thompson, *Sex in Middlesex: Popular Mores in a Massachusetts County, 1649–99* (Amherst: University of Massachusetts Press, 1986), 83–96; Lombard, *Making Manhood*, 80.

[86] *Journal of John Winthrop*, 56, 111, 374. Also see *Journal of John Winthrop*, 385.

[87] *Records of Massachusetts*, 1:275; 2:15, 207, 211–12; 3:398; 4 (pt. 1):255, 290, 322; *Records of Plymouth*, 3:206; 4:22, 140; 9:13, 29, 107–8; *Records of Connecticut*, 1:47–48, 105–6, 292, 350; 2:328; *New Haven's Settling*, 41–42; *Records of Rhode Island*, 1:13, 187, 330, 360–61; 3:435–37. Massachusetts's marriage laws applied to New Hampshire until 1693. See *Laws of New Hampshire*, 1:558–59; Howard, *History of Matrimonial Institutions*, 2:128–43.

[88] *Records of Massachusetts*, 1:92, 225, 301; 2:21; 4 (pt. 1):218–19; 4 (pt. 2):437–38; *Acts of Massachusetts*, 1:55–56, 171–72, 255, 296–97; 4:622; *Records of Plymouth*, 11:12, 94–95; *Records of Connecticut*, 1:77, 515; 2:20–21, 184, 189; 4:285; 6:26–28; *New Haven's Settling*, 18–19, 35; *Records of Rhode Island*, 1:173, 311–12; *Laws of New Hampshire*, 1:13, 15–16, 676–77; 2:124–25, 313–15. Adultery was not a capital crime in Rhode Island and New Hampshire. Also see "Capital Laws" (1660), in *The Colonial Laws of Massachusetts*, ed. William H. Whitmore (Boston: City Council of Boston, 1889), 55, 128–29, 153; "The Body of Liberties" (1641) in *American Historical Documents, 1000–1904*, ed. Charles W. Eliot (New York: Collier and Son, 1938), 66–84. Few people actually faced capital punishment for sexual offenses. See Howard, *History of Matrimonial Institutions*, 2:169–74; Thompson, *Sex in Middlesex*, 72–75, 128–29; *Court of Assistants*, 2:64, 81, 106, 121; Norton, *Founding Mothers and Fathers*, 347–57; Godbeer, "Cry of Sodom," 259–86; Thomas A. Foster, "Antimasonic Satire, Sodomy, and Eighteenth-Century Masculinity in the *Boston Evening-Post*," *William and Mary Quarterly*, 3rd ser., 60 (2003): 171–84; John Murrin, "'Things Fearful to Name': Bestiality in Early America," *Pennsylvania History*, special supplement to vol. 65 (1998): 8–43; Robert F. Oaks, "'Things Fearful to Name': Sodomy and Buggery in Seventeenth-Century New England," *Journal of Social History* 12 (1978): 268–81.

[89] William Bradford, *Of Plymouth Plantation, 1620–47*, ed. Samuel Eliot Morison (New York: Knopf, 1975), 316.

[90] *Journal of John Winthrop*, 629. Also see Godbeer, *Sexual Revolution*, 44–50.

[91] *Records of Massachusetts*, 1:92. On the marital status of a man as it related to adultery, see Bradford, *Of Plymouth Plantation*, 409; Samuel Willard, *A Compleat Body of Divinity in Two Hundred and Fifty Expository Lectures on the Assembly's Shorter Catechism* (Boston: Green and Kneeland, 1726), 681–82; Thompson, *Sex in Middlesex*, 129; Thomas, "Puritans and Adultery," 261–62; C. S. Firth and R. S. Raitt, eds., *Acts and Ordinances of the Interregnum, 1642–60*, 3 vols. (London: Wyman and Sons, 1911), 2:387–89. Also see *Court of Assistants*, 2:66, 70, 108, 139; Else L. Hambleton, "The Regulation of Sex in Seventeenth-Century Massachusetts: The Quarterly Courts of Essex County vs. Priscilla Willson and Mr. Samuel Appleton," *Sex and Sexuality in Early America*, ed. Merril D. Smith (New York: New York University Press, 1998), 89–115.

[92] Of 182 men presented at the Essex County Court for fornication from 1641 to 1685, 111 were married at the time of punishment. At the Plymouth General Court, 34 of 47 men presented for fornication between 1631 and 1680 were married. *Records of Essex County*, vols. 1–8; *Records of Plymouth*, vols. 1–6. Also see Thompson, *Sex in Middlesex*, 19; Howard, *History of Matrimonial Institutions*, 2:186–91.

[93] *Records of Massachusetts*, 2:22. Also see *Records of Plymouth*, 11:12; *Records of Connecticut*, 1:527; *New Haven's Settling*, 32; *Laws of New Hampshire*, 1:16. Rhode Island was alone in not allowing magistrates to enjoin a couple to marriage. *Records of Rhode Island*, 1:173, 355; 2:105.

[94] *Records of Essex County*, 1:180. Also see *Records of Essex County*, 4:106, 148–49; 5:133, 441; 7:162, 238; George Francis Dow, *History of Topsfield, Massachusetts* (Topsfield: Topsfield Historical Society, 1940), 44–45, 53, 54, 57, 66, 74, 436.

[95] *Records of Essex County*, 4:200; 8:295–96; Sidney Perley, *The History of Salem, Massachusetts*, 3 vols. (Salem: Perley, 1924–28), 3:32.

[96] Numbers of fornication cases listed in this section refer to records from the Massachusetts General Court, 1629–44, in *Records of Massachusetts*, vols. 1–5; Essex County (Massachusetts) Court, 1641–85, in *Records of Essex County*, vols. 1–8; Suffolk County (Massachusetts) Court, 1671–80, in *Records of Suffolk County*, vols. 1–2; and Plymouth General Court, 1631–80, in *Records of Plymouth*, vols. 1–6. Thompson finds three cases in Middlesex County, 1649–99. Thompson, *Sex in Middlesex*, 22, 64, 68.

[97] *Records of Suffolk County*, 1:254–55.

[98] *Records of Essex County*, 8:15. Also see *Records of Plymouth*, 5:265, 8:151; *Records of Essex County*, 8:15, 279.

[99] These figures omit Joseph Indian and Joseph Blake who were married to other women at the time of their presentations for fornication. *Records of Suffolk County*, 2:485, 518–19.

[100] *Records of Massachusetts*, 4 (pt. 2):143. Also see Carol F. Karlsen, *Devil in the Shape of a Woman: Witchcraft in Colonial New England* (New York: Norton, 1987), 198–202.

[101] *Records of Essex County*, 3:309.

[102] *Records of Massachusetts*, 4 (pt. 2):393–94.

[103] *Acts of Massachusetts*, 1:52; *The Book of the General Laws for the People within the Jurisdiction of Connecticut: Collected Out of the Records of the General Court* (Cambridge, Mass.: Green, 1673), 80; *Laws of New Hampshire*, 1:60, 678–79; *Records of Connecticut*, 4:411; *Records of Plymouth*, 5:99–100, 161–62, 260; 6:63–64, 177.

[104] *Records of Essex County*, 4:349; 5:38, 157. On sentences of child support, see *Records of Essex County*, 1:250, 337, 347; 2:54, 151, 372; 3:148, 198; 4:38–40, 342, 349; 6:171, 206, 256; 7:238, 315, 406, 410; 8:276; *Records of Suffolk County*, 2:719, 915–16; *Court of Assistants*, 2:137.

[105] *Records of Plymouth*, 6:177. Cornelia Hughes Dayton, *Women before the Bar: Gender, Law, and Society in Connecticut, 1639–1789* (Chapel Hill: University of North Carolina Press, 1995), 159, 186–87, 202–7; Howard, *History of Matrimonial Institutions*, 2:193. Also see David Flaherty, "Law and the Enforcement of Morals in Early America," *Perspectives in American History* 5 (1971): 225–45; Hendrik Hartog, "The Public Law of a County Court: Judicial Government in Eighteenth Century Massachusetts," *American Journal of Legal History* 20 (1976): 282–329; R. W. Roetger, "The Transformation of Sexual Morality in 'Puritan' New England: Evidence from New Haven Court Records, 1639–98," *Canadian Review of American Studies* 15 (1984): 243–57.

[106] Willard, *Compleat Body of Divinity*, 674. Also see Godbeer, *Sexual Revolution*, 52–83; Harry S. Stout, *The New England Soul: Preaching and Religious Culture in Colonial New England* (New York: Oxford University Press, 1986), 103–4.

[107] Richard Hakluyt, "A Discourse Concerning Western Planting" [1584], *Collections of the Maine Historical Society*, 2nd ser., 2 (1877): 152–61. Also see Horn, *Adapting to New World*, 62–63; Beier, *Masterless Men*, 161–64; Griffiths, *Youth and Authority*, 360–62; Greene, *Pursuits of Happiness*, 41–43.

[108] Horn, *Adapting to New World*, 251–92; Carr and Menard, "Immigration and Opportunity," 206–42; Russell R. Menard, "From Servant to Freeholder: Status Mobility and Property Accumulation in Seventeenth-Century Maryland," *William and Mary Quarterly*, 3rd ser., 30 (1973): 37–64; Lois Green Carr, Russell R. Menard, and Lorena S. Walsh, *Robert Cole's World: Agriculture and Society in Early Maryland* (Chapel Hill: University of North

Carolina Press, 1991); Darrett B. Rutman and Anita H. Rutman, *A Place in Time: Middlesex County, Virginia, 1650–1750* (New York: Norton, 1984).

[109] *The Statutes at Large; Being a Collection of All the Laws of Virginia, from the First Session of the Legislature in the Year 1619,* ed. William Waller Hening, 13 vols. (New York: Bartow, 1819–23), 1:253–55, 274–75, 401, 438–40, 445, 517–18, 538; *Archives of Maryland,* ed. W. H. Browne et al., 72 vols. (Baltimore: Maryland Historical Society, 1883–1972), 2:523–28. Also see Steinfeld, *Invention of Free Labor,* 44–46; David W. Galenson, *White Servitude in Colonial America: An Economic Analysis* (Cambridge: Cambridge University Press, 1981); Christopher L. Tomlins, *Law, Labor, and Ideology in the Early American Republic* (Cambridge: Cambridge University Press, 1993), 249–53.

[110] "Proceedings of the Virginia Assembly, 1619," in *Narratives of Early Virginia, 1606–25,* ed. Lyon Gardiner Tyler (New York: Scribner's Sons, 1907), 263.

[111] Edmund S. Morgan, *American Slavery—American Freedom: The Ordeal of Colonial Virginia* (New York: Norton, 1975), 62, 66, 88; Richard B. Morris, *Government and Labor in Early America* (New York: Columbia University Press, 1946), 86–90; Abbot Emerson Smith, *Colonists in Bondage: White Servitude and Convict Labor in America, 1607–1776* (New York: Norton, 1971), 270–75; Susie M. Ames, ed., *County Court Records of Accomack-Northampton, Virginia, 1640–45* (Charlottesville: University Press of Virginia, 1973), 185–87, 218–19; Peter Charles Hoffer and William B. Scott, eds., *Criminal Proceedings in Colonial Virginia: [Records of] Fines, Examination of Criminals, Trials of Slaves, etc., from March 1710 [1711] to [1754] [Richmond County, Virginia]* (Atlanta: University of Georgia Press, 1984), 125–26.

[112] Carr and Menard, "Immigration and Opportunity," 211; Lorena S. Walsh, "'Till Death Us Do Part': Marriage and Family Formation in Seventeenth-Century Maryland," in *Chesapeake in Seventeenth Century,* 127, 152; Morgan, *American Slavery,* 163; Darrett B. Rutman and Anita H. Rutman, "'More True and Perfect Lists': The Reconstruction of Censuses for Middlesex County, 1668–1704," *Virginia Magazine of History and Biography* 88 (1980): 55. Also see Carr, Menard, and Walsh, *Robert Cole's World,* 18, 143; Horn, *Adapting to New World,* 136–38, 206; Rutman and Rutman, *Place in Time,* 77.

[113] "Proceedings of Virginia," 263; Norton, *Founding Mothers and Fathers,* 190–91. Howard Chudacoff incorrectly interprets this law as a legal restriction on single men. Howard P. Chudacoff, *The Age of the Bachelor: Creating an American Subculture* (Princeton: Princeton University Press, 1999), 25. Virginia's version of England's statutes of laborers and artificers blatantly ignored marital status.

[114] *Archives of Maryland,* 1:373–74.

[115] *Archives of Maryland,* 1:442; 2:397; 38:21.

[116] *Statutes of Virginia,* 1:253.

[117] *Statutes of Virginia,* 1:438.

[118] *Statutes of Virginia,* 2:115. Also see Horn, *Adapting to New World,* 210; Kathleen M. Brown, *Good Wives, Nasty Wenches, and Anxious Patriarchs: Gender, Race, and Power in Colonial Virginia* (Chapel Hill: University of North Carolina Press, 1996), 189; Walsh, "Till Death," 132.

[119] Carr and Menard, "Immigration and Opportunity," 210–11, 221, 227, 232; Brown, *Good Wives,* 84–85; Rutman and Rutman, *Place in Time,* 46, 113, 136. Also see Lorena S. Walsh, "The Historian as Census Taker: Individual Reconstitution and the Reconstruction of Censuses for a Colonial Chesapeake County," *William and Mary Quarterly,* 3rd ser., 38 (1981): 257n45.

[120] There has been considerable debate among historians as to how much marriage and family composition differed between England and the Chesapeake. See Horn, *Adapting to New World,* 204–22; Walsh, "Till Death," 129–30; Nuran Çinlar, "Marriage in the Colonial

Chesapeake, 1607–1770: A Study in Cultural Adaptation and Reformulation" (PhD diss., Johns Hopkins University, 2001), 21–62; Morgan, *American Slavery*, 120, 148, 164–70; Menard, "From Servant to Freeholder," 37–64.

[121] Norton, *Founding Mothers and Fathers*, 354. Also see Jonathan Katz, *Gay American History: Lesbians and Gay Men in the U.S.A.* (New York: Discus, 1976), 26–31; Edmund S. Morgan, "The First American Boom: Virginia 1618 to 1630," *William and Mary Quarterly*, 3rd ser., 28 (1971), 193; Robert Oaks, "Perceptions of Sodomy by Justices of the Peace in Colonial Virginia," *Journal of Homosexuality* 5 (1979): 35–65; Colin L. Talley, "Gender and Male Same-Sex Erotic Behavior in British North America in the Seventeenth Century," *Journal of the History of Sexuality* 6 (1996): 385–408.

[122] "Maryland Rent Rolls," *Maryland Historical Magazine* 19 (1924): 350; 20 (1925): 281; 21 (1926): 337; 23 (1928): 274; 24 (1929): 232; Louis Dow Scisco, "Baltimore County Records of 1668 and 1669," *Maryland Historical Magazine* 25 (1930): 261; Donnell MacClure Owings, "Private Mansions: An Edited List," *Maryland Historical Magazine* 33 (1938): 319; Arthur L. Keith, "Berry Family of Charles County," *Maryland Historical Magazine* 23 (1928): 16; William Bose Marye, "The Place-Names of Baltimore and Harford Counties," *Maryland Historical Magazine* 25 (1930): 337; Arthur L. Keith, "Smallwood Family of Charles County," *Maryland Historical Magazine* 22 (1927): 142–43. Also see Çinlar, "Marriage in Colonial Chesapeake," 27; George R. Stewart, *Names on the Land: The Classic Story of American Placenaming*, 4th ed. (San Francisco: Lexikos, 1982), 123, 460.

[123] John Winthrop, *The History of New England From 1630 to 1649*, ed. James Savage, 2 vols. (Boston: Little, Brown, 1853), 1:468, 470; Edmund Berkeley Jr., "Three Philanthropic Pirates," *Virginia Magazine of History and Biography* 74 (1966): 440; "Commission Book, 82," *Maryland Historical Magazine* 26 (1931): 140; Aubrey C. Land, *The Dulanys of Maryland: A Biographical Study of Daniel Dulany, the Elder (1685–1753) and Daniel Dulany, the Younger (1722–97)* (Baltimore: Maryland Historical Society, 1955), 105.

[124] Charles F. Mullet, "The Bachelors of Virginia Thank Lieutenant-Governor Nicholson," *Virginia Magazine of History and Biography* 49 (1941): 339–41. On Nicholson, see Stephen Saunders Webb, "The Strange Career of Francis Nicholson," *William and Mary Quarterly*, 3rd ser., 23 (1966): 513–48; Dorothy Louise Noble, "Life of Francis Nicholson" (PhD diss., Columbia University, 1958); Fairfax Downey, "The Governor Goes A-Wooing: The Swashbuckling Courtship of Nicholson of Virginia, 1699–1705," *Virginia Magazine of History and Biography* 55 (1947): 6–19.

[125] *The Records of the Virginia Company of London*, ed. Susan Myra Kingsbury, 4 vols. (Washington, D.C.: Government Printing Office, 1906–35), 1:256. Also see *Records of Virginia Company*, 1:269; H. R. McIlwaine, "The Maids Who Came to Virginia in 1620 and 1621 for Husbands," *Reviewer* 1 (1921): 105–13; David R. Ransome, "Wives for Virginia, 1621," *William and Mary Quarterly*, 3rd ser., 48 (1991): 3–18; Brown, *Good Wives*, 80–83. Likewise, Robert Rich was adamant that single men would not be appropriate settlers for Bermuda. See *Letters from Bermuda, 1615–46: Eyewitness Accounts Sent by the Early Colonists to Sir Nathaniel Rich*, ed. Vernon A. Ives (Toronto: University of Toronto Press, 1984), 50.

[126] Quoted in Wilcomb E. Washburn, *The Governor and the Rebel: A History of Bacon's Rebellion in Virginia* (Chapel Hill: University of North Carolina Press, 1957), 69.

[127] Thomas Jefferson Wertenbaker, *Torchbearer of the Revolution: The Story of Bacon's Rebellion and Its Leader* (Princeton: Princeton University Press, 1940), 47–54, 63–64, 130–31; Susan Westbury, "Women in Bacon's Rebellion," in *Southern Women: Histories and Identities*, ed. Virginia Bernhard et al. (Columbia: University of Missouri Press, 1992), 38–43; Stephen Saunders Webb, *1676: The End of American Independence* (New York: Knopf, 1984), 26–27, 50–53, 68–69; Brown, *Good Wives*, 162–64; Rutman and Rutman, *Place in Time*, 82–83.

[128] "Nathaniel Bacon's Victory over the Indians, April 1676," in *The Old Dominion in the Seventeenth Century: A Documentary History of Virginia, 1606–89*, ed. Warren M. Billings (Chapel Hill: University of North Carolina Press, 1975), 268. Also see "Charles City County Grievances, 1676," *Virginia Magazine of History and Biography* 3 (1895): 137, 170–72.

[129] Quoted in Brown, *Good Wives*, 165.

[130] Aphra Behn, *The Widow Ranter, or, the History of Bacon in Virginia: A Tragi-Comedy*, ed. Aaron R. Walden (New York: Garland, 1993), 5.3.69; Washburn, *Governor and Rebel*, 3.

[131] Morgan, *American Slavery*, 235–36. For critiques of Morgan's thesis regarding single men, see Carr and Menard, "Immigration and Opportunity," 230–31, 237, 240; Rutman and Rutman, "More True and Perfect Lists," 59–62. For Morgan's reaction, see David T. Courtwright, "Fifty Years of American History: An Interview with Edmund S. Morgan," *William and Mary Quarterly*, 3rd ser., 44 (1987): 358. For an attempt to reconcile the competing interpretations, see Allan Kulikoff, "The Colonial Chesapeake: Seedbed of Antebellum Southern Culture?" *Journal of Southern History* 45 (1979): 515–17, 531–33; Allan Kulikoff, *Tobacco and Slaves: The Development of Southern Cultures, 1680–1800* (Chapel Hill: University of North Carolina Press, 1986), 35–37.

[132] Brown, *Good Wives*, 137–86.

2. The Bachelor Laws

[1] *The Colonial Laws of New York from the Year 1664 to the Revolution*, 5 vols. (Albany: Lyon, 1894), 1:550. Also see Michael Kammen, *Colonial New York: A History* (New York: Oxford University Press 1975), 142–45. On taxation in colonial New York, see Alan Tully, *Forming American Politics: Ideals, Interests, and Institutions in Colonial New York and Pennsylvania* (Baltimore: Johns Hopkins University Press, 1994), 53, 219–24; John Christopher Schwab, *History of the New York Property Tax: An Introduction to the History of State and Local Finance in New York* (Baltimore: Guggenheim and Weil, 1890), 35–66.

[2] The classic exploration of the affectionate patriarch is Lawrence Stone, *The Family, Sex, and Marriage in England 1500–1800* (New York: Harper and Row, 1977). Also see Alan Macfarlane, *Marriage and Love in England: Modes of Reproduction, 1300–1840* (Oxford: Basil Blackwell, 1986).

[3] Wesley Frank Craven, "An Introduction to the History of Bermuda," *William and Mary Quarterly*, 2nd ser., 17 (1937): 329. Also see Virginia Bernhard, *Slaves and Slaveholders in Bermuda, 1616–1782* (Columbia: University of Missouri Press, 1999), 7–9, 24–26.

[4] *Early Records of the Town of Dedham, Massachusetts*, 6 vols. (Dedham: Dedham Historical Society, 1886–1936), 3:21.

[5] The headright system made no reference to marital status. Edmund S. Morgan, *American Slavery—American Freedom: The Ordeal of Colonial Virginia* (New York: Norton, 1975), 171–73; *The Old Dominion in the Seventeenth Century: A Documentary History of Virginia, 1606–89*, ed. Warren M. Billings (Chapel Hill: University of North Carolina Press, 1975), 135; *North Carolina Higher-Court Records, 1670–1701*, ed. Mattie Erma Edwards Parker, 2 vols. (Raleigh: State Department of Archives and History, 1971); *The Colonial Records of the State of Georgia*, ed. Allen D. Candler et al., 28 vols. (Atlanta: Franklin et al., 1904–71), 18:191–96, 627–36, 743–48; 19 (pt. 2): 53–58.

[6] *Records of the Governor and Company of the Massachusetts Bay in New England*, ed. Nathaniel B. Shurtleff, 5 vols. (Boston: White, 1853–54), 1:93.

[7] *Records of the Colony of New Plymouth in New England*, ed. Nathaniel B. Shurtleff et al., 11 vols. (Boston: White, 1855–61), 11:17. Also see *Records of Massachusetts*, 2:221–24; *The Acts and Resolves, Public and Private, of the Province of the Massachusetts Bay*, 21 vols. (Boston: Wright and Potter, 1869–1922), 1:130–31; 5:448; *The Public Records of the Colony of*

Connecticut, ed. J. Hammond Trumbull et al., 15 vols. (Hartford: Case, Lockwood, and Brainard et al., 1859–90), 1:542; 3:430; 5:73; *Laws of New Hampshire Including Public and Private Acts and Resolves and the Royal Commissions and Instructions*, ed. Albert Stillman Batchellor et al., 10 vols. (Manchester: Clarke et al., 1904–22), 1:222, 537–38; 2:287; 4:42–43; *Charter to William Penn, and Laws of the Province of Pennsylvania, Passed Between the Years 1682 and 1700*, ed. Staughton George, Benjamin M. Nead, and Thomas McCamant (Harrisburg: Hart, 1879), 42; *Laws of New York*, 1:53. Neither England nor Rhode Island made mention of marital status in their military laws.

8   *The Statutes at Large; Being a Collection of All the Laws of Virginia, from the First Session of the Legislature in the Year 1619*, ed. William Waller Hening, 13 vols. (New York: Bartow, 1819–23), 1:263, 525; 3:13–14, 338; 4:120; 5:17–21; *Archives of Maryland*, ed. W. H. Browne et al., 72 vols. (Baltimore: Maryland Historical Society, 1883–1972), 1:347; 3:99–101, 345; 7:54–55, 189; 13:554–59; 22:562–63; 26:269–70; 30:277–78; 39:113–14; 52:452–56.

9   Barry Levy, *Quakers and the American Family: British Settlement in the Delaware Valley* (New York: Oxford University Press, 1988), 86–119, 150–51.

10   *The Papers of William Penn*, ed. Mary Maples Dunn and Richard S. Dunn, vol. 2, *1680–84* (Philadelphia: University of Pennsylvania Press, 1982), 149. Also see Gary B. Nash, *Quakers and Politics: Pennsylvania, 1681–1726* (Princeton: Princeton University Press, 1968), 28–47. Penn was not alone in these ideas. See *Papers of William Penn*, 168, 175; *Minutes of the Provincial Council of Pennsylvania*, vol. 1 (Harrisburg: Penn, 1838), 38.

11   *The Statutes at Large of Pennsylvania from 1682 to 1801*, ed. James T. Mitchell and Henry Flanders, 17 vols. (Harrisburg: Busch et al., 1896–1915), 2:7.

12   *Charter to Penn*, 109–10. Also see Barry Levy, "'Tender Plants': Quaker Farmers and Children in the Delaware Valley, 1681–1735," *Journal of Family History* 3 (1978): 116–35.

13   *Statutes of Pennsylvania*, 2:8. Offutt finds that a quarter of criminal proceedings from 1680 to 1710 involved morals charges, about half of which were sex crimes. See William M. Offutt Jr., *Of "Good Laws" and "Good Men": Law and Society in the Delaware Valley, 1680–1710* (Urbana: University of Illinois Press, 1995), 192–94. Also see *Records of the Courts of Quarter Sessions and Common Pleas of Bucks County, Pennsylvania, 1684–1700* (Meadville, Penn.: Tribune, 1943), 21; Herbert William Keith Fitzroy, "The Punishment of Crime in Provincial Pennsylvania," *Pennsylvania Magazine of History and Biography* 60 (1936): 242–62.

14   *Statutes of Pennsylvania*, 2:490.

15   *Statutes of Pennsylvania*, 2:178–84; 3:199–221; *Laws of the Commonwealth of Pennsylvania, from the Fourteenth Day of October, One Thousand Seven Hundred, to the Twentieth Day of March, One Thousand Eight Hundred and Ten*, vol. 2 (Philadelphia: Bioren, 1810), 533. Reference to marital status in the adultery law was removed in 1700. *Statutes of Pennsylvania*, 2:6.

16   *Statutes of Pennsylvania*, 2:181.

17   *Acts of Massachusetts*, 1:332. Also see Robert A. Feer, "Imprisonment for Debt in Massachusetts before 1800," *Mississippi Valley Historical Review* 48 (1961): 252–69; Peter J. Coleman, *Debtors and Creditors in America: Insolvency, Imprisonment for Debt, and Bankruptcy, 1607–1900* (Madison: State Historical Society of Wisconsin, 1974), 40–41; Charles E. Grinnell, *A Study of the Poor Debtor Law of Massachusetts and Some Details of Its Practice* (Boston: Little Brown, 1883), 317–30. When England began emptying its debtors' prisons at the turn of the eighteenth century, it did not extend clemency to men under the age of forty unless they agreed to join the army and fight in France. *Statutes of the Realm, Printed by Command of His Majesty King George the Third, in Pursuance of an Address of the House of Commons of Great Britain; from Original Records and Authentic Manuscripts*, 9 vols. (London: Eyre and Strahan, 1810–22), 7 & 8 Gul. III, c. 12; 1 Ann., c. 19; 2 & 3 Ann., c. 10.

[18] *Statutes of Pennsylvania*, 2:250.

[19] *Statutes of Pennsylvania*, 4:211–12. Also see *Statutes of Pennsylvania*, 6:392–93; 9:5–8; Coleman, *Debtors and Creditors*, 141–45; Richard B. Morris, *Government and Labor in Early America* (New York: Columbia University Press, 1946), 355. The New York law was passed in 1730 and repealed in 1732. The idea entered the Delaware statutes in 1734 but the laws tended to skirt the issue of marital status by demanding service from those "not having a charge of such small children." *Laws of New York*, 2:675, 753–56; *Anno Regni Georgii II Regis Magnae Britanniae, Franciae, & Hiberniae, Septimo: At a General Assembly of the Counties of New-Castle, Kent and Sussex upon Delaware, Begun and Holden at New-Castle, the Twentieth Day of October, Anno Dom. 1733* (Philadelphia: Franklin, 1734), 3–17; *Laws of the State of Delaware*, 4 vols. (New Castle: Adams et al., 1797–1816), 1:196–209, 282–84, 444–46; 4:215–18; Virginia D. Harrington, *The New York Merchant on the Eve of the Revolution* (New York: Columbia University Press, 1935), 122–24; Coleman, *Debtors and Creditors*, 106–7, 208–10. New Jersey may also have granted relief to insolvent debtors although the language of the law is unclear.

[20] *Acts of Massachusetts*, 2:658. Massachusetts removed the provision allowing creditors to put debtors into service in 1737. *Acts of Massachusetts*, 2: 831–33. State laws did not specifically exempt women from imprisonment for debt until the nineteenth century. See Coleman, *Debtors and Creditors*, 45, 62, 68, 77–78, 119, 138, 149, 177, 224, 235, 250; Deborah A. Rosen, *Courts and Commerce: Gender, Law, and the Market Economy in Colonial New York* (Columbus: Ohio State University Press, 1997), 52–54.

[21] On taxes placed on the unmarried in early America, see Arthur W. Calhoun, *A Social History of the American Family*, 3 vols. (Cleveland: Clark, 1917–19), 1:67–68, 245–46; 2:202; Joseph Kirk Folsom, *The Family and Democratic Society* (New York: Wiley and Sons, 1943), 2, 32, 117; Fairfax Downey, *Our Lusty Forefathers: Being Diverse Chronicles of the Fervors, Frolics, Fights, Festivities, and Failings of Our American Ancestors* (New York: Scribner's Sons, 1947), 34; Herbert Moller, "Sex Composition and Correlated Culture Patterns of Colonial America," *William and Mary Quarterly*, 3rd ser., 2 (1945): 113n1; Thomas P. Monahan, *The Pattern of Age at Marriage in the United States* (Philadelphia: Stephenson Brothers, 1951), 51, 77–78; Mark E. Kann, *A Republic of Men: The American Founders, Gendered Language, and Patriarchal Politics* (New York: New York University Press, 1998), 61; Howard Chudacoff, *The Age of the Bachelor: Creating an American Subculture* (Princeton: Princeton University Press, 1999), 24–25. For a broader interpretation of the implicit meaning of tax policy, see Glenn W. Fisher, *The Worst Tax? A History of the Property Tax in America* (Lawrence: University of Kansas Press, 1996); Carolyn Webber and Aaron Wildavsky, *A History of Taxation and Expenditure in the Western World* (New York: Simon and Schuster, 1986); Charles Adams, *For Good and Evil: The Impact of Taxes on the Course of Civilization*, 2nd ed. (Lanham, Md.: Madison, 1999). Several writers have noted the connection between gender and taxation in present-day laws, including how marital status affects an individual's tax burden. See Ruth Ruttenberg and Amy A. McCarthy, "Women and Tax Policy," in *Gender Differences: Their Impact on Public Policy*, ed. Mary Lou Kendrigan, 125–51 (Westport, Conn.: Greenwood, 1991); R. Michael Alvarez and Edward J. McCaffery, "Gender and Tax," in *Gender and American Politics: Women, Men, and the Political Process*, ed. Sue Tolleson-Rinehart and Jyl J. Josephson (Armonk, N.Y.: Sharpe, 2000), 91–113.

[22] *The Laws of Plato*, trans. Thomas L. Pangle (New York: Basic Books, 1980), 108–9.

[23] Lex Iulia et Papia was two pieces of legislation: Lex Iulia de maritandis ordinibus approved in 18 BC and Lex Papia Poppaea from AD 9. Pál Csillag, *The Augustan Laws on Family Relations* (Budapest: Akadémiai Kiadó, 1976), 77–78, 81–113; Percy Ellwood Corbett, *The Roman Law of Marriage* (Oxford: Clarendon Press, 1930), 30–42, 51–53, 112–21; Naphtali

Lewis and Meyer Reinhold, eds., *Roman Civilization: Selected Readings*, vol. 2, *The Empire* (New York: Columbia University Press, 1955), 52. Also see *Dio's Roman History*, trans. Earnest Cary, 9 vols. (Cambridge: Harvard University Press, 1914–27), 6:222–23, 320–25; 7:4–25; Gaius Suetonius Tranquillus, *The Twelve Caesars*, trans. Robert Graves (Baltimore: Penguin, 1957), 73–74; Richard I. Frank, "Augustus' Legislation on Marriage and Children," *California Studies in Classical Antiquity* 8 (1976): 41–52; Karl Galinsky, "Augustus's Legislation on Morals and Marriage," *Philologus* 125 (1981): 126–44. In the early second century, the satirist Juvenal called Lex Iulia et Papia "dormant" and the third-century Christian writer Tertullian labeled them "most futile." Despite flagrant violations of the law, Lex Iulia et Papia remained on the books until the sixth century. See Lewis and Reinhold, *Roman Civilization*, 47, 253–54; *The Epistles of Pliny*, ed. Clifford H. Moore, trans. William Melmoth, vol. 3 (Boston: Bibliophile Society, 1925), 104–5; Corbett, *Roman Law of Marriage*, 121; Csillag, *Augustan Laws*, 77–79, 229.

[24] See chapter 3 for a more complete discussion of the bachelor tax in English literature.

[25] *Statutes of the Realm*, 12 Car. II, c. 9. Also see Ronald Hutton, *The Restoration: A Political History of England and Wales, 1658–67* (Oxford: Clarendon Press, 1985), 138–39. On English taxation in the seventeenth and eighteenth centuries, see Roy Douglas, *Taxation in Britain since 1660* (New York: St. Martin's Press, 1999); Michael J. Braddick, *The Nerves of State: Taxation and the Financing of the English State, 1558–1714* (Manchester: Manchester University Press, 1996); John Sinclair, *The History of the Public Revenue of the British Empire*, 3rd ed., 3 vols. (London: Strahan, 1803); Stephen Dowell, *A History of Taxation and Taxes in England from the Earliest Times to the Present Day*, 2nd ed., 4 vols. (London: Longmans Green, 1888).

[26] *Statutes of the Realm*, 12 Car. II, c. 10. Also see *Statutes of the Realm*, 16 Car. I, c. 9; M. J. Braddick, *Parliamentary Taxation in Seventeenth-Century England: Local Administration and Response* (Woodbridge: Boydell Press, 1994), 231–41; Conrad Russell, *The Causes of the English Civil War* (Oxford: Clarendon Press, 1990), 173; E. A. Wrigley and R. S. Schofield, *The Population History of England, 1541–1871: A Reconstruction* (Cambridge: Harvard University Press, 1981), 263–64; Ann Kussmaul, *Servants in Husbandry in Early Modern England* (Cambridge: Cambridge University Press, 1981), 33.

[27] Lysander Salmon Richards, *History of Marshfield*, vol. 1 (Plymouth, Mass.: Memorial Press, 1901), 30. Also see Alice Morse Earle, *Customs and Fashions in Old New England* (New York: Scribner, 1893), 36–38; John Demos, *A Little Commonwealth: Family Life in Plymouth Colony* (New York: Oxford University Press, 1970), 77–79.

[28] Wilfred H. Munro, *The History of Bristol, R.I.: The Story of the Mount Hope Lands, from the Visit of the Northmen to the Present Time* (Providence: Reid, 1880), 114; Maurice H. Robinson, *A History of Taxation in New Hampshire* (New York: Macmillan, 1902), 163–64; William T. Davis, ed., *Records of the Town of Plymouth, Published by Order of the Town*, vol. 1, *1636 to 1705* (Plymouth: Avery and Doten, 1889), 117.

[29] *Statutes of the Realm*, 18 & 19 Car. II, c. 1. Also see Sinclair, *History of Public Revenue*, 1:303; Hutton, *Restoration*, 255–57; D. T. Witcombe, *Charles II and the Cavalier House of Commons, 1663–74* (New York: Barnes and Noble, 1966), 42–60.

[30] *Statutes of the Realm*, 29 & 30 Car. II, c. 1. For subsequent instances of similar language, see *Statutes of the Realm*, 1 Gul. & Mar., c. 13; 2 Gul. & Mar., st. 2, c. 7; 3 Gul. & Mar. c. 6; 5 & 6 Gul. & Mar., c. 14; 9 Gul. III, c. 38; 1 Ann., c. 6.

[31] *Charter to Penn*, 147. Also see *Charter to Penn*, 138, 182–83; *Statutes of Pennsylvania*, 2:105–9; 3:26–27.

[32] *Charter to Penn*, 222. Also see *Charter to Penn*, 254, 257, 280–82; *Statutes of Pennsylvania*, 2:109–13, 280; 3:83, 128, 180; 4:14; Charles P. Keith, *Chronicles of Pennsylvania from the*

English Revolution to the Peace of Aix-la-Chapelle, 1688–1748 (Philadelphia: Patterson and White, 1917), 298–301; Nash, *Quakers and Politics*, 211. The provisions of the 1696 act were renewed in the provincial tax acts of 1699 and 1700.

[33] *Charter to Penn*, 221, 257. Also see *Charter to Penn*, 138, 146–47, 182–83, 233; *Statutes of Pennsylvania*, 2:105–9; 3:26–27; Lemuel Molovinsky, "Continuity of the English Tax Experience in Early Pennsylvania History," *Pennsylvania History* 46 (1979): 233–44; Lemuel Molovinsky, "Taxation and Continuity in Pennsylvania during the American Revolution," *Pennsylvania Magazine of History and Biography* 104 (1980): 365–78; Keith, *Chronicles of Pennsylvania*, 167–68, 266; Clair W. Keller, "The Pennsylvania County Commission System, 1712 to 1740," *Pennsylvania Magazine of History and Biography* 93 (1969): 372–82; Nash, *Quakers and Politics*, 143–44, 156–60.

[34] Provincial rates with poll taxes on single freemen, 1700–81: *Statutes of Pennsylvania*, 2:115, 374, 389; 3:84, 128–29; 5:202, 294–96, 380; 6:8, 345; 8:379; 9:102, 152, 363–64; 10:330–31. County levies with poll taxes on single freemen, 1700–99: *Statutes of Pennsylvania*, 2:35; 3:180–81, 296; 4:14; 9:403; 16:379–80. The singles tax was incorporated into other tax schemes in the middle of the eighteenth century. See *Statutes of Pennsylvania*, 5:34; 6:205; 7:284–85; 8:105–6.

[35] Consistent with other studies of colonial Pennsylvania, Chester County here excludes those townships that became Lancaster County in 1729 but includes those that formed Delaware County in 1789.

[36] James T. Lemon and Gary B. Nash, "The Distribution of Wealth in Eighteenth-Century America: A Century of Change in Chester County, Pennsylvania, 1693–1802," *Journal of Social History* 2 (1968): 1–24; James T. Lemon, *The Best Poor Man's Country: A Geographical Study of Early Southeastern Pennsylvania* (Baltimore: Johns Hopkins University Press, 1972); Billy G. Smith, "Inequality in Late Colonial Philadelphia: A Note on Its Nature and Growth," *William and Mary Quarterly*, 3rd ser., 41 (1984): 629–45; Lucy Simler, "Tenancy in Colonial Pennsylvania: The Case of Chester County," *William and Mary Quarterly*, 3rd ser., 43 (1986): 542–69; Paul G. E. Clemens and Lucy Simler, "Rural Labor and the Farm Household in Chester County, Pennsylvania, 1750–1820," in *Work and Labor in Early America*, ed. Stephen Innes, 106–43 (Chapel Hill: University of North Carolina Press, 1988); Lucy Simler and Paul G. E. Clemens, "The 'Best Poor Man's Country' in 1783: The Population of Rural Society in Late-Eighteenth-Century Southeastern Pennsylvania," *Proceedings of the American Philosophical Society* 133 (1989): 234–61; Lucy Simler, "The Landless Worker: An Index of Economic and Social Change in Chester County, Pennsylvania, 1750–1820," *Pennsylvania Magazine of History and Biography* 114 (1990): 163–99; Jack D. Marietta, "The Distribution of Wealth in Eighteenth-Century America: Nine Chester County Tax Lists, 1693–1799," *Pennsylvania History* 62 (1995): 532–45; Karin Wulf, "Assessing Gender: Taxation and the Evaluation of Economic Viability in Late Colonial Philadelphia," *Pennsylvania Magazine of History and Biography* 121 (1997): 201–35; Jack D. Marietta and G. S. Rowe, "Violent Crime, Victims, and Society in Pennsylvania, 1682–1800," *Pennsylvania History* 66 supplement (1999): 24–54.

[37] Chester County, Pennsylvania: Board of County Commissioners, Chester County Archives, County Taxes, 1718–1800, Historical Society of Pennsylvania. Justices of the peace set the county rates until 1718 when the county commissioners assumed the task. See Tully, *Forming American Politics*, 337.

[38] There is considerable variation in the value of estates. This estimate is derived from the provincial tax records for Chester County. See Chester County, Pennsylvania: Board of County Commissioners, Provincial Taxes, 1765, 1768, and 1770, Historical Society of Pennsylvania.

[39] Chester County, County Taxes, 1718–1800, specifically: 1721, 1730, 1740, 1750, 1760, and 1771. In 1721, 917 of 1,147 (80%) of estates paid less than twelve shillings in property taxes, that year's county levy on single freemen. The figure rose to 94% when 2,451 of 2,607 estates were assessed less than six shillings. It remained between 80% and 86% until 1771, but dropped to 47% in 1781 and to 30% in 1788. For more statistical information and complete tables, see John Gilbert McCurdy, "Taxation and Representation: Pennsylvania Bachelors and the American Revolution," *Pennsylvania Magazine of History and Biography* 129 (2005): 283–315.

[40] "Transcript of Taxables in the County of Bedford for the Year 1775," *Pennsylvania Archives*, 3rd ser., 22 (1897): 85–116; "Returns for the Sixteenth, Eighteen-Penny Tax for the County of Lancaster, 1773," *Pennsylvania Archives*, 3rd ser., 17 (1897): 323–487. The Bedford figure excludes uncultivated lands in the county that were taxed.

[41] On estimating the size of households from tax records, see Rodger C. Henderson, *Community Development and the Revolutionary Transition in Eighteenth-Century Lancaster County, Pennsylvania* (New York: Garland, 1989), 224; Evarts B. Greene and Virginia Harrington, *American Population before the Federal Census of 1790* (New York: Columbia University Press, 1932). On Pennsylvania's population, see Robert V. Wells, *The Population of the British Colonies in America before 1776: A Survey of Census Data* (Princeton: Princeton University Press, 1975), 143.

[42] Concord, 1740 and 1750, in Chester County, County Taxes, 1718–1800. Bachelor taxes as a portion of total taxes paid rose from about 15% in Concord and the neighboring townships of Darby, Chester, and Kennett in the 1710s. The percentage then declined after 1760 but still constituted more than a quarter of the total county rates.

[43] Chester County, County Taxes, 1718–1800. Also see Simler, "Landless Worker," 175–177; Lemon, *Best Poor Man's Country*, 93–96.

[44] *Charter to Penn*, 99. The law was issued again in late 1682. *Charter to Penn*, 122–23. Also see Cortlandt F. Bishop, *History of Elections in the American Colonies* (New York: Columbia College, 1893), 46–97; Tully, *Forming American Politics*, 29–32.

[45] Tully, *Forming American Politics*, 71–73, 79–80.

[46] *Statutes of Pennsylvania*, 2:24. These voting requirements remained largely unchanged until 1776. See *Statutes of Pennsylvania*, 7:35; 8:334. Also see Albert Edward McKinley, *The Suffrage Franchise in the Thirteen English Colonies in America* (Philadelphia: University of Pennsylvania Press, 1905).

[47] *Charter to Penn*, 127. Also see *Charter to Penn*, 204; *Statutes of Pennsylvania*, 2:18, 359; 3:31.

[48] James H. Kettner, *The Development of American Citizenship, 1608–1870* (Chapel Hill: University of North Carolina Press, 1978), 65–172.

[49] *Laws of the Royal Colony of New Jersey, 1703–45*, ed. Bernard Bush, in *New Jersey Archives*, 3rd ser., vol. 2 (Trenton: Archives and History Bureau of the New Jersey State Library, 1977), 119. Also see *Laws of New Jersey*, 215, 232, 279, 343; Edwin P. Tanner, *The Province of New Jersey, 1664–1738* (New York: Columbia University, 1908), 519–39; Frederick R. Black, "Provincial Taxation in Colonial New Jersey, 1704–35," *New Jersey History* 95 (1977): 21–47; Brendan McConville, *These Darling Disturbers of the Public Peace: The Struggle for Property and Power in Early New Jersey* (Ithaca: Cornell University Press, 1999), 203–6.

[50] *Laws of the State of Delaware, from the Fourteenth Day of October, One Thousand Seven Hundred, to the Eighteenth Day of August, One Thousand Seven Hundred and Ninety-Seven*, vol. 1 (New Castle: Adams, 1797), 261. Also see Robert A. Becker, *Revolution, Reform, and*

the Politics of American Taxation, 1763–83 (Baton Rouge: Louisiana State University Press, 1980), 46.

[51] *Acts of Massachusetts*, 1:213.

[52] *Acts of Massachusetts*, 1:278. Single women made up almost 15% of householders in Boston in 1695, 80% of whom were widows. Tax and Census Records, 1657–1795 (Box 1, Folder 1) in Boston, Mass. Papers, 1634–1893, American Antiquarian Society.

[53] Allan Kulikoff, *Tobacco and Slaves: The Development of Southern Cultures in the Chesapeake, 1680–1800* (Chapel Hill: University of North Carolina Press, 1986), 165–204; Daniel Blake Smith, *Inside the Great House: Planter Life in Eighteenth-Century Chesapeake Society* (Ithaca: Cornell University Press, 1980), 25–125; Trevor Burnard, *Creole Gentlemen: The Maryland Elite, 1691–1776* (New York: Routledge, 2002), 103–38; Kathleen M. Brown, *Good Wives, Nasty Wenches, and Anxious Patriarchs: Gender, Race, and Power in Colonial Virginia* (Chapel Hill: University of North Carolina Press, 1996); Kenneth Lockridge, *On the Sources of Patriarchal Rage: The Commonplace Books of William Byrd and Thomas Jefferson and the Gendering of Power in the Eighteenth Century* (New York: New York University Press, 1992); Carole Shammas, *A History of Household Government in America* (Charlottesville: University of Virginia Press, 2002).

[54] *Archives of Maryland*, 38:368, 371.

[55] *Archives of Maryland*, 36:596–97; 39:135–36, 299–300; 40:27; 46:50, 90; 59:lix–lx, 48–49, 59, 69–70, 181–82, 194–95, 278–82; 61:72–73, 251–52, 472–73; 62:163–64, 449; 63:276–77, 328–29, 380, 409–10; 64:xxx, 405–6, 415–19.

[56] Coleman, *Debtors and Creditors*, 131, 160.

[57] Rhys Isaac, *Landon Carter's Uneasy Kingdom: Revolution and Rebellion on a Virginia Plantation* (New York: Oxford University Press, 2004), 277–81; Smith, *Inside the Great House*, 82–125.

[58] *Records of Massachusetts*, 2:173–74; 3:116–18, 4 (pt. 1):154–55; *Acts of Massachusetts*, 1:29–30, 91–95, 165–69, 185–88, 197–201, 213–16, 239–45, 257–62, 277–81, 301–5, 337–42, 358–62, 386–91, 413–17; *Records of Connecticut*, 1:548–49; 3:401; *Laws of New Hampshire*, 1:27, 28, 39, 40, 47, 64, 70, 86–87, 184–85, 246, 524–25, 554–55; *Records of the Colony of Rhode Island and Providence Plantations*, ed. John Russell Bartlett, 10 vols. (Providence: Greene, 1856–65), 1:384, 395, 422, 426, 480–82; 2:288–89, 338, 358–62, 412–16, 510–12; 3:21–22, 235–37, 247–48. Also see Julian Gwyn, "Financial Revolution in Massachusetts: Public Credit and Taxation, 1692–1774," *Historie sociale—Social History* 17 (1984): 59–77; Catherine S. Menand, "The Things That Were Caesar's: Tax Collecting in Eighteenth-Century Boston," *Massachusetts Historical Review* 1 (1999): 49–77; Michael J. Puglisi, "'An Insupportable Burden': Paying for King Philip's War on the Massachusetts Frontier," *Historical Journal of Massachusetts* 16 (1988): 187–203; Lawrence Henry Gipson, *Connecticut Taxation, 1750–75* (New Haven: Yale University Press, 1933).

[59] *Archives of Maryland*, 1:449. Also see *Archives of Maryland*, 1:313, 342, 359, 417, 536–38; 2:399; 7:159, 166, 168, 187; *Statutes of Virginia*, 1:305–6, 345; 2:84, 170, 257, 479–80, 492; William Zebina Ripley, *The Financial History of Virginia, 1609–1776* (New York: Columbia College, 1893), 18, 24–32, 38–45; Becker, *Revolution, Reform, and Politics*, 82–91; Percy Scott Flippin, *The Financial Administration of the Colony of Virginia* (Baltimore: Johns Hopkins University Press, 1915), 9–20; Brown, *Good Wives*, 116–28. On taxes in the Carolinas and Georgia, see *The Statutes at Large of South Carolina; Edited, Under the Authority of the Legislature*, ed. Thomas Cooper and David J. McCord, 10 vols. (Columbia: Johnston, 1836–41), 2:16, 182–85, 207, 229–32; Edward McCrady, *The History of South Carolina under the Proprietary Government, 1670–1719* (New York: Macmillan, 1901), 482–83;

The State Records of North Carolina, ed. William L. Saunders et al., 26 vols. (Raleigh: Hale et al., 1886–1907), 23:72–73, 210–12, 345–46, 526–31; *Records of Georgia*, 18:66–73, 164–71, 240–52, 337–50, 392–408; 19 (pt. 1):29–53, 100–137, 161–98, 449–505. Georgia only collected poll taxes on free blacks and slaves.

[60] *Archives of Maryland*, 75:313.

[61] Fred Anderson, *Crucible of War: The Seven Years' War and the Fate of Empire in British North America, 1754–66* (New York: Knopf, 2000), 11–49; James Titus, *The Old Dominion at War: Society, Politics, and Warfare in Late Colonial Virginia* (Columbia: University of South Carolina Press, 1991), 5–45; Lawrence Henry Gipson, *The British Empire before the American Revolution*, 15 vols. (New York: Knopf, 1939–70), 6:24.

[62] *Statutes of Virginia*, 6:438, 465; 7:14, 70. Also see *Statutes of Virginia*, 5:95; 6:527; Titus, *Old Dominion at War*, 59–61; Morgan, *American Slavery*, 340.

[63] *The Official Records of Robert Dinwiddie, Lieutenant-Governor of the Colony of Virginia, 1751–58*, ed. R. A. Brock, 2 vols. (Richmond: Virginia Historical Society, 1883–84), 1:74–75.

[64] Samuel Davies, *Religion and Patriotism the Constituents of a Good Soldier: A Sermon Preached to Captain Overton's Independent Company of Volunteers, Raised in Hanover County, Virginia, August 17, 1755* (Philadelphia: Buckland, 1756), 6, 20.

[65] Samuel Davies, *The Curse of Cowardice: A Sermon Preached to the Militia of Hanover County, in Virginia, at a General Muster, May 8, 1758, with a View to Raise a Company for Captain Samuel Meredith* (London: Buckland, 1758), 18–19.

[66] Davies, *Religion and Patriotism*, 28–29; Davies, *Curse of Cowardice*, 21, 22, 26. Also see Harry S. Laver, "Refuge of Manhood: Masculinity and the Militia Experience in Kentucky," in *Southern Manhood: Perspectives on Masculinity in the Old South*, ed. Craig Thompson Friend and Lorri Glover (Athens: University of Georgia Press, 2004), 1–21.

[67] *Letters to Washington and Accompanying Papers*, ed. Stanislaus Murray Hamilton, vol. 1 (Boston: Houghton Mifflin, 1898), 361–62. For other accounts of drafting men for the Seven Years' War, see James Patton, Augusta County, Virginia, to Governor [Robert Dinwiddie, Williamsburg, Virginia], July 2, 1754, in Preston Family Papers, 1727–1896, no. 135, Virginia Historical Society; Letter from Nathaniel Walthoe, March 8, 1758, Lee Family Papers, Section 96, Virginia Historical Society.

[68] *Records of Dinwiddie*, 2:480; Titus, *Old Dominion at War*, 78–80, 98–103; Gipson, *British Empire*, 6:51–54.

[69] *Letters to Washington*, 336–39.

[70] Titus, *Old Dominion at War*, 33–35, 91–92, 122.

[71] *Letters to Washington*, 362; *The Papers of George Washington: Colonial Series*, ed. W. W. Abbot et al., 8 vols. (Charlottesville: University Press of Virginia, 1983–93), 4:265.

[72] *Papers of Washington*, 306. Also see Titus, *Old Dominion at War*, 103–6, 109–13; *Letters to Washington*, 343, 364; *Papers of Washington*, 81; *Records of Dinwiddie*, 2:248; "Journal of Captain Charles Lewis of the Virginia Regiment, Commanded by Colonel George Washington in the Expedition Against the French, October 10—December 27, 1755," *Virginia Historical Society, Its Collections*, 3rd ser., 11 (1892): 203–18.

[73] Titus, *Old Dominion at War*, 120–25; Anderson, *Crucible of War*, 208–16, 267–85; *Statutes of Virginia*, 7:163–69. The other colonies paid bounties instead of drafting recruits.

[74] *Pennsylvania Gazette*, December 31, 1754.

[75] *Pennsylvania Gazette*, August 25, 1757. Also see *Pennsylvania Gazette*, March 30, 1758.

[76] *Pennsylvania Gazette*, February 2, 1764.

[77] *Statutes of the Realm*, 30 Geo. II, c. 25.

[78] Craig W. Horle et al., *Lawmaking and Legislators in Pennsylvania: A Biographical Dictionary*, vol. 2 (Philadelphia: University of Pennsylvania Press, 1991–97), s.v. "Langhorne, Jeremiah."

[79] *Statutes of the Realm*, 6 & 7 Gul. & Mar., c. 6; Colin Brooks, "Projecting, Political Arithmetic and the Act of 1695," *English Historical Review* 97 (1982): 31–53; Tom Arkell, "An Examination of the Poll Taxes of the Later Seventeenth Century, the Marriage Duty Act and Gregory King," in *Surveying the People: The Interpretation and Use of Document Sources for the Study of Population in the Later Seventeenth Century*, ed. Kevin Schurer and Tom Arkell (Oxford: Leopard's Head Press, 1992), 142–80.

[80] *Statutes of the Realm*, 8 & 9 Gul. III, c. 20; 9 Gul. III, c. 32; 9 & 10 Gul. III, c. 35; *Instructions to Be Held and Observed by the Several Surveyors Appointed for the Better Ascertaining the Duties upon Houses, and upon Marriages, Births, Burials, and upon Batchelors and Widowers, Pursuant to the Act of Parliament in That Behalf* (London: Bill, 1697); Sinclair, *History of Public Revenue*, 2:12–13. The rates on births, marriages, and burials were renewed in 1705 without the taxes on bachelors and widowers. See *Statutes of the Realm*, 4 Ann., c. 12.

[81] Molovinsky, "Continuity of Tax Experience," 233–44; Marvin L. Michael Kay, "The Payment of Provincial and Local Taxes in North Carolina, 1748–71," *William and Mary Quarterly*, 3rd ser., 26 (1969): 218–40; Jessica Kross, "Taxation and the Seven Years' War: A New York Test Case," *Canadian Review of American Studies* 18 (1987): 351–66.

[82] *Archives of Maryland*, 52:503–4. This passage was printed in the *Maryland Gazette*, July 1, 1756. Also see Charles Albro Barker, *The Background of the Revolution in Maryland* (New Haven: Yale University Press, 1940), 205–8, 239–55. For contemporaneous taxes in Virginia, see Becker, *Revolution, Reform, and Politics*, 78; Titus, *Old Dominion at War*, 113–14.

[83] Francis L. Hawks, *Contributions to the Ecclesiastical History of the United States*, vol. 2 (New York: Harper and Brothers, 1839), 244; Edward Ingle, *Parish Institutions of Maryland: With Illustrations from Parish Records* (Baltimore: Johns Hopkins University Press, 1883), 21; Calhoun, *Social History of Family*, 1:245–46; Julia Cherry Spruill, *Women's Life and Work in the Southern Colonies* (Chapel Hill: University of North Carolina Press, 1938), 137; Gerald Eugene Hartdagen, "The Anglican Vestry in Colonial Maryland" (PhD diss., Northwestern University, 1965), 180–87; Stephanie Coontz, *The Social Origins of Private Life: A History of American Families 1600–1900* (London: Verso, 1988), 83; Kann, *Republic of Men*, 61; Chudacoff, *Age of the Bachelor*, 24–25; Nuran Çinlar, "Marriage in the Colonial Chesapeake, 1607–1770: A Study in Cultural Adaptation and Reformulation" (PhD diss., Johns Hopkins University, 2001), 189–218.

[84] *Archives of Maryland*, 52:333. Members of the Committee of Laws voted 5–2 to remove the marriage fees when the measure was first proposed. *Archives of Maryland*, 52:347, 353–54. Maryland archivist J. Hall Pleasants also suggested a relationship between the rejection of the marriage license fee and the adoption of the bachelor tax. See *Archives of Maryland*, 52:xxii.

[85] On the relative wealth of the population, see Burnard, *Creole Gentlemen*, 7–10; David Curtis Skaggs, "Maryland's Impulse toward Social Revolution: 1750–76," *Journal of American History* 54 (1968): 771–86.

[86] Calhoun, *Social History of Family*, 1:246.

[87] St. Paul's Church, North Sassafras Parish, Cecil County, Maryland, "Vestry Minutes, 1693–1804," Microfilm 1363, pp. 217–18, Maryland Historical Society.

[88] St. Anne's Protestant Episcopal Church, Annapolis, Maryland, "Transcripts and Vestry Proceedings, 1704–1818, and Parish Register, 1681–1796," Microfilm 1012, pp. 320–60, Maryland Historical Society; St. Mary Anne's Parish, Cecil County, Maryland, "Vestry Book of Records, 1713–99," Microfilm 153, pp. 75–117, Maryland Historical Society; Prince

George Parish, Frederick County, Maryland, "Vestry Minutes, 1719–1832," Microfilm 261, pp. 69–92, Maryland Historical Society; St. Martin's Protestant Episcopal Church, Worcester County, "Records Collection, 1722–1925," Microfilm 9598, pp. 93–112, Maryland Historical Society. For other attempts to analyze vestry records, see Calhoun, *Social History of Family*, 1:246; Hartdagen, "Anglican Vestry," 185–87; Çinlar, "Marriage in the Chesapeake," 214–15. On differences in wealth in Maryland's regions, see Burnard, *Creole Gentlemen*, 5–7.

[89] *Archives of Maryland*, 52:325–26; 55:534–37; 56:245–47; 58:49–50, 274–76.

[90] *Archives of Maryland*, 38:20; Hartdagen, "Anglican Vestry," 217–21, 225–39.

[91] St. Mary Anne's Parish, "Vestry Book of Records," 107. Also see St. Mary Anne's Parish, "Vestry Book," 78, 81–82.

[92] Edward C. Papenfuse et al., *A Biographical Dictionary of the Maryland Legislature, 1635–1789*, 2 vols. (Baltimore: Johns Hopkins University Press, 1979–85); Ethan Allen, *Historical Notices of St. Ann's Parish in Ann Arundel County, Maryland, Extending from 1649 to 1857, a Period of 208 Years* (Baltimore: Des Forges, 1857), 71–74; "Records of the Homony Club of Annapolis," *American Historical Record* 1 (1872): 299; Edna Agatha Kanely, *Directory of Ministers and the Maryland Churches They Served, 1634–1990*, 2 vols. (Westminster, Md.: Family Line, 1991), 1:373; 2:77, 371; William K. Paynter, *St. Anne's Annapolis: History and Times* (Annapolis, Md.: St. Anne's Parish, 1980), 19–23, 113–17; *The History of the Ancient and Honorable Tuesday Club by Dr. Alexander Hamilton*, ed. Robert Micklus, 3 vols. (Chapel Hill: University of North Carolina Press, 1990), 1:lxxix–cv.

[93] Papenfuse, *Maryland Legislature*, vols. 1–2; *Archives of Maryland*, 52:347.

[94] St. Anne's Church, "Transcripts and Vestry Proceedings," 320. Also see "Vestry Proceedings, St. Ann's Parish, Annapolis, Maryland," *Maryland Historical Magazine* 9 (1914): 288–89.

[95] *Archives of Maryland*, 56:291.

[96] *Archives of Maryland*, 56:lxii–lxiii, lxvi–lxviii, 489, 496; 58:xxxi–xxxii, xxxviii–xlvi, 109–11, 310, 316, 547; Becker, *Revolution, Reform, and Politics*, 79–80, 89–92.

[97] *Statutes of Pennsylvania*, 6:358. Also see *Statutes of Pennsylvania*, 5:202, 295–96, 339, 380; 6:8.

[98] Chester County, Provincial Taxes, 1765 and 1770.

3. Literary Representations of the Bachelor

[1] James Edward Oglethorpe, *Some Account of the Design of the Trustees for Establishing Colonys in America*, ed. Rodney M. Baine and Phinizy Spalding (Athens: University of Georgia Press, 1990), 3–4, 6, 12, 26–29, 40–41.

[2] John Brewer, *The Pleasures of the Imagination: English Culture in the Eighteenth Century* (Chicago: University of Chicago Press, 1997), 129–66; David S. Shields, *Civil Tongues and Polite Letters in British America* (Chapel Hill: University of North Carolina Press, 1997).

[3] Stephanie Coontz, *Marriage, a History: From Obedience to Intimacy or How Love Conquered Marriage* (New York: Viking, 2005), 143–244. The shift is sometimes termed the coming of "companionate marriage," although historians remain divided on the application and the timing of this social development. See Lawrence Stone, *The Family, Sex, and Marriage in England 1500–1800* (New York: Harper and Row, 1977), 325–404; Alan Macfarlane, *Marriage and Love in England: Modes of Reproduction, 1300–1840* (Oxford: Basil Blackwell, 1986); Carl N. Degler, *At Odds: Women and the Family in America from the Revolution to the Present* (New York: Oxford University Press, 1980), 9–12; Anya Jabour, *Marriage in the Early Republic: Elizabeth and William Wirt and the Companionate Ideal* (Baltimore: Johns Hopkins University Press, 1998); Trevor Burnard, *Creole Gentlemen: The Maryland Elite, 1691–1776* (New York; Routledge, 2002), 120–21.

[4] Ned C. Landsman, *From Colonials to Provincials: American Thought and Culture, 1680–1760* (New York: Twayne, 1997), 31–56; Michael Warner, *The Letters of the Republic: Publication and the Public Sphere in Eighteenth-Century America* (Cambridge: Harvard University Press, 1990).

[5] Thomas A. Foster, *Sex and the Eighteenth-Century Man: Massachusetts and the History of Sexuality in America* (Boston: Beacon Press, 2006), 102. Also see Mark E. Kann, *A Republic of Men: The American Founders, Gendered Language, and Patriarchal Politics* (New York: New York University Press, 1998), 62–72; Richard Godbeer, *Sexual Revolution in Early America* (Baltimore: Johns Hopkins University Press, 2002), 278–88. For a rare alternative reading of literary depictions of bachelors, see Scott Slawinski, *Validating Bachelorhood: Audience, Patriarchy, and Charles Brockden Brown's Editorship of the* Monthly Magazine and American Review (New York: Routledge, 2005).

[6] At a time when the total population of Georgia was between 1,200 and 2,120, James Oglethorpe estimated that there were 700 more men then women in the colony. James Oglethorpe to the Trustees, February 12, 1743, in *General Oglethorpe's Georgia: Colonial Letters, 1733–43*, ed. Mills Lane, 2 vols. (Savannah, Ga.: Beehive Press, 1975), 2:660–61; Robert V. Wells, *The Population of the British Colonies in America before 1776: A Survey of Census Data* (Princeton: Princeton University Press, 1975), 170–71.

[7] Amos Aschbach Ettinger, *James Edward Oglethorpe: Imperial Idealist* (Oxford: Clarendon Press, 1936), 255–56; Rodney M. Baine and Mary E. Williams, "James Oglethorpe in Europe: Recent Findings in His Military Life," in *Oglethorpe in Perspective: Georgia's Founder after Two Hundred Years*, ed. Phinizy Spalding and Harvey H. Jackson (Tuscaloosa: University of Alabama Press, 1989), 112–21; Edwin L. Johnson, "The Search for Authentic Icons of James Edward Oglethorpe," in *Oglethorpe in Perspective*, 179.

[8] E. A. Wrigley and R. S. Schofield, *The Population History of England, 1541–1871: A Reconstruction* (Cambridge: Harvard University Press, 1981), 160–70, 207–15, 248–65; Macfarlane, *Marriage and Love*, 20–27.

[9] Wrigley and Schofield, *Population History of England*, 219–28, 260, 263–64; Roger Schofield, "English Marriage Patterns Revisited," *Journal of Family History* 10 (1985): 2–20; David R. Weir, "Rather Never Than Late: Celibacy and Age at Marriage in English Cohort Fertility, 1541–1871," *Journal of Family History* 9 (1984): 340–54; E. A. Wrigley, "The Growth of Population in Eighteenth-Century England: A Conundrum Resolved," *Past and Present* 98 (1983): 121–50.

[10] William Petty quoted in Charles Emil Stangeland, *Pre-Malthusian Doctrines of Population: A Study in the History of Economic Theory* (New York: Columbia University, 1907), 143.

[11] John Graunt, *Natural and Political Observations Mentioned in a Following Index, and Made upon the Bills of Mortality*, in *The Economic Writings of Sir William Petty Together with the Observations upon the Bills of Mortality More Probably by Captain John Graunt*, ed. Charles Henry Hull, 2 vols. (Cambridge: Cambridge University Press, 1899), 2:374–78; Stangeland, *Pre-Malthusian Doctrines of Population*, 138–43; Gregory King, *Natural and Politicall Observations and Conclusions upon the State and Condition of England*, in *Two Tracts by Gregory King*, ed. George E. Barnett (Baltimore: Johns Hopkins University Press, 1937); D. V. Glass, "Two Papers on Gregory King," in *Population in History*, 159–220; Joyce Oldham Appleby, *Economic Thought and Ideology in Seventeenth-Century England* (Princeton: Princeton University Press, 1978), 133–37. On fears of depopulation, see J. G. A. Pocock, *The Machiavellian Moment: Florentine Political Thought and the Atlantic Republican Tradition* (Princeton: Princeton University Press, 1975), 423–27; Rachel Weil, *Political Passions: Gender, the Family and Political Argument in England, 1680–1714* (Manchester: Manchester University Press, 1999), 28–31.

[12] William Petty, *A Treatise of Taxes and Contributions*, in *Writings of William Petty*, 1:47. Also see E. A. J. Johnson, *Predecessors of Adam Smith: The Growth of British Economic Thought* (New York: Prentice-Hall, 1937), 93–113.

[13] William Temple, *Of Popular Discontents*, in *The Works of Sir William Temple, Bart.*, vol. 3 (London: Rivington, 1814), 57.

[14] Charles Davenant, *An Essay upon the Probable Methods of Making a People Gainers in the Balance of Trade*, in *The Political and Commercial Works of That Celebrated Writer Charles D'Avenant, LL.D.*, ed. Charles Whitworth, vol. 2 (London: Horsfield, 1771), 184; D. Waddell, "Charles Davenant (1656–1714)—A Biographical Sketch," *Economic History Review*, ser. 2, 11 (1958–59): 279–88; Pocock, *Machiavellian Moment*, 436–46.

[15] Graunt, *Natural and Political Observations*, 2:377. Also see Weil, *Political Passions*, 30; Margaret Sommerville, *Sex and Subjection: Attitudes to Women in Early-Modern Society* (London: Arnold, 1995), 150–61.

[16] William Petty, *Multiplication of Mankind*, in *The Petty Papers: Some Unpublished Writings of Sir William Petty*, ed. Marquis of Lansdowne, vol. 2 (London: Constable, 1927), 51.

[17] *Marriage Promoted in a Discourse of Its Ancient and Modern Practice, Both under Heathen and Christian Common-Wealths, Together with Their Laws and Encouragements for Its Observance and How Far the Like May Be Practicable and Commodious in the Preservation of These Kingdoms, by a Person of Quality* (London: Baldwin, 1690), 27. For Gregory King's numbers, see King, *Natural and Politicall Observations*, 23.

[18] Temple, *Popular Discontents*, 58; Thomas Sheridan, *A Discourse of the Rise and Power of Parliaments, of Law's, of Courts of Judicature, of Liberty, Property, and Religion, of the Interest of England in Reference to the Desines of France; of Taxes and of Trade* ([London], 1677), 179–80; Appleby, *Economic Thought and Ideology*, 137.

[19] "Sodomitical Scandals and Subcultures in the 1720s," *Men and Masculinities* 1 (1999): 365–84; Stephen Shapiro, "Of Mollies: Class and Same-Sex Sexualities in the Eighteenth Century," *In a Queer Place: Sexuality and Belonging in British and European Contexts*, ed. Kate Chedgzoy, Emma Francis, and Murray Pratt, 155–76 (Hampshire: Ashgate, 2002); Richard Godbeer, "'The Cry of Sodom': Discourse, Intercourse, and Desire in Colonial New England," *William and Mary Quarterly*, 3rd ser., 52 (1995): 259–86; "The Mollies Club," in Edward Ward, *A Compleat and Humorous Account of All the Remarkable Clubs and Societies in the Cities of London and Westminster, from the R—l S—y down to the Lumber-Troop, &c.*, 7th ed. (London: Wren, 1756), 265; Cameron McFarlane, *The Sodomite in Fiction and Satire, 1660–1750* (New York: Columbia University Press, 1997).

[20] Thomas Starkey, *A Dialogue between Reginald Pole and Thomas Lupset*, ed. Kathleen M. Burton (London: Chatto and Windus, 1948), 141. Also see G. R. Elton, *Studies in Tudor and Stuart Politics and Government: Papers and Reviews, 1946–72* (Cambridge: Cambridge University Press, 1974), 252.

[21] James Harrington, *Oceana*, in *The Political Works of James Harrington*, ed. J. G. A. Pocock (Cambridge: Cambridge University Press, 1977), 226–27. Harrington was a bachelor when he wrote *Oceana*.

[22] Davenant, *Essay upon Trade*, 191. Also see Brooks, "Projecting, Political Arithmetic," 40; *Marriage Promoted*, 3–24.

[23] Petty, *Multiplication of Mankind*, 50.

[24] Temple, *Popular Discontents*, 58. Also see *Marriage Promoted*, 55–56; Temple, *Popular Discontents*, 58; Sheridan, *Discourse of Rise*, 180–82.

[25] Johnson, *Predecessors of Adam Smith*, 136–37, 253. For a direct refutation of Bacon without reference to a bachelor tax, see John Cockburn, *The Dignity and Duty of a Marriage State, in a Sermon Preach'd at the Celebration of a Marriage in the English Episcopal*

Church in Amsterdam, 2nd ed. (London: Hills, [1710?]), 10–11. Also see *A Critical Essay Concerning Marriage* (London: Rivington, 1724); John Wesley, *Thoughts on a Single Life* (London: Paramore, 1784); *Reflections on the Caelibacy of Fellows of Colleges* (Cambridge: Deighton, 1798).

[26] *A Proposal for a Tax for the Supplies of the War, That Will Be Useful and Easy, Not Affect Trade, and Will Have a Tendency to Increase the Political Strength of the Nation* (London: Davidson, 1748), 16.

[27] Daniel Defoe, *Some Considerations upon Street-Walkers with a Proposal for Lessening the Present Number of Them in Two Letters to a Member of Parliament* (London: Moore, [1726]), 6–7, 14. Also see *Single Life Discouraged, for the Publick Utility: or, an Essay on Ways and Means for the Supplies of the Government* (n.p., 1761).

[28] *Proposal for a Tax,* 14.

[29] John Sekora, *Luxury: The Concept in Western Thought, Eden to Smollet* (Baltimore: Johns Hopkins University Press, 1977), 58–59, 72, 226–27, 246–47, 256–65, 271; Bernard Bailyn, *The Ideological Origins of the American Revolution,* enlarged ed. (Cambridge: Harvard University Press, 1992), 50–51, 86–87; Gordon S. Wood, *The Creation of the American Republic, 1776–89* (Chapel Hill: University of North Carolina Press, 1969), 114–18; Linda K. Kerber, *Women of the Republic: Intellect and Ideology in Revolutionary America* (Chapel Hill: University of North Carolina Press, 1980), 31.

[30] *Proposal for a Tax,* 8, 16–18, 26. Also see *An Enquiry into the Nature, Foundation, and Present State of Publick Credit* (London: Carpenter, 1748); *Proposals for Raising an Annual Sum of Money for the Service of His Majesty* (n.p., [1748?]); Corbyn Morris, *Observations on the Past Growth and Present State of the City of London* (London: Millar, 1759).

[31] Ian Watt, *The Rise of the Novel: Studies in Defoe, Richardson, and Fielding* (Berkeley: University of California Press, 1957), 138–51; Katherine V. Snyder, *Bachelors, Manhood, and the Novel, 1850–1925* (Cambridge: Cambridge University Press, 1999), 20–46. Also see Kate Sanborn, *My Favorite Lectures of Long Ago, For Friends Who Remember* (Boston: Case, Lockwood, and Brainard, 1898), 61–107.

[32] *The Batchelors Ballad, or a Remedy against Love* (London: Brooksby, [1677]). Also see *The Country-mans Care in Choosing a Wife, or, a Young Batchelor Hard to Be Pleased* (London: Brooksby, [1685?]); *The Cuckold's Lamentation of a Bad Wife* (London: Brooksby, [1680?]); *Fore-warn'd, Fore-arm'd, or, a Caveat to Batchelors, in the Character of a Bad Woman* (London: Snowden, 1684); *Advice to Young Gentlemen, or, an Answer to the Ladies of London* (London: Back, [1685–88]); *Advice to Batchelors, or, a Caution to Be Careful in Their Choice* (London: Brooksby, [1686?]).

[33] *The Maids Answer to the Batchelors Ballad, or, Love without Remedy* (London: Brooksby, [1681?]). Also see *The Daughters Complaint, to Her Mother, for a Husband* (London: Brooksby, [1650–1700]); *The Maids Complaint against Batchelors, or, the Young Mens Unkindness Made Known* (London: Coniers, [1650–1700]).

[34] *The Maidens Fairing, or, a Pattern Pickt Out Against Young Men* (London: Clark, [1675]).

[35] *The Maids Complaint against the Batchelors, or an Easter-Offering for Young Men and Apprentices* (London: Coniers, 1675).

[36] *The Batchellors Answer to the Maids Complaint or the Young Men's Vindication* (London: Coniers, 1675).

[37] *The Petition of the Ladies of London and Westminster to the Honourable House of Husbands* (London: Want-man, 1693).

[38] *An Humble Remonstrance of the Batchelors, in and about London, to the Honourable House, in Answer to a Late Paper, Intituled* A Petition of the Ladies for Husbands (London: Bookselling Batchelors, 1693).

[39] *The Young Mens Answer to the Ladies of London's Petition to the Parliament of Women, Shewing That It Is Not Reasonable, That They Should Be Fined, or Forced to Marry Against Their Inclinations* (London: Blare, [1683–1706]).

[40] *The Petition of the Widows, in and about London and Westminster for a Redress of Their Grievances* (London: Use of the Wide—o's, 1693).

[41] *The Levellers: A Dialogue between Two Young Ladies, Concerning Matrimony, Proposing an Act for Enforcing Marriage, for the Equality of Matches, and Taxing Single Persons, with the Danger of Celibacy to a Nation*, in *Mundus Foppensis (1691) and The Levellers (1745, First Edition 1703)*, ed. Michael S. Kimmel (Los Angeles: William Andrews Clark Memorial Library, University of California, Los Angeles, 1988), 416–33. For a rare exception in which an old bachelor called for a bachelor tax, see *A Scheme to Pay Off, in a Few Years, the National Debt, by a Repeal of the Marriage Act, Humbly and Seriously Hinted, to the Leg—re of G—r B—n, Now in Par—t Assem—d* (London: Beckett and DeHondt, 1767).

[42] On authorship in such works, see Shields, *Civil Tongues*, 262–65.

[43] Calhoun Winton, *Captain Steele: The Early Career of Richard Steele* (Baltimore: Johns Hopkins University Press, 1964), 76–77, 81, 85–86, 86–90; Peter Smithers, *The Life of Joseph Addison*, 2nd ed. (Oxford: Clarendon Press, 1968), 137–40, 364–72.

[44] *The Spectator*, ed. Donald F. Bond, 5 vols. (Oxford: Clarendon Press, 1965), 1:1, 8; *The Tatler*, ed. Donald F. Bond, 3 vols. (Oxford: Clarendon Press, 1987): 2:30, 60–61, 90, 188, 402.

[45] *Spectator*, 1:4–5. See Landsman, *Colonials to Provincials*, 39.

[46] *Tatler*, 3:323–24.

[47] Erin Mackie, *Market à la Mode: Fashion, Commodity, and Gender in* The Tatler *and* The Spectator (Baltimore: Johns Hopkins University Press, 1997); Shawn Lisa Maurer, *Proposing Men: Dialectics of Gender and Class in the Eighteenth-Century English Periodical* (Stanford: Stanford University Press, 1998).

[48] *Spectator*, 2:295–98.

[49] *Spectator*, 2:295; 4:384.

[50] *Spectator*, 2:510–12. Jack Afterday mimicked George Heartwell, the title character in Congreve's *The Old Batchelor*. See William Congreve, *The Old Batchelor*, in *The Complete Plays of William Congreve*, ed. Herbert Davis (Chicago: University of Chicago Press, 1967); Anita Sieber, *Character Portrayal in Congreve's Comedies* The Old Batchelour, Love for Love, *and* The Way of the World (Lewiston, N.Y.: Mellen, 1996). The play was mentioned in both periodicals. See *Tatler*, 1:79; *Spectator*, 4:389.

[51] *Tatler*, 3:324.

[52] *Spectator*, 1:12.

[53] *Spectator*, 4:390–91. Also see *Spectator*, 4:183–84; Mackie, *Market à la Mode*, 176–78.

[54] *Spectator*, 4:382–84. A response was written by "Bellmour" who claimed that Welladay's letter had convinced him of marriage and "I am so truly become a Convert that I hate to live alone any longer." The letter was never published. See *Spectator*, 5:237–38.

[55] *The Guardian*, in Robert Lynam, *The British Essayists*, vol. 10 (London: Dove, 1827), 22.

[56] *Universal Spectator, and Weekly Journal*, September 18, 1731; George S. Marr, *The Periodical Essayists of the Eighteenth Century* (New York: Appleton, 1924), 194–95.

[57] "The Rake's Fortune," *Gentleman's Magazine* 2 (1732): 853. Also cited in *Weekly Register*, July 15, 1732. Also see "The Choice of a Batchelor's Wife," *Gentleman's Magazine* 36 (1736): 661.

[58] *Universal Spectator*, February 13, 1731. Also see *Gentleman's Magazine* 1 (1731): 60–61; *Westminster Journal*, March 15, 1746; *Gentleman's Magazine* 16 (1746): 150–52.

[59] Thomas L. Purvis, *Colonial America to 1763* (New York: Facts on File, 1999), 251–59; Landsman, *Colonials to Provincials*, 31–38; Jon Butler, *Becoming America: The Revolution before 1776* (Cambridge: Harvard University Press, 2000), 110–14.

[60] Kevin J. Hayes, *The Library of John Montgomerie, Colonial Governor of New York and New Jersey* (Newark: University of Delaware Press, 2000), 79, 85, 107, 164, 168; Kevin J. Hayes, *The Library of William Byrd of Westover* (Madison, Wis.: Madison House, 1997), 110, 114, 117–18, 121, 156, 164, 173, 225, 285, 302, 307; *Diary of Cotton Mather*, in *Massachusetts Historical Society Collections*, 7th ser., vol. 8 (Boston: Massachusetts Historical Society, 1912), 227; Elizabeth Christine Cook, *Literary Influences in Colonial Newspapers, 1704–50* (New York: Columbia University Press, 1912); Henning Cohen, *The South Carolina Gazette, 1732–75* (Columbia: University of South Carolina Press, 1935), 213–20; Martha C. Howard, "The Maryland Gazette: An American Imitation of the *Tatler* and the *Spectator*," *Maryland Historical Magazine* 29 (1934): 295–98; Robert Manson Myers, "The Old Dominion Looks to London: A Study of English Literary Influences upon the *Virginia Gazette* (1736–66)," *Virginia Magazine of History and Biography* 54 (1946): 195–217; Ernest Cassara, *The Enlightenment in America* (Lanham, Md.: University Press of America, 1988), 42–43; Landsman, *Colonials to Provincials*, 39; Michal Rozbicki, *The Complete Colonial Gentleman: Cultural Legitimacy in Plantation America* (Charlottesville: University of Virginia Press, 1998), 39, 57, 62, 65, 115, 138.

[61] *Boston Evening-Post*, April 17, 1749. Also see *New-York Gazette*, March 20, 1749; Cohen, *South Carolina Gazette*, 225, 225n163; "From an Epistle from a Society of Young Ladies," *New-York Evening Post*, October 28, 1751; "Humorous Proposal for a Female Administration," *Boston Chronicle*, November 6, 1769; Foster, *Sex and Eighteenth-Century Man*, 103–4.

[62] *Boston Evening-Post*, August 4, 1746.

[63] *Female Grievances Debated: In Six Dialogues between Two Young Ladies, Concerning Love and Marriage* (Boston: Fleet, [1731–58]).

[64] *New-England Courant*, August 7, 1721; January 22, 1722. Also see Shields, *Civil Tongues*, 259; Cook, *Literary Influences*, 5–7; Landsman, *Colonials to Provincials*, 38–42.

[65] *Proteus Echo (1727–28)*, ed. Bruce Granger (Delmar, N.Y.: Scholars' Facsimiles and Reprints, 1986), 14, 64, 120. Also see Shields, *Civil Tongues*, 236–49; Foster, *Sex and Eighteenth-Century Man*, 103.

[66] "A Bachelor's Will," *Boston Chronicle*, March 28, 1768. Also see "A Bachelor's Will," *New-Hampshire Gazette, and Historical Chronicle*, April 8, 1768.

[67] *Pennsylvania Gazette*, April 5, 1775.

[68] *Massachusetts Spy*, August 22, 1771. Also see *New-England Weekly Journal*, February 9, 1730; December 4, 1739; *Boston Post Boy*, July 15, 1751; *Boston Weekly News-Letter*, September 18, 1760; January 29, 1770; March 14, 1771; *Boston Gazette, and Country Journal*, July 16, 1764; *Pennsylvania Gazette*, August 15, 1771.

[69] Daniel Lewes, *The Sins of Youth, Remembered with Bitterness* (Boston: Kneeland, 1725), 6; Cotton Mather, *The Pure Nazarite: Advice to a Young Man* (Boston: Fleet, 1723), 2.

[70] *The Loyal American's Almanack* (Boston: N.C., 1715), October. Also see *The Virginia Almanack* (Williamsburg: Purdie and Dixon, 1768), August; *The Virginia Almanack* (Williamsburg: Purdie and Dixon, 1770), February; *The Virginia Almanack* (Williamsburg: Purdie and Dixon, 1772), February.

[71] "The Batchelor's Soliloquy," *Maryland Gazette*, August 19, 1762; "The Batchelor's Soliloquy," in Thomas Fox, *The Wilmington Almanack* (Wilmington, Del.: Adams, 1762), 34. Also see Godbeer, *Sexual Revolution*, 274–75; Nuran Çinlar, "Marriage in the Colonial Chesapeake, 1607–1770: A Study in Cultural Adaptation and Reformulation" (PhD diss.,

Johns Hopkins University, 2001), 178. A different version appeared in Britain twenty years earlier. See "The Batchelor's Soliloquy," *Gentleman's Magazine* 14 (1744): 218.

[72] Sir John Dillon, *The Pleasures of the Single Life, or, the Miseries of Matrimony* (Philadelphia: Steuart, 1763), 4, 6. Also see "The Batchelor's Reasons for Taking a Wife," *American Magazine or, General Repository* 1 (March 1769), 91–92; "Reflections on Celibacy and Marriage," *Boston Post Boy*, September 14, 1772.

[73] *The Autobiography of Benjamin Franklin*, ed. Leonard W. Labaree et al. (New Haven: Yale University Press, 1964), 53.

[74] Carl Van Doren, *Benjamin Franklin* (New York: Viking, 1938), 18–27; Cook, *Literary Influences*, 29; Janette Seaton Lewis, "'A Turn of Thinking': The Long Shadow of the *Spectator* on Franklin's *Autobiography*," *Early American Literature* 13 (1978–79): 268–77; Albert Furtwangler, "Franklin's Apprenticeship and the *Spectator*," *New England Quarterly* 52 (1979): 377–96; George F. Horner, "Franklin's *Dogood Papers* Re-examined," *Studies in Philology* 37 (1940): 501–23; James A. Sappenfield, *A Sweet Instruction: Franklin's Journalism as a Literary Apprenticeship* (Carbondale: Southern Illinois University Press, 1973), 36–37; Warner, *Letters of the Republic*, 82–86.

[75] *The Papers of Benjamin Franklin*, ed. Leonard W. Labaree et al., 36 vols. (New Haven: Yale University Press, 1959–2001), 1:11–12.

[76] *Papers of Franklin*, 1:14, 38.

[77] *Autobiography of Franklin*, 69–70.

[78] *Papers of Franklin*, 1:240–48; Van Doren, *Benjamin Franklin*, 106. On Franklin's take on women, see Ruth H. Bloch, *Gender and Morality in Anglo-American Culture, 1650–1800* (Berkeley: University of California Press, 2003), 111–18.

[79] *Autobiography of Franklin*, 71, 128; Van Doren, *Benjamin Franklin*, 73–80, 91–94; Sheila Skemp, "Family Partnerships: The Working Wife, Honoring Deborah Franklin," in *Benjamin Franklin and Women*, ed. Larry Tise, 19–36 (University Park: Pennsylvania State University Press, 2000).

[80] Sappenfield, *Sweet Instruction*, 128; Bloch, *Gender and Morality*, 115.

[81] Benjamin Franklin [Richard Saunders, pseud.], *Poor Richard: The Almanacks for the Years 1733–58* (New York: Heritage, 1964), 3, 4, 9, 116, 118, 240. Also see Van Doren, *Benjamin Franklin*, 107–15. The 1733 verse was subsequently reprinted in several almanacs; see Theophilus Wreg, *The Virginia Almanac* (Williamsburg: Royle, 1762); Abraham Weatherwise, *Father Abraham's Almanack* (Philadelphia: Dunlap, 1764). Promarriage and antibachelor remarks in *Poor Richard's Almanac* were not out of the ordinary for almanacs. See James Franklin [Poor Robin, pseud.], *The Rhode-Island Almanack* (Newport: Franklin, 1729), 5; Titan Leeds, *The American Almanack* (New York: Bradford, 1733), 3–4.

[82] *Papers of Franklin*, 2:21–24.

[83] *Gentleman's Magazine* 17 (1747): 175–76. Also see Max Hall, *Benjamin Franklin and Polly Baker: The History of a Literary Deception* (Chapel Hill: University of North Carolina Press, 1960). Cornelia Dayton finds that Franklin's charges were not that far off. Cornelia Hughes Dayton, *Women before the Bar: Gender, Law, and Society in Connecticut, 1639–1789* (Chapel Hill: University of North Carolina Press, 1995), 210n108, 227n138.

[84] Bloch, *Gender and Morality*, 116. Also see "Old Mistresses Apologue," in *Papers of Franklin*, 3:27–31; Van Doren, *Benjamin Franklin*, 150–209.

[85] *Papers of Franklin*, 1:35–36, 437–41.

[86] *Papers of Franklin*, 4:225–34. Also see *Papers of Franklin*, 5:456–63; 6:75–82; 20:522–28; Van Doren, *Benjamin Franklin*, 216–17.

[87] Van Doren, *Benjamin Franklin*, 711–12; T. H. Breen, *The Marketplace of Revolution: How Consumer Politics Shaped American Independence* (New York: Oxford University Press, 2004), 172–82.

[88] Robert V. Wells, "The Population of England's Colonies in America: Old English or New Americans?" *Population Studies* 46 (1992): 91–93. Also see Foster, *Sex and Eighteenth-Century Man*, 8–9.

[89] Dennis Hodgson, "Benjamin Franklin on Population: From Policy to Theory," *Population Development and Review* 17 (1991): 639–61. Also see Thomas Malthus, "Essay on the Principle of Population (1798)," in *Thomas Robert Malthus: An Essay on the Principle of Population (Norton Critical Editions)*, ed. Philip Appleman (New York: Norton, 1976), 45–47; David Hume, "Of the Populousness of Antient Nations (1752)," in *Thomas Robert Malthus*, 3; Robert Wallace, "A Dissertation on the Numbers of Mankind in Antient and Modern Times (1753)," in *Thomas Robert Malthus*, 4–5; Adam Smith, "An Inquiry into the Nature and Causes of the Wealth of Nations (1776)," in *Thomas Robert Malthus*, 6.

[90] Baron de Montesquieu, *The Spirit of the Laws*, trans. Thomas Nugent, 2 vols. (New York: Hafner, 1949), 2:6. Also see Montesquieu, *Spirit of the Laws*, 2:2–25, 68–72; Stangeland, *Pre-Malthusian Doctrines of Population*, 118–37, 267–90.

[91] On gender and the work of Malthus, see Randi Davenport, "Thomas Malthus and Maternal Bodies Politic: Gender, Race, and Empire," *Women's History Review* 4 (1995): 415–39; Libby Schweber, *Disciplining Statistics: Demography and Vital Statistics in France and England, 1830–85* (Durham: Duke University Press, 2006); Bruce Curtis, *The Politics of Population: State Formation, Statistics, and the Census of Canada, 1840–75* (Toronto: University of Toronto Press, 2001).

[92] *Papers of Franklin*, 9:175.

[93] *Papers of Franklin*, 15:184. Also see *Papers of Franklin*, 10:209–15, 411–16; 19:83–84, 111; 35:572–74.

[94] *Papers of Franklin*, 30:313. Also see *Papers of Franklin*, 29:283–84, 318–19.

[95] Skemp, "Family Partnerships," 26; Jan Lewis, "Sex and the Married Man: Benjamin Franklin's Families," in Tise, ed., *Benjamin Franklin and Women*, 67–82.

[96] *Virginia Gazette*, November 28, 1745; June 27, 1751; March 28, 1766.

4. Living Single in Early America

[1] *The Papers of Robert Treat Paine*, ed. Stephen T. Riley and Edward W. Hanson, 2 vols. (Boston: Massachusetts Historical Society, 1992), 1:287–89. Also see Clifford K. Shipton et al., *Sibley's Harvard Graduates*, 17 vols. (Cambridge, Mass.: Sever et al., 1873–1975), 12:462–82.

[2] *Papers of Robert Paine*, 1:358; 2:114, 461n1.

[3] *Maryland Gazette*, August 19, 1762.

[4] *The Diaries of John Hull*, in *Transactions and Collections of the American Antiquarian Society* 3 (1857): 141–43. Also see *Memoirs of Capt. Roger Clap* (Boston: Green, 1731), 17–24, 55.

[5] Robert A. Fothergill, *Private Chronicles: A Study of English Diaries* (New York: Oxford University Press, 1974), 19. Also see Rhys Isaac, *Landon Carter's Uneasy Kingdom: Revolution and Rebellion on a Virginia Plantation* (New York: Oxford University Press, 2004), xiv–xvii, 340–41; Nancy Armstrong and Leonard Tennenhouse, *The Imaginary Puritan: Literature, Intellectual Labor, and the Origins of Personal Life* (Berkeley: University of California Press, 1992); Patricia Meyer Sparks, *Privacy: Concealing the Eighteenth-Century Self* (Chicago: University of Chicago Press, 2003). Early commonplace books are hardly more revealing. See Jonathan Corwin, *Account Books, 1649–85*, American Antiquarian Society.

[6] Anne S. Lombard, *Making Manhood: Growing up Male in Colonial New England* (Cambridge: Harvard University Press, 2003), 18–45. On young men's occupations, especially teaching school, see Jackson Turner Main, *The Social Structure of Revolutionary America* (Princeton: Princeton University Press, 1965), 91–95, 141–44; Lisa Wilson, *Ye Heart of a Man: The Domestic Life of Men in Colonial New England* (New Haven: Yale University Press, 1999), 24–25, 107–10.

[7] Thomas Augst, *The Clerk's Tale: Young Men and Moral Life in Nineteenth-Century America* (Chicago: University of Chicago Press, 2003), 1–11. On the changing motivations for keeping diaries, see Fothergill, *Private Chronicles*, 64–94.

[8] John May Diary, 1708–66, American Antiquarian Society, entries for December 16, 1710 and January 18, 1711. Also see Frances K. Goldscheider and Calvin Goldscheider, *Leaving Home before Marriage: Ethnicity, Familism, and Generational Relationships* (Madison: University of Wisconsin Press, 1993).

[9] Williams Family Diaries, 1714–41, American Antiquarian Society, entry for December 13, 1713.

[10] Thomas Robie Diary, 1710, American Antiquarian Society, entry for February 20.

[11] William Williams Diaries, 1710–58, American Antiquarian Society, entry for June 5, 1710.

[12] Robie Diary, entry for May 20. Also see Shipton, *Sibley's Harvard Graduates*, 5: 450–51.

[13] William Williams, *The Duty of Parents to Transmit Religion to Their Children and of the Children of God's Covenant People, to Know and Serve the God of Their Fathers* (Boston: Green, 1721), vii.

[14] May Diary, entry for December 18, 1711.

[15] Judith S. Graham, *Puritan Family Life: The Diary of Samuel Sewall* (Boston: Northeastern University Press, 2000), 24, 167–80; *The Diary of Ebenezer Parkman, 1703–82*, ed. Francis G. Walett (Worcester, Mass.: American Antiquarian Society, 1974), 5.

[16] Lombard, *Making Manhood*, 76, 81.

[17] John Ballantine Diary, 1737–43, 1753–74, transcribed by Joseph D. Bartlett, American Antiquarian Society, entry for March 7, 1737.

[18] Elisha Odlin Diary, 1729, American Antiquarian Society, entry for November 6.

[19] Lombard, *Making Manhood*, 77–83.

[20] Diary for 1754, Nathan Fiske Papers, 1750–99, American Antiquarian Society, entry for February; Nathaniel Ames, *An Astronomical Diary* (Boston: Draper, 1754).

[21] Rogers Family Papers, 1731–1804, American Antiquarian Society, entry for June 25, 1731; Shipton, *Sibley's Harvard Graduates*, 7:554.

[22] Stephen Peabody Diaries, 1767–1814, Massachusetts Historical Society, entry for July 15, 1767. For diaries of other Harvard students, see Samuel Baldwin, Diaries, 1749/50, 1772, American Antiquarian Society; Nathaniel Lovejoy, Diaries, 1762–1809, American Antiquarian Society.

[23] *The Diaries of Benjamin Lynde and Benjamin Lynde, Jr.* (Boston: Houghton, 1880), 132, 135.

[24] John Burt Diaries, 1737, 1739, American Antiquarian Society, entries for April 12 and December 21, 1737; Shipton, *Sibley's Harvard Graduates*, 10:29.

[25] Abner Bayley Diary, 1745, American Antiquarian Society, entries for January 31 and February 14; Nathaniel Ames, *An Astronomical Diary* (Boston: Draper, 1745). The anxiety of being a bachelor on Valentine's Day is captured in "Poet's Corner," *Connecticut Courant*, April 30, 1771.

[26] Lombard, *Making Manhood*, 89.

[27] Notebook, 1750–95, Fiske Papers, 2, 29, 31. On interpreting commonplace books, see Kenneth A. Lockridge, *On the Sources of Patriarchal Rage: The Commonplace Books of William Byrd and Thomas Jefferson and the Gendering of Power in the Eighteenth Century* (New York: New York University Press, 1992), 1–5; *Milcah Martha Moore's Book: A Commonplace Book from Revolutionary America*, ed. Catherine La Courreye Blecki and Karin Wulf (University Park: Pennsylvania State University Press, 1997).

[28] Quoted in Shipton, *Sibley's Harvard Graduates*, 8:482. Also see Ballantine Diary, entry for July 6, 1737.

[29] Burt Diary, entry for February 27, 1737; Lombard, *Making Manhood*, 80.

[30] Ballantine, Diary, entries for March 7 and August 4, 1737; March 1740.

[31] E. Harlow Russell, "Thoreau's Maternal Grandfather Asa Dunbar: Fragments from His Diary and Commonplace Book," *Proceedings of the American Antiquarian Society* 19 (1908): 70. Also see Asa Dunbar Diary, 1771–78, American Antiquarian Society.

[32] Lombard, *Making Manhood*, 97.

[33] On identity, see Ronald Hoffman, Mechal Sobel, and Frederika J. Teute, eds., *Through a Glass Darkly: Reflections on Personal Identity in Early America* (Chapel Hill: University of North Carolina Press, 1997); Kathleen Wilson, *The Island Race: Englishness, Empire and Gender in the Eighteenth Century* (London: Routledge, 2003); Teresa A. Toulouse, *The Captive's Position: Female Narrative, Male Identity, and Royal Authority in Colonial New England* (Philadelphia: University of Pennsylvania Press, 2007).

[34] *The Holyoke Diaries, 1709–1856*, ed. George Francis Dow (Salem, Mass.: Essex Institute, 1911), xii–xiv, 21–22.

[35] Marilyn J. Easton, *Passionate Spinster: The Diary of Patty Rogers, 1785* (Exeter, N.H.: Exeter Historical Society, 1999), 106. Also see Lee Virginia Chambers-Schiller, *Liberty, a Better Husband: The Generations of 1780–1840* (New Haven: Yale University Press, 1984), 114–16; Karin Wulf, *Not All Wives: Women of Colonial Philadelphia* (Ithaca: Cornell University Press, 2000).

[36] Easton, *Passionate Spinster*, 47, 50–51.

[37] Easton, *Passionate Spinster*, 89. Also see Mary Beth Norton, *Liberty's Daughters: The Revolutionary Experience of American Women, 1750–1800* (Ithaca: Cornell University Press, 1996), 52–53.

[38] Priscilla Holyoke, Diary, 1766, American Antiquarian Society, preface and entry for September 2.

[39] Mary Seccombe 1769 and 1770 Diaries, Seccombe Family Diaries, 1753–70, American Antiquarian Society, entries for June 16, July 2, October 25 and 30, 1769; November 18, 1770. Also see Shipton, *Sibley's Harvard Graduates*, 8:481–90; Mather B. DesBrisey, *History of the County of Lunenburg*, 2nd ed. (Toronto: Briggs, 1895), 256–68.

[40] On gender and diarists, see Fothergill, *Private Chronicles*, 87–94. On the perceived passionlessness of single women, see Chambers-Schiller, *Liberty, a Better Husband*, 21–22.

[41] Bailey finds that 169 of the 1,848 (9.2%) eighteenth-century Yale graduates for whom marital status is known died unmarried, although only twenty-six of these bachelors lived to age fifty. Shipton's biographies suggest similar figures for Harvard. William B. Bailey, "A Statistical Study of Yale Graduates, 1701–92," *Yale Review* 16 (1907–8): 400–26; Shipton, *Sibley's Harvard Graduates*, vols. 1–17.

[42] For a more complete discussion of the Pickerings, see John Gilbert McCurdy, "'Your Affectionate Brother': Complementary Manhoods in the Letters of John and Timothy Pickering," *Early American Studies* 4 (2006): 512–45.

[43] "Diary for the Year 1759 Kept by Samuel Gardner of Salem," *Essex Institute Historical Collections* 49 (1913): 1–22.

[44] *The Diary of William Bentley, D.D., Pastor of the East Church, Salem, Massachusetts,* 4 vols. (Gloucester, Mass.: Smith, 1962), 4:42–43.

[45] Charles A. Waehler, *Bachelors: The Psychology of Men Who Haven't Márried* (Westport, Conn.: Praeger, 1996).

[46] Timothy Pickering to John Pickering, January 26, 1786, Pickering Papers, 5:380–80A, Massachusetts Historical Society; *Diary of William Bentley,* 4:41. Farber figures the sex ratio in Salem before 1800 was eighty-seven men for every one hundred women among people aged sixteen to forty-five. Bernard Farber, *Guardians of Virtue: Salem Families in 1800* (New York: Basic Books, 1972), 143.

[47] Shipton, *Sibley's Harvard Graduates,* 6:331–36.

[48] John Pickering to Timothy Pickering, July 4, 1778, Pickering Papers, 17:175–76A.

[49] John Pickering to Timothy Pickering, July 4, 1778, Pickering Papers, 17:175–76A; John Pickering to Timothy Pickering, April 28, 1781, Pickering Papers, 18:91–92.

[50] *Diary of William Bentley,* 1:400.

[51] Timothy Pickering to John Pickering, April 24, 1777, Pickering Papers, 5:44; John Pickering to Timothy Pickering, September 4, 1777, Pickering Papers, 17:31–31A. On Timothy Pickering, see Octavius Pickering and Charles W. Upham, *The Life of Timothy Pickering,* 4 vols. (Boston: Little Brown, 1867–73); Edward Hake Phillips, "The Public Career of Timothy Pickering, Federalist, 1745–1802" (PhD diss., Harvard University, 1952); Gerard H. Clarfield, *Timothy Pickering and American Diplomacy, 1795–1800* (Columbia: University of Missouri Press, 1969); Gerard H. Clarfield, *Timothy Pickering and the American Republic* (Pittsburgh: University of Pittsburgh Press, 1980); David McLean, *Timothy Pickering and the Age of the American Revolution* (New York: Arno Press, 1982).

[52] Pickering and Upham, *Life of Timothy Pickering,* 1:212, 527.

[53] John Pickering to Timothy Pickering, September 29, 1788, Pickering Papers, 19: 144–45A.

[54] Howard Chudacoff, *The Age of the Bachelor: Creating an American Subculture* (Princeton: Princeton University Press, 1999).

[55] George Webb, *Batchellors-Hall; A Poem* (Philadelphia: [Franklin], 1731). Also see David S. Shields, *Civil Tongues and Polite Letters in British America* (Chapel Hill: University of North Carolina Press, 1997), 35–36, 94; *Pennsylvania Gazette,* January 13, 1743; December 9, 1746; March 15, 1748; Townsend Ward, "North Second Street and Its Associations," *Pennsylvania Magazine of History and Biography* 4 (1880): 179–80; "Plan of Batchelor Hall Lott, Survey by John Sukens, [1779]," Logan Papers, Historical Society of Pennsylvania.

[56] Information on Concord Township's taxed bachelors from Chester County, Pennsylvania: Board of County Commissioners, County Taxes, 1718–1800, Historical Society of Pennsylvania; *Collections of the Genealogical Society of Pennsylvania: Chester County Tax List, 1693–1740,* 8 vols., Gilbert Cope Collection, Historical Society of Pennsylvania; Gwen Boyer Bjorkman, *Quaker Marriage Certificates: Concord Monthly Meeting, Delaware County, Pennsylvania, 1679–1808* (Bowie, Md.: Heritage, 1991), 52; Concord Monthly Meeting Records, Delaware County, Pennsylvania, Historical Society of Pennsylvania. On Concord Township, see J. Smith Futhey and Gilbert Cope, *History of Chester County, Pennsylvania, with Genealogical and Biographical Sketches* (Philadelphia: Everts, 1881); Robert P. Case, *Prosperity and Progress: Concord Township, Pennsylvania, 1683–1983* (Concordville, Penn.: Concord Township Historical Society, 1983).

[57] Of 264 legible surnames, 138 (52.3%) match names of people rated for property taxes or poll taxes in Concord Township.

[58] Futhey and Cope, *History of Chester County,* 612; Concord Monthly Meeting Records, 194; Bjorkman, *Quaker Marriage Certificates,* 103; Rosemary Sweeney Warden, "The

Revolution in Political Leadership in Chester County, Pennsylvania, 1765–85" (PhD diss., Syracuse University, 1979), 316.

[59] Ann Kussmaul, *Servants in Husbandry in Early Modern England* (Cambridge: Cambridge University Press, 1981), 52.

[60] Concord Monthly Meeting Records, 250.

[61] Barry Levy, *Quakers and the American Family: British Settlement in the Delaware Valley* (New York: Oxford University Press, 1988), 248. Jack Marietta and G. S. Rowe found that single men were not responsible for a disproportionate number of violent offenses before the Revolution. Jack D. Marietta and G. S. Rowe, "Violent Crime, Victims, and Society in Pennsylvania, 1682–1800," *Pennsylvania History* 66 supplement (1999): 37–39.

[62] Concord Monthly Meeting Records, 273; Case, *Prosperity and Progress*, 103–8. See Jack Marietta, *The Reformation of American Quakerism, 1748–83* (Philadelphia: University of Pennsylvania Press, 1984), 6–7.

[63] The ages of only sixteen Concord bachelors could be determined but they correlate to previous studies, suggesting a broader trend. See Robert V. Wells, "The Population of England's Colonies in America: Old English or New Americans?" *Population Studies* 46 (1992): 88–89; Robert V. Wells, "Quaker Marriage Patterns in a Colonial Perspective," *William and Mary Quarterly*, 3rd ser., 39 (1972): 429; Levy, *Quakers and American Family*, 273; Rodger C. Henderson, *Community Development and the Revolutionary Transition in Eighteenth-Century Lancaster County, Pennsylvania* (New York: Garland, 1989), 51, 59–60, 105–8, 190–91, 287–89.

[64] Of 264 legible names, fifty-five (20.8%) were later rated for property in Concord Township and twenty-seven (10.2%) for property in other Chester County townships.

[65] Mary M. Schweitzer, *Custom and Contract: Household, Government, and the Economy in Colonial Pennsylvania* (New York: Columbia University Press, 1987), 26–29.

[66] Levy, *Quakers and American Family*, 248–51.

[67] *To the Commissioners and Assessors of Chester County, for the Year 1764*, American Broadsides, Library Company of Philadelphia. "Thrave" was a measurement of straw or fodder.

[68] In 1684, the assembly passed a law empowering local justices to set the wages, but there is little evidence that the measure was ever enforced. Richard B. Morris, *Government and Labor in Early America* (New York: Columbia University Press, 1946), 86.

[69] *Pennsylvania Gazette*, January 23, 1766. Also see *Pennsylvania Gazette*, January 3, 1771 and April 18, 1778.

[70] James T. Lemon, *The Best Poor Man's Country: A Geographical Study of Early Southeastern Pennsylvania* (Baltimore: Johns Hopkins University Press, 1972), 179; Lucy Simler, "The Landless Worker: An Index of Economic and Social Change in Chester County, Pennsylvania, 1750–1820," *Pennsylvania Magazine of History and Biography* 114 (1990): 185.

[71] Simler, "Landless Worker," 182–84; Schweitzer, *Custom and Contract*, 25.

[72] *The Statutes at Large of Pennsylvania from 1682 to 1801*, ed. James T. Mitchell and Henry Flanders, 17 vols. (Harrisburg: Busch et al., 1896–1915), 2:395–96.

[73] Linda K. Kerber, *No Constitutional Right to Be Ladies: Women and the Obligations of Citizenship* (New York: Hill and Wang, 1998), 81–123.

[74] Wilson Somerville, *The Tuesday Club of Annapolis (1745–56) as Cultural Performance* (Athens: University of Georgia Press, 1996), 147. Also see Shields, *Civil Tongues*, 175–208; J. A. Leo Lemay, *Men of Letters in Colonial Maryland* (Knoxville: University of Tennessee Press, 1972), 248–54; Robert Micklus, "'The History of the Tuesday Club': A Mock-Jeremiad of the Colonial South," *William and Mary Quarterly*, 3rd ser., 40 (1983): 42–61; Robert Micklus, *The Comic Genius of Dr. Alexander Hamilton* (Knoxville: University of Tennessee Press, 1990); Elaine G. Breslaw, "Wit, Whimsy, and Politics: The Uses of Satire by the Tuesday Club of Annapolis, 1744 to 1756," *William and Mary Quarterly*, 3rd ser., 33

(1975): 295–306; Elaine G. Breslaw, "The Chronicle as Satire: Dr. Hamilton's History of the Tuesday Club," *Maryland Historical Magazine* 70 (1975): 129–48.

[75] Quoted in Elaine G. Breslaw, "A Perilous Climb to Social Eminence: Dr. Alexander Hamilton and His Creditors," *Maryland Historical Magazine* 92 (1997): 449.

[76] Quoted in Lemay, *Men of Letters*, 216–17. On Hamilton, see Elaine G. Breslaw, "Dr. Alexander Hamilton and the Enlightenment in Maryland" (PhD diss., University of Maryland, 1973), 2–31; Elaine G. Breslaw, "From Edinburgh to Annapolis: Dr. Alexander Hamilton's Colonial Maryland Medical Practice," *Maryland Historical Magazine* 96 (2001): 400–420; Micklus, *Comic Genius*, 19–40; Carl Bridenbaugh, ed., *Gentleman's Progress: The Itinerarium of Dr. Alexander Hamilton 1744* (Chapel Hill: University of North Carolina Press, 1948).

[77] *Records of the Tuesday Club of Annapolis, 1745–56*, ed. Elaine G. Breslaw (Urbana: University of Illinois Press, 1988), 5.

[78] *Records of Tuesday Club*, 8.

[79] *The History of the Ancient and Honorable Tuesday Club by Dr. Alexander Hamilton*, ed. Robert Micklus, 3 vols. (Chapel Hill: University of North Carolina Press, 1990), 1:129–30.

[80] *Records of Tuesday Club*, 13. For biographies of the members, see *History of Tuesday Club*, 1:lxxix–cv; *Records of Tuesday Club*, xiii–xxxvii; Somerville, *Tuesday Club of Annapolis*, 10–18.

[81] *Records of Tuesday Club*, 7, 21.

[82] *History of Tuesday Club*, 1:151–52. This might be an allusion to an incident in Xenophon's *Symposium* mentioned in *Spectator* issue 500. See *The Apology and Crito of Plato and the Apology and Symposium of Xenophon*, trans. Raymond Larson (Lawrence, Kan.: Coronado, 1980), 109; *The Spectator*, ed. Donald F. Bond, 5 vols. (Oxford: Clarendon Press, 1965), 4:272–73.

[83] *History of Tuesday Club*, 1:255–56; *Records of Tuesday Club*, 50; John Barry Talley, *Secular Music in Colonial Annapolis: The Tuesday Club, 1745–56* (Urbana: University of Illinois Press, 1988), 77–78.

[84] *History of Tuesday Club*, 1:161–65.

[85] *Records of Tuesday Club*, 377; *History of Tuesday Club*, 3:89.

[86] Somerville, *Tuesday Club of Annapolis*, 141–42; Breslaw, "Hamilton and Enlightenment," 47–50; Micklus, *Comic Genius*, 53–56.

[87] *Records of Tuesday Club*, 49.

[88] Quoted in Micklus, *Comic Genius*, 53–54.

[89] *Records of Tuesday Club*, 322; Talley, *Secular Music*, 94–96.

[90] *Records of Tuesday Club*, 185, 194.

[91] *History of Tuesday Club*, 1:294, 294n3.

[92] *Records of Tuesday Club*, 138–39, 529.

[93] St. Anne's Protestant Episcopal Church, Annapolis, Maryland, "Transcripts and Vestry Proceedings, 1704–1818, and Parish Register, 1681–1796," Microfilm 1012, p. 320, Maryland Historical Society.

[94] Quoted in Joseph Chandler Morton, "Stephen Bordley of Colonial Annapolis" (PhD diss., University of Maryland, 1964), 211. Also see Edward C. Papenfuse et al., *A Biographical Dictionary of the Maryland Legislature, 1635–1789*, 2 vols. (Baltimore: Johns Hopkins University Press, 1979–85), s.v. "Bordley, Stephen."

[95] *History of Tuesday Club*, 2:325–28; Somerville, *Tuesday Club of Annapolis*, 147.

[96] *Maryland Gazette*, July 7, 1757; *History of Tuesday Club*, 1:lxxxiv; F. Edward Wright, *Anne Arundel County Church Records of the Seventeenth and Eighteenth Centuries* (Westminster, Md.: Family Line Publications, 1989), 99. Hamilton claimed that Cole was the oldest

member of the club, which would mean that he was older than Robert Gordon, who was sixty-nine when he was admitted in 1745. See *History of Tuesday Club*, 1:lxxxix, 51–52.

[97] *History of Tuesday Club*, 136–38.

[98] *History of Tuesday Club*, 1:143–44.

[99] *History of Tuesday Club*, 1:194, 342, 388. Compare with single women's petitions in *Boston Evening-Post*, April 17, 1749; *New-York Gazette*, March 20, 1749; Henning Cohen, *The South Carolina Gazette, 1732–75* (Columbia: University of South Carolina Press, 1935), 225, 225n163.

[100] *History of Tuesday Club*, 2:37, 335.

[101] *History of Tuesday Club*, 2:347–98.

[102] Thomas Foster, *Sex and the Eighteenth-Century Man: Massachusetts and the History of Sexuality in America* (Boston: Beacon, 2006), 101–27.

[103] Chudacoff, *Age of the Bachelor*, 114–15, 233–38; George Chauncey, *Gay New York: Gender, Urban Culture, and the Making of the Gay Male World, 1890–1940* (New York: Basic Books, 1994), 76–86.

[104] *History of Tuesday Club*, 3:210.

[105] *History of Tuesday Club*, 1:lxxxiii–lxxxiv; Wright, *Anne Arundel County Records*, 104.

[106] Foster, *Sex and Eighteenth-Century Man*, 101–27; Mark E. Kann, *A Republic of Men: The American Founders, Gendered Language, and Patriarchal Politics* (New York: New York University Press, 1998), 52–62.

5. The Single Man and the American Revolution

[1] Stephen Salisbury to Samuel Salisbury, January 8, 1768, Salisbury Family Papers, Box 1, Folder 3, American Antiquarian Society; Samuel Salisbury to Stephen Salisbury, June 21, 1769, Salisbury Family Papers, Box 2, Folder 1, American Antiquarian Society; Stephen Salisbury to Samuel Salisbury, June 22, 1769, Salisbury Family Papers, Box 2, Folder 1, American Antiquarian Society. Also see Charles L. Nichols, "Samuel Salisbury—A Boston Merchant in the Revolution," *Proceedings of the American Antiquarian Society* 35 (1925): 46–63; Thomas A. Foster, *Sex and the Eighteenth-Century Man: Massachusetts and the History of Sexuality in America* (Boston: Beacon Press, 2006), 105–6.

[2] William Maccarty Apprentice Indenture, August 9, 1769, Salisbury Family Papers, Box 2, Folder 1, American Antiquarian Society.

[3] Samuel Salisbury to Stephen Salisbury, January 18, 1770, Salisbury Family Papers, Box 2, Folder 2, American Antiquarian Society.

[4] On manhood and the Revolution, see Michael Kimmel, *Manhood in America: A Cultural History* (New York: Free Press, 1996), 13–21; E. Anthony Rotundo, *American Manhood: Transformation in Masculinity from the Revolution to the Modern Era* (New York: Basic Books, 1993), 10–18; Mark E. Kann, *A Republic of Men: The American Founders, Gendered Language, and Patriarchal Politics* (New York: New York University Press, 1998); David Hackett Fischer, *Paul Revere's Ride* (New York: Oxford University Press, 1994), 149–64; Robert A. Gross, *The Minutemen and Their World* (New York: Hill and Wang, 1976); Janet Moore Lindman, "Acting the Manly Christian: White Evangelical Masculinity in Revolutionary Virginia," *William and Mary Quarterly*, 3rd ser., 57 (2000): 393–416; Wayne Bodle, "Soldiers in Love: Patrolling the Gendered Frontiers of the Early Republic," in *Sex and Sexuality in Early America*, ed. Merril D. Smith (New York: New York University Press), 217–39.

[5] *Diary and Autobiography of John Adams*, ed. L. H. Butterfield, vol. 1 (Cambridge: Harvard University Press, 1961), 74, 280. Also see *Diary of John Adams*, 92–93, 97; *Adams Family Correspondence*, ed. L. H. Butterfield, 4 vols. (Cambridge: Harvard University Press, 1963–73), 1:263; 4:370–71.

[6] Henry Belcher, *The First American Civil War: First Period, 1775–78*, vol. 1 (London: Macmillan, 1911), 249. Also see Don Higginbotham, *The War of American Independence: Military Attitudes, Policies, and Practice, 1763–89* (New York: Macmillan, 1971), 44–48, 123–25; Kann, *Republic of Men*, 69–73; Edward E. Curtis, *The Organization of the British Army in the American Revolution* (New Haven: Yale University Press, 1926); Reginald Hargreaves, *The Bloodybacks: The British Serviceman in North America and the Caribbean, 1655–1783* (New York: Walker, 1968).

[7] William V. Wells, *The Life and Public Services of Samuel Adams*, vol. 3 (Boston: Little Brown, 1865), 222, 261.

[8] Paul D. Brandes, *John Hancock's Life and Speeches: A Personalized Vision of the American Revolution, 1763–93* (Lanham, Md.: Scarecrow, 1996), 212, 215–16.

[9] "For the New-Jersey Gazette from the Original Letter of Monsieur de Lisle," *New-Jersey Gazette*, April 23, 1778. Also see "Bp Berkeley's Maxims Concerning Patriotism," *Boston Chronicle*, November 2, 1769; Kann, *Republic of Men*, 53–56; "General Matuskin's Marriage to the Widow in Tears," *Massachusetts Magazine, or, Monthly Museum of Knowledge and Rational Entertainment* (Boston), December 1789, 755.

[10] Quoted in Lisa Wilson, *Ye Heart of a Man: The Domestic Life of Men in Colonial New England* (New Haven: Yale University Press, 1999), 87. Also see Higginbotham, *War of American Independence*, 45; Charles Royster, *A Revolutionary People at War: The Continental Army and American Character, 1775–83* (Chapel Hill: University of North Carolina Press, 1979), 25–53.

[11] Israel Keith to J. P. Palmer, November 19, 1776, Israel Keith Manuscripts 2 (1760–1803), Massachusetts Historical Society.

[12] Jean B. Lee, *The Price of Nationhood: The American Revolution in Charles County, Maryland* (New York: Norton, 1994), 125.

[13] Clifford K. Shipton et al., *Sibley's Harvard Graduates*, 17 vols. (Cambridge, Mass.: Sever et al., 1873–1975), 12:216–18; 13:127–30; 15:280–81, 356–58; Franklin Bowditch Dexter, *Biographical Sketches of the Graduates of Yale College with Annals of College History*, 6 vols. (New York: Holt, 1885–1912), 2:698–99; "Biography of William Gardner," Gardiner-Whipple-Allen Family Papers, Volume 2 (Disbound), 2:42, Massachusetts Historical Society; Walter B. Edgar, ed., *Biographical Directory of the South Carolina House of Representatives*, 5 vols. (Columbia: University of South Carolina, 1974–92), 3:38, 50.

[14] "Estimate of Losses of Daniel Oliver, 1775," Hutchinson and Oliver Papers, Volume 2, Massachusetts Historical Society; Edgar, *South Carolina House*, 3:38, 50.

[15] John A. Schutz, *Legislators of the Massachusetts General Court, 1691–1780: A Biographical Dictionary* (Boston: Northeastern University Press, 1997); Craig W. Horle et al., *Lawmaking and Legislators in Pennsylvania: A Biographical Dictionary*, 2 vols. (Philadelphia: University of Pennsylvania Press, 1991–97); Edgar, *South Carolina House*, vols. 2 and 3; Robert G. Ferris and Richard E. Morris, *The Signers of the Declaration of Independence* (Flagstaff, Ariz.: Interpretive Publications, 1982); Robert G. Ferris and Richard E. Morris, *The Signers of the Constitution* (Flagstaff, Ariz.: Interpretive Publications, 2001).

[16] "Philadelphia, June 9," *Essex Gazette*, June 22, 1773.

[17] *Songs and Ballads of the American Revolution*, ed. Frank Moore (New York: Appleton, 1856), 114. Also see "The Patriotic Lover," *Gentlemen and Ladies Town and Country Magazine* (Boston), December 1789, 565–67.

[18] Edward C. Papenfuse and Gregory A. Stiverson, "General Smallwood's Recruits: The Peacetime Career of the Revolutionary War Private," *William and Mary Quarterly*, 3rd ser., 30 (1973): 121–23; Henry A. Gemery, "The White Population of the Colonial United States, 1607–1790," in *A Population History of North America*, ed. Michael R. Haines and Richard H. Steckel (Cambridge: Cambridge University Press, 2000), 154.

[19] Charles Patrick Neimeyer, *America Goes to War: A Social History of the Continental Army* (New York: New York University Press, 1996), 12. Also see John Shy, *A People Numerous and Armed: Reflections on the Military Struggle for American Independence*, rev. ed. (Ann Arbor: University of Michigan Press, 1990), 165–79; Fred Anderson, *A People's Army: Massachusetts Soldiers and Society in the Seven Years' War* (Chapel Hill: University of North Carolina Press, 1984).

[20] Geoffrey L. Hudson, "Disabled Veterans and the State in Early Modern England," in *Disabled Veterans in History*, ed. David A. Gerber, 117–44 (Ann Arbor: University of Michigan Press, 2000); William Henry Glasson, *History of Military Pension Legislation in the United States* (New York: Columbia University Press, 1900), 12–24; Gary B. Nash, *The Urban Crucible: The Northern Seaports and the Origins of the American Revolution*, abridged ed. (Cambridge: Harvard University Press, 1979), 39, 117–21, 154–55, 159–60; Ruth Wallis Herndon, *Unwelcome American: Living on the Margin in Early New England* (Philadelphia: University of Pennsylvania Press, 2001), 166–70.

[21] *The Acts and Resolves, Public and Private, of the Province of the Massachusetts Bay*, 21 vols. (Boston: Wright and Potter, 1869–1922), 5:775. The law was repealed in 1782. See *Acts and Laws, Passed by the Great and General Court or Assembly of the Commonwealth of Massachusetts, Begun and Held at Boston, in the County of Suffolk, on Wednesday the Twenty-Ninth Day of May, 1782; and from Thence Continued by Adjournment to Wednesday the Eighteenth Day of September Following, and Then Met* (Boston: Edes and Sons, 1782), 841.

[22] *The Statutes at Large of Pennsylvania from 1682 to 1801*, ed. James T. Mitchell and Henry Flanders, 17 vols. (Harrisburg: Busch et al., 1896–1915), 9:23, 27. Pennsylvania later pondered drafting singles. See *Pennsylvania Gazette*, September 20, 1797.

[23] *The Statutes at Large; Being a Collection of All the Laws of Virginia, from the First Session of the Legislature in the Year 1619*, ed. William Waller Hening, 13 vols. (New York: Bartow, 1819–23), 9:338–39. Also see *Statutes of Virginia*, 9:90–91, 588–92; 10:214–15.

[24] John E. Selby, *The Revolution in Virginia, 1775–83* (Williamsburg, Va.: Colonial Williamsburg Foundation, 1988), 132, 135–36, 209–10, 214; *Statutes of Virginia*, 10:82–83, 214–15, 257–62, 326–37. Also see Rhys Isaac, *The Transformation of Virginia, 1740–90* (Chapel Hill: University of North Carolina Press, 1982), 275–77; Woody Holton, *Forced Founders: Indians, Debtors, Slaves, and the Making of the American Revolution in Virginia* (Chapel Hill: University of North Carolina Press, 1999), 202.

[25] *Votes and Proceedings of the House of Delegates of the State of Maryland, March Session 1778, Being the Second Session of the Assembly* (Annapolis: [Green], 1778), 80; Arthur J. Alexander, "How Maryland Tried to Raise Her Continental Quota," *Maryland Historical Magazine* 42 (1947): 184–96; Neimeyer, *America Goes to War*, 2.

[26] *Archives of Maryland*, ed. W. H. Browne et al., 72 vols. (Baltimore: Maryland Historical Society, 1883–1972), 47:434–35.

[27] *Laws of Maryland, Made and Passed at a Session of Assembly, Begun and Held at the City of Annapolis, on Monday the Eighth of November, in the Year of Our Lord One Thousand Seven Hundred and Seventy-Nine* (Annapolis: Green, [1780]), chap. 36. The Continental Congress made no reference to marital status in its calls for soldiers. See *Journals of the Continental Congress, 1774–89*, 34 vols. (Washington: U.S. Government Printing Office, 1904–37), 7:262; 10:200.

[28] This discussion is based on James H. Kettner, *The Development of American Citizenship, 1608–1870* (Chapel Hill: University of North Carolina Press, 1978); Linda K. Kerber, *No Constitutional Right to Be Ladies: Women and the Obligations of Citizenship* (New York: Hill and Wang, 1998); Gordon S. Wood, *The Creation of the American Republic, 1776–89* (Chapel Hill: University of North Carolina Press, 1969); Marc W. Kruman, *Between Authority and*

Liberty: State Constitution Making in Revolutionary America (Chapel Hill: University of North Carolina Press, 1997); Michael Schudson, *The Good Citizen: A History of American Civic Life* (Cambridge: Harvard University Press, 1998); Alexander Keyssar, *The Right to Vote: The Contested History of Democracy in the United States* (New York: Basic Books, 2000).

[29] Steven Rosswurm, *Arms, Country, and Class: The Philadelphia Militia and "Lower Sort" during the American Revolution, 1775–83* (New Brunswick, N.J.: Rutgers University Press, 1987), 49–51. Also see Robert J. Steinfeld, *The Invention of Free Labor: The Employment Relation in English and American Law and Culture, 1350–1870* (Chapel Hill: University of North Carolina Press, 1991), 121; Kettner, *Development of American Citizenship*, 122–24, 194–96.

[30] "The Petition of the Privates of the Military Association of the City and Liberties of Philadelphia," *Pennsylvania Archives*, 8th ser., vol. 8 (Harrisburg: Department of Property and Supplies, 1935), 7406. Also see Rosswurm, *Arms, Country, and Class*, 52–75; Richard Alan Ryerson, *The Revolution Is Now Begun: The Radical Committees of Philadelphia, 1765–76* (Philadelphia: University of Pennsylvania Press, 1978), 117–47; Gregory T. Knouff, *The Soldiers' Revolution: Pennsylvanians in Arms and the Forging of Early American Identity* (University Park: Pennsylvania State University Press, 2004).

[31] *Pennsylvania Gazette*, May 1, 1776.

[32] *Pennsylvania Gazette*, June 7, 1770.

[33] *Pennsylvania Packet, or the General Advertiser*, April 29, 1776. Also see *Pennsylvania Gazette*, May 1, 1776; Rosswurm, *Arms, Country, and Class*, 89–90; Kruman, *Between Authority and Liberty*, 98–99; Chilton Williamson, *American Suffrage: From Property to Democracy, 1760–1860* (Princeton: Princeton University Press, 1960), 79–82; Keyssar, *Right to Vote*, 14.

[34] "Proceedings of the Conference of Committees of the Province of Pennsylvania, Held at Carpenter's Hall, Philadelphia, from June 18 to June 25, 1776," *Pennsylvania Archives*, 2nd ser., vol. 3 (Harrisburg: Meyers, 1890), 560–61; Ryerson, *Revolution Is Now Begun*, 232–34; Glenn W. Jacobsen, "Politics, Parties, and Propaganda in Pennsylvania, 1776–88" (PhD diss., University of Wisconsin—Madison, 1976), 33.

[35] Richard R. Beeman, *The Varieties of Political Experience in Eighteenth-Century America* (Philadelphia: University of Pennsylvania Press, 2004), 273.

[36] *Statutes of Pennsylvania*, 9:590. On the constitutional convention, see Rosswurm, *Arms, Country, and Class*, 100–108; Ryerson, *Revolution Is Now Begun*, 207–46. On the Pennsylvania Constitution of 1776, see Charles H. Lincoln, *The Revolutionary Movement in Pennsylvania, 1760–76* (Philadelphia: University of Pennsylvania Press, 1901); J. Paul Selsam, *The Pennsylvania Constitution of 1776: A Study in Revolutionary Democracy* (Philadelphia: University of Pennsylvania Press, 1936); Robert L. Brunhouse, *The Counter-Revolution in Pennsylvania, 1776–90* (Harrisburg: Pennsylvania Historical Commission, 1942); Theodore Thayer, *Pennsylvania Politics and the Growth of Democracy, 1740–76* (Harrisburg: Pennsylvania Historical and Museum Commission, 1953); David Hawke, *In the Midst of a Revolution* (Philadelphia: University of Pennsylvania Press, 1961). On the 1776 Constitution in the national context, see Wood, *Creation of American Republic*, 83–90, 226–37; Kruman, *Between Authority and Liberty*, 24–28, 37, 39, 92–93, 99, 101; Beeman, *Varieties of Political Experience*, 268–75.

[37] Ryerson, *Revolution Is Now Begun*, 234. Also see Rosswurm, *Arms, Country, and Class*, 100; Ryerson, *Revolution Is Now Begun*, 9. These figures reflect the electorate for delegates to the constitutional convention. The percentages for elections after 1776 were probably slightly smaller as the constitution demanded that voters had *paid* taxes rather than just being *assessed* them.

[38] Stella H. Sutherland, *Population Distribution in Colonial America* (New York: Columbia University Press, 1936), 124–34; Pennsylvania: Board of County Commissioners, State Taxes, 1777–91, Historical Society of Pennsylvania; "Effective Supply Tax of the City of

Philadelphia, 1779," *Pennsylvania Archives*, 3rd ser., 14 (1897): 469–561. For a breakdown of the figures referenced here, see John Gilbert McCurdy, "Taxation and Representation: Pennsylvania Bachelors and the American Revolution," *Pennsylvania Magazine of History and Biography* 129 (2005): 283–315.

[39] "Transcript of the Seventeenth Eighteenth Pence Rate for the County of Chester, 1774," *Pennsylvania Archives*, 3rd ser., 12 (1897): 1–124; "Returns for the Sixteenth Eighteen-Penny Tax for the County of Lancaster, 1773," *Pennsylvania Archives*, 3rd ser., 17 (1897): 323–487. This refutes the arguments of Wood and Williamson that the expansion of the electorate during the Revolution was not remarkable. See Williamson, *American Suffrage*, 96; Wood, *Creation of American Republic*, 167.

[40] *Statutes of Pennsylvania*, 9:601. Also see Anthony Mario Joseph, "The Pennsylvania Legislature, 1776–1820" (PhD diss., Princeton University, 1999), 151–58.

[41] *Statutes of Pennsylvania*, 9:598. The constitutional provision became statutory law in August 1776. See *Statutes of Pennsylvania*, 9:5–8.

[42] Rosswurm, *Arms, Country, and Class*, 103–8, 310n138; William H. Egle, "The Constitutional Convention of 1776: Biographical Sketches of Its Members," *Pennsylvania Magazine of History and Biography* 3 (1879): 96–101, 194–201, 319–30, 438–46; 4 (1880): 89–98, 225–33, 361–72; Beeman, *Varieties of Political Experience*, 272–74; Hawke, *In the Midst of Revolution*, 176–77; Robert Gough, "Notes on the Pennsylvania Revolutionaries of 1776," *Pennsylvania Magazine of History and Biography* 96 (1972): 89–103.

[43] *Letters of Benjamin Rush*, ed. L. H. Butterfield, 2 vols. (Princeton: Princeton University Press, 1951), 1:148. Also see *Letters of Rush*, 1:114–15, 137, 150, 240, 244, 333, 498–99, 532–33; George W. Corner, *The Autobiography of Benjamin Rush, His "Travels Through Life" Together with His Commonplace Book for 1789–1813* (Princeton: Princeton University Press, 1948), 141–42, 158, 161; Brunhouse, *Counter-Revolution in Pennsylvania*, 221–27.

[44] *The Papers of Benjamin Franklin*, ed. Leonard W. Labaree et al., 36 vols. (New Haven: Yale University Press, 1959–2001), 15:184. Also see *Papers of Franklin*, 10:57–58; Carl Van Doren, *Benjamin Franklin* (New York: Viking, 1938), 554.

[45] *Letters of Rush*, 1:465–66, 576.

[46] *The Works of James Wilson*, ed. Robert Green McCloskey, vol. 1 (Cambridge: Harvard University Press, 1967), 406–7. Also see Geoffrey Seed, *James Wilson* (Millwood, N.Y.: KTO Press, 1978).

[47] Quoted in J. Paul Selsam and Joseph G. Rayback, "French Comment on the Pennsylvania Constitution of 1776," *Pennsylvania Magazine of History and Biography* 76 (1952): 317. Also see Johnson Kent Wright, *A Classical Republican in Eighteenth-Century France: The Political Thought of Mably* (Stanford: Stanford University Press, 1997).

[48] *The Works of John Adams, Second President of the United States*, ed. Charles Francis Adams, 10 vols. (Boston: Little, Brown, 1850–56), 9:377.

[49] *Statutes of Pennsylvania*, 9:587, 600. This usage of *single* here probably does not translate simply as *unmarried*, although its juxtaposition with *family* raises the distinct possibility that it was attempting to speak to a growing class of bachelors. Also see Burton Alva Konkle, *George Bryan and the Constitution of Pennsylvania, 1731–1791* (Philadelphia: Campbell, 1922), 127–28.

[50] Beeman, *Varieties of Political Experience*, 272.

[51] *Statutes of Pennsylvania*, 9:102, 153, 232–33, 363–64, 402–3, 447; 10:240, 330–31; 11:90. Also see Brunhouse, *Counter-Revolution in Pennsylvania*, 84–89, 108–10, 121–22, 133–34, 157, 162.

[52] Similarly, in 1786, Republicans charged that members of the the Constitutionalist Party kept mechanics disfranchised by keeping them off the tax rolls. See Brunhouse, *Counter-Revolution in Pennsylvania*, 192.

[53] Ruth H. Bloch, *Gender and Morality in Anglo-American Culture, 1650–1800* (Berkeley: University of California Press, 2003), 136–53; Kerber, *No Constitutional Right*, 3–46, 81–123.

[54] Kann, *Republic of Men*, 52–62.

[55] Keyssar, *Right to Vote*, 339, 342.

[56] Colonial South Carolina allowed taxpayer suffrage although the taxes one had to pay to vote placed the franchise out of reach for men with less than two hundred acres of land or two slaves. See W. Roy Smith, *South Carolina as a Royal Province, 1719–76* (New York: Macmillan, 1903), 95–98, 115–17, 282–84; Keyssar, *Right to Vote*, 5, 16–19, 328–36.

[57] Henry G. Connor and Joseph B. Cheshire Jr., *The Constitution of the State of North Carolina Annotated* (Raleigh: Edwards and Broughton, 1911), lxx. All legislators and electors also had to be residents of their respective districts for at least twelve months. Also see Cortlandt F. Bishop, *History of Elections in the American Colonies* (New York: Columbia College, 1893), 79, 88–90; Robert L. Ganyard, *The Emergence of North Carolina's Revolutionary State Government* (Raleigh: Division of Archives and History of the North Carolina Department of Cultural Resources, 1978), 68–89.

[58] *The State Records of North Carolina*, ed. William L. Saunders et al., 26 vols. (Raleigh: Hale et al., 1886–1907), 24:202. Also see Robert A. Becker, *Revolution, Reform, and the Politics of American Taxation, 1763–83* (Baton Rouge: Louisiana State University Press, 1980), 94–99, 189–94; Coralie Parker, *The History of Taxation in North Carolina during the Colonial Period, 1663–1776* (New York: Columbia University Press, 1928), 97–124.

[59] The North Carolina bachelor tax was revised several times before 1784. See *Records of North Carolina*, 24:258, 260, 390–91, 432, 435–36, 438.

[60] Bertie County, Taxables, 1772–84, County Records 010.701.3, North Carolina State Archives; Chowan County Taxables, 1780–85, County Records 024.701.4, North Carolina State Archives; Tax Lists: Craven County, 1779, General Assembly Papers, 30.1, North Carolina State Archives; Cumberland County, List of Taxables, 1777–83, County Records 29.701.1, North Carolina State Archives.

[61] *Records of North Carolina*, 24:543.

[62] *Laws of Maryland, Made and Passed at a Session of Assembly, Begun and Held at the City of Annapolis, on Thursday the Tenth of May, in the Year of Our Lord One Thousand Seven Hundred and Eighty-One* (Annapolis: Green, [1781]), ch. 24, § 17. Also see Becker, *Revolution, Reform, and Politics*, 183–87, 193, 212–17; Beverly W. Bond Jr., *State Government in Maryland, 1777–81* (Baltimore: Johns Hopkins University Press, 1905), 58–75; Ronald Hoffman, *A Spirit of Dissension: Economics, Politics, and the Revolution in Maryland* (Baltimore: Johns Hopkins University Press, 1973), 207–10. On the adoption of the tax, see *Votes and Proceedings of the Senate of the State of Maryland, May Session, 1781, Being the Second Session of this Assembly* ([Annapolis: Green, 1781]), 66–72.

[63] Bettie Carothers, *1783 Tax List of Maryland, Part I: Cecil, Talbot, Harford, and Calvert Counties* (Silver Spring, Md.: Family Line Publications, 1977); Robert W. Barnes and Bettie Stirling Carothers, *1783 Tax List of Baltimore County, Maryland* (Lutherville, Md.: Carothers, 1978).

[64] *Proceedings of the Convention of the Province of Maryland, Held at the City of Annapolis, on Wednesday the Fourteenth of August, 1776* (Annapolis: Green, [1776]), 297, 349. Also see Philip A. Crowl, *Maryland during and after the Revolution: A Political and Economic Study* (Baltimore: Johns Hopkins University Press, 1943), 29–40; *Maryland Gazette*, August 15, 1776; Kruman, *Between Authority and Liberty*, 95, 99–100; Williamson, *American Suffrage*, 81; Keyssar, *Right to Vote*, 16–17, 331. The last Maryland bachelor tax was approved in 1786. See *Laws of Maryland, Made and Passed at a Session of Assembly, Begun and Held at the City*

of Annapolis, on Monday the Seventh of November, in the Year of Our Lord One Thousand Seven Hundred and Eighty-Five (Annapolis: Green, [1786]), chap. 83, § 16.

[65] "The Constitution of the State of New Jersey," in *New Jersey in the American Revolution, 1763–83: A Documentary History*, ed. Larry R. Gerlach (Trenton: New Jersey Historical Commission, 1975), 214. Also see *Acts of the General Assembly of the State of New-Jersey, at a Session Begun at Trenton on the 28th Day of October 1777 and Continued by Adjournments, Being the Second Sitting of the Second Session* (Trenton: Collins, 1778), 57; *Votes and Proceedings of the General Assembly of the State of New-Jersey, at a Session Begun at Trenton on the 28th Day of October, 1777, and Continued by Adjournments until the 8th of October, 1778, Being Their Second Session* (Trenton: Collins, 1779), 59–60, 72–74, 85–87; Charles R. Erdman Jr., *The New Jersey Constitution of 1776* (Princeton: Princeton University Press, 1929), 55–57; Leonard Lundin, *Cockpit of the Revolution: The War for Independence in New Jersey* (Princeton: Princeton University Press, 1940), 139, 143–44, 191, 227–29; Richard P. McCormick, *The History of Voting in New Jersey: A Study of the Development of Election Machinery, 1664–1911* (New Brunswick, N.J.: Rutgers University Press, 1953), 67; Williamson, *American Suffrage*, 85; J. R. Pole, "Suffrage Reform and the American Revolution in New Jersey," *Proceedings of the New Jersey Historical Society* 74 (1956): 184–85.

[66] *Private and Temporary Acts: Acts of the Forty-Third General Assembly of the State of New-Jersey, at a Session Begun at Trenton, on the Twenty-Seventh Day of October, One Thousand Eight Hundred and Eighteen, Being the Second Sitting* (Trenton: Justice, 1819), 69; Becker, *Revolution, Reform, and Politics*, 166–73; Keyssar, *Right to Vote*, 331–32.

[67] *Pennsylvania Gazette*, September 12, 1792.

[68] Keyssar, *Right to Vote*, 20, 54; Mary Beth Norton, *Liberty's Daughters: The Revolutionary Experience of American Women, 1750–1800* (Ithaca: Cornell University Press, 1996), 191–93.

[69] "The Dreamer, No. XV," *Massachusetts Magazine*, September 1790, 518.

[70] Johann David Schoepf, *Travels in the Confederation [1783–84]*, ed. and trans. Alfred J. Morrison, vol. 2 (Philadelphia: Campbell, 1911), 202. It is possible that Schoepf confused the Carolinas because the poll tax collected on white males in South Carolina from 1786 to 1788 made no reference to marital status. See *The Statutes at Large of South Carolina*, ed. Thomas Cooper and David J. McCord, 10 vols. (Columbia: Johnston, 1836–41), 4:729; 5:25.

[71] *Journal of the House of Delegates of Virginia [May 5–June 28] Anno Domino, 1777* (Williamsburg: Purdie, 1777), 69. Also see Fred Shelley, ed., "The Journal of Ebenezer Hazard in Virginia, 1777," *Virginia Magazine of History and Biography* 62 (1954): 407, 422.

[72] "The Plan of Government as Originally Drawn by George Mason," in *The Papers of Thomas Jefferson*, ed. Julian Boyd, vol. 1 (Princeton: Princeton University Press, 1950), 366, 369. Also see Williamson, *American Suffrage*, 114; "The Constitution as Adopted by the Convention," in *Papers of Jefferson*, 379.

[73] *The Laws of the Northwest Territory, 1788–1800*, ed. Theodore Calvin Pease (Springfield: Illinois State Historical Library, 1925), 201, 205.

[74] *Laws of a Public and General Nature, of the District of Louisiana, of the Territory of Louisiana, of the Territory of Missouri, and of the State of Missouri, up to the Year 1824* (Jefferson City: Lusk and Son, 1842), 732. Also see *The Laws of Indiana Territory, 1801–9*, ed. Francis S. Philbrick (Springfield: Illinois State Historical Library, 1930), 69, 187, 481; *The Laws of Indiana Territory, 1809–16*, ed. Louis B. Ewbank and Dorothy L. Riker (Indianapolis: Indiana Historical Society, 1934), 278; *Governors' Messages and Letters: Messages and Letters of William Henry Harrison*, ed. Logan Esarey, vol. 1, 1800–1811 (Indianapolis: Indiana Historical Commission, 1922), 305–6, 321; *Acts Passed by the General Assembly of the Territory of Arkansas, at the Session in October, 1823* (Little Rock: Woodruff, 1824), 34.

[75] *Acts of Massachusetts*, 5:448; *Laws of New Hampshire Including Public and Private Acts and Resolves and the Royal Commissions and Instructions*, ed. Albert Stillman Batchellor et al., 10 vols. (Manchester: Clarke et al., 1904–22), 6:442.

[76] *Acts and Laws of the Commonwealth of Massachusetts* (Boston: Adams and Nourse, 1788), 99; *Laws of New Hampshire*, 6:693.

[77] *Laws of the Commonwealth of Pennsylvania, from the Fourteenth Day of October, One Thousand Seven Hundred, to the Twentieth Day of March, One Thousand Eight Hundred and Ten*, vol. 2 (Philadelphia: Bioren, 1810), 533.

[78] Richard Godbeer, *Sexual Revolution in Early America* (Baltimore: Johns Hopkins University Press, 2002), 227–63; Cornelia Hughes Dayton, *Women before the Bar: Gender, Law, and Society in Connecticut, 1639–1789* (Chapel Hill: University of North Carolina Press, 1995), 157–230; Clare A. Lyons, *Sex among the Rabble: An Intimate History of Gender and Power in the Age of Revolution, Philadelphia, 1730–1830* (Chapel Hill: University of North Carolina Press, 2006), 186–236.

[79] *Statutes of Pennsylvania*, 3:221–22. On the poor in Pennsylvania, see Billy G. Smith, *The "Lower Sort": Philadelphia's Laboring People, 1750–1800* (Ithaca: Cornell University Press, 1990); Peter J. Parker, "Rich and Poor in Philadelphia, 1709," *Pennsylvania Magazine of History and Biography* 99 (1975): 3–19.

[80] *Statutes of Pennsylvania*, 4:266–77; 5:79–86; 7:75–79, 159–61, 310; 8:75–96, 474; 9:228–29; George Wharton Pepper and William Draper Lewis, *A Digest of the Laws of Pennsylvania, 1700–1907, the Constitution of the United States and the Constitution of Pennsylvania with Notes and References to the Decisions Bearing Thereon and a Chronological Table of Acts 1683 to 1907*, 2nd ed. (Philadelphia: Johnson, 1910), 5742; *Laws of Pennsylvania*, 1:332–50; *Supplement to Purdon's Digest: A Digest of the Statute Law of the State of Pennsylvania for the Years 1917–21*, 13th ed. (Philadelphia: Bisel, 1923), 8920–37.

[81] *Statutes of Pennsylvania*, 16:379.

[82] The singles tax remained when the law on county rates was rewritten in 1834. See *Laws of the General Assembly of the State of Pennsylvania, Session 1833–34, in the Fifty-Eighth Year of Independence* (Harrisburg: Welsh, 1834), 512; *Supplement to Purdon's Digest*, 9176–77.

[83] Kann, *Republic of Men*, 52–78; Godbeer, *Sexual Revolution*, 227–334; Foster, *Sex and Eighteenth-Century Man*, 17–22, 42–43, 63–64; Rodney Hessinger, "'Insidious Murderers of Female Innocence': Representations of Masculinity in the Seduction Tales of the Late Eighteenth Century," in *Sex and Sexuality*, 262–82; Howard P. Chudacoff, *The Age of the Bachelor: Creating an American Subculture* (Princeton: Princeton University Press, 1999), 21–44.

[84] Scott Slawinski, *Validating Bachelorhood: Audience, Patriarchy, and Charles Brockden Brown's Editorship of the* Monthly Magazine and American Review (New York: Routledge, 2005); Arthur Scherr, *"I Married Me a Wife": Male Attitudes toward Women in the* American Museum, *1787–92* (Lanham, Md.: Lexington Books, 1999).

[85] "Character of a Bachelor," *American Museum, or Repository of Ancient and Modern Fugitive Pieces* (Philadelphia), January 1787, 42–43. Also published in *Monthly Repository of Useful Information* (Concord, N.H.), September 1793, 239–40; *Philadelphia Minerva*, March 3, 1798, 18; "Distresses and Complaints of a Bachelor," *American Museum*, October 1789, 293. Also see "The Bouquet," *Massachusetts Magazine*, February 1791, 110; "To the Ragged Old Bachelor," *Philadelphia Minerva*, May 9, 1795, 4; "The Bachelor," *Rural Magazine* (Newark, N.J.), May 5, 1798, 5; "The Bachelor," *Philadelphia Minerva*, June 23, 1798, 84. For other humorous takes, see "The Bachelor's Meditation In a Love-Fit Hour," *New-Jersey Gazette*, May 31, 1780; "The Bachelor's Address to Modesty," [Benjamin West], *Bickerstaff's New-England Almanack, for the Year of Our Lord 1792* (Norwich, Conn.: Trumbull, 1791), 20; "The Old Maid's Reply To an Old Batchelor, Who Told Her She Would Lead Apes In Hell,"

Massachusetts Magazine, February 1794, 120; "Written by a Bachelor, Who Married in Spite of the Laugh of His Brother Bachelors," *Philadelphia Minerva,* December 9, 1797, 3.

[86] "The Pitiable Case of an Old Bachelor," *American Museum,* January 1787, 56–57; *Rural Magazine or, Vermont Repository* (Rutland, Vt.), January 1795, 21–22.

[87] *Georgia Gazette* quoted in "Trivia," *William and Mary Quarterly,* 3rd ser., 31 (1974): 139–40.

[88] J. G. A. Pocock, *The Machiavellian Moment: Florentine Political Thought and the Atlantic Republican Tradition* (Princeton: Princeton University Press, 1975), 383–97; Bernard Bailyn, *The Ideological Origins of the American Revolution,* enlarged ed. (Cambridge: Harvard University Press, 1992), 34–35, 75, 210, 365.

[89] *Papers of Jefferson,* 504. Also see Wood, *Creation of American Republic,* 169.

[90] "The Old Bachelor's Lamentation," in Benjamin West, *The New-England Almanack, or Lady's and Gentleman's Diary, for the Year of Our Lord Christ 1780* (Providence, R.I.: Carter, 1779), 21. Also see "An Old Batchelor's Reflections on Matrimony," *Columbian Magazine* (Philadelphia), March 1789, 197–98.

[91] "To the Honourable the Delegates of the United States in Congress Assembled," *American Museum,* April 1787, 348.

[92] M. L. Weems, *Hymen's Recruiting-Serjeant: or the New Matrimonial Tat-too, for the Old Bachelors* (Philadelphia: Maxwell, 1800). Reprinted in *Virginia and North Carolina Almanac, for the Year of Our Lord 1800* (Fredericksburg, Va.: Green, [1799]). Also see Lewis Leary, *The Book-Peddling Parson: An Account of the Life and Works of Mason Locke Weems Patriot, Pitchman, Author, and Purveyor of Morality to the Citizenry of the Early United States of America* (Chapel Hill, N.C.: Algonquin, 1984), 54–80.

[93] "The Old Bachelor, [Number I,]" *Pennsylvania Magazine or, American Monthly Museum* (Philadelphia), March 1775, 113.

[94] "An Account of the Burning of Bachelor's Hall, By the Old Bachelor, [Number II,]" *Pennsylvania Magazine,* April 1775, 168; "The Bachelor, [Number VIII,]" *Pennsylvania Magazine,* December 1775, 552, 554.

[95] Kettner, *Development of American Citizenship,* 174–75. For a rejection of gentle persuasion, see "Letters on Marriage, Ascribed to the Reverend John Witherspoon, Late President of Princeton College," in *A Series of Letters on Courtship and Marriage: To Which Are Added, Witherspoon's Letters on Marriage; Mrs. Piozzi's Letter to a Gentleman Newly Married; Swift's Letter to a Newly Married Lady; Marriage, a Vision, by Cotton; Nugent's Epistle to a Lady* (Elizabeth-Town, N.J.: Kollock, [1796]), 69.

[96] "The Candid Acknowledgment of an Old Batchelor," *New-York Weekly Magazine,* January 4, 1797, 213.

[97] "Letter On Marriage," *American Museum,* January 1788, 50–51. Also see "Thoughts On the Choice of a Wife; In a Letter to a Young Bachelor," *Universal Asylum and Columbian Magazine* (Philadelphia), March 1792, 176–79. For other mournful bachelors, see "The Batchelor's Wish," *Pennsylvania Magazine,* January 1776, 43; September 14, 1796, 88; "The Bachelor's Last Shift," *Pennsylvania Magazine,* May 1776, 226; "The Batchelor," *Columbian Magazine,* March 1787, 343–44; "To the Editors of the *New-York Magazine,*" *New-York Magazine or, Literary Repository,* February 1790, 79; "Letter From an Old Bachelor," *New-York Magazine,* August 1795, 483–86; "The Batchelor's Wish," *New-York Magazine,* September 14, 1796, 88; "Selected Poetry Written By a Disappointed Old Bachelor," *Time Piece and Literary Companion,* March 9, 1798, 4. Some bachelors blamed their condition on the poor quality of young women. See *Pennsylvania Chronicle, and Universal Advertiser,* August 20, 1770, reprinted in T. H. Breen, *The Marketplace of Revolution: How Consumer Politics Shaped American Independence* (New York: Oxford University Press, 2004), 282.

[98] Hessinger, "Insidious Murderers," 262–82; Godbeer, *Sexual Revolution*, 264–98. Also see Jay Fliegelman, *Prodigals and Pilgrims: The American Revolution against Patriarchal Authority, 1750–1800* (Cambridge: Cambridge University Press, 1982); Cathy N. Davidson, *Revolution and the Word: The Rise of the Novel in America* (New York: Oxford University Press, 1986), 110–50.

[99] "A Plan for the Establishment of Public Schools," *Pennsylvania Gazette*, May 10, 1786.

[100] "To the Editor of the Columbian Magazine," *Columbian Magazine*, February 1789, 102.

[101] "Geographical Description of Bachelor's Island," *Universal Asylum*, April 1790, 213; "Geographical Description of the Isle of Matrimony," *Universal Asylum*, August 1791, 102. "Bachelor's Island" first ran in *The European Magazine*, March 1782, and was subsequently published in *Boston Magazine*, December 1783, 8. See E. W. Pitcher, "Fiction in *The Boston Magazine* (1783–86): A Checklist with Notes and Sources," *William and Mary Quarterly*, 3rd ser., 37 (1980): 477. For other defenses of bachelorhood, see "To the Editor of the *Columbian Magazine*," *Columbian Magazine*, May 1789, 314; "The Batchelor's Defence," *Massachusetts Magazine*, December 1796, 680; "The Bachelor's Advocate," *North Carolina Star* (Raleigh), April 19, 1810.

[102] Slawinski, *Validating Bachelorhood*, 17–58.

[103] "Arguments in Favour of Celibacy," *American Universal Magazine* (Philadelphia), March 6, 1797, 301–5. Reprinted as "An Old Bachelor's Reflections on Matrimony," *New Star* (Concord, N.H.), August 29, 1797.

[104] "Oration in Praise of Deliberate Batchelors, Delivered at the Public Commencement in the University of Pennsylvania, July 8th, 1790, by Mr. James Stuart," *Universal Asylum*, August 1790, 83–85. On Stuart, see *University of Pennsylvania: Biographical Catalogue of the Matriculates of the College Together with Lists of the Members of the College Faculty and the Trustees Officers and Recipients of Honorary Degrees, 1749–1893* (Philadelphia: Society of the Alumni, 1894), 31. Also see *The Old Bachelor's Masterpiece: To Which Are Added Several Pieces of Poetry Never Before Published* (Fairhaven, Conn.: Spooner, 1797).

[105] Lee Virginia Chambers-Schiller, *Liberty, a Better Husband: The Generations of 1780–1840* (New Haven: Yale University Press, 1984); Karin Wulf, *Not All Wives: Women of Colonial Philadelphia* (Ithaca: Cornell University Press, 2000).

[106] Jonathan Fisher Diary, transcribed by Gaylord C. Hall, Jonathan Fisher Papers, 1791–1826, American Antiquarian Society, entry for May 24, 1795. Also see Mary Ellen Chase, *Jonathan Fisher: Maine Parson, 1768–1847* (New York: Macmillan, 1948).

[107] Fisher Diary, entries for April 23, 1821 (sandwiched between December 1795 and January 1796) and February 4, 1796.

[108] Moses Bond Wheelock Diary, 1788–89, American Antiquarian Society, entries for February 4 and March 30, 1789.

[109] Foster, *Sex and Eighteenth-Century Man*, 106–7.

[110] James Tufts Diary, 1789–91, American Antiquarian Society, entries for May 22 and 29, 1790 and May 9, 1791.

[111] Stephen Peabody Jr., Diary, 1796–97, American Antiquarian Society, entries for December 9, 1796 and March 20, 1797.

[112] Daniel Scott Smith and Michael S. Hindus, "Premarital Pregnancy in America, 1640–1971: An Overview and Interpretation," *Journal of Interdisciplinary History* 5 (1975): 537–70.

[113] Susan E. Klepp, "Revolutionary Bodies: Women and the Fertility in the Mid-Atlantic Region, 1760–1820," *Journal of American History* 85 (1998): 910–45; Richard Godbeer,

Sexual Revolution, 299–334; Lyons, *Sex among the Rabble*, 186–236. Also see Mary Beth Sievens, *Stray Wives: Marital Conflict in Early National New England* (New York: New York University Press, 2005).

[114] See Thomas Phillibrown Diary, 1739–58, Virginia Historical Society; George Carlyle Papers, 1744–52, Virginia Historical Society; "Copy of Sketch of John Coalter in His Own Hand Writing," *Augusta County Historical Society Bulletin* 4 (1968): 17–19; William Robertson Diary, 1771, Virginia Historical Society. On masculinity in the antebellum South, see Craig Thompson Friend and Lorri Glover, eds., *Southern Manhood: Perspectives on Masculinity in the Old South* (Athens: University of Georgia Press, 2004).

[115] William Bolling Diary, 1794–95, Virginia Historical Society, entries for May 17 and June 18, 1794. Also see *Dictionary of Virginia Biography*, ed. Sara B. Bearess et al., vol. 2 (Richmond: Library of Virginia, 2001), s.v. "Bolling, William"; Manning C. Voorhis, "Bollingbrook," *William and Mary Quarterly*, 2nd ser., 16 (1936): 545–53; Betty Miller Unterberger, "The First Attempt to Establish an Oral School for the Deaf and Dumb in the United States," *Journal of Southern History* 13 (1947): 556–66; W. G. Strand, "Randolph Family," *William and Mary Quarterly*, 1st ser., 9 (1901): 182–83. An intriguing diary that discusses a seduction of a young woman is *The Journal of John Harrower, an Indentured Servant in the Colony of Virginia, 1773–76*, ed. Edward Miles Riley (Williamsburg, Va.: Colonial Williamsburg, 1963).

[116] Bolling Diary, entries for June 10, December 2 and 8, 1795.

[117] Kenneth Lockridge, *The Diary, and Life, or William Byrd II of Virginia, 1674–1744* (Chapel Hill: University of North Carolina Press, 1987); Kenneth Lockridge, *On the Sources of Patriarchal Rage: The Commonplace Books of William Byrd and Thomas Jefferson and the Gendering of Power in the Eighteenth Century* (New York: New York University Press, 1992); Richard Godbeer, "William Byrd's 'Flourish': The Sexual Cosmos of a Southern Planter," in *Sex in Early America*, 135–62.

[118] Richard N. Venable Diary, 1791–92, Virginia Historical Society, entries for February 20 and 22, 1791. Also see Richard Harrison, *Princetonians, 1776–83: A Biographical Dictionary*, vol. 3 (Princeton: Princeton University Press, 1981), s.v. "Venable, Richard N."; Joseph J. Casey, "Venable Family," *William and Mary Quarterly*, 1st ser., 15 (1907): 246–49.

[119] Venable Diary, entries for January 8 and 9, 1792. It is unclear what became of Elizabeth Williams.

[120] Venable Diary, entry for May 22, 1792. Archibald Alexander, "List of Marriages February to May 1797, Recorded," Carrington Papers, Section 7, Virginia Historical Society.

[121] Nichols, "Samuel Salisbury," 56–63.

Epilogue: Bachelors since 1800

[1] *James Buchanan, His Doctrines and Policy as Exhibited by Himself* (New York: Greeley and McElrath, 1856), 15–16. Also see Philip C. Auchampaugh, "James Buchanan, the Bachelor of the White House: An Inquiry on the Subject of Feminine Influence in the Life of Our Fifteenth President," *Tyler's Quarterly Magazine* 20 (1938–39): 154–66, 218–34.

[2] "Bachelors, Look Out!" *National Trades Union*, May 16, 1835; *Roswell Register* (Roswell, New Mexico), April 17, 1903; Nancy F. Cott, *Public Vows: A History of Marriage and the Nation* (Cambridge: Harvard University Press, 2000), 191–93, 223–24; Richard W. Stevenson, "House Passes Bill to Reduce Taxes for the Married," *New York Times*, February 11, 2000; Paul Krugman, "For Richer, for Poorer," *New York Times*, August 9, 2000.

[3] "Bachelors—Taxation," *Lady's Book* (Philadelphia), August 1839, 53; Carolyn Davidson, *The Bachelor Tax* (Toronto: Harlequin, 2000). Also see "A Bachelor's Dissipation,"

Boston Lyceum, March 15, 1827, 120–25; *Report of the Committee of the House of Assembly, on Petition of William McElroy, of the County of Warren, the Same Having Been Referred to a Committee of Bachelors and Widowers* (Trenton: Justice and Son, 1837).

4 Washington Irving, *Diedrich Knickerbocker's History of New-York* (Norwalk, Conn.: Heritage Press, 1940); William L. Hedges, "Knickerbocker, Bolingbroke, and the Fiction of History," *Journal of the History of Ideas* 20 (1959): 317–28; James Fenimore Cooper, *Notions of the Americans: Picked up by a Travelling Bachelor*, ed. Gary Williams (Albany: State University of New York Press, 1991); William Wirt, *The Old Bachelor (1814): A Photoreproduction with an Introduction by Bruce Granger* (Delmar, N.Y.: Scholars' Facsimiles and Reprints, 1985); Jay B. Hubbell, "William Wirt and the Familiar Essay in Virginia," *William and Mary Quarterly*, 2nd ser., 23 (1943): 136–52; William Robert Taylor, "William Wirt and the Legend of the Old South," *William and Mary Quarterly*, 3rd ser., 14 (1957): 477–93; Anya Jabour, *Marriage in the Early Republic: Elizabeth and William Wirt and the Companionate Ideal* (Baltimore: Johns Hopkins University Press, 1998); Bob Pepperman Taylor, *America's Bachelor Uncle: Thoreau and the American Polity* (Lawrence: University Press of Kansas, 1996). Also see Vincent J. Bertolini, "Fireside Chastity: The Erotics of Sentimental Bachelorhood in the 1850s," *American Literature* 68 (1996): 706–37; Phillip Lopate, *Bachelorhood: Tales of the Metropolis* (Boston: Little Brown, 1978), 249–81.

5 Daniel Haynes, *An Address Pronounced at Natick, May 27, 1824, Before the Society of Bachelors in That Place* (Boston: Haynes, 1824); Arthur C. Cole, "The Puritan and the Fair Terpsichore," *Mississippi Valley Historical Review* 29 (1942): 27; N. J. Cooper, "Bachelor's Ball" [Jefferson, N.Y.: n.p., 1845]; C. Lenschow, "A Bachelors Polka for the Piano Composed and Dedicated to the Junior Bachelors Association of Philada," (Philadelphia: Lee and Walker, 1849); "Alexandria's Old Bachelor's Club," *Fireside Sentinel* (Alexandria Library, Lloyd House Journal), 6 (1992): 127–28; T. Michael Miller, ed., *Manuscripts of an Old Bachelor: Reminiscences of Alexandria* (n.p., 1987); *The Bachelors' Journal* (Boston), September 18, 1828; *Old Bachelor* (Boston), July 1843.

Index